PROBLEMATIC PARADIGMS

Latinx: The Future Is Now

A series edited by Lorgia García Peña, Nicole M. Guidotti-Hernández, and Maritza E. Cardenas

BOOKS IN THE SERIES

Guadalupe Escobar, *Decolonial Witnessing: Cold War Afterlives in Latin American and Latinx Testimonios*

Irene Mata, *Beyond the Moment: Connecting Histories of Latinx Performance and Resistance*

PJ DiPietro, *Sideways Selves: Travesti and Jotería Struggles across the Americas*

Sony Coráñez Bolton, *Dos X: Disability and Racial Dysphoria in Latinx and Filipinx Culture*

Marcos Gonsalez, *Revolting Indolence: The Politics of Slacking, Lounging, and Daydreaming in Queer and Trans Latinx Culture*

Sharina Maíllo-Pozo, *Bridging Sonic Borders: Popular Music in Contemporary Dominican/Dominicanyork Literature*

Frank García, *Clicas: Gender, Sexuality, and Struggle in Latina/o/x Gang Literature and Film*

Regina Marie Mills, *Invisibility and Influence: A Literary History of AfroLatinidades*

Jason Ruiz, *Narcomedia: Latinidad, Popular Culture, and America's War on Drugs*

Rebeca L. Hey-Colón, *Channeling Knowledges: Water and Afro-Diasporic Spirits in Latinx and Caribbean Worlds*

Tatiana Reinoza, *Reclaiming the Americas: Latinx Art and the Politics of Territory*

Kristy L. Ulibarri, *Visible Borders, Invisible Economies: Living Death in Latinx Narratives*

Marisel C. Moreno, *Crossing Waters: Undocumented Migration in Hispanophone Caribbean and Latinx Literature and Art*

Yajaira M. Padilla, *From Threatening Guerrillas to Forever Illegals: US Central Americans and the Cultural Politics of Non-Belonging*

Francisco J. Galarte, *Brown Trans Figurations: Rethinking Race, Gender, and Sexuality in Chicanx/Latinx Studies*

PROBLEMATIC PARADIGMS AND THE CONTOURS OF US LATINIDAD

ESSAYS BY

SILVIO TORRES-SAILLANT

EDITED BY NANCY KANG AND
MICHAEL NIETO GARCIA

University of Texas Press *Austin*

Printed in the United States of America
First edition, 2026

Complete information regarding publishing credits and history is available in the back-matter.

♾ The paper used in this book meets the minimum requirements of ANSI/NISO Z39.48–1992 (R1997) (Permanence of Paper).

Library of Congress Cataloging-in-Publication Data

Names: Torres-Saillant, Silvio, author. | Kang, Nancy, editor. | Garcia, Michael Nieto, editor.
Title: Problematic paradigms and the contours of US Latinidad / essays by Silvio Torres-Saillant ; edited by Nancy Kang, Michael Nieto Garcia.
Other titles: Latinx (Series)
Description: First edition. | Austin : University of Texas Press, 2026. | Series: Latinx: the future is now | Includes bibliographical references and index.
Identifiers: LCCN 2025030753 (print) | LCCN 2025030754 (ebook)
ISBN 978-1-4773-3403-4 (hardcover)
ISBN 978-1-4773-3404-1 (paperback)
ISBN 978-1-4773-3405-8 (pdf)
ISBN 978-1-4773-3406-5 (epub)
Subjects: LCSH: Torres-Saillant, Silvio—Criticism and interpretation. | Hispanic Americans—Race identity. | Latin Americans—United States—Ethnic identity. | Dominican Americans—Ethnic identity. | Multiracial people—United States—Ethnic identity. | Cultural pluralism—United States. | Group identity—United States. | African diaspora—Influence. | Intellectuals—Hispanic Americans. | Hispanic American scholars—United States—Biography. | Hispanic Americans—Study and teaching.
Classification: LCC HT1523 .T67 2026 (print) | LCC HT1523 (ebook)
LC record available at https://lccn.loc.gov/2025030753
LC ebook record available at https://lccn.loc.gov/2025030754

doi:10.7560/334034

To Changho Charles Kang
우리 아버지: 존경스러운 평생의 노력

To the Humanities, Languages, and Arts:
foundation of a liberal education,
pillars of humanism

CONTENTS

NOTE ON TERMINOLOGY

LATINO, LATINA/O, LATIN@, LATINX, LATINE, AND WHATEVER COMES NEXT

Considering Multiple Identity Labels

Although this book appears in the Latinx: The Future Is Now series, many of the chapters use *Latino* or *Latina/o* instead of *Latinx* or the more recent *Latine*. As editors, we felt that historical accuracy compelled us to retain selectively (for instance, in chapter titles) whichever term the author used at the time of original publication. Doing so honors the Zeitgeist and terminologies of those who came before us by refusing to impose retroactively (but not unproblematically) the lexicon currently in vogue. We would be remiss to gloss over any of the intricate tensions informing the past usages, based on current preferences, themselves a product of generative and necessary conversations about diversity and inclusion. Our respect for the social and historical situatedness of the original texts overruled the push for orthographical consistency or normalization regarding terminology. Insisting on uniformity would be the kind of "foolish consistency" that Ralph Waldo Emerson dubbed "the hobgoblin of little minds" (537)—or in this case, of editorial self-assertion.

We would also acknowledge that while the shifting of terms (along with the values and demographics they represent) often feels like a direct line of moral progress in the present moment, it is likely that many of our current usage preferences may not last. For example, in the African American community, the term *black* was once disparaged as an identity label but revitalized and reclaimed during the Black Power and Black Arts movements. While some still balk at the term *African American*, based largely on unfamiliarity or tenuous ties to African roots, others contend that the term underscores a specifically US identity, helping to differentiate black Americans from their African diaspora immigrant counterparts. In his memoir *Colored People* (1994), for instance, literary scholar Henry Louis Gates, Jr., recalls his application essay for Yale University, which stated, "My grandfather was colored, my father was Negro, and I am black" (201). This compact array of terms captured his formative years and generational inheritance of civil rights struggle in Piedmont, West Virginia.

Perhaps for its own compelling reasons, such as convenience or familiarity, we might see a similar turn back toward the term *Latino*, which was replaced by *Latina/o* and *Latin@*, then *Latinx*, and subsequently *Latine* to resist rigid binaries of gender and a long history of patriarchy, as well as to ensure a space for plurality and difference within Latinidad. As Katy Steinmetz points out in her *Time* magazine article, "The letter *X* can refer to unknown locations or quantities and has a rebellious patina" that plants the term squarely between the competing forces of tradition and future-mindedness. Lourdes Torres, former editor of the journal *Latino Studies*, observes that while the interdisciplinary publication has "accepted all iterations of terminology in circulation, including Latino, Latina/o, Latina and Latino, and Latin@, as well as Hispanic," the issue of naming remains fraught:

> When we first started receiving submissions that included "Latinx," in 2015, some external reviewers and members of our editorial board felt it was gimmicky, trendy, and probably a passing fad. One person commented that it sounded like a laundry detergent. Another suggested (jokingly?) that they would quit the board if we ever adopted it. On the other hand, others agreed that "Latinx" signaled an important recognition of nonbinary gender identifications, and while they had not embraced its use in their own scholarship, they recognized that it was becoming more common in the writing of their students and colleagues on social media and, increasingly, in academic spaces. ("Latinx?" 283)

As Torres's words attest, there is currently no clear consensus among academics on which of the competing terms is the favored identity label. Likewise, it is too soon to tell how widely adopted the terms *Latinx* and *Latine* will become in popular usage, given the difficulty, for instance, that some have even in pronouncing these terms. Furthermore, a great divide exists between the term that is handiest for academic use and what members of the populations themselves prefer to be called. Subgroup diversity may take precedence over wider identity labels. Hesitation over which spelling of the panethnic label to use may heighten the tendency of some to self-identify by asserting the more familiar ethnonyms based on distinct national origins (such as Dominican American) instead. In short, there is an ongoing need for flexibility when approaching identity labels, which are, by nature, provisional, negotiable, and often highly volatile given the unpredictable force of personal preference.

We should also consider how competing rationales exist for choosing one identity label over another. For activists, that choice depends precisely on political resonance and strategic concerns, such as group values, perceived consensus, and ease of access. But politicizing identity labels can prove counterproductive. Further considerations arise regarding recognition and overall accessibility. Among these is the argument that the term *Latinx* is orthographically—if not aesthetically—challenging. It also seems that the term is not favored by most Latinos.[1] These and other practical factors largely explain the continuing preference for the consistent and long-standing term *Hispanic* by the media and bureaucratic bodies. Though its colonial underpinnings make some social justice advocates bristle at its use, the term has done well to establish a clearly recognizable identity category for census and demographic purposes for a group that does not share a common race, national origin, or ethnic background. In other words, it may be the least complicated option, though not necessarily the best one.

As academics and literary critics, our response to this ongoing taxonomic question is one of fascination and watchful waiting. This is a stance of "Yes, and . . ." combined with the critical inclusivity of "All of the above." We embrace the incredible diversity within the Latino community that this collection of essays and the Latinx: The Future Is Now series seek to address. We acknowledge the multifaceted, overlapping dynamics that the *x* in the Latinx series signifies, and in that spirit, we see little reason in this volume to discriminate against some alternative terms in favor of others. As editors, we are compelled to respect the demands of the rhetorical situation and particular moment of the text's composition.

Decisions do need to be made, of course. When planning the February 2020 conference of the University of Houston's Recovering the US Hispanic Literary Heritage ("Recovery Project"), some animated discussion arose among board members around the choice to specify *Latinas* in the title of the event and the call for papers. A couple of colleagues suggested that doing so would efface contributions of non-Latinas, including men and nonbinary individuals. As director of Arte Público Press and the Recovery Project, Nicólas Kanellos made the executive decision that the specific term *Latinas* would be used, considering that women would be the focus of scholarly inquiry—but not to the exclusion of others who have made contributions to feminist and women-centered causes. The conference ultimately ran with the title Histories and Cultures of Latinas: Suffrage, Activism and Women's Rights, and the program featured an array of perspectives by diverse presenters, not just Latinas. To his credit, Kanellos has also used the terms *Hispanic writers*, *Hispanic literature*, and *Latino literature* in his much-heralded anthologies, encyclopedias, and other reference works.

Overall, flexibility of mind is what we are striving to capture in *Problematic Paradigms*. As noted, we have preserved the identifiers for titles (for instance, "Afro-Latinos and the Racial Wall") that appeared in the original version of each selection. We also use the terms *Latino*, *Latina/o*, and *Latinx* somewhat interchangeably in our introduction, as well as in the headnotes that precede each chapter. However, for consistency's sake, in the actual chapters, we have retained "Latino" to describe what are generally nonhuman abstractions (for example, "Latino literature," "Latino politics") and embraced "Latina/o" when referring specifically to human subjects (for example, "Latina/o writers," "the history of Latina/os"). As scholars, we look forward to the ongoing conversation about competing identity labels, academic versus popular usage, and the stimulating exchange of ideas that these debates about preferences and appropriate use encourage. As musings on usage are constantly being shared both on and off the page, we welcome these differences of opinion and greet them in the spirit of civility, appreciation, respect, and forbearance, and hope others will do the same.

Notes

1. Southern California–based cultural-insights entrepreneur Mario Carrasco conducted a poll in which participants were asked, "Which of these terms do you prefer to describe your ethnicity?" Forty-four percent of US Hispanics who responded chose "Hispanic," 24 percent preferred "Latino/Latina," and 2 percent chose "Latinx" ("Progressive Latino Pollster"). See Meraji for Pew Research Center poll results where only 3 percent of the adults surveyed nationally use "Latinx." As counterpoint, journalist Paola Ramos's *Finding Latinx: In Search of the Voices Redefining Latino Identity* (2020) contends that the *x* gives rise to a highly unifying sense of community: "I noticed that Latinx was able to capture what other terms had not in the past—it captured the stories of all these people under one umbrella, spanning so many separate identities" to give birth to "a type of collective solidarity I hadn't experienced in my lifetime" (11–12).

PROBLEMATIC PARADIGMS

INTRODUCTION

ON PROBLEMATIC PARADIGMS AND THE POETICS OF IDENTITY

NANCY KANG AND MICHAEL NIETO GARCIA

Problematic Paradigms is an unexpected title. Surely a collection of writings by a long-standing figure in the field of Latino studies,[1] someone widely regarded for decades of groundbreaking work as a pioneering scholar of Caribbean and Dominican diaspora literature, should convey something more definitive, emphatic, and settled. As will become evident upon reading the essays in this collection, Silvio Torres-Saillant is not that kind of thinker. Though a foundational scholar in the field, he resists the temptation, all too common among founders and figureheads, to staunchly defend traditional views (including ones from early in their careers), or to adopt too quickly the trendiest catchphrases in an attempt to stay relevant. Rather, Torres-Saillant ceaselessly interrogates the dominant discourses and "problematic paradigms" of the day, including his own presuppositions and guiding claims. His roles as founding director of the Dominican Studies Institute at the City University of New York (CUNY) and associate editor for over two decades of the preeminent journal *Latino Studies* notwithstanding, he continues to relish investigating—and dissecting—the received wisdom and convenient narratives informing his multiple fields of interest and specialization.

Rather than providing definitive answers, Torres-Saillant wrestles with major questions of identity, representation, and cultural production as someone too curious to settle for the glib ideologies of the day. He is a deep and wide-ranging thinker, not a channeler of fashionable views. These essays investigate the dominant interpretative templates, not only in mainstream society, but also from within the ethnoracial communities that *Latinidad* comprises. The author dares to confront sacrosanct models, generating readings that some scholars may have automatically written off, fearing controversy or accusations of datedness. It is this kind of verve that makes his scholarship worthy of examination. It is intellectual labor based on a stalwart commitment to rigorous critical inquiry, wherever it might lead.

The selected essays in this volume break out of the presentist mold, the groupthink of any given cultural moment, the rush to judge, condemn, or denounce those with views contrary to our own. At times, they arrive at unexpected conclusions. They surprise and delight with a telling aside or a stunning "minor" point, such as how Richard Rodriguez and Gloria Anzaldúa "both pastoralized" the view of amalgamation advocated by Mexican thinker José Vasconcelos in his racist tract *La raza cósmica* (1925).

These meditations deftly dispense with unexamined shibboleths and beliefs that others let pass, such as the field's all-too-common invocation of cultural essentialism (that is, treating cultural characteristics as if they were fixed rather than fluid). Typically accomplished with sensitivity and nuance, Torres-Saillant's explorations of such narratives also tend to model effective critical thinking about the most challenging issues in the discipline. Likewise, his invocations of Spanish as well as Latin or Greek coinages shake readers out of the limited perspective of a monolingual lexicon. What else could we expect from a multilingual, Caribbean-born, classically trained US scholar who takes the long view, and who has toiled in these vineyards for longer than many of us have seen the sun?

While the study of literature and history is fraught with its own perils and biases, scholarship is all the more challenging around matters of ethnic identity. *Problematic Paradigms* appraises the prevailing modes of representation of the US Latinx population in academic, political, and literary contexts. The essays correspond to the portion of the author's heterogeneous output that most explicitly ponders the difficulty of formulating large truth claims about a panethnicity with such disparate points of origin and varied manners of incorporation into the US population. This facet of Torres-Saillant's writings probes the tension between the ad hoc certainties that the struggle for sociopolitical advancement seems to call for, and the critical caution required for serious scholarly inquiry when speaking about historically complex panethnic formations.

Eschewing convenient caricatures, Torres-Saillant explores the question of ethnic identity in its complexity and complications, relentlessly exposing untidy corners and inconvenient contradictions. Particularly characteristic of his oeuvre is a concern with larger social issues balanced against an unshakeable belief in upholding intellectual honesty. The reader will find that deep passion for justice tempered by the scholar's dedication to maintaining a requisite degree of emotional detachment when practicing critical inquiry. It is a tricky balance; some activists paint themselves into antirealist positions or make absurd claims when they allow personal leanings to cloud scholarly judgment. Torres-Saillant largely avoids intellectual posturing, instead grappling with the thorniest points around the topics of race, class, and ethnicity with uncommon open-mindedness and candor.

Many of these essays reflect the writer's abiding interest in public outreach, community awareness, and transformative pedagogy from the point of view of a frontline participant in the growth of Latinx studies in the US academy. As inaugural director of the Latino-Latin American Studies program at Syracuse University and cofounder of La Casita Cultural Center, a thriving off-campus cultural and educational hub in Central New York, he helped envision and facilitate collaborations between the city's population of Latin American ancestry and various sectors of the campus and community at large. In addition to being associate editor of *Latino Studies* from its founding in 2003 until the summer of 2024, he was a senior editor for the landmark six-volume *Oxford Encyclopedia of Latinos and Latinas in the United States* (2005), among other projects that set out to conceptualize the field and frame the bodies of knowledge pertinent to it. Since the early 1990s, he has served on the board of editorial advisors of the University of Houston's Recovering the US Hispanic Literary Heritage project, and decades later he joined the board of advisors to the Smithsonian Institution's Molina Family Latino Gallery from the outset to its public opening in 2022. He also became a member of the scholarly advisory committee to the Smithsonian's National Museum of the American Latino, an undertaking created by an act of Congress in December 2021.

These endeavors showcase a history of local as well as national engagement in cocreating a living record of Latinx peoples in a truthful, accessible, and public-facing fashion. Torres-Saillant's experience in such pursuits has endowed him with an advantageous perspective from which to examine the field panoptically, as the writings in this collection amply suggest. The essays we included in this volume also illuminate the advantages of taking the long view about present concerns, as well as the evolution of his thought over decades. To capture the author's line of inquiry, information on publication date, venue, and original context of earlier versions of chapters can be found in the Credits and Publication History section of this book.

On Symbolic Capital and the Signifiers of Racial Discourse

A trademark of Torres-Saillant's methodological approach is careful attention to historical narratives, strategic media representations, and engagement with the symbolic realm more broadly. This includes an interrogation of influential social templates and popular discourses, particularly as they align with racial and ethnic concerns. In Torres-Saillant's oeuvre, readers will find skillfully woven discussions of Dominican and Dominican American literature; meditations on the history and lived realities of blackness; the ties between ethnicity, racialization, and diaspora; the problems undergirding nationalism and nationhood; and the ways in which all of the above are conveyed in the wide and tangled net of media representations, from the Latin Grammys to singer Ricky Martin's appearance at the Republican National Convention in 2000.

One abiding theme in Torres-Saillant's work is the extent to which blackness has often been excluded from, or marginalized within, Latinx scholarship. In relation to this historical diminishment, he points to a large degree of *negrophobia*—a combination of cultural attitudes, problematic assumptions, and generalized contempt for blackness—in both Latin America and the United States. The first thing to strike the reader may be the term invoked to explain this phenomenon. US Anglophone scholars may initially be taken aback by negrophobia's prefix, *negro*, any use of which has become somewhat taboo in recent years without clear and specific historical contextualization. The term should be changed, some might say, to *white racism* or *antiblackness*, so as to fit better into the new lexicon arising from antiracist advocacy. At the very least, some may say, a word like *negrophobia* is démodé, anachronistic, and even downright offensive for some.

First, the term is indeed appropriate from the perspective of a Caribbean-born native Spanish speaker who studied Latin, reads French, and writes in English. Alas, monolingual preconceptions about word origins can lead to erroneous assumptions about linguistic connotations of terms from other languages and cultures, as well as about the "correct" usage of material imported from other tongues. Second, it is precisely that aforementioned resistance to intellectual trendiness and passing fads that makes Torres-Saillant's contributions so vital. Third, the term has a rich philological and intellectual heritage that identifies the author's roots in Caribbean thought.

Negrophobia can be traced back as Latin cognate (in Spanish and French) to the conceptual influence of the Martinican psychoanalyst and social theorist Frantz Fanon, who in *Black Skin, White Masks* (1952) endeavored "to determine what are the constituents of Negrophobia" in consonance with the precedent set by Jean-Paul Sartre, who had undertaken, in Fanon's view, a masterful exploration of anti-Semitism (160). As a psychoanalyst, Fanon engages the pathology of black-white relations in France as well as in the Antilles, contending that the anti-Semite is typically also a "negrophobe" (Fanon 98). Arguing for a sexual dimension to antiblack racism, he posits, for instance, the "abnormal sexual life of the female negrophobe" (128), while attributing the negrophobia of blacks towards themselves to their socialization in a colonial regime intent on inferiorizing them.

As someone who had attended middle and high school at night, while working days in a *zapatería* (shoe factory) from his early teens, Torres-Saillant has not valued all of Fanon's teachings in the same way. When, as an aspiring scholar, he opted to pursue graduate studies in comparative literature at New York University, he already felt more attracted to the social aspects of Fanon's interpretations than to their psychoanalytic counterparts. While acknowledging the Martinican as a key Caribbean thinker, with the intellectual and moral strength to call out the racial regimes of the Christian West, his own analyses entail varied forays into the literacies and pedagogies whereby the colonizing world powers have, over the last five centuries, poisoned human interactions across differences of phenotype and ancestry. Identifying racist dogma as an enemy of us all, our author prefers to scrutinize white supremacy's fundamentalist character as one whose power all people of goodwill should seek to dismantle. He identifies the social realm, *not* the psyche, as the primary battleground on which racialized peoples should wage their war against threats to inclusion, equality, and justice. One could conjecture that Fanon would not quarrel with Torres-Saillant's choosing to think, for instance, that black and brown children who see themselves as less pretty or smart than their lighter-complexioned peers are probably less influenced by stimuli stemming from their psyche than by a deleterious learning inflicted upon them by social sites within and beyond the classroom. The author also uses negrophobia (or its corresponding variants) to account for the unique status and social location of people of Afro-Latinx ancestry, the matter of racial heterogeneity within the panethnicity, and the ongoing need to dismantle the racial walls and ceilings that divide and stratify US society to the detriment of all.

From Caribbean Poetics to Latinx Studies

As a product of the Caribbean who eventually turned his scholarly gaze toward the region, Torres-Saillant came to a surprising conclusion: the rootedness of his identity and related research had primed him to be comfortable with a global perspective. This alignment is evident in *An Intellectual History of the Caribbean* (2006), which analyzes the formative influence of his background.

Indeed, over the long arc of his career, Torres-Saillant has tirelessly advocated for treating the Caribbean experience as the cradle of modernity. If we are to "speak holistically about human society," he argues, Caribbean literature and culture must no longer be "exclud[ed] from the mega-narratives of humanity and the condition of the world" (*Intellectual History* 3). His insistence on the inclusion of the Caribbean experience extends to the field of Latinx studies too; when Hispanophone literatures and cultures have been sidelined or ignored, what results is an egregious knowledge deficit, both in the United States and beyond.

Having arrived in New York City as an adolescent, Torres-Saillant spent decades orchestrating voices from Hispaniola and the diaspora. He founded the CUNY Dominican Studies Institute shortly after completing his doctorate at NYU. He repeatedly played an active role in seeking recognition for people of Dominican ancestry as legitimate constituents of the Latinx panethnicity. His advocacy has involved unearthing traces of a US Dominican presence to counter the early impulse of Latinx leaders to exclude the group from local or national agendas on grounds of recency and insufficient evidence of civic engagement. Combatting the charge that Dominicans only care about politics in their ancestral homeland, the author set forth diasporic identity as a framework to rebut the notion that Dominicans had little interest in building community with other Latinx and minoritized populations. He has also sought to rectify the dismissal of his coethnics as illegitimate or uncommitted partners in the panhemispheric struggle against negrophobia, doing so by excavating the history of black resistance in the part of Hispaniola that is now the Dominican Republic.

True to the multiple forms of bridging represented by his personal story, the titles of early works, such as *Caribbean Poetics* (1997) and *An Intellectual History of the Caribbean* (2006), indicate an ethnic and area studies approach to Caribbean literature and culture. Indeed, attention to what he describes as the intricacies of "ethnic studies undertakings" has been a hallmark of his scholarship (*Intellectual History* 3). Likewise, his lifelong focus on global influences and the Dominican diaspora forms a natural linkage with Latinx studies (3). The breadth and variety of his influences range from Aristophanes to Max Weber, from Julia Alvarez to Ofelia Zepeda. Torres-Saillant approaches his subjects armed with the resources of someone who has taken full advantage of his schooling, including a hands-on political and class education in factories and other sites of menial labor. His formal learning consisted of early contact with ancient Mediterranean and European cultures, training in Latin and Greek in college, eager absorption of medieval and Renaissance European letters, and eventual discovery of the Caribbean as a site of scholarly reckoning and conceptual investment. He accomplished all these forays as a second-language speaker of English who often thinks in Spanish but undertakes most of his writing in English. Early on, he recognized the false dichotomy between town and gown and nurtured an abiding sympathy for those from the less empowered sectors of society. These sensibilities greatly influenced his trajectory in the professoriate of various academic departments, including those with the benefit of privileged access to Latinx-studies networks, projects, communities, and debates.

Broadly, Torres-Saillant's theoretical influences have emanated from comparative cultural studies, ethnic studies, critical race theory, and reflections on the postcolonial. His approach tends to be eclectic and deeply interdisciplinary. That his work transcends the boundaries of any one academic field or critical perspective seems almost inevitable, considering that his early work sought to understand a diverse region (the Caribbean), fragmented in terms of languages, literatures, cultures, and colonial experiences. When turning his scholarship to Latinx studies, this interdisciplinary approach again proved illuminating, as it mirrored the equally fragmented nature of his new scholarly undertaking: analyzing the histories, cultures, and trajectories of Latinx peoples, whose diasporic heritage reflects geographic divisions based on place of origin and site of destination (and eventual settlement) in the United States.

Torres-Saillant has been vocal in noting the limitations of a single, reductive lens. While deploying anti- and postcolonial approaches in his own unique way, he still reserves the right to criticize the dominance of the latter in defining the Caribbean. The work of the region's thinkers is often flattened and refurbished according to the current dominant paradigm, whether that be postcolonialism or the latest "theoretical intervention." The writer finds this flimsiness particularly troubling vis-à-vis his primary influences among Caribbean and Afro-diaspora intellectuals. To name a few: Aimé Césaire on *Négritude* and the challenge to the Christian West's self-assigned monopoly to speak about the nature of the human; Kamau Brathwaite on creolization; Édouard Glissant on the poetics of relationality as a transformative mode of being; Fanon on independence struggles in Africa and its diaspora while minding the deleterious effects of residual regimes on the psychopathology of the colonized; and C. L. R. James on the power of pan-African anticolonial struggle and other liberatory social movements, such as those models offered by revolutions in Haiti and Cuba, respectively.

Glissant is perhaps the starkest example of a Caribbean intellectual whose work tends to be oversimplified. As Torres-Saillant notes, despite the "originality" of his scholarship and speculative inquiry, Glissant "now gets established through his presumed rapport with postcolonial theory" (*Intellectual History*

43). The "surrender" to the epistemic might of the postcolonialists by some Caribbeanists is troubling, and in some ways "indicates the erosion of the region's intellectual self-confidence" (43). It is no wonder that when imparting his own vision of Caribbean history, culture, and destiny—in an attempt to extract some coherence out of the region—Torres-Saillant sidesteps an overreliance on theory, in light of "the problematic rapport the theoretical has had with the Caribbean region and its people" (7).

The writer stresses how differences should not be erased in the quest for a unified group identity. The resonances between critical approaches to the Caribbean and to Latinx studies have become increasingly apparent in recent years as the latter field grapples with complex issues—broached much earlier in Caribbean studies—such as the regional, racial, and cultural variations within the diaspora. Recognition of Caribbean creolization, for instance, leads us to a richer understanding of the ethnoracial admixture commonly known as *mestizaje*. In the landmark 2003 essay "Dominican Blackness and the Modern World," the author posited that a conceptual bridge between Dominican culture—"black awareness with a Dominican difference"—and the US context may inform racial thought in a salutary way (285). In the United States, Caribbean and Latin American migrants are often surprised to find themselves cast into "racial polarities" that defy the greater nuance and "accommodation of racial difference" of their home countries. As indicated by the Dominican poet Sherezada "Chiqui" Vicioso's comment, "Until I came to New York, I didn't know I was black," the volatile dynamics of race in the US may defy the "complexity of their own national experience regarding interracial relations" ("Dominican Blackness" 284–285). Torres-Saillant's scholarship thus advances novel ways of thinking about hybridity and interethnic tensions without compromising the challenge of interpreting race, cultures, and variegated experiences among Latinx peoples.

Latinx Oneness and Diversity: The Seesaw of Group Identities

Among Torres-Saillant's major themes is an urgency to respect and understand the particularities comprising Latinx identity. He insists that without expending the labor needed to theorize the rapport among these differentiated subgroups, a de facto assumption of oneness has often led to large truth claims about "the community" and its supposed political, cultural, or ethnic agenda. These claims typically fail to account for the multiple sites and planes of difference within a population of over sixty-five million in the United States. He weighs the need for people of Latinx ancestry to figure in public discourse as a group and to have a shared sense of place in this country, while at the same time advocating for the critical recognition of internal divisions, stratifications, and self-identifications within Latinidad.

Alongside such contemporaries as Frances R. Aparicio, Marta Caminero-Santangelo, Agustín Laó-Montes, Roberto Márquez, Yolanda Martínez-San Miguel, Suzanne Oboler, Mérida M. Rúa, José David Saldívar, and Lourdes Torres, among others, Torres-Saillant directly tackles the major challenges informing contemporary Latinidad. This composite label often seems to attempt to fashion a shared cultural identity among the Latin American-descended and Spanish-speaking diaspora in the US, but without invoking any single or essential trait to culturally or politically unify a population of widely diverse races, classes, social locations, geographic origins, and locations of diasporic settlement. Given the inherent difficulties—some would even say *impossibility*—of making any foolproof claims about a shared identity among such a diverse population, Latinidad, as both a theoretical concept and social construct, has been duly interrogated and critiqued in recent scholarship.

Foremost among the problematic paradigms associated with this concept is the notion of a composite identity and culture: the assumption of Latinx oneness. Torres-Saillant raises concerns about uncritical invocations of such oneness, which could discourage the serious work required to catalyze any sense of unity among the population in question. Indeed, such an assumption would seem to conspire *against* the potential for panethnic unity, since it may sanction overcertain and self-appointed spokespersons to proceed as if panethnic unity were an axiomatic good that one can and should take for granted. Furthermore, wholesale identity claims undermine genuine efforts aimed at promoting integration and solidarity. Presuppositions of cultural unity among the Latinx population also diminish the need to get to know and understand one another better. Likewise, outside of academic discourses, totalizing formulations of communal identity and culture, as they relate to race, class, gender, language, forms of worship, family dynamics, and the like, normally meet with tension—even protest—from distinct segments of the panethnicity that have experienced exclusion. Many tend not to see themselves in the generalizations put forward. Resolving the contradictions of invoking oneness out of political expediency may prove, again, impossible. An honest account of Latinx identity must demand recognition of internal plurality and respect the fundamental intricacies of human lives.

Torres-Saillant contends that if we cannot overcome the inherent contradictions of assuming a unified "community" for political purposes while simultaneously safeguarding the complexity stemming from their humanity (including by fending off the homogenizing gaze of others), we might settle for Latinidad as a rhetorical concept rather than a reifying claim. That is, any sense of coherence within the Latinx population would look something like Austrian philosopher Ludwig Wittgenstein's "family resemblances" model: peoples related through various traits, though not necessarily one in particular, all collected under a useful banner that may be deployed strategically for political purposes. This setup would circumvent the temptation to embrace metaphysical concepts such as biological or cultural essentialism.

Such an approach honors both the differences and the dimensions of similarity within the panethnicity. Torres-Saillant imparts how this "both/and" type of analysis (Latinidad as both a social construct and a reflection of real coherence within the group) rather than an "either/or" position (either Latinidad describes actual Latinx unity, or it is just a convenient fiction to label what is actually a heterogeneous population) may best address the ethical and metaphysical problem for scholars. Being cognizant of the messy ongoing reality of actual Latinx lives means irresolution can be highly productive, despite being unsettling. After all, our trade as purveyors of knowledge, unlike that of politicians, requires us to substantiate our claims based on evidence, reason, and accountability, as well as openness to possible truths that leave room for creative thinking.

While preparing this volume, the editors enjoyed many memorable conversations with Torres-Saillant. In one, he invited us to envision the oneness-diversity paradigm through the metaphor of a seesaw, with its up-and-down, give-and-take configuration: "On a seesaw, the player at one end pushes against the ground to swing up, thereby lowering the player at the other end, who can reverse the action by doing likewise. A third relational position manifests when they become balanced on par, thus level with each other on the ground. A pivot point balances the plank at the middle, such that both players are linked in a flexible dynamic." Likewise, rival formulations of assumed *oneness* or a unity-defying *diversity* among Latinx peoples may take rhetorical turns in the up position as required by the social context. Thus, either political expediency or epistemic integrity (to the fact of diversity within the group) may assert itself by turns. The two opposing forces may even find a balance point, at which competing goals can—at least temporarily—be held in suspension. We asked him to elaborate, and he obliged as follows:

> In this model, the tension between the rival formulations becomes a creative force, in that the rhetorical turns remain inextricable from one another, with each option having a provisional use and neither claiming absolute power over the other. Likewise, neither claim can permanently overwhelm or annul recognition of the other. The seesaw model

allows for the utterance of commonplace essentialisms about Latinx identity for strategic aims, such as to reassure coethnic audiences at times when they find themselves dismissed or belittled. A similar dynamic applies to the in-group's embrace of ethnic stereotypes, such as when Latinx audiences take pride in their reputation for greater displays of affection compared to "cold" Anglos, or when boasting of their stronger family ties than those of other groups.[2]

The Poetics of Prose: Signature Style, Voice, and Approach

Torres-Saillant shares a perspective that is gratifying in terms of argument, form, and approach. Among these is his tendency to emphasize a historical perspective. This hallmark is on full display in his excavation of US Dominican literary history in the chapter "Before the Diaspora." Likewise, one will find an almost anthropological description of cultural legacies, discourses, and paradigms in many of the essays in this volume, such as the unearthing of identitarian manifestations in "Afro-Latinos and the Racial Wall" and of Latinx nationalism in "A Tenuous Community: Latino Identity, Nationalism, and *Latinidad*." By unearthing and tracing the genesis of key concepts and notable cultural traditions, Torres-Saillant's analysis empowers us to question often-outmoded ways of thinking, being, and doing as they relate to the "givens" that we uncritically assume to be true.

A particular delight of reading these texts is Torres-Saillant's signature voice and style, features of which include the following: quaint archaisms and idiosyncratic diction (e.g., "mingle carnally with"; "decalogues of distinct characteristics"); a "foreignized," capacious lexicon befitting a multilingual scholar; and a tendency toward sinuous phrasing that winds up slowly to land a punchy takeaway. At times, the diction may strike some as awkward, even stuffy. But a chapter or two in, we realize the fault may lie in our quickness to judge, as we begin to discern a pleasing poetics and signature voice at play. Soon we begin to appreciate terms, phrases, or syntax we initially dismissed as ornate or stilted. What results is an altogether fascinating flux, a combination of welcome surprises and the expansion of our vocabulary—followed by revisions of our own assumptions and readerly expectations.

Surprises and Challenges: The Promise of Scholarship

The present collection is a compendium of heterodox views, illuminating insights, and timely challenges to dominant discourses in the field. For example, we encounter the critique of "essentialized, hardened, and therefore simplified ideas of identity" in the chapter "Afro-Latinos and the Racial Wall." By recovering forgotten histories and excavating cultural legacies, these chapters let some much-needed oxygen into the wine, including for us of more recent vintage or for those who appreciate the tastes of the present while anticipating the harvests of the future. One of the editors (Garcia) is reminded of the time when, as a naive graduate student at Cornell, he corrected a quite senior professor who, while relating a story, identified Rio de Janeiro as the capital of Brazil.

> YOUNG GARCIA, *with unchecked certainty and the overconfidence of youth*. Rio isn't the capital of Brazil. The capital of Brazil is Brasília.
> AGING PROFESSOR, *with wry humor*. Don't be such a presentist! At the time of the story, the capital of Brazil *was* Rio.

Garcia stands dumbfounded, awareness of his historical ignorance slowly dawning. Like a Zen master, the professor waits patiently until he sees comprehension on the young man's face. Then they laugh, uproariously, together.

Without the intervention of the senior scholar's wisdom, and without the benefit of that object lesson in grace and intellectual humility, Garcia would have continued in his error for who knows how long. Like the "Zen master" professor in the story, Torres-Saillant vibrates with a similar grace and deep erudition—both in person and on the page. We need scholars who take the winding path, whose wealth of experience and knowledge extend beyond the current moment, and whose scholarship supersedes the narrow confines of a single discipline. In Torres-Saillant's writing we discover the intellectual riches of someone who helped to build the field, but whose thinking is not defined by it.

Without scholars willing to call it as they see it, based on evidence and a fair-minded assessment of the case, our "scholarship" is reduced to a doom loop of groupthink, regurgitated dogma, and discipline-enforced orthodoxy. Torres-Saillant calls it as he sees it, but not as uninformed opinion. Whatever the topic at hand, he brings to bear the wide-angle lens of a historian, the creative versatility of a literary critic, and his own singular perspective—all tempered by conscientious self-reflection. Rather than a producer of instant scholarship, he is a painstaking and patient writer.

These essays are to be savored, even as they unsettle. They unseat the familiar, challenge our assumptions, and radically contextualize atomized facts. The chapters of *Problematic Paradigms* also reflect Silvio Torres-Saillant's evolving participation in the political and rhetorical development of US Latinidad. They set forth a rigorous exploration of one thinker's careful interventions into issues that continue to affect us all, especially in a time of fractured and apocalyptic national consciousness. What results, at least for us as editors, is a cautious optimism and renewed awareness of the urgency to pursue transformative thinking in Latinx studies.

Notes

1. Torres-Saillant's main intellectual formation occurred before the advent of *Latinx*, or, more recently, *Latine*, as preferred terms. His usage of the term *Latino* acknowledges the history behind the term as well as the preference of some, especially older generations, for that earlier usage—or for the more inclusive variants *Latina/o* or Latin@. Later essays in the book use a combination of these terms, so as to accurately reflect the historical and intellectual context in which each essay was originally written. See the "Note on Terminology."

2. Private conversation, 21 Feb. 2025, in Torres-Saillant's office at Syracuse University.

PART I

APPROACHES TO DOMINICAN STUDIES

History, Literature, and Culture

CHAPTER 1

BEFORE THE DIASPORA

Early Dominican Literature in the United States

In this piece of literary recovery, Torres-Saillant seeks to correct the "faulty chronology" that had afflicted the temporality of US Dominican writing. Many had represented that literary record as a relatively recent phenomenon that emerged in the mid-twentieth century as an outgrowth of pivotal historical events taking place in the Dominican Republic at the time. In contrast, Torres-Saillant situates Dominican letters within the larger schema of the US Hispanic literary heritage, a repository of cultures and politics dating back to periods prior to the birth of the United States. "Once we accept the idea that there was *a Dominican literary presence in the United States during the 115 years prior to the Great Exodus of the mid-1960s forwards," he argues, "it becomes automatically plausible to encounter texts by Dominicans worthy of being recovered."*

The nineteenth-century forerunners to such contemporary Dominican American writers as Junot Díaz, Rhina P. Espaillat, and Julia Alvarez include diplomats, exiles, and notable individuals whose travels to the US yielded fruitful reflections on their lives and times. Using examples such as the Henríquez Ureña family, Torres-Saillant stresses the impact of the Dominican nationals who made their mark in the US before the founding of the Dominican Republic in 1844. This "long literary presence" also preceded the formation of Hispanic ethnic enclaves in the US Northeast, such as El Barrio and Washington Heights in Manhattan. The chapter covers writers who self-published and formed literary communities in New York shortly after the large Dominican migration began in the 1960s. These creatives undertook the "task of bearing witness to the traumatic immigrant experiences of their people with imaginative verve," paving the way for complex Dominican-US interactions on and off the page, within and beyond borders.

Cultural Invisibility

The state of knowledge about the cultural life of Dominicans in the United States is rather dismal. Most reference publications that allegedly cover the various ethnic groups that make up the US population, including those dealing specifically with Hispanics, omit Dominicans. Over four decades ago, a book entitled *Spanish-Speaking Groups in the United States* (1954), by John H. Burma, made no mention of Dominicans, focusing instead on Mexican Americans, Hispanos of New Mexico, Puerto Ricans, and Filipinos. Nearly twenty years later in 1976, the Hispanic chapter of a guide to media and materials covering US ethnic minorities still omitted Dominicans, limiting the survey to Cubans, Puerto Ricans, and Mexican Americans (L. M. King). In the same year, *A Comprehensive Bibliography for the Study of American Minorities* carried a section titled "From the Islands," which included the "Puerto Rican–American Experience" and the "Cuban American Experience" but mentioned nothing of Dominican life in the United States (Miller 757). Still in the 1990s, the place accorded to Dominicans in reference sources remained so meager that it seemed possible to compile a voluminous *Hispanic Almanac* covering virtually every field of endeavor and yet give under five pages to Dominican personalities and events.[1]

The invisibility of Dominicans in the reference sources seems incongruous with their numerical presence in many populous cities in the Northeast. One example would be New York City, where people from the Dominican Republic have outnumbered all other immigrant groups in their rate of arrival, as well as in school enrollment and naturalization, evincing the community's desire to integrate into the larger US society. But as so often happens with disempowered communities in this country, the arbiters of culture have found it difficult to acknowledge, let alone valorize, Dominicans, despite their considerable presence. The already trite expression "Out of sight, out of mind" takes on a bitter aftertaste when applied to Dominicans, who have remained generally "out of mind" despite being "in sight." The complaint against the omission of Dominicans and their experiences, particularly from literary histories, anthologies, and related compilations of Hispanic or US experience broadly, has been articulated in public forums since at least the start of the 1990s (Torres-Saillant, "La literatura" 139–140). During this decade, major collections of US Latino literature appeared, such as *The Latino Reader: An American Literary Tradition from 1542 to the Present* (1997), edited by Harold Augenbraum and Margarite Fernández Olmos, and *The Hispanic Literary Companion*, edited by Nicolás Kanellos (1997), that failed to include a single Dominican voice.

The Literary Productivity of the Diaspora

Excluding Dominicans from the literary history of US Latina/os seems hardly defensible, given the visibility enjoyed for over a decade now by Julia Alvarez, a poet and fiction writer born in New York to Dominican parents in 1950. Alvarez spent her early childhood in her parents' homeland, where she attended Carol Morgan, an American school, coming back to New York in 1960 when the family felt the need to flee the regime of Rafael Leónidas Trujillo. A longtime resident of Vermont, Alvarez has served as professor and writer-in-residence at Middlebury College. Her literary career began in full force in 1984 when Grove Press published her book of poems *Homecoming*, which garnered recognition for combining narrative with lyrical verse. The volume features a speaker who searches for her identity as a woman through an exploration of her mother's teachings about housekeeping and through an understanding of the worldviews informing her maternal culture. "Orchids," the last poem in "Housekeeping" (the first section) interrogates the theme of the woman artist who achieves self-realization through her craft but loses touch with her creativity after marriage. The third section of *Homecoming*, titled "33," uses the sonnet form to examine the angst of a childless divorced woman confronting solitude, sexual desire, and the indignities of living in a persistently patriarchal world. These realizations become more poignant considering her omnipresent awareness of aging and its effects on her self-concept and self-worth.

Alvarez has continued writing verse, publishing *The Other Side* in 1995 and *Homecoming: New and Collected Poems* in 1996, both with Penguin Books. The importance attributed to her verse may be illustrated by her selection for inclusion in the exhibition "The Hand of the Poet," a display of "original manuscripts by 100 masters" at the New York Public Library. The second part of the exhibit, which displayed manuscripts of poets from e. e. cummings to Alvarez herself, remained open to the public from August 16, 1996, through February 15, 1997. Her poetry had already received unmistakable recognition in a 1987 anthology edited by Robert M. Bender and Charles L. Squier. *The Sonnet: A Comprehensive Selection of British and American Sonnets from the Renaissance to the Present* surveyed practitioners of the form ranging from Sir Thomas Wyatt of the English Renaissance to Alvarez as representative of contemporary American verse. While she was lauded for her poetic acumen, it was Alvarez's fiction that propelled her to the international status she now enjoys. Her first two novels, *How the García Girls Lost Their Accents* (1991) and *In the Time of the Butterflies* (1994), became bestsellers, with the latter being made into a 2001 feature film starring Salma Hayek. The debut novel was named Notable Book of 1991 by the *New York Times Book Review* and by the American Literature Association. It also received the PEN Oakland / Josephine Miles Award for excellence in literature. The second work of fiction was nominated for the 1995 National Book Critics Circle Award. A third novel, *¡Yo!*, has earned favorable reviews since it first appeared in 1997. Alvarez's works in fiction and nonfiction have received multiple prizes and honors both at home and abroad, including a National Medal of Arts in 2013 during the second term of President Barack Obama's administration.

Coming one generation earlier than Alvarez, another contemporary Dominican American writer who uses English as her medium of expression is Rhina Polonia Espaillat, who was born in Santo Domingo in 1932. Her family fled the Trujillo dictatorship, and she arrived in the United States as a toddler, eventually residing in New York City with her working-class parents. Though she writes primarily in English, she has fully retained her Spanish, publishing poems in newspapers of the Dominican Republic while undertaking extensive translation work both to and from her mother tongue. Espaillat studied as an undergraduate at Hunter College, earning a bachelor's degree in English. For her graduate work, she attended Queens College, also part of the City University of New York system. After receiving her master's degree, she worked as an English teacher in public high schools until her retirement, which was a pivotal moment for her to resume her commitment to her poetic craft and revive the fame she had first enjoyed during adolescence. When she and her late husband, sculptor Alfred Moskowitz, moved away from New York City to be closer to their adult children, they settled in Newburyport, Massachusetts. She has not always been well known among Dominicans in the United States, probably due to her starting her publication track in English and delaying the release of her book-length texts until age sixty. Even before then, Espaillat had several hundred poems published in literary magazines and journals.

At sixteen, Espaillat became the youngest person ever to have been inducted into the Poetry Society of America. Decades later, the Society would honor her twice, in 1986 and 1989, with its Gustav Davidson Memorial Award. The British magazine *Urbis* also distinguished her with two awards for literary excellence (R. Fernández 79). In 1992 she published her first book of poems, *Lapsing to Grace*, which included her own line drawings to accompany the text. The numerous compilations and anthologies that have published Espaillat's poems include *Looking for Home: Women Writing about Exile* (1990), *Sarah's Daughters Sing: A Sampler of Poems by Jewish Women* (1990), *A Formal Feeling Comes: Poems in Form by Contemporary Women* (1994), and *In Other Words: Literature by Latinas of the United States* (1994). Many of her poems evoke memories of childhood and wrestle with distant images of Dominican life, conjuring the complex interaction of contemporary poetic versatility of themes and diction with primarily classical prosody.

One of the most memorable literary developments among Dominican writers in recent times has been the celebrity of Junot Díaz, an author born in Santo Domingo in 1969. He came to the United States at the age of seven, spending the rest of his childhood and adolescence in New Jersey, where he attended high school and college. A graduate of Rutgers University, he went on to study creative writing at Cornell University. When he left, MFA degree in hand, he had already published short fiction in the well-known literary magazine *Story*. Within a month, between the end of 1995 and the beginning of 1996, *The New Yorker* published two of his short pieces. The January 15, 1996, issue of *Newsweek* carried a feature on the "overnight success" of the young Díaz, celebrating his impressive "six-figure" contract with Riverhead Books, a division of Penguin, for a collection of stories and a novel. Díaz's short fiction has earned him inclusion in such competitive compilations as *The Best American Short Stories: 1996* and *The Best American Short Stories: 1997*, testifying to an ongoing interest from peers as well as the general public. Named a Notable Book of 1996 by *The New York Times Book Review*, the collection *Drown* established Díaz as a vigorous new voice in contemporary American fiction.

Drown appeared midway through that year, earning immediate praise from reviewers in *The New York Times*, *The Village Voice*, *Publishers Weekly*, and even in fashion and entertainment magazines, such as *Elle* and *Mirabella*. Showing a keen intellectual sensibility, the author delves unsentimentally into slice-of-life experiences centering Dominican characters. Whether in the Caribbean or the US, they face misery and uprooting. With an exceptional command of figurative and colloquial language, Díaz communicates complex emotions and warring states of mind through concrete images and vivid tropes. The grown-ups in *Drown* struggle against unfriendly destinies while their children, as diasporic creatures, bear the weight of the American Dream thrust upon them by their parents. We also confront the stress inherent in the interaction between the individual and the collective that frames social identity.

Successful Dominican writers working in the United States do not abound. Indeed, few have transcended the limitations posed by the social marginality that has typified their community in general. Most Dominican authors write predominantly in Spanish, for the virtually exclusive consumption of small literary circles in Dominican neighborhoods. These literary artists grapple with a dearth of publication opportunities. Normally, they must finance, supervise the production of, and distribute their own books. They hardly have any chance of being integrated into mainstream literary markets or at least of attaining a level of prestige outside of their immigrant enclaves. Yet, many have proven tenacious in their dedication to the craft and have continued to publish despite the odds. A sample list of the authors who were the most active during the 1990s, committing their poems, novels, and short fiction to print during that time, includes Carlos Rodríguez, Marianela Medrano, Alexis Gómez Rosa, Franklin Gutiérrez, Miriam Ventura, León Félix Batista, Rei Berroa, Juan Rivero, José Carvajal, Josefina Báez, Tomás Modesto Galán, Julio Alvarado, Maitreyi Villamán Matos, Norberto James Rawlings, Juan Torres, Teonilda Madera, Diógenes Abreu, Yrene Santos, Félix Darío Mendoza, Juan Matos, José Segura, Ynoemia Villar, and Dagoberto López. Whether or not their works have withstood the test of time, the community remains indebted to them for assuming the task of bearing witness to the traumatic immigrant experiences of their people with imaginative verve and unbridled creativity.

The glaring exception to the fate of literary works written in Spanish by writers from the Dominican community is the remarkable case of Viriato Sención's *They Forged the Signature of God* (1995), as translated into English by Asa Zatz for the Connecticut-based Curbstone Press. The original Spanish edition, *Los que falsificaron la firma de Dios,* written by Sención in the South Bronx, has broken the Dominican Republic's sales records since it appeared there in 1992. Dominican readers, including people who had shown no interest in literature before, took to bookstores in droves. A tale of intrigue, corruption, and deceit set in contemporary times, the novel features characters bearing an unmistakable resemblance to Trujillo and his political heir Joaquín Balaguer, the best known of the country's military chiefs, and the latter's influential relatives and associates. The characters represented the whole gamut of the political scene in the Dominican Republic during those tumultuous decades. The novel lays bare the mendacity of the country's ruling class and government officials. Its indictment proved so biting that President Balaguer himself publicly endorsed the minister of education's decision to revoke the 1993 National Prize for Fiction that a panel of experts had awarded the work.

The English translation by Zatz received noteworthy reviews in *Publishers Weekly*, *The Washington Post Book World*, *Choice*, and the *Latino Review of Books*, among others. During the 1996 presidential election in the Dominican Republic, *The New York Times* quoted various fragments from *They Forged the Signature of God* to illustrate the behavior of some of the contenders. Sención wrote the novel after living in New York for nearly fifteen years. Though the book deals with political situations of the homeland, its scathing indictment of the Dominican power structure reflects an inherently diasporic perspective. Inside the country, such representations would be inconceivable in light of the government's firm and endemic control of the media, the publishing industry, and the venues meant for transmission of intellectual discourse. It was arguably the distance from his native land that sharpened the author's memory and activated his critical sensibilities. This text captures an important stage in the Dominican community's coping with the political events that, for many, constituted the chief impetus for emigration.

The Case for a New (or Revised) Chronology

In view of the meagre place accorded by current Latino literary historiography to Dominican authors, despite the achievements of Alvarez, Díaz, Sención, and Espaillat, one can easily imagine the state of knowledge about US Dominican writing prior to the settlement of large Dominican neighborhoods in Northeastern cities starting in the mid-1960s. Indeed, the prevailing assumption appears to have been that the cultural and artistic presence of Dominicans in this country was an exceedingly recent phenomenon. The scholar William Luis composed a noteworthy meditation on Cuban, Puerto Rican, and Dominican writing in the United States for the second volume of *The Cambridge History of Latin American Literature*. Luis begins his account of Puerto Rican writers by examining figures who visited but did not stay in the mainland United States during the first half of the twentieth century. These included René Marqués and José Luis González ("Latin American [Hispanic Caribbean] Literature" 538–539). He opens the Cuban portion of his chronicle by tracing the trajectory of such prominent visitors as José María Heredia, Cirilo Villaverde, and José Martí throughout the nineteenth century. When Luis moves on to Dominicans, however, he radically shortens the temporal reach of his account: "Dominicans are the most recent group of Hispanic Caribbean authors to write in the United States. The Dominican Republic and its writers have been marked by two vital events: the end of the Trujillo dictatorship and the US invasion of the island" (554). Guided by that chronology, the critic predictably makes reference to Dominican literary artists in the United States beginning in the mid-1970s.

The chronology adopted by Luis fails to account for a long history of interactions between Quisqueya and North America prior to the 1965 US invasion. It is these interactions that underlie the emergence of large Dominican settlements in this country. When one considers that background, which includes a legacy of political and cultural exchange, it becomes possible to trace the literary activity of Dominicans in the United States back to the founding of this Caribbean nation. Prior to the proclamation of the Dominican Republic on February 27, 1844, Juan Pablo Duarte, the ideological architect of Dominican independence, spent time in New York, where, according to his sister Rosa, he studied English (Duarte 40). Duarte regularly produced verse, prose, and plays—some now lost, some still extant—and no evidence exists to rule out his having added to the bulk of his writings during his North American sojourn. It seems fit to conjecture that the man continued writing while stateside. But no conjecture is really needed to show the literary presence of Dominicans in the US during the nineteenth century. Following the official beginning of the Dominican Republic as an independent state, the Dominicans who ventured north of the Caribbean were likely to have literary interests and aptitudes, since they generally belonged to the educated class. Those who came from the ruling elite tended to be indistinguishable from the literati. Illustrative of that interrelationship is the book *Los próceres escritores*, by Balaguer (1947), in which the author surveys the literary activities of most of the well-known political leaders in nineteenth-century Dominican history.

US-Dominican Relations

Contact between Dominicans and the United States began as soon as Santo Domingo's creole elite succeeded in implementing the juridical emancipation of their country—roughly two-thirds of the island known as Hispaniola—which had for the preceding twenty years been politically unified under Haitian rule. The leaders of the incipient nation-state found it necessary to seek the recognition of their neighbor to the north. The newborn republic urgently needed commercial and diplomatic credibility to meet the challenge of surviving on the world's economic stage. As a result, the Dominican government sent an emissary to Washington in December 1844, the same year as independence, to secure the establishment of formal relations between the two countries. John C. Calhoun, then secretary of state, advocated for the recognition of the small Caribbean country (Welles 76). But no further developments occurred because the issue had arisen at the very end of President John Tyler's administration.

The situation changed when Tyler's successor, President James K. Polk, arrived at the White House in March 1845. Polk's secretary of state, James Buchanan, appointed a man named John Hogan to serve as American agent in Santo Domingo and sent him there to assess the country. Two other American envoys would arrive in the capital before the end of Polk's term in office: Francis Harrison and Jonathan Elliot. In a letter to Secretary Buchanan, dated May 2, 1849, an enthusiastic Hogan reported a conversation with

Dominican president Manuel Jimenes regarding the possibility of annexing the country to the United States. After Polk, virtually every new American chief of state—Zachary Taylor, Millard Fillmore, Franklyn Pierce, and James Buchanan—dealt in varying degrees with the need to articulate a policy toward the Dominican Republic. The administration of President Abraham Lincoln, immersed in the throes of the Civil War, could not afford to tackle the Dominican question. However, the context of the war and the prevailing sense of national despair that ensued created an emotional ambience that favored the enterprise of William Cazneau and Joseph Fabens, two veterans of the Texas wars (1836–1846) who hoped to make money by selling land to their troubled compatriots in the Dominican Republic. The two American adventurers, having obtained sizable land concessions from the Dominican government, set up an American colony in Santo Domingo and sought to promote migration to that country as an escape from the sorrows of the war and a safe pathway to prosperity and wealth.

After the Civil War, President Andrew Johnson, upon the advice of Secretary of State William H. Seward, renewed the US government's interest in the Dominican Republic. This time, Washington had its eyes on the acquisition of Samaná Bay, with plans to install a naval base there that would ward off the danger of European aggression in the Caribbean. Johnson even worked the Dominican question into his fourth annual message to Congress on December 9, 1868. At that point, on his way out, as it were, he plainly endorsed the annexation of Santo Domingo (Welles 355). This occurred less than twenty years after the Guadalupe Hidalgo Treaty of February 2, 1848. The United States had not yet ceased to expand territorially. Thus, when President Ulysses S. Grant came to the White House, he embraced Johnson's exhortation with vehement obstinacy. He sought by various means to deflect the opposition posed by political sectors both at home and in the Dominican Republic. Due to the effective challenge of vigorous voices in Congress, such as that of Senator Charles Sumner, Grant failed to receive congressional approval for the annexation of Santo Domingo. Pleading his case with the legislature, he finally prevailed upon the Senate to authorize him to appoint a commission of inquiry to visit the country and prepare a report on the conditions there for the benefit of Congress. With a young Frederick Douglass as recording secretary, the commission featured three US senators: Benjamin F. Wade, Samuel G. Howe, and Andrew D. White (who would subsequently move on to serve as Cornell University's founding president).

The Dominican Republic did not become a territory of the United States. However, the decades that followed witnessed the growing influence of this northern neighbor in the country's economic, social, political, and cultural spheres. The United States, by the end of the nineteenth century, had become the predominant foreign influence in the nation, having displaced what historian Frank Moya Pons calls "European interests that had traditionally dominated Dominican commerce" (272). The trend took on a momentum of its own, and by 1905, Washington found it necessary to assume control of all fiscal transactions in the land, via the establishment of a customs receivership under direct supervision by American officials. In 1916 the management of Dominican life by the United States escalated further, with the formal declaration of a US military occupation, whereby Washington would rule the small republic until 1924. When they withdrew after eight years of governance, the occupying forces left a radically Americanized country. They had created several social and political institutions, including a National Guard, one of whose most clever graduates, Rafael Leónidas Trujillo, would perpetrate thirty years of the most ruthless tyranny against the Dominican people. As the saying goes, the rest is history: Trujillo met his death in 1961; democracy raised its hopeful head in 1962; the old Trujillo oligarchy overthrew the constitutional government in 1963. The people revolted, demanding democracy in 1965. The US intervened militarily to quell the popular uprising. In 1966, the elusive Balaguer, Trujillo's craftiest servant, became president of the republic. The great exodus of Dominicans to the United States thus began and continued unabated for decades thereafter.

Nineteenth-Century Dominican Presence in the US

The foregoing overview of US-Dominican relations crams many decades into a few paragraphs, seeking to provide a historical framework to affirm the plausibility of a Dominican presence in the United States, just as there was an American one in the Dominican Republic, since 1844. When channels of communication between two countries open, the movement that follows normally occurs in both directions. One thinks, for instance, of Tomás Cocco y Alum, born in New Orleans, Louisiana, in 1843, who settled in Puerto Plata, where he eventually earned distinction as a Dominican patriot. No less meaningfully, Federico Lithgow, born in Puerto Plata in 1842, had parents who were themselves natives of the United States. His father, Arturo Lithgow, came from Augusta, Maine, and his mother, Ana María Pellegrín, was a native of New Orleans (Rodríguez Demorizi, *Próceres* 72, 173).

Washington was as necessary to Dominican politicians and entrepreneurs as Santo Domingo was to their US counterparts. The North was a place where prominent Dominicans could come when expelled from their country by powerful political rivals. For instance, on June 13, 1866, the dictator Buenaventura Báez in St. Thomas wrote to his brother Damián Báez, asking him to arrange a meeting for him in New York with some potential business associates (Rodríguez Demorizi, *Papeles* 459). In a February 5, 1867, letter to a friend's daughter named Corinne, the exiled statesman wrote about his having recently arrived in Curaçao from New York (203). On December 25, 1875, corresponding from Curaçao with his sibling Damián, the shrewd caudillo complained about his having been detained "in New York when [he] was there having [his] eye illness treated" (my trans.; 465).

Political rivalry was not the only motive for people from the Dominican Republic to venture northward. A different example of a Dominican presence in the United States is suggested by Captain José Gabriel Luperón, the older brother of General Gregorio Luperón, probably the most venerated of nineteenth-century Dominican patriots. According to the testimony of his younger brother, Captain Luperón participated in the American Civil War on the side of the North and received the rank of captain from President Lincoln: "He was the courageous soldier who cut the chain that had blocked the way of the North's naval vessels at the entrance of the Mississippi" (my trans.; Rodríguez Demorizi, *Próceres* 185).

The awareness that Dominicans traveled to the United States as political exiles or as individual talents in search of wider horizons during the nineteenth century may help to overcome the faulty chronology that has hampered the dissemination of knowledge about the Dominican contribution to the US Hispanic literary heritage. A modification of that chronology would put us closer to historical truth, enabling us to see a long Dominican literary presence in the United States prior to the massive immigration that began in the mid-1960s. I would venture to affirm, further, that the Dominican portion of the US Hispanic literary heritage is ample and significant enough to warrant its inclusion in recovery efforts of the kind marshaled by Nicolás Kanellos at the University of Houston. In the sections that follow, I will map schematically some of the areas of research that may prove fruitful for scholars interested in reconstructing the thus-far neglected Dominican presence in the US prior to the formation of bustling Dominican enclaves in this country.

I begin by looking closely at the Dominican presence in New York in connection with the independence movement of the Antilles. Dominicans were invariably at the center of the movement. We have the testimony of the most prominent Hispanic Caribbean thinkers Ramón Emeterio Betances, Eugenio María de Hostos, and José Martí themselves to support this contention. Once nineteenth-century Dominican Antilleanists are identified, one needs to examine their writings, including their correspondences, to isolate the portion pertaining to their stays in North America. A salient example is fiction writer and essayist Alejandro Angulo Guridi (1822–1906), who arrived in the United States in the 1840s and stayed continuously until 1852. He became a US citizen and had his second marriage recorded in Charleston, Virginia. Subsequently, Angulo Guridi returned to the Dominican Republic, where he became reintegrated into political life but retained contact with North America. On December 31, 1863, he traveled to Washington as an assistant to Dominican secretary of state Pablo Pujol. His pamphlet advocating against the annexation of the Dominican land to the Spanish empire, *Santo Domingo y España* (1864), appeared in New York under the auspices of Imprenta de M. W. Siebert (Vallejo de Paredes 65). Also at that time, he was "writing a lot in English" in his role as correspondent for the *New York Herald* and the *Daily News*, as described in a letter dated March 10, 1865. The epistle was addressed to Don Ulises Francisco Espaillat, an intellectual who would years later become president of the Dominican Republic (my trans.; Rodríguez Demorizi, *Próceres* 21–23).

Many prominent Dominicans came to the United States in the nineteenth century simply to comply with diplomatic assignments, as was the case with General José Billini, Dr. José Caminero, and the aforementioned Pablo Pujol. Others, such as General Matías Ramón Mella, one of the three patriots generally recognized as founders of Dominican nationhood, used experiences in the US as a stepping stone to return to their home country's political arena. Having been exiled to Liverpool by dictator Pedro Santana, Mella made his way back via the United States, whence he journeyed to Puerto Rico before reaching Santo Domingo in 1848 (Rodríguez Demorizi, *Próceres* 40–41, 203, 269). Still others succeeded at building alliances in the North American territory with Cuban and Puerto Rican counterparts who were also devoted to the cause of national liberation. In 1865 the Sociedad Democrática de los Amigos de América printed the pamphlet *Las Colonias españolas y la República Dominicana*, penned by the Cuban nationalist Juan Manuel Macías. Founded by Macías, the Sociedad included the Puerto Rican physician José J. Basora and the Cuban novelist Cirilo Villaverde among its prominent members. By the same token, on December 15, 1870, the New York–based periodical *El Demócrata* featured a long obituary authored by Cuban patriot J. M. Ferregur in homage to one of the original leaders of the Dominican independence movement, Pedro Alejandrino Pina, who had died several months prior. Ferregur's ardent appraisal highlighted not only Pina's devotion to Dominican causes, but also his invaluable support of the Cuban independence struggle, which was consistent with the spirit of regional solidarity that characterized the typical attitudes of nineteenth-century Antillean leaders (Rodríguez Demorizi, *Próceres* 186, 259–260).

In addition to political motives, some Dominicans had personal reasons for settling in the United States in the nineteenth century. Juan de Dios Tejada, a Dominican who, in 1897, lived in New York, where he occupied an apartment at 49 East 99th Street, is a case in point. Earlier that year, while traveling to Santo Domingo from New York, Tejada's wife and four children had perished in a shipwreck. Despite his bereavement, the widower endeavored to remarry only a few months after the tragedy. Mindful of the heavy reproach that this decision would elicit, he wrote a letter on December 24, 1897, to Ramona Ureña, an old family friend, in a clear effort to plead for the understanding of someone whose moral judgment he either feared or respected. In a telling passage, he gives the following rationale for rushing to the altar: "The life one leads here is pitiful or extremely risky for a man in my condition. I am still young, and in order to avert the cold dryness of an old bachelor or the unnatural temptations that here one is besieged by every minute, I decided to marry" (my trans.; 281–283). The power of Tejada's letter lies in its presentation of a predictably human drive to seek commiseration from others for decisions we have made on our own, including for selfish reasons. The document lays bare the personal drama of an individual Dominican who had made his home in New York during the late nineteenth century and sought to fit in, at least to a degree, amid the pressures of his "pitiful or extremely risky" environment.

The Twentieth Century: The Henríquez Ureña Family

The twentieth century, of course, offers the most fertile ground for the excavation of Dominican literary artifacts from North American soil. At the very beginning of the century, one finds distinguished Dominicans who came to this country in pursuit of personal objectives, namely the Henríquez Ureña family. The young Pedro Henríquez Ureña and his brothers, upon completing their secondary education in their hometown of Santo Domingo, traveled to New York on February 19, 1901. Their father, Francisco Henríquez y Carvajal, had sent them there for their college education. As he acknowledges in a 1902 letter to Pedro, he hoped they would "become acquainted with the American spirit" before moving on to complete their graduate studies in Europe (my trans.; Henríquez y Carvajal 291). During their stay in New York, the young men attended Columbia University and lived in the vicinity of the campus. They spent the whole month of August 1901 in Buffalo, New York, in the company of a Dominican writer from Puerto Plata named Mercedes Mota. In 1902, Pedro and his brothers received the regrettable news from their father about the loss of his government position. He could no longer afford to provide for them in New York and asked them to return home. However, with a temerity befitting their youth, the young men chose to stay abroad and fend for themselves. Pedro found a job in retail sales, while his younger brother, Max, entertained restaurant patrons on the piano. Pedro worked long hours, studied hard, and wrote assiduously (de Lara 25).

It was arguably in New York that Pedro Henríquez Ureña, the Dominican literary figure with by far the most international reputation, began his writing career. In that respect, one could contend that it was in the context of his US experience that he, devoid of parental supervision and protection, made the serious decision to become a professional wordsmith and literary scholar. Many of the earliest of Henríquez Ureña's extant compositions come from these New York years. The poems written in his youth appeared posthumously in a slim volume titled *Poesías juveniles* (1949). The book includes twenty-two poems, of which eight identify New York as their place of composition. Written between 1901 and 1904, they appear in the following order: "Flores de otoño," "En la cumbre" (dedicated to the aforementioned Mercedes Mota), "Mariposas negras," "Intima," "Música moderna," "Frente a las 'Palisades' del Hudson" (whose reference to New York could not be more obvious), "Ensueños," and "Escorzos." Not only did Henríquez Ureña affirm his commitment to writing at the time of these early poems, but from his correspondence it also becomes clear that he and his brothers did not live in isolation from other important Dominicans in the Northeastern US metropolis. Addressing his maternal aunt Ramona Ureña in a letter dated July 5, 1902, he names many friends from his social circles back home, among them writers, who were also in New York and who had already visited him there ("De Pedro Henríquez Ureña" 289–290).

According to Pedro's testimony, he and his brothers found "various Dominicans" upon arriving in New York. These included "the ex-President D. Alejandro Woss y Gil, a man of subtle intelligence and good friend of my father as well as of my cousin Enrique, the Consul Leonte Vásquez, brother of the then Vice President Horacio; the students Floricel Rojas and *Niño* Alfonseca; that remarkable character Abelardo A. Moscoso, an energetic man, not entirely uncouth but of somewhat bizarre ideas and feelings on account of his long years of struggle in exile; and many more whom we had less to do with" (my trans.; qtd. in Roggiano xiii). The young brothers frequented the libraries as well as the theaters of the city. As a regular feature of their social life, they visited educational and cultural institutions as well as "the hotels and houses that lodged the Dominicans who came to New York for their summer vacation, whose number increased every year" (my trans.; Roggiano xxviii). The young men's decision to stay in New York provides us with a case study of Dominican youths fending for themselves in the metropolis at the very beginning of the twentieth century. In 1903 they ventured into renting their own flat, one located on West 15th Street in Manhattan, where other compatriots would board as well. Among them were Virgilio Ortea, a family friend who had come to New York "to work in commerce," and his brother Julio, whose parents had sent him so that he could "become Americanized" (my trans.; xxix). The brothers inhabited a neighborhood that "teemed with Dominican exiles who now increasingly headed for New York" (my trans.; xxxi).

Over the next decade, Pedro and his brothers moved from New York to Cuba to Mexico and back to Cuba again. Only in 1914 did Pedro return to the United States. He traveled to Washington, DC, first, working as a correspondent for the newspaper *Heraldo de Cuba*, writing under the pen name E. P. Garduño. He kept his column until April 1915, when he relocated to New York to join the staff of the periodical *Las Novedades*, headed at the time by the Dominican intellectual and entrepreneur Francisco José Peynado. Pedro wrote prodigiously for *Las Novedades* until mid-1916 (de Lara 38). New York appears to have been a site of much intellectual activity for Dominicans who enjoyed positions of privilege. A letter from his father, during Pedro's second sojourn in the United States, refers to meetings in the city with other well-known Dominican writers, such as Tulio M. Cestero. His father's eager inquiry about the possibility of "developing in New York the publication of books in Spanish" gives grounds for supposing that the Hispanophone cultural life must have been considerable at the time (my trans.; Henríquez y Carvajal 657).

El nacimiento de Dionisos (1916), a dramatic prose composition in which Henríquez Ureña aims to reconstruct the form of Greek tragedy "during the period immediately before Aeschylus," appeared in New York under the book-publishing branch of Las Novedades (my trans.; P. Henríquez Ureña, *El nacimiento* 63). Though probably written in Mexico, as biographer Juan Jacobo de Lara claims, the text waited until the author returned to New York to be committed to print (38). In Mexico, Pedro had studied law; now back in the United States, on September 27, 1916, he began teaching in the Romance Languages Department of the University of Minnesota, Minneapolis, while also pursuing a graduate degree there. In June 1917, he received his master of arts in Spanish, having produced a thesis titled "The Irregular Stanza in the Spanish Poetry of the XVI and XVII Centuries" (orig. in English; de Lara 40). Immediately after receiving his MA, Henríquez Ureña proceeded to enroll in a doctoral program at the same institution. After obtaining permission to write his dissertation in Spanish, he proposed to conduct a more advanced and in-depth study of the topic of his MA thesis. The outcome of this effort was a major scholarly project that subsequently earned the praise of the eminent Spanish humanist Ramón Menéndez Pidal and the cadre of distinguished philologists then associated with Madrid's Centro de Estudios Históricos. *La versificación irregular en la poesía castellana* was published in 1920 in the Spanish capital, precisely under the imprint of the Centro de Estudios Históricos. This rigorous investigation by Henríquez Ureña surveys poetry written in Spanish from the medieval epics and romances through the twentieth century with an eye on metrical arrangements. His panoramic quest abundantly confirmed the premise that "metrics in Spanish poetry is a lot less simple than scholars have thus far noted" (my trans.; *La versificación* 13).

In 1921, Henríquez Ureña left Minnesota to settle in Madrid, after which professional engagements took him to Mexico, Argentina, and, for a period of less than two years, his native Dominican Republic. The last time he came to the United States was to serve as the Charles Eliot Norton visiting professor at Harvard University during academic year 1940–1941 (M. Henríquez Ureña xlix–l). During this third and final stay in North America, Henríquez Ureña continued to be the prolific writer that he had been since 1901. In addition to his other scholarly output, his lectures at Harvard, delivered in English, would appear in book form in 1945 from Harvard University Press titled *Literary Currents in Hispanic America*. A cultural survey of Latin America from the moment of conquest to the present, the book bore a biographical error on the inside flap, alleging that "these lectures by a South American scholar mark a real milestone." The editorial oversight, which essentially changed the author's nationality, strangely presaged the invisibility that Dominican writers would have to endure in subsequent accounts of Hispanic literatures in the United States.

After completing this teaching opportunity, Henríquez Ureña would leave the United States, never to return. Yet it is clear from the foregoing overview, despite its brevity, that the writings he produced during three prolonged stays in this country constitute a major Dominican contribution to the US Hispanic literary heritage. The selections contained in Alfredo A. Roggiano's anthology *Pedro Henríquez Ureña en los Estados Unidos* (1961) bear witness to the fruit that recovery efforts directed at this eminent humanist's work can yield. An extensive search of the annals of *Heraldo de Cuba*, *Las Novedades*, *El Fígaro*, *Romanic Review*, *Revue Hispanique*, and other periodicals, plus those books in his oeuvre whose composition, regardless of place of publication, can be traced to the years he spent in American cities, could reveal a sizeable body of work by an author who ranks among the top essayists in twentieth-century Latin American literature

When Henríquez Ureña received his doctorate from the University of Minnesota in June 1918, another Dominican was graduating at the same time, namely his sister Camila Henríquez Ureña (1894–1973), who received her MA degree at the same ceremony (de Lara 41). She, like her brother, became a literary scholar and essayist. Upon graduating, she traveled back to Cuba, where she had lived prior to pursuing her postbaccalaureate education in the United States. It was in Cuba that she was most productive, except for a seventeen-year span (1941–1958) when she lived in the United States. She taught in the Spanish Department at Vassar College in Poughkeepsie, New York, also offering courses occasionally at Middlebury College in Vermont. The work of recovering the literary texts produced by Camila during her seventeen years in North America has yet to begin in earnest. The voluminous compilation *Estudios y conferencias* (1982), published posthumously in Cuba under her name, comes strictly from sources found in the archives of the Cuban Academy of Science's Institute of Literature and Linguistics. Looking at that significant collection, one cannot help but wonder about the rich potential of undertaking a comparable search for Camila's texts with a focus on her North American years.

Dominican Writers in New York through the 1950s

At this point, I will list a few other Dominican literary artists who wrote and published in the United States, primarily in New York, during the early twentieth century. José M. Bernard (1873–1954), a highly regarded poet in his lifetime, released the collection *Renuevos* in 1907 through the New York–based Imprenta Hispano-Americana. In 1908, also in this city, a volume of short fiction titled *Cuentos frágiles* (1908), by Fabio Fiallo, appeared. Fiallo (1866–1942) was a poet and short-story writer who enjoyed great renown in Latin America. He was a close friend of Rubén Darío and other towering literary figures of the continent. Another important name among Dominican writers being mapped here is Manuel Florentino Cestero (1879–1926), who had lived in the United States with his family since early in the century, when a sudden loss of privilege caused by the fall of a government that had favored him led to his permanent exile (Martínez 119). In New York he published a book of poems, *El canto del cisne* (1915), printed by Las Novedades, and a short period later, he is said to have written a fiction work, titled *El amor en Nueva York*, reportedly published in 1920. The actual existence of the text remains unverified.

An intense period of Dominican literary productivity in the United States was connected to the large presence of middle-class exiles who lived here during the thirty years of the ruthless Trujillo dictatorship. Jesús de Galíndez, the Basque writer whose murder at the hands of Trujillo's henchmen on March 12, 1956, caused an international uproar, attested to the numerical significance of anti-Trujillo Dominican exiles active in New York during the 1940s (Galíndez 252). The year 1946 witnessed the publication in the city of the tract *¡Yo también acuso!*, by Carmita Landestoy, a former collaborator of the regime who later became an opponent. Andrés Requena, a well-known fiction writer who fell out of favor with the dictatorship and ended up joining the opposition, wrote the novel *Cementerio sin cruces* (1951) while exiled in New York. This text was published by Editorial Veracruz in Mexico (Silfa 332). The novel, plus his other writings in the anti-Trujillo paper *Pluma y espada*, published occasionally in New York by its editor, José R. López Cestero, as well as in the periodical *Patria*, which Requena co-edited with Juan M. Díaz, cost the author his life (Galíndez 279). The consul general of the Dominican Republic in New York, Félix W. Bernardino, an angel of death whom Trujillo appointed specifically to silence opposition abroad, supervised his killing.

The fiction writer Angel Rafael Lamarche (1899–1962) also resided in New York during the 1940s. Here, he wrote *Los cuentos que Nueva York no sabe* (1949) and *El Nueva York de un iberoamericano*, whose publication date remains unknown. The former was released by the publisher Talleres Gráficos de la Carpeta in Mexico, earning him considerable praise in the literary circles of Santo Domingo. Lamarche is not known to have joined the opposition to the Trujillo regime in New York, but it is clear that most of the publications by Dominicans in the city from 1930 through 1961 were informed by an awareness of the dictatorship's actions. In addition to the Dominican-led periodicals cited above, we should underscore the prominent presence of Dominican authors in the pages of widely known Hispanic publications, such as *Visión*, *La Prensa*, and *El Diario de Nueva York* (Galíndez 136–137). Significantly, Stanley Ross, who was the editor of *El Diario de Nueva York* in the 1950s, had lived in the Dominican Republic, where he founded the daily *El Caribe* (Silfa 426). A search for Dominican texts in those invaluable sources would likely prove rewarding for recovery-minded scholars. Hector J. Díaz (1910–1952), the Dominican poet whose work is most often recited among nonliterary audiences in his native land, spent the last years of his life in New York. It would be useful to survey the totality of his verse to determine whether a meaningful portion of his oeuvre can be isolated as dating from his years in the city.

Recovering Early US Dominican Texts: A Legacy in Process

Whether these early Dominican writers composed in verse or prose, and whether they produced creative or expository texts, one would need to weigh carefully how much of their work falls under the category of what we term the

"US Hispanic literary heritage" today. I believe that once we accept the idea that there *was* a Dominican literary presence in the United States during the 115 years prior to the Great Exodus of the mid-1960s forward, it becomes automatically plausible to encounter texts by Dominicans worthy of being recovered. The point of my remarks here, ultimately, is that the literary activity of Dominicans in the United States already had generations of forerunners prior to the late 1970s, when Dominican writers were putatively seen as part of an ethnic community of recent immigrants. For the most part, today's Dominican American writers know little of that earlier history. A vital task of future explorations of this topic would be to identify and evaluate resonances between present and past Dominican writers in the United States across the chasms of class origins, generations, genders, sexualities, and historical circumstances, as well as differences in their language of literary communication. Much labor remains to be undertaken in the overall recovery project of Dominican literary history in this country.

Notes

1. See Kanellos, *Hispanic Almanac*. See also Kanellos, *The Hispanic Literary Companion*, which does not include any Dominicans. This initial paragraph and early commentary in the chapter draw extensively from "Forging a US Dominican Culture," chapter 4 of *The Dominican Americans* (1998), which Torres-Saillant coauthored with Ramona Hernández.

CHAPTER 2

VISIONS OF DOMINICANNESS IN THE UNITED STATES

This chapter takes a bird's-eye view of commonalities and differences between groups that contribute to pan-Latino identity in the United States. The author points to "a composite of diverse historical realities, national experiences, and collective existential traumas" that bring people together. The ground-level view focuses specifically on self-definition for Dominicans, namely, those who either migrated to the US or were born there, as well as those living in the Dominican Republic. This dichotomy in and of itself also invites commentary, as ongoing tensions have fomented competition and disunity. The chapter also interrogates stereotypical views of Latina/os in the mainstream, simultaneously identifying their shared social location as a basis for commonality. Torres-Saillant argues that while "the language of unity thus appears to function as an instrument of survival," specificities cannot be ignored, since solidarity and kinship bonds are not guaranteed.

Thus, the chapter investigates the dynamics and limits of panethnic discourse as it relates to the legacies of colonization, intergroup relationships, and the ongoing pressures of globalization. Shared concerns, such as the politics of borders, as well as immigrant vulnerabilities and triumphs, remain crucial to self-definition. More specifically for the Dominican community, Torres-Saillant asks, "Which and whose perceptions are privileged when examining things Dominican?" The voice reflects a moment when Dominican studies and its usually Dominican practitioners did not enjoy any particular cachet in the US academy. At that time, valuing lived experience and community welfare was key to empowering Dominicans to speak for themselves. Torres-Saillant takes pains to refute historical impressions of the Dominican Republic, as well as contemporary media stereotypes that tended to associate US-based Dominicans with drugs, gangs, and criminality. He does so with an awareness of the historical constructions that depicted the country as a paradise to be conquered and exploited by enterprising outsiders in collusion with scheming political insiders.

What is the Dominican perspective on the Latino community and the global society? The inclusion of a Dominican voice among this conference's presenters says a great deal about the rise of people connected by ancestry or birth to the Dominican Republic as a core branch of the US Hispanic population.[1] It may also acknowledge that tackling the difficult challenges currently facing our communities requires a plurality of voices. The adoption by the United States of economic and political measures prompted by the imperatives of globalization can be expected to shake up the relationship of Latina/os to the mainstream society. But an equally important concern is the extent to which the logic of the global society will make it possible for Latina/os to see themselves as a diverse yet unifiable human formation—a community capable of speaking with a complex but hopefully integrated and ideally harmonious voice.

One ultimate consequence of the relaxation of national borders implicit in the North American Free Trade Agreement (NAFTA, 1994) and other such treaties may be a weakening of our claim, as a US minority, to entitlements and services based on our contributions to the larger society. Many of us have "paid our dues" over the course of an arduous immigrant experience. Even within a national group, competition for resources in the quest for survival may create traumas or trigger the return of old ones. Imagine a scenario in which—borders having been made flexible by some regional accord—Dominicans may come to the United States straight from the home country and gain easy access to the social and economic spaces that US Dominicans have struggled for, over the course of many years. One can only speculate on the consequences for both Dominicans in the United States and those in the ancestral land.

Latina/os and Diasporic Identity

Latina/os in the United States are a composite of diverse historical realities, national experiences, and collective existential traumas. Before emigration from the native land, which for each distinct group corresponded to different sociohistorical and geopolitical events, one did not see oneself as Latina/o or Hispanic but as Puerto Rican, Cuban, Colombian, or Dominican, to name only some of the most visible groups in my current base of operation, New York. As members of diasporic communities, however, we have become unified in significant ways. We share the experience of being uprooted by large socioeconomic forces in our original homelands. We come from societies with a history of unequal association with the United States, a country that has influenced and sometimes even dictated political behavior in Latin America. The metaphor of the "backyard," often invoked by US policymakers to identify Latin America's geographical proximity to the United States, entails a qualitative view that constructs the region not as a partner but as a subordinate.

By the third decade of the twentieth century, a good many Latin American nations already had ascertained, through the incursion of US armed forces into their territory, the concrete realities resulting from the inequality of their relationship with their North American overseer. They had also become acquainted with the ideologies and assumptions that informed these military invasions. For instance, Senator Albert J. Beveridge of Indiana, speaking before the Senate in 1901, declared, "God has made us the master organizers of the world to establish systems where chaos reigns. He has made us adept in government that we may administer government among savages and senile people" (qtd. in Welles 916). Similarly, President Theodore Roosevelt is known to have publicly decried the social and political lives of Cubans, Dominicans, Haitians, and Nicaraguans. The famous "corollary to the Monroe Doctrine" in his annual message to Congress in 1904 hints at the US sense of moral and political superiority over the peoples of Latin America: "Chronic wrongdoing or an impotence which results in a general loosening of the ties of civilized society, may in America, as elsewhere, ultimately require intervention by some civilized nation, and in the Western Hemisphere the adherence of the United States to the Monroe Doctrine may force the United States, however reluctantly, in flagrant cases of such wrongdoing or impotence, to the exercise of an international police power" (qtd. in Black 23).

The popular view of the Spanish-speaking inhabitants of the hemisphere that prevailed in the United States during the first half of the century is reflected in a poll conducted in 1940 by the Office of Public Opinion Research. The questionnaire gave respondents nineteen adjectives with which to describe "Latins." "Dark-skinned" came first, chosen by 80 percent of the respondents, followed by "quick-tempered," "emotional," "religious," "backward," "lazy," "ignorant," and "suspicious," chosen by 40 to 50 percent of those who answered. At the very bottom, chosen by a mere 5 percent, "efficient," preceded by the adjectives "progressive," "generous," "brave," "honest," "intelligent," and "shrewd," none of which obtained a ranking higher than 16 percent (Black 61). The assumptions held by respondents to this questionnaire foreshadowed the treatment awaiting Latin Americans upon their arrival in the United States.

Coming, as we do, from subaltern nations, it is no wonder that we occupy not the center but the margins of US society. This peripheral location has intensified; most of us, except for Mexicans and Puerto Ricans, immigrated at a time when the country's economy was less expansive than during earlier waves. The arrival of Dominicans, Cubans, Colombians, and Central Americans, among others, coincided with the notable transformation of economic life in former industrial centers, such as New York City, where the service sector has become the primary area of employment. Instead of fostering integration, this arrangement has produced a widening gap between recent Latina/o immigrants and the mainstream of productive economic life. New York exhibits what scholars have called a "dual city" model,[2] where recent Spanish-speaking immigrants almost invariably occupy the less prosperous side of the divide, with clear implications for their sense of identity and belonging. Political, economic, and cultural marginality relegates them to a condition of "otherness" with respect to the dominant economic and social structures.[3]

The awareness of such alterity vis-à-vis the US mainstream would lead a Colombian or Dominican to assert their commonality with Latina/os of other national origins on the grounds that they share a comparable socioeconomic condition, especially as they encounter linguistic, religious, and historical interactions across various groups. The experience of diasporic uprooting and the sense of living outside the dominant realm of the receiving society permeate the core of Latino identity. Even though Mexicans, Puerto Ricans, and Dominicans became ethnic communities in the United States through profoundly different processes, they are bound by political imperatives to see themselves as one. Ironically, Simón Bolívar's desideratum of a unified Latin American nation and the ideal upheld by Eugenio María de Hostos of an Antillean federation find in US Latina/os a strange kind of fulfillment. They have come to articulate a collective identity, not in their native homelands, as Bolivár and Hostos had dreamed, but within the insecure space of the diaspora. The feeling that they inhabit a contested terrain, that they do not inherit their social space but must carve it out for themselves in the face of adversity, leads them to hoist the banner of their oneness, despite the different circumstances under which each subgroup came to the United States. The language of unity functions as an instrument of survival.

Dominicans in the Latin American Diaspora

The encompassing Latino identity described above does not, however, satisfy the need for each of the national groups to articulate its own sense of itself as product of a particular historical experience. It is within this frame that I will discuss some of the issues now faced by the Dominican portion of the Latino population. After three decades of massive migration to the United

States, Dominicans are passing through a stage where it is necessary for the community to define itself. US Dominicans have lost the privilege of individuality, namely, the ability of a person of Dominican descent to commit a crime or perform an act of charity and be judged individually, rather than as an instance of the collective behavior or personality of the national group. Therefore, many Dominicans, especially academics and others with the potential to influence public discourse, have begun the quest for self-definition. In the mid-1990s, a group of scholars and educators agreed to create a Dominican Studies Association, with one of their clearest goals being to ensure that the image of Dominicans in American society is drawn by knowledgeable and sensitive spokespersons.

A central purpose of this enterprise was to ensure that the Dominican community held some power over the prism through which they were seen. The Bildner Center for Western Hemisphere Studies at the Graduate Center of the City University of New York, for instance, had for years conducted a series of seminars on Dominican issues. The organizers were non-Dominicans, and the speakers invariably had been scholars brought from the Dominican Republic or from parts of the United States that did not have a recognizable Dominican immigrant community. The sole Dominican scholar listed by the Bildner Center as collaborator was one who, perhaps not incidentally, lived and worked for many years in Mexico and could not claim strong ties to any of the New York Dominican enclaves. This selectivity had worried New York–based Dominican scholars, many of whom were committed to the idea that the study of the Dominican experience must encompass not only the production of knowledge but also a research agenda aimed at securing the spiritual well-being and material survival of the population. Any venture into this field of study that did not exhibit a recognizable vision of the future of—and by—US Dominicans was cause for concern.

Which and whose perceptions are privileged when examining things Dominican? Dominicans in the diaspora have serious reasons for wanting a say in the answer to this question. For example, in her best-selling *Out of the Barrio: Toward a New Politics of Hispanic Assimilation*, Linda Chavez contrasts the neighborhoods of Dominicans and other Latina/os with those of Puerto Ricans. She magnifies the prosperity of Dominicans in New York to strengthen her case about the inadequacy of Puerto Ricans. She writes, "The vibrant commercial areas, even the manner in which the people moved on the street, attested to the vitality of neighborhoods. By contrast, the streets of the South Bronx were filled with men and women whose bearing suggested they had no place to go" (150). To diminish the effects of racism on the labor participation of Puerto Ricans, she claims that "other Hispanic groups who share

Puerto Ricans' mixed racial background, most notably Dominicans, face the same labor market conditions and yet managed to find jobs and retain a far higher degree of labor market attachment. This is so even among women who are single heads of households" (153). Dominican scholars from the diaspora would likely take issue with Chavez's representation of Dominicans, since it pits them against Puerto Ricans, arguably their most crucial ally in the struggle for survival in the Northeast.

Similarly, when scholars arrange the socioeconomic profile of Dominicans in the United States, their work has political implications. The literature on Dominican migration already reveals divergent views on the condition of the community, with striking differences corresponding to the particular emphases of individual scholars.[4] One can also point to a body of knowledge that has denormalized Dominicans, describing the members of the community in terms characteristic of zoological observation. Defamatory portrayals of Dominicans in the press have seriously detrimental effects on the community. These negative images affect the collective's lobbying power and bring about a loss of influence with political institutions. On a related note, corporate lawyers from the Dominican Republic, allied with counterparts in the US, have made inroads into important sectors of the American economy. For several years, the Santo Domingo–based Dominican American Assistance Fund celebrated its "Dominican Week" in Washington, DC; Miami; and various cities in New Jersey and New York. The initiative, which has enlisted the support New York Governor Mario Cuomo, Congressman Charles Rangel, and state department officials, was led by prominent individuals committed to attracting US investors to the Dominican Republic. Could their agendas coexist with the interests and needs of the US Dominican population, or will a time come when the members of the diaspora are forced to compete with their island-based compatriots as both seek to attract the attention of stateside business and government sectors?

These concerns suggest that the definition of Dominican identity is not unproblematic. The question of identity is compounded by history; the identity of Dominicans as a community in North America is developing in the context of prevalent and longstanding perceptions that took root before Dominicans established an immigrant settlement in the United States. Societal perceptions of immigrant groups normally correspond to shifts in the relationship between the host and the sending countries. In placing this discussion within the framework of community formation and interdependence for Latina/os in the United States, it is useful to keep in mind that every immigrant group inherits historical baggage from earlier stages of the relationship between ancestral homeland and country of civic belonging.

The "pre-history" of Dominican migration to the United States may shed some light on the process by which an immigrant group's self-definition (which necessitates a measure of political empowerment) comes into being on the battleground of an existing discourse and as a corrective challenge to perceptions deemed oppressive to them. The Dominican community's articulation of its identity encounters unsavory images (including media stereotypes) found in American public discourse. The resulting dynamic not only adds a measure of complexity to Dominican immigrants' drive to control their own representations, but also colors their interactions with other segments of the Latino population, as well as with Dominicans in the native land.

Global Order and National Identity

In the second decade of the twentieth century, with the Dominican Republic under direct rule by an American military government, the legal scholar Otto Schoenrich saw in the Dominican case "a striking illustration of the rule that large bodies attract nearby smaller or weaker bodies whether in the world of physics or in international politics" (389). For him, the US Army's occupation of the Dominican land came as no surprise: Once Puerto Rico and Cuba were occupied, "the attraction exerted on Santo Domingo was powerfully increased." From then on, "the Dominican Republic was in fact a protectorate of the United States, though neither American nor Dominican statesman would have admitted it" (389). He gave his book the telling title *Santo Domingo: A Country with a Future* (1918). The "future" he imagined was inextricably linked to the future of the United States. He predicted that the North American country would continue to shape the life of the smaller Caribbean nation "with greater strength than ever, despite all that may be said or done, on either side, to oppose it," since the historical dynamics in question transcended the will of politicians and citizens. He summarizes, "Conditions in Santo Domingo, in the United States, and in the world at large are the causes of this force of attraction, for which the government of neither country is responsible" (390).

Schoenrich was speaking about the imperatives of the global economic order as it manifested itself around 1918, the year his book was published. At the time, of course, it was not called "the global economy." The young Fidel Castro, for instance, invoked the founder of Cuban nationhood, with his own interpretation of international relations: "[José] Martí had already, in 1895, pointed to the danger hovering over America and called imperialism for what it was: imperialism" (my trans.; 101). For Latina/os in the United States, the most pertinent difference between the present and former versions of the global economic order is the emergence in the core countries of immigrant communities from peripheral nation-states that have assumed a diasporic identity. In carving out an existential and political space to speak for and name themselves, US Dominicans, consciously or unconsciously, contend with the images projected by commentators from a former era in US-Dominican relations. They must come to terms with an extant body of narratives fashioned by the likes of Schoenrich long before the massive exodus of Dominicans to the United States that surged during the 1960s. In short, they must wrestle with a skewed discursive history that has its roots in over a century of unequal relations between their land of origin and the land of their civic belonging.

Schoenrich believed fervently that the Dominicans' best hope lay in yielding to the inexorable power of the United States. In his view, every treaty or agreement transacted between the two nations served merely to avert or delay a direct annexation. Indirect control of a protectorate was the preferable option for Americans, insofar as it would afford "the advantages of annexation without its responsibilities, without the undesirable feature of bringing into our body politic a people foreign in race, language, and customs" (392). Schoenrich anticipated no sadness in this inevitable fate, for he expected it to bring greater benefits to Dominicans than they could possibly imagine. Indeed, only under the tutelage of the United States could they aspire to achieve peace, without which no prosperity would be possible: "All the troubles which have befallen the Dominican Republic" stem "directly or indirectly" from "the state of civil disorder which has so long been the bane of the country" (393–394). In his estimation, American military rule of the Dominican land had ended violent strife among political factions vying for control of the small country:

> When we think of the vast resources of Santo Domingo . . . we must be glad that the clouds which have so long shrouded the land in darkness are definitely dissipated at last and that the sun of peace and prosperity has begun to shine. . . .
>
> A new era has begun for beautiful Quisqueya, in which, under the protection of the Stars and Stripes, it is destined to enjoy a greater measure of freedom, progress and prosperity than its inhabitants have ever dreamed. (394–395)

The Dominican Republic did not morph into "one of the richest gardens of the West Indies," as Schoenrich had predicted (394). When the Americans relinquished rule of the country in 1924, the nation still had grave economic and social problems, and violence remained a political constant. The difference was that now the power to perpetrate such violence lay principally in the hands of social sectors trained or favored by the United States, since the occupying forces had succeeded in disarming the civilian population and enhancing the effectiveness of the armed forces. Thus, in February 1930, less than six years after American rule formally ended, General Rafael Leónidas Trujillo came to power and initiated a thirty-year reign of terror. He had been trained by the National Guard, a police force created by the occupying US Army. From 1916 to the present, there has been more bloodshed, corruption, and cynicism in Dominican society than during all previous years of republican life. Since 1916, however, by dint of the celebrated disarmament, the powers of coercion and destruction have resided almost exclusively among the most conservative sectors of society. This includes, not incidentally, economic violence, which was primarily responsible for the great exodus of Dominicans from their homeland and their subsequent emergence as immigrant communities in the diaspora.

Early American Images of Dominicans

The perception that Dominicans would secure their future by embracing North American control and protection was preceded by a stage in the public discourse that saw in the Dominican land a chance for US citizens themselves to realize their future. More than four decades before Schoenrich, W. S. Courtney, in a book suggestively titled *The Gold Fields of St. Domingo*, had announced "the development of the vast mineral, agricultural, manufacturing and commercial resources of the Spanish part of the Island of Santo Domingo" (9). This project was an ideal outlet for the "surplus of mental and physical energy" of his compatriots (8). The author warded off any suspicion that the inhabitants of Santo Domingo might, by virtue of their tropical habitat, be deemed "semi-barbarous" (10). He insisted, instead, on their civility, politeness, and affability, and their abiding honesty, demonstrated by the complete absence of robbery or theft "within the limits of the State" (14). The following passage captures this impression:

> Travelers, utter strangers to each other, meet at the inns, lay their money, watches and other valuables together on the table, swing their hammocks in the same room, retire, some rising to pursue their different journeys, while others sleep, and a single instance of a larceny under such circumstances of temptation, has never been known. (14)

Undergirding Courtney's benign representation of the Dominican character was a sense of these people being good-natured noble savages, relatively devoid of human complexity. They had neither vice nor virtue; they would not harm others, but neither could they help themselves. Without the "mental and physical energy" of white Americans, people in Santo Domingo, Courtney found, "wholly lack that thrift and industry necessary to their own material well-being, and the redemption of their country from the desolation into which it has fallen" (132). With a questionable temperament inherited from their Spanish ancestors, Dominicans seemed apathetic to the demands of capitalist accumulation: "No allurements of wealth will arouse them from their indolence and lethargy" (138). Americans, namely those of Anglo-Saxon background, with their "herculean energies and [their] inherent genius and skill," were urged to take advantage of this land that Providence had brought forth just for them (143). In addition to being a highly profitable enterprise, adding the Dominican land to the area over which the US had jurisdiction was, for Courtney, inescapable:

> That this gem of the Western Seas will sooner or later, through the enterprize of the Anglo-American be rescued from desolation, its valleys and plains transformed into elysian gardens and blooming fields, its mountains made to yield their golden stores and its now solitary rivers and pensive bays thronged with commerce, is inevitable. (143–144)

Many enterprising Americans did indeed view the Dominican Republic as a land of milk and honey. Joseph Warren Fabens and William Leslie Cazneau, in 1859, negotiated with Dominican president Pedro Santana a concession of land on which to build houses for Americans in order to encourage migration (Tansill 343). Cazneau's wife, Jane Maria McManus Cazneau, who participated in the entrepreneur's business dealings, authored a small book titled *Our Winter Eden* (1878), under the pen name Cora Montgomery. In it, she re-creates the pastoral experience of living in Santo Domingo as an American settler. Fabens's *In the Tropics* (1863) purports to show the success of a young American after twelve months of working the land there. Richard B. Kimball's introduction calls attention to the book's utility in teaching the reader "what Nature—not the stern old parent of Our North, but Nature young and prodigal and Eden-like—brings forth in the charmed circle of her tropical home" (3–4). Fabens, for his part, observes that "hundreds of the working classes are seeking new homes in countries where *intelligent* labor can best be made to supply the want of capital" (302). In a subsequent edition, published a decade later with the title *Life in Santo Domingo*, Kimball enhanced the Edenic scenario by adding a supplementary chapter about the Samana Bay Company of Santo Domingo, which was "inaugurated in this country, with headquarters in the City of New York, on a large and comprehensive scale, by a number of our leading capitalists." Anyone wishing to travel to "the island for the purposes of husbandry" would "go literally among his countrymen, and will receive protection and all necessary aids in founding his new home" (307–308).

Fabens and Cazneau were partners in various economic ventures in Santo Domingo. The most curious was the importation of thirty camels to ensure excellent transportation in the Monte Cristi area (Tansill 247). More enduring and large-scale was a project to annex the Dominican Republic, an idea that had interested various American presidents but reached the level of a passion with Ulysses S. Grant. The American Civil War hero, in collaboration with Dominican president Buenaventura Báez, invested much energy and time in pursuing the acquisition of the Dominican territory. To that end he appointed his personal secretary, General Orville E. Babcock, commissioner in the Dominican Republic.

At times, the commitment to annexation meant that the US government took sides in political struggles among Dominican factions. On July 10, 1869, Secretary of the Navy George M. Robeson ordered Commander Owen of the USS *Seminole* to capture a steamer used by General Gregorio Luperón, a nationalist insurgent leader who opposed the Báez government. Robeson's dispatch contended that Luperón's vessel had been "interfering with American commerce and sailing upon the high seas without legal authority" (qtd. in Welles 370–371). But the ulterior motive was to protect Báez's government and secure a safe course for the annexationist scheme. Indeed, the American commercial agent Sommer Smith lost his position in the Dominican Republic for holding "unfavorable opinions" regarding annexation, just as his substitute, Major Raymond H. Perry, would be permitted to resign when he, too, proved to be less than cooperative to the cause (Welles 374–375).

So great was the urgency to finalize the proceedings that in February 1870, the steamship *Albany* took possession of the Province of Samaná in the name of the United States. Babcock appointed Fabens to be American agent there. President Grant's nemesis, Senator Charles Sumner, the chairman of the Senate Committee on Foreign Relations, led the opposition that ultimately defeated the project. "Báez," Sumner declared, "is sustained in power by the Government of the United States that he may betray his country" (159). He denounced Cazneau and Fabens as "political jockeys" who, along with Babcock, were conspiring to defraud both the Dominican Republic and the nation back home. In light of these political maneuvers, the image of Dominicans as an essentially mild breed, good-natured and too indifferent or lazy to interfere with any foreigners eager to reap the wealth of their land, survived.

The imagery recurred throughout the American press and travel books of the nineteenth century. Journalist De B. Randolph Keim remarked, "The character of the people, generally, is that of an easy, thoughtless, inoffensive set who would prefer to live in listless forgetfulness of the duties or responsibilities of life. Their notions are exceedingly primitive, and their wants exceedingly few" (316). When President Grant sent a commission to the Dominican Republic to study the viability of annexing it, the members found "the physical, mental, and moral condition of the inhabitants of Santo Domingo to be much more advanced than had been anticipated" (United States 13).

Generally, Dominicans appeared denormalized in the public discourse of nineteenth-century United States. This was a portrayal that remained current until the early part of the twentieth century. They were "an honest and inoffensive people," according to a "sketch" published in New York in 1906 to garner support for a pending treaty whereby President Roosevelt sought to formalize US financial control over the Dominican Republic (*Santo Domingo* 19). Contrastively, when needing to present Dominicans as an essentially good, harmless people, American authors tended to present them as predominantly Caucasian to render them acceptable to white American readers at a time of rampant negrophobia. Thus the 1906 sketch states that while "the black race is in complete ascendancy" in Haiti, among the Dominican people "white blood preponderates" (*Santo Domingo* 18). Henry J. Hancock, another supporter of the treaty that would subsequently be known as the Dominican-American Convention, declared that in the Dominican Republic the "inhabitants are, with very few exceptions, white" (50).

The Colonizer, the Colonized, and the Individual

Nineteenth-century images, for the most part, distorted and falsified the Dominican collective profile. The practice may be inherent in the interaction between colonizer and colonized, as one gathers from prominent sociologist Frank Bonilla's discussion of US government spokespersons' appraisals of Puerto Ricans after the American occupation of 1898. Puerto Ricans saw themselves "coldly assessed by various agents of the overlord," through images that invariably rendered them devoid of nuance and human complexity. In the eyes of these official witnesses, Puerto Ricans were either "a gentle, patient, uncomplaining lot, living in ignorance and penury, generally polite, and willing to work in a plodding, undemonstrative way," as perceived by a certain Captain Macomb, or, in the contrasting profile advanced by one Lieutenant Blunt, "lazy and dirty" with the capacity to be "very sharp and cunning" ("Beyond Survival" 453–454). Bonilla places these representations within "a mind warping exchange that has disfigured and scarred mentalities among both rulers and ruled. This fragmentary and distorted self-knowledge continues a crippling heritage from which, I believe, none of us has so far achieved more than partial deliverance" (454).

We have not yet mapped the dimensions of the scars produced by the damaging images of Dominicanness disseminated by the agents of the imperial overlord. One might suppose the disfigurement to be less extreme in the Dominican Republic, a virtual protectorate, than in Puerto Rico, where the northern neighbor executed a classic colonial regime. But one notes a striking resemblance between the logic of US observers and that of the Dominican ruling elite in the discourse on progress, national resources, race, ethnicity, and the role of foreigners in the country's development. Even the language Dominicans used to assess their interactions with neighboring Haitians may have been mediated by the rhetoric of American overseers during the nineteenth century. This chapter is not the place to explore the full range of implications of Bonilla's "crippling heritage" as applied to the Dominican Republic. Rather, one might conclude with some thoughts on its implications for the Dominican diaspora in the United States.

The early images of Dominicans formed by US observers were hardly complimentary, but neither were they wholly disparaging. The predominant gaze is friendly in a paternalistic way. It was merely disrespectful; outright scorn and violent defamation would come later. At the time, Americans travelled to the Dominican Republic to pursue their own interests, which were economically and politically expedient. But since they did not undertake to colonize the country formally, they could sever their ties to Dominicans anytime at their convenience. This loose arrangement, in which Americans had much to gain and hardly anything to lose, did not foster the kind of tension that generates adversarial sentiments. Within such a context, it would not seem odd for individual Dominicans to gain ascendancy in the United States, with some even becoming stars.

The actress María Móntez came from Barahona to New York and rose to prominence through such successful Hollywood productions as *Arabian Nights* (1942) and *Cobra Woman* (1943). She found herself elevated to "world cult status" (Susann 4). In the late 1940s, New York's high society followed the adventures of Porfirio Rubirosa, a Dominican who developed an international reputation as a playboy by romancing wealthy and famous women. His multiple conquests included tobacco heiress Doris Duke, actress Zsa Zsa Gabor and her sister Eva, and Barbara Hutton, granddaughter of the founder of the Woolworth Company. The highly celebrated fashion designer Oscar de la Renta, notable for dressing celebrities (including several First Ladies), as well as the legendary pitcher Juan Marichal, inducted into the Baseball Hall of Fame in 1983, are also renowned Dominicans. All four, coming to the United States and carving out names for themselves as individuals, were generally able to pursue their ambitions unimpeded by strong anti-Dominican rhetoric. However, sociohistorical events of subsequent decades significantly reduced the opportunities for Dominicans to attain visibility relatively unencumbered by ethnic barriers. Once Dominicans emerged in the United States as an ethnic minority vying for political and economic space, they challenged entrenched sectors (including other minority groups) whose own political and economic fortunes appeared even more precarious by the empowerment of Dominicans and other Latina/os.

Migration and Demonization

The death of the dictator Trujillo in 1961, another American military invasion in 1965, and US congressional passage of the Immigration and Nationality Act of 1965 collectively paved the way for the massive exodus of Dominicans to the United States. Today, Dominicans are among the largest new immigrant cohorts in the United States. From 1982 to 1989, the Dominican Republic ranked seventh among countries sending migrants to the United States, and Dominicans ranked ninth in terms of naturalization, with 43,333 becoming citizens during those eight years (Salvo 27). In New York City during this period, Dominicans' naturalization rate outpaced all other communities (587). They constituted 42 percent of all Caribbean immigrants settling in the city and, along with the Chinese, accounted for 58 percent of all "new" immigrants in the borough of Manhattan. Impressive as they are, these statistics tell an incomplete story about the numerical significance of Dominicans in New York and the US broadly. A large portion of Dominican migration to this country has been undocumented or through informal channels. The actual size of that immigrant group can only be approximated.

As with earlier immigrant populations, the increase in Dominican arrivals provoked xenophobia from the mainstream media. During the 1980s, Washington Heights and its mostly Dominican inhabitants were associated almost exclusively with drugs and violent crime in the New York press. The *New York Post* frequently devoted pages to articles that spoke of Dominicans as "a community where three of the biggest sources of income are drugs, loan sharking, and money laundering" (McAlary, "Framing" 2). Such unflattering portrayals of the community, which date back to the 1980s, increased in frequency and vitriol since the summer of 1992, when the death of José "Kiko" García at the hands of a police officer from the 34th Precinct sparked three days of upheaval in Washington Heights. The journalist Mike McAlary painted the community as follows: "The Dominican Republic has always exported talent to the United States. The sports pages are filled with statistics of Dominican baseball heroes in the Major Leagues. But for every George Bell and Pedro Guerrero, Stan Javier and Julio Franco thrilling American audiences, there are now a dozen lethal drug dealers from San Francisco de Macorís terrorizing neighborhoods in upper Manhattan" ("Washington Heights" 3).

To prove the prevalence of crime among Dominicans and its roots in the homeland, McAlary, with the backing of the *New York Post*, embarked on a four-day trip to the Dominican Republic. He assessed the prevailing moral climate of San Francisco de Macorís this way: "There is a hint of dark evil in every gold-toothed smile, and the sound of sinister laughter in the pock-marked streets" ("Washington Heights" 3). In April 1994, when officers from the 30th Precinct were arrested for various forms of corruption, including collusion with drug dealers, it turned out that one member of the "dirty dozen," Alfonso Comprés, was a Dominican. This sufficed for McAlary to shift the focus of his coverage from corruption in the New York Police Department to Dominican criminality. The title of his article for the *New York Daily News*, "The Tragic Legacy of a 'Narco Village,'" alludes to the city where Comprés was born and where he presumably planned to return: "If the cops moved in, he could always go back to San Francisco de Macorís. This is the way of the Dominican York" (5).

"Dominican York," a term that refers to Dominicans in the Big Apple, parallels the term "Nuyoricans" for Puerto Ricans in the City. For their part, Dominicans have endured slanderous representations from public figures as prominent as Staten Island borough president Guy Molinari and police union boss Phil Caruso. In his campaign to unseat incumbent David Dinkins, New York City mayoral candidate Rudolph Giuliani condemned his opponent's expression of sympathy for a Dominican mother whose son had died at the hands of the NYPD. Giuliani construed the gesture as siding with "urban terrorists" (Torres-Saillant and Hernández, "Community" 3). These examples reveal the vulnerability of Dominican immigrants and their US-born children who must, for the time being, endure undeserved criticism without being able to challenge their detractors directly or on equal terms. The turning point will come, one expects, when the Dominican community has gained so much economic and political power that denigrating its members would be strategically unwise. One also hopes that by then, Dominicans will have enough access to English-language print and electronic media, including radio and television, to have significant influence over the construction of their public image.

The negative image of Dominicans may have a deleterious effect on efforts to build alliances with other Latino subgroups. During a literary colloquium at the Ollantay Center for the Arts in Queens during the late 1980s, the Puerto Rican fiction writer Edgardo Vega Yunqué (better known as Ed Vega) highlighted the inevitability of intra-Latino divisions, so long as the current economic scenario prevailed: "If all Latinos were from Ecuador the same thing would happen because the question is economic. Period. In other words, 90% of the wealth is controlled by 10% of the population. Then, a few crumbs are given to 90% of the people so they can fight amongst themselves" (71–72). Dominicans face, in addition to intra-Latino animosity, the dangers of tension with their compatriots in Hispaniola. Powerful Dominicans from the homeland, without a clear knowledge of or identification with the diaspora, may find it easier than US Dominicans to win the ear of important domestic spokespersons, including leaders of government agencies, cultural foundations, and major corporations. This special access, often rooted in questionable assumptions about authenticity, might well provoke the resentment of US Dominicans toward their brothers and sisters back on the island, particularly since the immigrant community has also experienced its share of rejection in the homeland (Torres-Saillant, "El concepto" 165–167). Nor can we ensure that the negative images of Dominicans currently prevalent in US public discourse will be rejected when they make landfall in the native land. These frictions are all the more worrisome when we consider that in the restructured global economy, Dominicans in the United States and those in the Dominican Republic may find themselves increasingly in a position of rivalry.

It will be key for those of Dominican ancestry going forward, whether situated in the Caribbean or North America, to examine the complexities of the historical, economic, and representational legacies they have inherited. For non-Dominicans and Dominicans alike, the challenge will be to avoid overgeneralizing Latino communities via convenient or sensational stereotypes (whether negative or positive) and seek instead to educate ourselves using a multiplicity of perspectives, reliable knowledge, and critical distrust of essentialism.

Notes

1. This chapter started as a revised and augmented version of "Visions of Dominicanness: Changing Images, Community Formation, Diasporic Identity, Precarious Associations," a paper presented at the Global Society and the Latino Community Conference sponsored by the Inter-University Program for Latino Research, held at the Rockefeller Foundation's Bellagio Conference Center, Bellagio, Italy, 12–16 Dec. 1994. It first appeared in print under the title "Visions of Dominicanness in the United States," in *Borderless Borders: US*

Latinos, Latin Americans, and the Paradox of Interdependence, edited by Frank Bonilla and the other conveners of the Bellagio conference for Temple University Press (2000).

2. I first presented this idea at the 1989 Latin American Studies Association Conference in Miami. See Torres-Saillant, "The Construction of the Other."

3. See, for instance, Mollenkopf and Castells.

4. See, for example, the contrasting perspectives offered by Pessar and by R. Hernández et al.

CHAPTER 3

PILGRIMS OF HUMANE REMEMBRANCE AT THE BORDERLANDS

This chapter blends literary analysis, personal reflection, and historical critique into an emphatic call for renewed awareness of the 1937 massacre of Haitians and Haitian Dominicans at the border between the two countries that share the island of Hispaniola. It was originally published in The Border of Lights Reader *(2021), a compendium of works by artists, activists, scholars, and observers meditating on the disturbing event. The essay pinpoints the legacy of denial, ignorance, and complicity that often characterizes official Dominican responses to the massacre. Because the mass killings were orchestrated by the Trujillo regime, working to rectify the residual impact of* trujillismo cultural *(continued allegiance to the exclusionary view of nation bequeathed by the scribes of the dictatorship) will be key to truth-telling and efforts at reconciliation. The end goal of such a reckoning, according to this short piece, is humane remembering, including the rehabilitation of public memory from the narratives woven and disseminated by the Trujillo regime and its offshoots.*

Torres-Saillant stresses the need to acknowledge different types of remembering. Some of us absorb historical lessons in a rote way while going through the motions of formal education; others do so as an obligation, often anchored in fear, to stand in allegiance to a particular administration or ideological machine. There is also, however, constructive and humane remembering, which entails more complex, more nuanced, and less unitary interpretations of history. This kind of remembering seeks to understand and make judgments in a more balanced, dispassionate way. Citing key examples from works by such writers as Jacques Stéphen Alexis, René Philoctète, Edwidge Danticat, and Freddy Prestol Castillo, Torres-Saillant encourages a renewed commitment to mutual respect, human dignity, and the right to safety and prosperity for all.

Since 2012, parents, children, students, teachers, members of the clergy, community organizers, cultural activists, artists, and scholars have convened in early October at several sites that straddle the arrondissement of Ouanaminthe in Haiti and the Dominican city of Dajabón. These souls come from various places on both sides of the Massacre River on the island of Hispaniola as well as from numerous cities overseas, especially in the United States, home of large diasporic communities of both Dominican and Haitian ancestry. These individuals come to participate in peaceful acts of subversive remembering. During a two-day program of activities (discussion sessions, readings, arts-and-crafts exhibitions, prayers, performances, and community service), they commune with their neighbors across the borderline. They assert their shared humanity over the national difference that the political partition of the island prescribes and its governments emphasize. Through various reflective tasks, they commit to remembering the past with an eye on increasing their chances of realistically envisioning a future of wholeness for Haitians and Dominicans alike. Their yearly pilgrimage seeks to establish sites of commemoration that put memory in the service of healing rather than triggering. They gather to come to terms with and transcend a ghastly chapter in the history of the hemisphere. They call their convergence a "Border of Lights," which they rightly juxtapose with the forces of darkness that have often impeded communication between the two polities that share the island, with especially deleterious consequences for Dominicans of Haitian ancestry.

The intersection of Ouanaminthe and Dajabón, where Dominicans and Haitians of good will have gathered annually, stands out among the key border points that in October 1937 witnessed the slaying of some fifteen thousand men, women, and children of Haitian ancestry, both immigrant and Dominican-born. It was the seventh year in the thirty-year rule of Dominican dictator Rafael Leónidas Trujillo. Machete-wielding soldiers and hired civilians hewed down lives quietly, swiftly, and messily in order to avoid the noise that firearms would have made. Despite the stealth, the Dominican government's genocidal violence shocked many in the hemisphere, and several pan-American conferences ensued shortly thereafter to address the looming crisis. Arbitration occurred among the region's heads of state, and an accord emerged that required Trujillo's administration to make amends, without formally admitting to sanctioning or committing the acts. The Dominican government agreed to pay reparations to the administration of Haitian president Sténio Vincent. As "arbitrated" during the negotiations, the Vincent government would receive $750,000 to spend on a series of "colonies agricoles" ("agricultural colonies") to accommodate Haitian refugees who had escaped the slaughter.

Literature has done a nuanced job of urging the peoples of Hispaniola and the rest of the world to contend with the memory of what transpired at the island's borderlands in 1937, a time when, still counting on US support, the Trujillo regime literally got away with murder. Literary texts have pointed to the Vincent government's odd interest in maintaining a cozy relationship with the Dominican dictator, thereby failing to press hard enough to secure the justice that the victims of the massacre deserved. *Les semences de la colère* (1949), a novel by Anthony Lespès, recounts a story of the agricultural colonies in a way that leaves readers understanding the deep despair endured by the refugees upon their return to Haitian territory. They generally had to fend for themselves in the face of obstacles stemming from the arbitrary choice of the area assigned to them, the climate, the suitability of the soil, and the broad impact of institutional neglect. In his review of *Les semences*, the African American scholar Mercer Cook observed that when he lived in Haiti in the early 1940s, it was widely known that Trujillo had ended up paying less than the $750,000 negotiated during the talks, and that the absurdly small amount actually disbursed reached only a handful (474).

The revolutionary Haitian writer Jacques Stéphen Alexis chose the 1937 bloodshed as the vehicle by which to conclude the difficult lives of his main characters, Hilarion and his wife, Claire-Heureuse, in his gripping debut novel *Compère Général Soleil* (*General Sun, My Brother*; 1955). After surviving earlier trials, the couple see their infant son, Désiré, die in the attack by Trujillo's henchmen and their dogs. When the pair finally reaches the Haitian border, Hilarion derives some satisfaction from dying in Haiti ("the domain of Ayiti Toma. He closed his eyes and smiled"), while his wife must go on alone (290). Carrol F. Coates, who translated the novel into English, observes that the "'missing' third subsection of part 3 might logically have been an exposé of the reasons for President Vincent's failure to protest the massacre or a glimpse of Claire-Heureuse's return" (xxxi). Coates remarks that the novel gestures to the author's awareness of secret correspondence between Trujillo and Vincent. In addition to his owing major favors to Trujillo, Vincent had apprehensions that limited his public response to the mass killings. In a letter to his compatriot Élie Lescot, he explained, "Having attested before the Haitian people to the sincerity and the solidity of our relations with the neighboring State and also to my personal friendship with President Trujillo, I admit that I am rather embarrassed by this sad event which, in all conscience, seems to me to go beyond ordinary border matters" (Vega, *Trujillo* 446; qtd. in Coates xxxviii).

The novel *Le peuple des terres mêlées* (1989), by the avant-garde Haitian poet and literary trailblazer René Philoctète, evokes the horrors of 1937 in a manner that invites reflection on the cultural fusion and border-bending practices of those living where the two countries of Hispaniola meet and diverge. The French adjective "mêlée," stemming from the verb "*mêler*" ("blend," "combine," or "mix" in English), can also, in its noun form, denote a clash or skirmish between combatants. In English usage, it also suggests more generally the confusion of a free-for-all. These nuances all seem to apply to the variegated and asymmetrical cosmos inhabited by the characters in Philoctète's novel, beginning with the protagonists: Dominican labor organizer Pedro Brito and his Haitian wife, Adèle Benjamin, a native of the commune of Belladère in the arrondissement of Lascahobas. Philoctète was a leader, alongside his celebrated compatriot Frankétienne, of Spiralisme, a Haitian literary school that upheld a poetics characterized by narrative defiance of logical progression and a mode of utterance that pays no heed to common sense. He captures the carnage in a manner that allows the magical to reign supreme. We encounter machetes with minds of their own and an oversized raptor-like bird that hovers in the sky above the Dominican province of Elías Piña, as if supervising the affair and providing support to the perpetrators on the ground. The bloodshed takes on a nightmarish form in scenes involving Pérez Agustín de Córdoba, a local boss of Elías Piña, who serves doubly as a killer and captain to murderous gangs. In a frenzy, Agustín charges at the powerless Haitian throng, stabbing and maiming the bodies while re-creating in his mind moments of memorable sex with his former Haitian mistress, Emmanuela. Through the thick fog of the horror, however, the love story of Pedro and Adèle shines forth with luminous clarity. Their tragedy, too, stands out starkly, as Pedro, in the end, fails to save his partner from the cruel blades of his own compatriots.

In her preface to *The Massacre River* (2005), the English translation of *Le peuple des terres mêlées*, Haitian American fiction writer Edwidge Danticat draws attention to the way in which Philoctète's novel lingers on the struggles of the people living in the borderlands, the points where the two nations come together while drifting apart. She revisits her own findings about those lands, including her realization that "sandwiched between the two borders was a group of people who tried to make a new world, people who were as fluid as the waters themselves, the people of the Massacre River." Like Pedro and Adèle, they not only suffered, but also sang, as they do in the pages of Philoctète's book (Danticat, Preface 8). By the time Danticat wrote her preface, she had already become widely known as the author of *The Farming of Bones* (1998), her own successful novel evoking the massacre. This text delves into the complex quandaries and plights of regular people who were not deliberate henchmen of the dictatorship, but who often found themselves complicit in atrocities not of their own making.

The Farming of Bones privileges a focus on individuals variously connected to the narrator, Amabelle Désir, who survives the killings by narrowly escaping to Haiti. We learn of her lover, Sebastien Onius, her acquaintances, and the Dominican family she lived with up until the unfortunate event. We take an especially close look at Doña Valencia, "the lady of the house" ("la dueña"), whom Amabelle comes back to visit years later. It is clear to the protagonist that Doña Valencia wishes to absolve herself from the horrors perpetrated by her people. Amabelle had even assisted during the lady's parturition to bring la dueña's daughter Rosalinda into the world. The former domestic feels conflicted while hearing Doña Valencia's assurances about the Haitians she harbored from imminent death. Doña Valencia attests to her own humanity with such statements as, "I hid many of your people. I hid a baby who is now a student at the medical school with Rosalinda" (299). Señor Pico, Valencia's deceased husband, had actively partaken in the extermination efforts, and she knows that Amabelle has him in mind. As if answering an impending—though unasked—question, the older woman declares, "Amabelle, I live here still. If I denounce this country, I denounce myself. I would have had to leave the country if I'd forsaken my husband. Not that I ever asked questions. Not trusting him would have been like declaring that I was against him" (299).

By dramatizing Amabelle's journey to Haiti with the band of refugees that formed precipitously, as they all sought to escape the carnage, Danticat's novel depicts the appalling conditions in which the characters find themselves, regardless of which side of the island they are from. Without a state to back them up, they are left to fend for themselves. Yves, a member of the band, resents the apparent impunity with which the Dominican government has harmed them and asks, "Tell me, why don't our people go to war because of this?" and "Why won't our president fight?" (197). On the Haitian side, while standing in line to submit testimonials that would qualify them for whatever pittance the survivors can apply for, the refugees find themselves treated with disdain. The narrator observes the similarity of the military garb on both sides of the island: "The soldiers from the Police Nationale . . . [have] the same khaki uniforms as the Dominican soldiers—a common inheritance from their training during the Yanki invasion of the whole island" (234). They gaze upon a giant photograph of President Vincent, "a sophisticated looking man," wearing "a gentleman's collar with a bowtie, the end of which touched the shiny medal of the Grand Cross of the Juan Pablo Duarte Order of Merit, given to him by the Generalissimo as a symbol of friendship between our two people" (236). Danticat's novel, which in many ways pays tribute to *Les semences de la colère* by Lespès and *Compère Général Soleil* by Alexis, insists on evoking the horror of the massacre in a way that retains the humanity of victims and perpetrators alike, staying clear of caricatures of good and evil. In that respect, her text takes full advantage of the artistic and moral ambiguities permeating representations of the massacre in the literature of Haiti and its diaspora.

We encounter a notable contrast in the first and best-known literary text by a Dominican author exploring the same genocide, namely *El Masacre se pasa a pie*. This is a tale allegedly composed in 1937 and kept concealed for thirty-six years by Freddy Prestol Castillo, a magistrate sent to the border during the massacre. The text deviates from the model of humane remembering exemplified by Danticat's novel. When the author found it safe to publish his story, it appeared in print in 1973. The Dominican literati understood Prestol Castillo's piece to be a novel and praised it as one that presumably exposed the crimes perpetrated by the Trujillo dictatorship. This misrecognition is ironical in a work that, upon closer inspection, generally justifies the genocide by decrying the thievery of Haitian marauders in the border regions. In a nightmarish frame of mind, the narrator recreates all the elements of fundamentalist anti-Haitian historiography that he can think of as he witnesses the actual massacre. There is no differentiation between foreign Haitians and Dominicans of Haitian ancestry. He envisions the machete-wielding killers as avengers for the butchery that the schoolbooks taught him to ascribe to the troops of Jean-Jacques Dessalines in 1805, as they withdrew from the eastern part of the island, after having fallen under French military control. The 1802 Napoleonic invasion of Saint-Domingue came to Hispaniola to crush the insurrection of the enslaved population originally led by Toussaint Louverture. The rebels had defeated and expelled the French forces from the western side of the island and had created the Republic of Haiti there. However, the anti-French resistance lacked the manpower and resources to expel them from the eastern side as well, hence Dessalines's 1805 withdrawal. Using a narrator whose imagination works as if programmed to find, in the remote past, an act of Haitian violence against Dominicans for every atrocity committed at the present moment (and before his very eyes) by Dominicans against Haitians, the novel conditions readers to accept the claim by one character that "we are collecting on an old debt" (Torres-Saillant, *El tigueraje* 83). Owing to his rhetoric, which renders animalistic those whom he perceives to be ancestral Others (for instance, "the feet of Haitians, like those of cattle, are hoofs"), the narrator relegates this population to a lower rung of the human ladder. He even sneers at "the alphabet of smells of this primitive race," a visceral observation which seems to justify their extermination (Torres-Saillant, *El tigueraje* 83).

El Masacre appeared in 1973 under the imprint of Editora Taller, at the time managed by José Israel Cuello, a leftist who still claimed allegiance to a socialist creed. A quarter of a century later, in 1998, with the Socialist Bloc long gone, Cuello's press reissued the novel as one of the titles meriting inclusion in a permanent canon of Dominican letters. The text was thus placed in the series titled Biblioteca Taller Permanente. This elevation of Prestol Castillo's narrative occurred despite several literary scholars (chiefly Diógenes Céspedes, Iván Grullón, and Elissa Lister), having already analyzed the piece closely, revealing what they construed to be its unearned status as a national classic (Torres-Saillant, *El tigueraje* 83). In *On the Edge* (2018), a cultural history of representations of the Haitian-Dominican border in literature and other art forms, scholar Maria Cristina Fumagalli accomplished a notably balanced reading of Prestol Castillo's text. Staying clear of explicit indictment or praise, she identifies *El Masacre* as valuable primarily for the conflicts and contradictions that plague the mind of the author, as reflected in the psychopathology of the narrator (141). Here, as well as in her foreword to *You Can Cross the Massacre on Foot* (2019), the English translation of *El Masacre*, Fumagalli urges us to consider the political and moral impasse as central to the tale that Prestol Castillo set out to tell (xv). Like Doña Valencia in Danticat's novel, Prestol Castillo was trapped. A magistrate serving, like everybody else on the government payroll, at the pleasure of Trujillo, he apparently lacked the political will of those conscientious objectors who chose to go into exile. He would have nowhere to hide upon denouncing the regime. But it seems that he was not devoid of the degree of sensitivity necessary to respond to the large-scale pain inflicted on the innocents. The book recognizes the evil perpetrated by the regime, hence the narrative ambivalence and structural disarray of the writing, along with the morally fraught stance of an authorial voice that seems simultaneously to acknowledge and blame the victims. All this vacillating reflects his ambivalence toward the Trujillo regime, which he appears unwilling and unable to embrace fully, but which he also cannot resolutely reject (Fumagalli, *On the Edge* 141).

The challenge of Prestol Castillo's text, to a large extent, epitomizes the difficulty that the memory of the massacre presents to Dominicans. More than eight decades after the horrors, the task of engaging in constructive remembering remains an aspiration on the part of a citizenry that wishes to dismantle the historical mindset inculcated by the Trujillo era. The anti-Haitian ideology remains pervasive even to the present day. The yearning to humanize national memory forms the kernel of the book *Masacre de 1937, 80 años después: Reconstruyendo la memoria* (*80 Years after the Massacre: Reconstructing the Memory*), based on a seminar, held in Santo Domingo in October 2017. The editors of the volume articulate their hopes in a paragraph that merits quoting in full:

> The nation needs to delink from the negation or deformation of its history. It needs to stop accepting or validating each tyrannical myth and imposed silence or consensus. It needs to refrain from venerating false heroes and taking despicable crimes as patriotic epics. It needs to recognize itself, become reconciled with itself, and reconstruct its ethical system. To do that, it must contend with three pillars of reconciliation: memory, truth, and historical justice, which can help close our open wounds, culturally transcend the scars, and prevent them from continuing to replicate acts of brutality in whatever modality of the present. (my trans.; Bosch Carcuro et al. 13)

Remembering the killings—"el corte" ("the slashing") in Dominican parlance, "kout kouto-a" ("the stabbing") in Haitian Kreyòl, and the "Vísperas dominicanas" / "Vêpres dominicaines" ("Dominican vespers") in Trujillista diction—has been as hard for present-day Dominicans as it was for Prestol Castillo. An explanatory note on the vespers lays bare the mnemonic obstruction. Adopting the term *vespers* served the scribes of the Trujillo regime in aligning the mass murder of these unarmed people with an episode from European history that they construed to be a precedent for demonstrating patriotic indignation. They seized upon the Sicilian Vespers, the name conventionally given to the 1282 bloody uprising of residents of Sicily against the French-born King Charles I, who had ruled the kingdom without local support since 1266. The rebels proceeded by seeking to kill every French person in the land (civil servants and members of the clergy included), totaling some three thousand souls. The currency of the term in Trujillista discourse is acknowledged by historian Bernardo Vega, who mentions "Vísperas" in his amicable exchange with Danticat as they aired minor disagreements related to verisimilitude and logistics in her novel's depiction of the genocide ("Bernardo Vega"). Coates likewise refers several times to the "Dominican Vespers" in critical annotations to his translation of *Compère Général Soleil* (viii, xv, xxx, 295). The epithet also appears in the title of an article by Kevin Jenks, who contends that the massacre was among the root causes of Dominican migration to the United States. "Vêpres dominicaines" as a term arises in a well-written 2010 blog posting by user Morbraz that reviews *Le peuple des terres mêlées*.

Given the Eurocentric pretentions of the Dominican intelligentsia who operated as scribes for the dictatorship, the Sicilian precedent helped ennoble the carnage, rendering it patriotic and therefore something that the people ought to embrace. Whether or not the rhetorical gesture of glorifying mass murder worked, the fact remains that there was no alternative discourse to refute it. Lacking a sturdy national press with any semblance of intellectual autonomy, accounts of the events at the border came almost exclusively from the mouths and pens of the Trujillo regime. Ironically, while the government never admitted that the carnage had been a state action, ascribing it to the spontaneous indignation of peasant farmers in the borderlands, the massacre somehow provided the intelligentsia with a platform for systematically disparaging Haitians as racially, culturally, morally, religiously, and politically incapable of sustaining an organized society. Dominicans thus inhabited the roles of heroes waging an ongoing war to save their civilization from the encroachment of Haitian barbarians. In their aggregate discourse, these ideologues committed unapologetically to anti-Haitian dogma, voicing a concomitantly negrophobic creed, despite the overwhelming majority of their country's population being of African descent as well. The names Joaquín Balaguer, Manuel Arturo Peña Batlle, and Emilio Rodríguez Demorizi come to mind here, because of their proximity to Trujillo himself. But they represent only the tip of the iceberg. The discursive enterprise of the regime operated a "total war" (what we would call today a gigantic trolling campaign) that seeped into the media, school textbooks, church sermons, political speeches, and nearly every other arena relevant to mass communication, socialization, and the construction of public memory. In Dominican society, then, remembering the past was largely a rehearsal of the narratives woven and disseminated by the scribes of the dictatorship.

Even today, it remains difficult for the citizenry to extricate itself from the long shadow of Trujillo's pervasive cultural legacy. This persistence is a result not of the regime's discursive acumen, but rather of the near lack of an effective debunking effort. The dictatorship's discourse of patriotism and national identity has remained virtually unchallenged in Dominican society at the institutional level. During the 1960s and 1970s, from platforms at the Autonomous University of Santo Domingo and other progressive outposts, a new intelligentsia stepped up to rectify the monopoly on historical memory held by the dictatorship. They made available quantitative and qualitative data that effectively refuted the historical disinformation that the Trujillo intelligentsia had circulated for thirty years. But Trujillo's successor, the most influential politician after the dictatorship, happened to be none other than Balaguer, easily the most virulent anti-Haitian and most militantly negrophobic among the scribes in the dictator's court. During the twenty-two years of his rule after the death of the tyrant, *trujillismo cultural* continued to dominate

Dominican public discourse. The new knowledge produced by progressive scholars and thinkers from the 1960s onward remained relegated to the classrooms of left-leaning university professors and alternative fora for self-selected audiences and activist interlocutors. The *Balaguerato*, an ideological extension of the *Trujillato*, with the Catholic Church by its side, ensured the continued skewing of public memory about the massacre and the diverse ethnic makeup of the Dominican people (Balaguer, *La isla al revés*).

New and younger political leaders have come to the helm of the Dominican Republic in the decades following the rule of Balaguer. Politicians from the Partido Revolucionario Dominicano (PRD), a party founded in New York in 1939 by the anti-Trujillo resistance, governed for three four-year terms (1978–1982, 1982–1986, and 2000–2004). The ideological offspring of the progressive leader Juan Bosch, the Partido de la Liberación Domincana (PLD) ruled for the remaining presidential terms until August 2020. Neither of them, however, saw it fit to rehabilitate public memory. During a PRD government, the minister of culture gave the National Book Award (2002) to a negrophobic, anti-Haitian tract that warned that the Haitian presence in Dominican society represented an imminent threat to the nation's cultural identity. This threat was also compounded by the return migration of *dominicanyorks* (Dominican New Yorkers). Similarly, during a PLD government, the Ministry of Culture gave the lifetime achievement award in literature to Roberto Marcallé Abreu, the author of a trilogy of novels that extend a vision of future Dominican greatness, after resolving the "Haitian problem" by means of the extermination of large portions of the Haitian population in the country, combined with the sterilization and deportation of the remainder. Again, no distinction is made between Dominicans of Haitian ancestry, Haitian immigrants, and people in Haiti proper (Victoriano-Martínez).

We cannot overstate the value of what the borderlands pilgrims do. Those who trek to the Ouanaminthe-Dajabón site every year at the beginning of October propose salutary ways of remembering the horrors of the past, whether as the descendants of victims or of the perpetrators—or both. Unlike Germans who, with widely broadcast public displays, such as the Nuremberg Trials, had occasion to behold what the Third Reich had done in their name when it orchestrated its Final Solution, Dominicans of goodwill who have lacked exposure to humane remembering find themselves at a loss for words when they see their country indicted for the 1937 massacre. Unless they have been exposed to a multifaceted array of historical perspectives, Dominicans have no way of saying in retrospect to the Trujillo regime, "No, you did not do that for me. You did it for yourself to satisfy your own perverse desires. You did it *against* me, because you soiled the very idea of Dominicanness by linking it with mass murder. You are thus fundamentally anti-Dominican." When the Dominican government withdrew the citizenship of over 250,000 compatriots of Haitian ancestry, many well-meaning Dominicans were similarly tongue-tied when the international community began to indict their country. Some reacted instinctively by defending the Dominican government; they thus spoke as supporters of an action that, had they been asked, they would likely not have approved. Dominicans of goodwill would not support a government's decision to place a large segment of their country's population in stateless limbo, turning them into foreigners in their own birthplace. Were their historical memory not shaped by a racial ideology of national identity that enables them to recognize Dominicanness in some ancestries but not in others, they would not sit still while hundreds of thousands of their compatriots were rendered vulnerable to the whims of any *guardia* who could drag them to the nearest border point, for deportation to a country that might be entirely alien to them. Humane remembering can warn us about those ultranationalists who act in ways inimical to our ethics of national identity and belonging. Whoever invokes Dominican identity to justify or enable harm done to others, whether foreigners or compatriots of other ancestries, smears all Dominicans. Even if it is the national government itself doing it, there is a germ of anti-Dominicanness there, and subjects should owe no loyalty to rulers who invoke their name to commit and justify acts of evil.

The liberal governments that came after Balaguer did not promise to delink from the tenets of *trujillismo cultural*, probably because these ideological apparatuses were too useful. Such paradigms could come in handy at key political junctures. These ideas may, at any time, translate into good political capital that could help certain sectors win elections, stay in power, or elicit support for corrupt schemes. Anti-Haitianism worked in electoral campaigns that kept the PLD in power, and the denationalization law of 2013 bears every resemblance to a voter-suppression scheme given the precedent of Haitian Dominicans voting for the PRD in previous elections. One can traffic in hatred not only for hatred's sake, but simply because it is sure to work in a ploy motivated primarily by economic or political gain. The problem remains in the resulting legacy, namely the climate of social relations that such a ploy might leave to our children and generations thereafter.

There is nothing to guarantee that the carnage of 1937 will not be repeated. For as long as *trujillismo cultural* remains alive, no one can rest assured that Trujillo will not reappear with another name—or even with the same. Ramfis, the grandson of the dictator, was able to establish himself as a viable candidate for the 2019 election cycle without delinking from the family legacy. Ramfis vowed to set the record straight about his grandfather, whom he viewed as having unfairly suffered too many years of slander in Dominican society (Pereyra). The younger politician did not win a major nomination this time around, but we have not yet heard the last of him: the website *Trujillo Declassified* (which makes available a free e-book), dedicated to promoting his candidacy, denies all charges made in recent scholarship against his grandfather, in addition to publishing articles and documents that highlight the dictator's supposed virtues. There, Ramfis takes great pains to malign those he views as his grandfather's foes, be it Juan Bosch, the CIA, or the people involved in the tyrant's assassination. In the United States, a comparable discourse emerged from the emboldened atmosphere of self-righteous hatred brought to the White House via a candidate who proved himself the enemy of non-European immigrants and, in many cases, their descendants. He labelled Mexicans "rapists" and "murderers," and when in power, impugned several countries as being patently undesirable, among other incendiary comments with real-life consequences. One need only look at the exponential rise in racist violence against East Asians, especially Chinese Americans and others in the diaspora, following his coinage of the terms "China virus" and "kung flu" to describe COVID-19. In Brazil, the celebration of past dictatorships and the open indictment of Indigenous people and citizens of African descent helped propel Jair Bolsonaro to the country's presidency. Aware that words, actions, and representations matter, the Border of Lights pilgrims are agitating for a new humane logic of social relations in Hispaniola. In this global climate of crisis, conflict, and consternation, there is no greater need than that we come together for truthful—albeit painful—reconciliation with a past that we can no longer afford to remember in a partisan, exclusionary way.

PART II

LATINIDAD IN LITERATURE, CULTURE, AND POLITICS

CHAPTER 4

LATINO IDENTITY, NATIONALISM, AND LATINIDAD

A Tenuous "Community"

In this chapter, Torres-Saillant tackles the protean notion of "Latino community" and how its necessarily provisional and evolving status encompasses multiple identity locations. The term Latino *itself is an ethnoracial placeholder, replaceable with other terms that emphasize gender specificity or diversity (Latina, Latinx) or specific national origins (Puerto Rican, Ecuadorian American, Guatemalan, and so on) rather than a panethnic identity. Torres-Saillant reminds us of the historically subordinate positions inhabited by Latina/os in the United States, especially in the shadow of colonization, wars, forced or voluntary migration, systemic racism, and other key historical realities. He juxtaposes* Latinismo *with Hispanic and Latin American identities and broaches whether certain groups (Iberian Americans, for instance) fall under the category of* Latino. *He fleshes out the notions of Latinidad and Hispanidad, underscoring the importance of historical contexts and specific applications in politics, activism, and mass media. The writer also stresses that in-group solidarities are never guaranteed, especially considering the force of nationalism and the mutability of allegiances between diverse groups. He highlights the utility and attraction of panethnic formulations, insisting upon the need for specific lenses to be applied when assessing the balance of allegiance, competition, and willingness to self-identify as Latina/o, as opposed to aligning with any distinct regional or national grouping.*

Central to this chapter is a return to a major theme in this collection: the diversity within Latina/os as a group. Historical meditations predominate. We find here memorable illustrations detailing the complex genealogies of the Latino commu-

nity. Torres-Saillant claims, "The heterogeneity of Latinos stems from their varied national origins, the staggered process of their incorporation into the US population, and the peculiar historical circumstances characterizing not only the insertion of each subgroup, but also different stages of the process experienced within these subgroups as they settled in the United States." Despite the challenges of such an unwieldy project, Torres-Saillant notes in closing that even though a panethnic Hispanic community granting an equal sense of belonging to each of its constituent parts has yet to come into being, the desire to imagine such an outcome endures as a vital collective aspiration.

Defining *Latina/os*

Broadly conceived, *Latina/os* consists of a medley of disparate ancestries, historical experiences, cultural heritages, and varying circumstances of incorporation into the United States. Faced with such diversity within the group, some scholars discourage the representation of this segment of the US population as "even a relatively homogeneous 'ethnicity'" (Flores, "Living Borders" 199). However, at the level of public discourse, politicians, policymakers, media personalities, and community advocates often speak confidently about Latina/os as "a people," ascribing to them a shared identity meaningful enough to distinguish them from other segments of the US population, namely African Americans, Asian Americans, Euro-Americans (whites), and Native Americans, to use the principal categories established by the US census. This chapter provides a general overview of the group dynamics of Latina/os, seeking to set forth an interpretive framework that can assist readers in contextualizing the more specialized, in-depth discussions of Latino subgroups, as the need to balance the specific with the general arises. Whatever the circumstances that facilitate or hinder group cohesion, the notion of a US Latino community—tied transnationally to the Caribbean as well as to Central and South America—remains a convenience, an ideal, and an impossibility.

Origins: Races, Nations, and Languages

The term *Latinos* (and its gender-specific and diversity-informed variants, including the more recent *Latinx* and *Latine*) coexists with *Hispanics* as a label of ethnic self-identification. Members may use one or the other (or neither), often depending on regional, generational, or ideological differences. Latina/os are the segment of the US population that has ancestral ties to Mexico, Puerto Rico, Cuba, the Dominican Republic, and the Spanish-speaking countries of South and Central America. Scholars disagree on whether to extend the designation of Latino to US Hispanics linked by birth or immediate descent to the Iberian Peninsula, such as the philosopher George Santayana, born in Madrid in 1863, or novelist Felipe Alfau, born in Barcelona in 1902. Latina/os can boast multiple ancestral origins (or so-called races) through their links to Latin America, an area that, as a result of the conquest and colonization that followed the arrival of Christopher Columbus in 1492, witnessed a sizeable intermixing of peoples from across the globe. These included invaders from Spain and Portugal, Indigenous populations that had inhabited the region for millennia, diverse enslaved Africans transported to the Americas from 1502 onwards, indentured laborers brought there from Asia some time thereafter, and waves of European and Middle Eastern immigrants who came in search of economic opportunity. As such, while most Latina/os come from mixed racial backgrounds, a good many among them may be identified by predominant traits that match one or another of the US Census ethnoracial classification system.

Especially among those with traceable roots that link them to Indigenous ancestors in such countries as Ecuador, Guatemala, Bolivia, Mexico, and Peru, for instance, Latina/os may also trace their linguistic backgrounds to several of the diverse native languages spoken in the hemisphere, rather than Spanish alone. The question of ancestral languages becomes even more complicated when one considers Brazilians, one of the largest populations in Latin America, whose language is not Hispanophone but Lusophone. Some of the scholarship that deals with Latino identity has begun to tackle the matter of the proper place of Lusophone Latin Americans vis-à-vis the larger Latino designation.[1] Suffice it to say that in considering the Hispanic population of the United States, John H. Burma's pioneering *Spanish-Speaking Groups in the United States* (1954) confidently included Filipinos alongside Mexican Americans, Hispanos of New Mexico, and Puerto Ricans. Today, Filipino Americans are typically recognized as part of the larger Asian American and Pacific Islander (AAPI) population, although texts like Anthony Ocampo's *The Latinos of Asia: How Filipino Americans Break the Rules of Race* (2016) command attention.

Latina/os and Latin Americans

Understood broadly as a US panethnicity, Latina/os may be said to differ significantly from their Latin American ancestors in that members of the former have lived their socialization and formative experiences north of the Rio Grande. Latin Americans, as people inhabiting foreign countries located *south* of the Rio Grande, have lived as apart from Latina/os as have Africans from African Americans. Though useful, this distinction is complicated by the fact that, depending on the longevity of their subgroup's incorporation into American society, they may have close relatives in their respective ancestral homelands, including grandparents, aunts and uncles, and cousins. Connecting with the extended family may involve frequent travel to the Old Country. Under these circumstances, with close relatives spread across two or more nations, individuals may grow up regarding all these locations as part of the composite geography of their national belonging. In response to the recurrence of this scenario, since the 1990s, scholars have insisted on the emergence of a transnational identity among people whose everyday lives straddle two or more nation-states. Especially for people living in the cities located along the US-Mexico border, the nature of daily existence entails a certain proficiency in negotiating transnational dynamics. The interdependence of Latina/os in the United States and their relatives in Latin America notwithstanding, life for a Colombian in the homeland differs significantly from that of a Hispanic-born person in Texas or California.

With the exception of Indigenous and African-descended communities in the region that have increasingly asserted their differentiated ethnicity in response to discrimination, most Latin Americans tend to live in societies where they constitute the majority. The values, cultural heritage, and political yearnings of a middle-class person in Argentina, Paraguay, Guatemala, or Uruguay, for instance, would tend to correspond to the normative ideals of each respective society. When reading the works of Colombia's Gabriel García Márquez, Mexico's Elena Poniatowska, or Chile's Pablo Neruda, for example, people would not normally approach these writers' texts as representing utterances from the social periphery. Once these writers become well-known in their respective countries, they are subsumed by their national cultures as regular voices within the broader literary conversation. They are not "minority" voices in the way that Chicana poet Pat Mora or Nuyorican fiction writer Nicholasa Mohr in the United States is.

A further motivation for literary scholars to differentiate US Hispanics from the populations of countries south of the Rio Grande has to do with caution in view of the likelihood of historical tensions between the two. At times, Latina/os have had to contend with prejudiced appraisals coming from the intelligentsia and the press in the Latin American lands of their ancestors. Renowned Mexican poet Octavio Paz, in the first chapter of his book-length essay *The Labyrinth of Solitude* (1950), set forth a portrayal of the Pachuco, a social archetype in Mexican American urban youth culture at the time, with damning implications for the standing and pride of the entire community. Scathing representations of Puerto Ricans and US Dominicans by the intelligentsia and the popular press of their ancestral homelands have also become flashpoints. However, the need to recognize their difference does not, as suggested above, make the dividing line between the two any easier to draw, especially amidst the continuous immigration of people from Latin America. Those who come to the United States from the Hispanic Caribbean, South America, or Central America when young enough to be shaped by life in this country may overcome the mindset of the foreign exile who arrives as an adult and yearns to return home someday. The younger immigrants tend to develop a sense of belonging as members of an ethnic minority in American society. When that happens, the process of acculturation may be described as one whereby a Latin American immigrant gradually becomes a Latina/o. It remains to be seen to what extent the legislative move since the 1990s by Latin American political leaders to enable their émigré communities to retain their original citizenship (even after becoming naturalized US citizens) will discernibly affect the process whereby Hispanic immigrants morph into Latina/o ethnics. Nor can one overlook those immigrants who never shed their exilic state of mind, even while staying permanently in the United States.

Discontinuous Incorporations

Latina/os are a heterogeneous segment of the US population insofar as their formation as an ethnicity has occurred through a series of disparate and discontinuous historical episodes.[2] Indigenous Tejanos may be able to trace their roots back several centuries prior to the arrival of the Spanish, the first Europeans who entered Texas at the start of the conquest and colonization of North America. A Hispanic native of New Mexico may be able to cite ties to Spanish ancestors who came there as soldiers in Juan de Oñate's 1596 invasion. In addition to Texas, some Latina/os from Arizona, California, Colorado, and Utah may claim ancestral ties to the Spanish-speaking peoples who ruled those vast lands, or to the mestizo *vaqueros* and Indian *peones* who worked for them, prior to the 1848 Treaty of Guadalupe Hidalgo, whereby the United States seized those territories from the Republic of Mexico. The 1849 discovery of gold in San Francisco brought numerous Chileans and Peruvians to California in the mid-nineteenth century. There were people of Cuban origin in Tampa and of Puerto Rican origin in New York decades prior to the 1898 Spanish-American War, in which the United States annexed Cuba and Puerto Rico from imperial Spain. This was an event that unleashed a migratory flow from the islands to the North American mainland, resulting in the emergence of ethnic enclaves of both groups in various American cities. The involvement of the United States in the internal affairs of the Dominican Republic, beginning in the second half of the nineteenth century, eventually led to the rise of an early Dominican immigrant presence, already visible in New York by 1901. Mexican Americans, or Chicano/as, can also trace their beginnings in this country to different waves of northward migration, starting in 1880, through to the advent of the Bracero Program in the 1940s, and then via immigration in subsequent decades.

As part of a development strategy favored by the United States, the leaders of the Commonwealth of Puerto Rico in the 1940s promoted a massive exodus from the small Caribbean island to the North American mainland. The process had been made easier by the passage of the Jones Act (1917), which extended US citizenship rights to Puerto Ricans in their homeland. The Cuban Revolution that brought Fidel Castro to the head of the government in 1959 triggered a large-scale emigration of nationals who disapproved of the new regime's socialist policies. Most of those emigrants came to the United States, which encouraged their arrival as part of this country's campaign against leftist regimes in the hemisphere. The waves of Cuban exiles substantially augmented the size of their population stateside, transforming cities such as Miami, where they soon became the Latino majority. After World War II, the passing of the Immigration and Nationality Act of 1965 increased the volume of US visas granted to applicants from the Dominican Republic and countries in South and Central America. The presence of those groups increased dramatically, leading to the rise of additional ethnic enclaves, such as the iconic Dominican neighborhood of Washington Heights in Manhattan and the Colombian barrio in Jackson Heights, Queens. In sum, the heterogeneity of Latina/os stems from their varied national origins, the staggered process of their incorporation into the US population, and the peculiar historical circumstances characterizing not only the insertion of each subgroup, but also different stages of the process experienced by them as they settled in the United States.

Latino Ethnic Consciousness

The Latino population's diversity of national origins, cultural roots, linguistic backgrounds, and circumstances of incorporation into the United States would seem to justify the suspicion of those scholars who doubt that a collective ethnic label can effectively encompass such a heterogeneous gathering of subgroups.[3] It can thus be argued that the representation of Latina/os as a panethnic formation united by a commonality of interests is merely a desideratum. When spokespersons enunciate their commitment to a "Latino agenda" of socioeconomic and political empowerment, their actions constitute a project that can more accurately be called a Chicano, Puerto Rican, or Cuban agenda, depending on which subgroup wields the greatest power in a particular region at the moment in question. Also, since US Hispanics cannot claim to have entirely freed themselves from the white supremacist values that they inherited from their colonial past in Latin America and in the United States, Afro-Latina/os and Latina/os of Indigenous ancestry still suffer greater levels of disempowerment than their light-skinned mestizo and white counterparts. Asian Latina/os may find themselves omitted altogether. But despite the intergroup tensions, the rise of the all-inclusive panethnic label can be associated with a politically salutary mission. Examining the emergence of Latinismo in Chicago during the 1970s, scholar Felix Padilla's classic study *Latino Ethnic Consciousness* (1985) showcased some of the ways in which Mexicans and Puerto Ricans opted to organize under the alternative racialized banner of *Latina/os*. This coalition-building emerged in response to a racialized urban political space previously dominated by black and white perspectives and agendas.

Concomitantly, the United States government fostered the adoption of an inclusive ethnic label for all US Hispanics, along with the designations applied to the four other major populations, creating the classification system that scholar David Hollinger termed "the ethnoracial pentagon" (*Postethnic America* 33). In keeping with the mandate of the Voting Rights Act and Title VII of the Civil Rights Act, the government needed to collect racial statistics for the purpose of remedying the social disadvantage to which non-white ethnic minorities had been subjected for generations. As a result, in 1977, the Office of Management and Budget issued Statistical Directive 15, thus formalizing the breakdown of the population into the five existing branches. While the classification system was well intentioned, it also involved a rather arbitrary lumping together of peoples who otherwise may not have seen themselves as alike in relation to the other subgroups sharing the same panethnic category. Placing people of Mexican, Hispanic Caribbean, and Central and South American origin under the all-encompassing ethnoracial label *Hispanics* assumed, for many, an unrealistic homogeneity that overlooked the differences that set the various subgroups apart. Suzanne Oboler's *Ethnic Labels, Latino Lives* (1995) cogently explored the advent of the classifications that construed all peoples tracing their roots to the Latin American region as one coherent population and the impact of this taxonomy on those whom the term encompassed.

Negotiating Panethnicity alongside Nationalism

The naming that broke down the US population into five panethnic branches served its bureaucratic purpose by providing a mechanism whereby many Hispanics began to gain access to resources previously unavailable to them in the areas of employment, housing, health, education, and youth services. Granted, no wholesale classification system can do justice to the complexity of the human experience. The term *Native Americans,* for instance, purports to encompass hundreds of tribes and nations with distinct languages and cultural traditions that, prior to the European conquest, occupied the vast territory that is now the United States. Similarly, the label *Asian Americans* presumes to unify the numerous languages, heritages, worldviews, and historical realities of people who trace their ancestry to societies as distinct from one another as Pakistan, Cambodia, China, South Korea, Mongolia, India, Vietnam, Japan, and Indonesia. The value of each of the five ethnic labels is to be sought not in its ability to describe a segment of the population with unimpeachable accuracy, but in its ability to help US society redress the racial injustices of the past and its ongoing consequences. Until a more descriptively reliable classification system has come to replace it, the ethnoracial pentagon, as a legacy of the Civil Rights era, will remain a useful sociopolitical tool.

At the level of social practice, Latina/os have shown that they can benefit from the strategic embrace of a panethnic label to command the attention of non-Latina/os by boasting of their large numbers. They can claim the political purchase that might ensue from their becoming the largest ethnic minority in the country only if they allow themselves to be counted as one group. Taking advantage of this galvanizing classification for its political value in the national arena in no way hinders the ability of the various subgroups to assert their particularized agendas locally. Among themselves, Chicano/as, Puerto Ricans, Cubans, Dominicans, Colombians, Peruvians, and the other subgroups continue to assert their specificity, as determined by the peculiar circumstances they each face. In certain barrios of Los Angeles, the label *Chicano/Chicana* no doubt occurs to a greater degree than *Latino/Latina,* as is also the case with *Cuban* in Miami, *Puerto Rican* in New York City's Lower East Side, and *Dominican* in Manhattan's Washington Heights. With ready access to either a panethnic label or each subgroup's term for national origins, Latina/os do not need to choose, as one does not replace the other. Perhaps the panethnic label, inasmuch as it encourages every US Hispanic subgroup to conceive of an abstract community that welcomes people not linked to the same ancestral homeland, may induce a collaborative disposition.

A discussion of panethnicity cannot be complete without engaging *nation-*

alism. The term describes the attitude of citizens in those instances when the contours of the nation correspond to those of the state. This confluence need not always happen, as we observe in the Caribbean societies of Puerto Rico, the French Overseas Departments of Martinique, French Guiana, and Guadeloupe, as well as the countries within the former Netherlands Antilles. These locales, among others in the region, illustrate the phenomenon whereby people may inhabit a land to which they feel attached and from which they derive their sense of national belonging, while existing politically under the jurisdiction of a larger sovereign state. The latter may have a seat of power elsewhere as well. Whether upheld by members of a society where the nation is coterminous with the confines of the state or not, *nationalism* refers to an ideology that posits affiliation with a distinct homeland or ancestral origin as a person's principal social identity.[4]

Nationalist sentiment tends to subordinate other social identities that a person may claim, including those stemming from one's gender, sexuality, religion, class, culture, ethnic origin, race, or political creed. Thus, even if suffering marginalization as a minority group from exclusionary and hostile public policies imposed by their nation-state, most individuals will not easily renounce their national affiliation if given the choice. Often the poor, the disinherited, the ostracized, and the exiled may remain loyal to the nation that has denied them economic opportunities, political access and protection, an overall sense of equanimity and spiritual connectedness, and, most broadly, a genuine sense of belonging. One need only look to history, often to the nation-building stages of society, to understand the emergence of nationalism as a powerful force in determining how people ascertain the causes, concepts, and communities meriting their loyalty within the larger framework of the human family.

To speak about nationalism in relation to US Latina/os, one must adapt the term conceptually, insofar as the ideology cannot apply to the manner of one's affiliation within a distinct nation or nation-state as opposed to another. As a US minority group, Latina/os express any nationalist sentiment they may harbor through their differential rapport with other subsections of the population, namely the European-descended majority and fellow minorities of African, Asian, and Indigenous backgrounds. Latina/os must often share space, resources, responsibilities, and opportunities in American society with these latter groups. While their solidarity is not a given, coalition building has proven to be both useful and necessary in advancing mutual social-justice causes. Streaks of nationalism may also be visible in the relationships within Latino subgroups differentiated by national origins. Broadly speaking, nationalist sentiment or behavior will reveal themselves in the context of intergroup relations at moments of competition for political leadership, social prestige, cultural visibility, public funding, employment options, and control of "the Latino agenda" in any particular place and time. Nationalism, in short, may shape the way Latina/os interact amongst themselves as well as with non-Latina/os in the overall US body politic. As such, nationalism encompasses several locations of identity vis-à-vis an ethnoracial other in US society as a whole.

Panethnic Nationalism

The symbolic separatism implied in essentialist formulations about the warm spontaneity of Latina/os as compared with the cold calculatedness of Anglos involves a nationalist stance. Latina/os who have adopted such essentialist views may cheer for a particular politician who has attained national visibility, calling that person "one of our own," irrespective of the ideology upheld by the selfsame figure. A Latino nationalist perspective regards Marco Rubio, the conservative Cuban American who, in 2010, became a junior US senator for the State of Florida, or Julian Castro, the Mexican American liberal who, in 2009 assumed office as the youngest mayor ever of the city of San Antonio, Texas, as equally advancing the political empowerment of "the community." A type of Latino nationalism, embraced by scholars invested in conceptualizing *Latinidad*, a notion that posits an ontological commonality among peoples of Latin American origin, as well as by corporations rooted in the US Hispanic market (such as television networks Univision and Telemundo), takes a panhemispheric as well as panethnic view of "the community." This inclusivity corrals together US Hispanic populations—grouping immigrants alongside people with several generations of experience in the land—irrespective of national origins and the populations residing in the countries of Latin America.

In terms of single subgroup nationalism, construing Latina/os as a panethnic family with cherished values and salutary characteristics in common occasionally crumbles in the face of circumstances that appear to pit one subgroup against another. Depending on its degree of economic and political empowerment, a single subgroup, such as Chicana/os, Cubans, Puerto Ricans, Ecuadorians, Dominicans, or Hondurans (or South and Central Americans more broadly), may display a commitment to its own separate advancement and may even regard other Latino subgroups as competition for scarce resources locally, regionally, or nationally. This competition applies to popular media, often devoid of nuance to begin with, who will allot precious attention to a Latino celebrity from one group, assuming that the coverage suffices to satisfy all the groups. Contrastively, the relative political rise of Dominicans in New York since the 1990s may strike some as cutting into the domain of Puerto Ricans who long dominated the Hispanic "space" in municipal and state politics.

In the US academy, Chicano and Mexican American studies initiatives have long existed, producing significant bodies of knowledge prior to the emergence of a panethnic Latino identity and the birth of Latino studies as an academic field. The advent and establishment of full-fledged academic publications such as *El Grito: A Journal of Contemporary Mexican-American Thought* and *Aztlán: A Journal of Chicano Studies* date from as far back as the late 1960s and the start of the 1970s. Aware of the longevity and preeminence of the field, Chicano and Mexican American scholars of the past often failed to see any major benefits to their advocacy for embracing the panethnic academic formation. The departments and programs devoted to the study of the US Hispanic experience located in places where people of Mexican descent predominated describe themselves as "Chicano/a studies" or "Mexican American studies," with some settling for an integrative label, such as "Chicano/Latino studies." Such realities gesture to the panethnic Latino field while maintaining a sense of the primacy and distinctness of the Chicano/a experience.

Similarly, many of the Hispanic-based ethnic studies units that emerged in colleges and universities of the Northeast amid the climate of ethnic affirmation spurred by the Civil Rights Movement started out as "Puerto Rican studies" initiatives. By the first decade of the twenty-first century, the majority of them, attending to demographic shifts among the student population in their region, have widened their scope, making concession to the other US Hispanic groups and describing themselves more broadly as "Latino studies" programs even while retaining the Puerto Rican identification in their name (that is, "Puerto Rican/Latino Studies"). As with other minority-studies initiatives that have responded at their inception to a differentiated population's demand for inclusion, these scholarly fields have grown to assert themselves in the academy as areas of study that are of value to learners of any ancestry. At their later stages of development, they tend to transcend the nationalist impulse that may have prompted their initial creation.

Dual Nationalism

At the time of this writing, US Hispanics seem to have evolved into a flexible state of dual nationalism that enables them, depending on the situation, to identify with their coethnic and panethnic "communities" without significant contradictions. A high rate of intermarriage between different Latino subgroups—combined with ethnically transformative demographic shifts in their particular regions—may expand the contours of their belonging from ethnonational exclusivity to panethnic inclusivity. A major factor in the expansion may be the realization, especially among politicized cohorts of each subgroup, that Hispanophobia will most likely make no distinction between a Peruvian of Indigenous descent and an Afro-Dominican. This scenario may have prompted a twofold practice of collective belonging that enables Latina/os to balance an allegiance to the panethnicity even while remaining affiliated with "community causes" that relate specifically to their coethnics. The 2012 conference of the Puerto Rican Studies Association held at the State University of New York at Albany sought to tackle precisely the intersection of the coethnic and panethnic experience with the theme Boricuas and Other Border Crossers: Of Diasporas and Latinidades. The organizers strategically chose the distinguished Mexican American scholar Arturo Madrid, of Trinity University in San Antonio, Texas, as their keynote speaker.

Enduring Contests of Identity

The negotiation of multiple sites of identity has not eliminated the possible clash of nationalist loyalties between coethnic and panethnic affiliations. This scenario has emerged, for instance, when two Latino subgroups have found themselves competing for the leadership of a project of presumed common interest. Disagreement as to whether a Puerto Rican or a Chicano/a director would best serve the interests of the constituencies advocating for a Latino studies program at Cornell University caused rifts in the 1990s, arresting the development of the initiative for many years, according to participant informants. The conflicting loyalties of coethnic versus panethnic affiliations surfaced poignantly in 2002 with the appointment of Mexican-born museum administrator Julián Zugazagoitia as the first non–Puerto Rican director of El Museo del Barrio in New York City, a development that triggered protests from many spokespersons from the Puerto Rican community, including some scholars who otherwise identified as supporters of the panethnic field of Latino studies. The preference of coethnic solidarity over panethnic affiliation may have also operated in the contest over New York City's Thirteenth Congressional District during the June 2012 Democratic primary election. Dominican American state senator Adriano Espaillat had stood out as the most compelling contender that incumbent congressman Charles Rangel had ever faced in his forty-two years on the job. Born to an African American mother and a Puerto Rican father, Rangel identified solely with the African American side of his parentage, citing resentment about the treatment of his mother by his father. The Democratic Party's Latino establishment in New York opted to support Rangel, enabling him to defeat his Dominican challenger by less than a thousand votes.

Taking Rangel as an African American, in keeping with his preference, it seems that the contest over the congressional district showed an interruption of the expected logic of solidarity in a context of panethnic nationalism. The Democratic Party's Latino establishment, whose members were primarily Puerto Rican, found it more expedient to side with an old-guard politician from outside the panethnicity than with a rising newcomer from one of the Latino subgroups. Further exacerbating this situation, Dominican American state assemblyman Guillermo Linares, Espaillat's coethnic, also chose to cast his dice on the side of the African American incumbent. Overall, this intricate political scenario points to the unstable nature of ethnically inflected nationalist loyalty and logic. Neither good nor bad, nationalism can bring about benefit and harm separately and simultaneously. It serves a beneficial function when it mobilizes a people's resistance against state oppression or foreign aggression, but it can behave problematically when used to legitimize violence against, or neglect of, differentiated segments of a country's population. In the context of intergroup relations between ethnic components of the overall US population, Latino nationalism can be exclusionary and narrow-minded or inclusive and flexible, depending on the particular circumstances and the character of the leaders in any given group. New York City's congressional contest in June 2012 suggested that nationalist sentiment, whether of the panethnic or coethnic kind, does not present a reliable-enough predictor of inter- or intragroup solidarity. In the arena of social relations—group affiliations and identity locations notwithstanding—one cannot dismiss political expediency, individual ambitions, backroom deals, and outright opportunism as factors that influence our ultimate decision-making processes. Such a reality applies to Latina/os no less than to non-Latina/os.

Latinismo(s) and Latinidad

Latinidad, a term that signals a sense of pan-ethnic belonging across the US Hispanic population, despite their multiple national origins, phenotypes, and cultural heritages, names a political aspiration no less than a will to communal self-assertion. Many would warn against upholding definitions of Latinidad that uncritically lump together all peoples with ancestral roots in Latin America and Spain irrespective of culture, race, class, or the particular national histories that led to their integration into American society. Some would posit that the term obscures as much as it clarifies. To this point, some scholars categorically contend, in the words of Juan Flores and George Yúdice, that Hispanics are a "very heterogeneous medley of races and nationalities" that do not make up "even a relatively homogeneous 'ethnicity'" (Flores, "Living Borders" 199). Acknowledging the term's ongoing hermeneutic potential, literary scholar Marta Caminero-Santangelo devotes the introduction of her book *On Latinidad* (2007) to surveying the arguments and counterarguments regarding any assertion of Latino identity as consisting of a commonality of cultural backgrounds, worldviews, forms of association, and ways of interacting with other groups in US society.

According to the 2010 US Census, people of Hispanic descent made up the largest ethnic minority group in the country, and even proponents of a wholesale Latino identity would acknowledge the difficulty of generalizing about them. Ancestrally connected to all Latin American countries—from Argentina to Venezuela—US Latina/os cannot fit easily into a single panethnic category that encompasses all their historical, cultural, class, racial, linguistic, and religious differences. To this mix, one should add the longevity of their ancestral country's rapport with the United States and the distinct geopolitical features of their varied historical relationships. Thus, after exploring the diverse ways in which major Chicano/a, Cuban, Puerto Rican, and Dominican authors render their particular relationships to the notion of a Latino community, Caminero-Santangelo concludes, "As a singular 'people' Latinos cannot be said to exist; but Latino identity might well be found in the multiple alliances, along sometimes quite different pan-ethnic and transnational lines, that we make with each other" (219). She proposes that we might best understand Latinidad as our "commitment to attending to the historical and present differences among Latinos, as well as to the sometimes overlapping or analogous histories and current structural problems—which is another way of saying our commitment to solidarity" (219).

Grounding in North America

The compulsion for Hispanics in the United States to claim belonging to a large Latino panethnicity arguably has its roots in the social dynamics unleashed by Anglo-Spanish colonial competition on the North American mainland in the decades following the Jamestown settlement in 1607. By the late seventeenth century, powerful Anglo voices had set out to boast of the superior spiritual enlightenment of the English colonies over the benighted Spanish Catholics on the Pacific coast. The influential Puritan minister Cotton Mather of New England taught himself Spanish so that he could write the two texts that he published in that language, with the purpose of converting the people of New Spain (the "Spanish Indies") to the true Protestant faith of the English (Johnston 8). The one entitled *La Fe del Christiano: En Veyntequatro Artículos de la Institución de Christo* (1699) is addressed specifically "To the Spanish." The text on the title page explains why the Spanish need Mather's pastoral care: "So that they will open their eyes and that they will convert from the darkness to the light and from the power of Satan to that of God: So that through faith in Jesus Christ they may receive the remission of their sins and good fortune among the sanctified." Later, in his evangelical history of New England from 1620 to 1698, *Magnalia Christi Americana* (1712), the religious leader attempted to downplay the primacy of Spain in the discovery of America, a region that God had presumably concealed until people of the right faith arrived to make proper use of it. Given the difficulty of arguing that the Puritan presence in the hemisphere preceded that of their Catholic foes, Mather settled for emphasizing that the Almighty had the well-being of the former in mind when he emancipated the region from its long concealment.

In chronicling the longevity of Anglo animosity toward their Spanish counterparts in North America, the historian David J. Weber deploys the evocative term "Hispanophobia" (1992). Richard Henry Dana, traveling in the Mexican territory of California in the 1830s, unequivocally asserted the cultural superiority of his Anglo ethnicity over that of his host society. In Monterrey, he found the sole impediment to progress in "the character of the people," which also explained the rapid prosperity of the Anglos who had relocated there and married into the city's key families. These families, he claimed, had "more industry, frugality, and enterprise than the natives" (80). The ideological arsenal that sustained Hispanophobia would manifest itself politically in the 1836 Anglo takeover of Texas, which school textbooks would subsequently memorialize as a patriotic American struggle against Mexican oppression. Similarly, the US invasion of Mexico in 1846 would lead to the shrinking of that vanquished nation's landmass while enlarging the United States through the annexation of the territories now constituting the Southwest.

As the United States continued to expand through conquest, emerging as the preeminent political and economic power in the hemisphere, it quickly became the natural destination for migrants from the weakened Latin American republics south of the Rio Grande. With the United States establishing regional hegemony through its defeat of Spain in the war of 1898, Hispanics found their place in American society marked by a sense of deep political and cultural subordination. Whether as homegrown American citizens with roots in the land dating back to times prior to Anglo settlements, as immigrants, or as descendants of immigrants, they bore the stigma of conquest and geopolitical subalternity. They also endured the impact of Hispanophobic perceptions that restricted their ability to achieve full citizenship and productive belonging.

Hispanophobia, after all, preceded the birth of the United States and the Republic of Mexico. Later, when large numbers of Mexicans began to travel north as immigrants in the early twentieth century, debilitating prejudices awaited them. These biases stemmed from ideas widely disseminated by US journalists and writers.[5] Immigrants had to contend with the stereotyping, racism, criminalization, and distrust that preceded their arrival.

Not surprisingly, a poll conducted in 1940 by the Princeton University–based Office of Public Opinion Research revealed key findings about the unflattering views held by the US population about people of Hispanic descent. Respondents rated nineteen adjectives to describe "Latins." The first on the list, "dark-skinned," received 80 percent of the votes. The words "quick-tempered," "emotional," "backward," "religious," "lazy," "ignorant," and "suspicious" each received between 40 and 50 percent of the votes cast. Of the favorable adjectives (among them "progressive," "generous," "brave," "honest," "intelligent," and "shrewd"), none received a mark higher than 16 percent. The last positive adjective on the list, "efficient," received a mere 5 percent (Black 61). By the mid-twentieth century, the prevailing opinions about Hispanics remained largely negative, making little to no distinction between recent immigrants and those who could claim residency on the land for several generations.

Defining "Reactive Ethnicity"

The history of Hispanophobia played a key role in the emergence of the sense of Hispanic panethnicity that informs the notion of Latinidad. It created the necessary conditions for Latinidad to emerge as what Alejandro Portes and Rubén G. Rumbaut call a "reactive ethnicity." An adverse mainstream environment prompted the development of defensive identities to counter deleterious effects on the self and the collective (284). Reactive ethnicity may also be understood as a differentiated instance of what other scholars in the human sciences have more inclusively called "reactive identity" (McCall 20; Vetik et al. 1084–1085). Hispanics have thus nurtured a sense of themselves as a somewhat unified population, against the history of marginalization and outright aggression toward them by the US mainstream. The climate of antipathy that they endured gave rise to the appeal of the Robin Hood–like outlaw Joaquín Murieta, as a vindicator of Hispanics during the California Gold Rush era of the mid-1850s.

The same applies to the hostility that made farmer Gregorio Cortez a folk hero to Mexicans, especially after he killed Anglo sheriff W. T. Morris and evaded a posse of three hundred Texas Rangers for ten days in June 1901. These milestones of resistance evoke the oppositional location that Hispanics inhabited at these particular historical moments. In more recent memory, the 2008 killing of the undocumented Mexican immigrant worker Luis Eduardo Ramírez Zavala by white teenagers in Shenandoah, Pennsylvania, or the 2016 Pulse nightclub shootings in Orlando (on "Latin Night," with most of the casualties being LGBTQ-identified) indicate that intersecting forms of hatred and aggression against Latina/os have remained strong in the twenty-first century. In Ramírez Zavala's case, nothing encourages this impression more than the role of Shenandoah's police chief and a lieutenant in falsifying information related to the hate crime ("Two Former"). According to FBI statistics, hate crimes against Latina/os surged 40 percent nationwide since 2003. In 2008, Latina/os made up 62 percent of the victims attacked throughout the country on account of their ancestry or phenotype (Kashatus). Such a sociohistorical scenario would indeed make it hard for a differentiated subsection of the population not to recognize its location, even if vaguely, in a place of alterity. The degree of recognition would vary, of course, in accordance with every person's measure of political awareness.

Hispanophone Mass Media

The fraught relationship between Hispanics and Anglos in the United States only partially explains the concept of Latinidad. The colonial legacy in Latin American cultural discourse, with its strong tradition of asserting the heritage of Spain in the formation of the national identity of each of the countries in the region, provides an equally noteworthy source. That historical discourse largely explains the success of US Spanish-language media at establishing public voices that manage to speak influentially about "the community," even when they themselves may have had minimal contact with the long struggle of US Hispanics. Often, these public voices reflect the values and experiences of Latin American middle-class professionals or entrepreneurs who arrived in the United States looking to expand careers they had already started in their home countries. News anchor Jorge Ramos, for example, a native of Durango, Mexico, landed a job on the New York–based Spanish-language TV network Univision the year after he left his prominent position at a radio station back home to seek greater opportunities up north. Few Latino leaders have enjoyed similar ascendancy as a purported voice of "the community."

Similarly, Ramos's colleague at Univision, the Chilean entertainer Mario Luis Kreutzberger Blumenfeld, better known by his television moniker "Don

Francisco," became the preferred mouthpiece of the Social Security Administration to inform the US Hispanic population about this agency's offerings, in a series of public-service announcements. Although they ultimately represent the interests of the major (usually conservative-leaning) corporations that employ them, the likes of Ramos and Don Francisco command significant credibility as spokespersons for US Hispanics on account of their celebrity. They stand simultaneously as Latino and Latin American voices, since they remain active in the media and entertainment circles of their respective birthplaces. Don Francisco continued to exert influence in Chilean television through his long-running variety show, *Sábado Gigante*, to great international acclaim. Ramos aired his views on Latino political participation in his book *The Latino Wave: How Hispanics Will Elect the Next American President* (2004), which was directed at US readers. He can likewise address audiences in his birthplace about presidential elections there, hence his book *Los presidenciables* (2011), a collection of interviews with Mexican presidential candidates and former presidents. In view of the power of the television networks they represent, Ramos and Don Francisco inhabit the ultimate domain of Latinidad, one that aims to encompass not only all US Hispanics, whether recent immigrant or multigenerational US-born, but also the populations of Latin American countries and their diasporas.

Iberian Hispanidad

The panhemispheric ambition that informs the corporate imaginary of Univision, with its Latino–Latin American public voices, benefits from the survival of an older version of Latinidad, also known as *Hispanismo* or *Hispanidad*. This cultural ideology, formulated in Spain in the second half of the nineteenth century, acquired the forcefulness of a quasi-religious doctrine. Its most lasting articulation could be found in the editorial commentaries Marcelino Menéndez Pelayo appended to the selection of poems in his *Antología de poetas hispano-americanos* (1893–1895), a compilation prepared to commemorate four centuries of the Spanish presence in Latin America. As Arcadio Díaz Quiñones has shown, Menéndez Pelayo's survey of poetic achievement in Latin America served primarily to highlight the civilizing achievement of Spain in the region and to assert the "preeminence of Spain as legitimizing center for the national elites of Spanish-American countries" ("la preeminencia de España como centro legitimador de las élites nacionalistas 'hispano-americanas'"; my trans.; *Sobre los principios* 68). With its defeat by the United States in "the disastrous year" of 1898, the Spanish Empire's demise afflicted the intelligentsia not only of the Iberian Peninsula but also of the Latin American nations (Díaz Quiñones 68). Their deep sense of humiliation launched them into the widespread search for a panacea, particularly through the glorification of the spiritual virtues of the Iberian legacy as representing a more humane heritage than the materialistic mores of the Northern European–descended Yankees (78).

Prior to the war, many Iberian intellectuals had begun to meditate on the loss of Spain's former imperial glory. They envisioned a recovery outside the realm of economic and military competition. In his influential *Idearium español* (1897), Ángel Ganivet commented that Spain should look for its future in Africa, while cautioning against former methods of colonial domination. He simply did not think that the "African races," existing at "a lower degree of evolution" than the Native Americans and Asians who had fallen under European control during earlier colonial exploits, could withstand the full impact of Western civilization (my trans.; 149). He placed great faith in the allegiance of the Hispanophone peoples of the Western Hemisphere. As Ganivet looked to "our numerous family in America," he claimed to have never had the impression of dealing with "foreigners" while interacting with Latin Americans, leading him to imagine something like "inter-family law" as a more viable principle than "international law" to regulate the relations between Spain and Hispanic America (my trans.; 113, 122–123). The evocation of the former glory of Spain, the diffusion of its legacy across the globe, and the need to preserve the unifying values of the Hispanic world consumed a great deal of intellectual power in the Iberian Peninsula, with signal echoes in the words of Latin American writers and thinkers.

Spanish American Latinidad

The Iberian advocates of Hispanidad typically failed to consider the savage violence, mass enslavement, depopulation, genocide, and utter dehumanization involved in the colonial transaction that essentially created the Hispanic world. Their Latin American disciples embraced a hierarchical cultural doctrine, as reflected in their disdain for the non-Hispanic heritages and cultural legacies of the Indigenous and African-descended peoples of the hemisphere. Perhaps no text stands out as prominently in this regard as the book-length essay *Ariel* (1900), by the Uruguayan thinker José Enrique Rodó. Alluding to Shakespeare's play *The Tempest*, Rodó has Prospero deliver an impassioned speech about the virtues of the Western European humanistic values that Spain generously bestowed on the peoples of the Americas, "rectifying in superior men the tenacious vestiges of Caliban, symbol of sensuality and baseness" (26). The writer envisioned with horror the likelihood that Iberian America, under the throes of US domination, might become de-Latinized. Personified by the character of Caliban, the United States would usher in the rule of "equality in mediocrity" that Rodó associated with American democracy. The new order would threaten the prevailing aristocratic regime that had privileged the best minds devoted to the pursuit of beauty, disinterested cultivation of the intellect, and the highest values of the human spirit, all personified in the figure of the sprite, Ariel (101–102). In a passage that showcases his eugenicist credentials, Rodó mused about cranial size as indicative of the relative intellectual capacity of the "thinking races." Racist craniology at the time understood Indigenous peoples and blacks to be insufficiently endowed, in terms of skull size, for advanced thought (140). The classist, racist, elitist, and militantly Eurocentric tenor of Rodó's worldview did not prevent *Ariel* from becoming one of the most influential texts in Latin American intellectual history.

By the end of the eighteenth century, Spanish American ruling elites inhabited a divided society. Opposing the absolutism of the Bourbons in Spain, they also feared a rebellion of the slaves and the *castas* (ethnically or racially distinct segments of the population) at home. Toward the period of the Napoleonic domination of Spain, they came to see themselves as the "best custodians of their own interests, which meant protecting their social and economic positions. They fought for independence not so much against a feeble Spain as against their own subjects, until eventually they crossed the Rubicon of mobilizing their subjects against the empire" (Stavans and Jaksić 39). Just as the members of the Latin American intelligentsia did not frown upon the nefarious ideologies that informed the predominant vision of Hispanidad, the proponents of Latinidad in the United States have done very little to distance themselves ideologically from the ethnocentric and exclusionary texture of this early chapter of their formulation. Joan Ramon Resina describes the history of Hispanism as "a proselytizing enterprise," an assessment that Ilán Stavans echoes in viewing Hispanidad as "an ideological stance, maybe even an argumentative approach, that is, the use of the specific elements of Hispanic civilization for a political purpose" (Resina 161; Stavans and Jaksić 3). These critics view Latina/os in the United States as "an integral part of Hispanic civilization," noting that one out of every ten of the world's Hispanics lived in this country as of 2005. Stavans also points to the "cumbersome mutation" whereby "la hispanidad becomes *la latinidad*" in American society, paving the way for future interrogations of both provocative concepts (Stavans and Jaksić 2, 38).

Tenuous Ties

The problematic genealogy of the concept notwithstanding, several scholars in Latino studies have continued to assert the validity of Latinidad as a banner of panethnic identity for US Hispanics. Agustín Laó-Montes declares, "In spite of all the substantive differences among peoples hailed as Latinos, latinidad remains as a marker of otherness both in the core discourses of US identity and citizenship and in the ethnoracial hierarchies of New York's urban regimes" ("Niuyol" 124). He identifies struggles "against police brutality and for racial justice" in New York City during the 1990s as vibrant issues that mobilized Latinidad as a political stance (129). He insists on the role of Latino-centered projects as social movements that contribute to building Latinidad broadly, and frowns upon conservative Hispanic professionals, including business leaders, who would confine Latinidad to the realm of the private sphere rather than acknowledge its value as a political identity (127–133).

With a discernibly different conceptual agenda, Frances R. Aparicio has made the case for a sort of organic Latinidad rising from below, one that involves the US Hispanic population's own resourcefulness in the formation of its panethnic identity. She puts forth examples of five individuals of Latin American descent living in Chicago with meaningfully varied socioeconomic, cultural, ancestral, and ideological profiles. Their identities unfold differently from one another, and their experiences lead to divergent results in terms of material and psychological survival (Aparicio, "[Re]constructing" 41). Recalling the way their separate realities intersect in the capacious context of urban Chicago, Aparicio finds grounds for a demographic revolution whose dimensions "call for a recognition that the term 'Latino' is a real thing, an emerging social and cultural experience and experiment, and not just a label or construction imposed from the outside" (44).

Discussions of the emergence of Latinidad normally cite as foundational the formulation of the concept of *Latinismo* by sociologist Felix M. Padilla in his influential analysis of Mexican and Puerto Rican political coalitions in Chicago during the first half of the 1970s. One should note, however, that Padilla's primary aim was to document the emergence of Latino consciousness as a "contextual or situational" stance occurring when two or more Hispanic groups succeeded at transcending national origin–based allegiances to forge mutually beneficial coalitions (161). His research revealed the successful construction of intergroup solidarity through initiatives spearheaded by the Spanish Coalition for Jobs and the Latino Institute. He highlighted the issue-oriented dimensions of Latinismo operating favorably in an urban setting like Chicago at a moment in history when the groups in question recognized the benefits of asserting themselves as members of a larger ethnicity than simply Puerto Rican or Mexican (147, 163). Padilla helped to shed light on a special kind of praxis, namely, Hispanismo or Latinismo, as "an ethnic-conscious identity and behavior" (1).

In contrast, art historian Yasmín Ramírez reported a different outcome at the Smithsonian Institution's November 2002 National Conference on the Interpretation and Representation of Latino Cultures: Research and Museums. At this event, Ramírez expounded upon the issues surrounding the change of leadership and vision from a Puerto Rican to a panethnic focus, at El Museo del Barrio in New York City. A town hall meeting convened by the We Are Watching You Campaign on September 26, 2002, brought together community activists and members of El Museo's board of directors to talk about the organization's new direction. As mentioned earlier in this chapter, the board had selected the Mexican-born museum administrator Julián Zugazagoitia as new head of the institution, which had also reframed their mission statement: "to present and preserve the art and culture of Puerto Ricans and all Latin Americans in the United States." This objective signaled a shift from the original commitment to research and disseminate the cultural heritage of "the Puerto Rican community in El Barrio / East Harlem" that had founded the museum in 1971 (Ramírez). The tense and emotional meeting, during which many Puerto Rican cultural activists decried the new direction envisioned by the board, led to the formation of the Nuestro Museo Action Committee. The intent was to pressure board members to return to the organization's original focus. The analysis offered by Ramírez invites us to consider the layers of the committee's "atavistic demand" for a group-specific museum over a panethnic one, and to refrain from seeing the gesture as merely the expression of "narrow-minded nationalism." As a scholar with strong connections to the museum's history, Ramírez attests to her own identification with Nuestro Museo's demands, having come "to respect that sector of the Puerto Rican arts community which [had] decided to by-pass discourses of Latinidad for the moment."

No longer the primarily Puerto Rican enclave that it had been up to the 1980s, El Barrio has proven less permeable to panethnic projects like the coalition building that Padilla documented in early 1970s Chicago. Journalist Juan González tells the story of a woman from East Harlem who voiced her dismay at an icon of la Virgen de Guadalupe in her place of worship, the Church of Holy Agony, a religious institution serving Puerto Rican Catholics since the 1940s. The objector viewed the holy figure's presence as a sign of the Mexican takeover of El Barrio. Ironically, the Virgin of Guadalupe is not totally alien to

Puerto Ricans on the island, having been brought to Ponce by Spanish soldiers who had served in Mexico. As a child, the writer Rosario Ferré worshiped the dark-skinned virgin after discovering her through one of the housemaids. This sense of identification was a secret she had to keep from her parents, whose allegiance lay with the more mainstream, lighter-complexioned Inmaculada Concepción (Ferré 80, 84). If La Virgen de Guadalupe, primarily associated with Mexico but not entirely unfamiliar to the people of Puerto Rico, can find it hard to pass the ethnic pews on the way to the altar of a church in El Barrio, one can only imagine how much harder a time she might have had were she to venture into the domains of La Virgen de la Altagracia in the Dominican enclave of Washington Heights. The foregoing illustrations suggest that, as a banner of panethnic unity among US Hispanics, Latinidad always involves treading on precarious ground. Padilla captured a specific grassroots moment when conditions existed to engender trust between Puerto Ricans and Mexicans on the merits of working together in 1970s Chicago. This was a moment when the stakeholders realized that having an intergroup agenda would improve everyone's safety and well-being better than if they were working apart. However, at the level of identity formation to facilitate shared paradigms of belonging, Latinidad has not yet succeeded at holding much sway.

Little seems to have changed since 1991, when folklorist Laurie Kay Sommers published her foundational examination of unstable projects of panethnic solidarity through cultural performance among Hispanics in San Francisco. Sommers relied on data she gathered in 1983 to "explore the creation of Latino folklore of ethnicity and its role in inventing Latinismo." She was encouraged by the influence that "folk and popular traditions and vernacular languages" had enjoyed on the search for "overarching symbols of panethnic culture" throughout modern times (33–34). Long a stronghold of immigrant settlements from Mexico, the Mission District of San Francisco witnessed a demographic shift after the 1960s, when large numbers of Salvadoreans, Nicaraguans, and other Central Americans arrived in the neighborhood. Since that decade, neighbors had organized several festivals, initially to commemorate major Mexican holidays, such as Mexican Independence Day (September 16) or the Battle of Puebla (May 5). By 1983, with the greater ethnic mix in the barrio becoming obvious, Central Americans and others attempted various strategies to render the Mexican *fiestas patrias* flexible enough to accommodate the interests of a wider audience. One such attempt, the annual Cinco de Mayo / Latin American Fiesta Parade, sponsored by the Spanish Speaking Citizens Foundation, laid bare the difficulty of simultaneously advancing an ethnic and panethnic agenda without leaving everyone dissatisfied. Sommers interviewed the Nicaraguan-born organizer of the 1983 parade, who candidly admitted that his organization's intention "[had] never been to celebrate Cinco de Mayo" but rather had been to use the powerful symbolism of the Mexican holiday. He recognized that "politically they [the Mexicans] are stronger than we are," and also admitted to having raised suspicion among Mexicans who thought "that we [were] stealing their parade" (42).

Sommers's findings pointed to a bumpy road ahead on the way to achieving even temporary solutions to the conflicts that will arise when attempting to harmonize identities across multiple planes of difference. Nearly all of the key decisions related to curating the program for the festivities that Sommers explored prompted disagreements, including over the choice of music, cuisine, flags, traditional attire, speakers, and the topics of the speeches. She concluded that "Latino consciousness still remains chiefly at the level of rhetorical unity, a community that imagines itself as such only in certain strategic contexts" (49). But her study does allow for some optimism in those instances when, given the right enabling conditions and the will to unify, intergroup identifications have transpired successfully. She envisions the potential of festivals, performances, and the overall realm of expressive culture to bring about "a new folklore of panethnicity" that may one day help bring to fruition the vision of togetherness implicit in the doctrine of Latinidad (49). The words of literary scholar Marta Caminero-Santangelo, formulated nearly two decades after Sommers', set forth an understanding of Latinidad as an idea that hinges on a collective willingness to build solidarity and "to express, to ourselves and to others, our commitment to attending to the historical and present differences among Latinos" (219). Even though a panethnic Hispanic community granting an equal sense of belonging to each of its ethnic components has not yet materialized, the desire to imagine it as an inclusive and democratic ideal has proven to be an enduring goal.

Notes

1. See, for instance, Torres-Saillant, "The Unlikely Latinos."
2. See, for instance, Sánchez Korrol; see also Aparicio and Chávez-Silverman.
3. See Cabán; see also Torres-Saillant, "Inventing the Race."
4. See, for instance, Miščević.
5. See, for instance, González, *Harvest of Empire*.

CHAPTER 5

THE POLITICAL ESSAY AND LATINO AUTOBIOGRAPHY

This chapter acknowledges the crucial interplay of content and form in nonfiction writing. Torres-Saillant concentrates on two major nonfiction genres in Latino literature, one less prevalent (the essay) and one more so (the autobiography). He gauges the efficacy of each form to represent the voice of the ethnic American writer who exists individually as an artist and yet remains inextricably linked to the collective. The negotiation of belonging through narrative involves the careful interplay of allegiances and (dis)identifications with "the community" of the ethnic group or groups involved. Torres-Saillant generates an insightful overview of recognized—if often polarizing—Mexican American authors Richard Rodriguez and Jorge Ramos. He argues for a distinction between academics who write about Latino politics from a disciplinary perspective (usually as political scientists) and those popular voices who adopt the opinionated, interventionist guise of the political essayist.

In the section on autobiography, Torres-Saillant evaluates the contributions of various luminaries, including some underexamined early women writers, whose ancestral backgrounds include Puerto Rico, Cuba, Mexico, and the Dominican Republic. He does not omit the increasingly vital presence of South and Central American life stories as demographic patterns shift into the twenty-first century. Torres-Saillant bears witness to the continuing emergence of Latina/o autobiographers, whose narratives present their personal lives as examples of the ongoing imperative to capture the experience of traumatic history, frustrated homecomings, and still incomplete belonging in the United States. It is the mosaic, the mélange of "I"/eyes, that ultimately provides the most persuasive snapshot of what constitutes Latino identity back then and there, *as well as* right here and now.

Given the wide appeal of her books across the American reading public and her choosing the US territory as the setting for several of her stories, Peruvian-born Chilean writer Isabel Allende has appeared in several compilations of Latino literature. By 1997, when of her US-based texts only *The Infinite Plan* (1991) had been published, her work had already received coverage as the voice of a "Latina." In Frances Ann Day's reference book *Latina and Latino Voices for Children and Teenagers* (1997), a text for middle and high school students, Allende shares space comfortably with key US Latina/o authors, such as Julia Alvarez, Rudolfo Anaya, Gloria Anzaldúa, Judith Ortiz Cofer, and Pat Mora. Not everyone will agree with Day's decision to include Allende among this cadre of writers, a classification that more exacting scholars would reserve for those US authors of Hispanic descent born in this country or who immigrated while they were young enough to have been shaped by the experience of living as an ethnic minority in American society. This is clearly not the case with Allende, who was already a Latin American author of note when she chose to settle in California, having achieved an international reputation with her first novel *The House of the Spirits* (1982; English trans. 1985), followed by *Of Love and Shadows* (1984; English trans. 1987) and *Eva Luna* (1988; English trans. 1988). These absorbing novels gave her a firmer footing in contemporary Latin American literature than in any US canon. As a naturalized US citizen, Allende has received literary honors from Chile alongside accolades from her adopted country, including the 2014 Presidential Medal of Freedom, conferred by President Barack Obama, among various other distinctions of the highest order.

Even the details of Allende's biography place her quite apart from the community of writers typically called Latina/os. Her father, first cousin of Salvador Allende, the man who would, in 1970, become president of Chile, was a diplomat serving in Peru, where Isabel was born. She lived in her birthplace, Lima, until the age of three, when her mother relocated with the children to Santiago, Chile. In 1953 her mother remarried, to another diplomat, Ramón Huidobro, and his posts to foreign shores brought the family to live in Bolivia, where young Isabel attended an American private school, and in Lebanon, where she studied at a British private school. Returning to Santiago, Isabel continued her secondary education through to graduation, after which she obtained employment as a secretary at the Santiago branch of the UN Food and Agriculture Organization. Then came marriage in 1962, followed by extended periods of residence in Europe. After the overthrow of President Allende by a military coup on September 11, 1973, the family stayed in Santiago until they no longer felt safe. They moved to Caracas, Venezuela, where they resided for the next decade or so, while Isabel wrote for the national press until the breakthrough moment of her literary career with the 1982 publication of *The House of the Spirits* by a major press in Spain. But, as the inclusion of Allende's name in anthologies and compilations continues, scholars will have to consider revisiting the classification of "Latinos/as" to accommodate writers like her. To achieve belonging in the United States, people of Hispanic ancestry typically undergo a process of self-identification rather than exclusively adhering to labels based on descent.

Allende's peripatetic profile is an intriguing one. When writers, literary scholars, and cultural critics from racialized minority groups in the United States think of American literature, they tend to display two dissimilar but not mutually exclusive impulses: to assert their rightful place in the national corpus that the designation encompasses, and to challenge the sociocultural framework that first went into naming and setting parameters for inclusion or exclusion of texts. The tension between those two intentions must remain alive, as it encourages a diversity of languages, expressive forms, ethnoracial engagements, and intersectional commentaries based on class, gender, sexuality, and culture that poignantly defy rigid notions of literature as well as Americanness. The following chapter, divided into two parts, seeks to open the American literary mind by dismantling the protocols of confinement that the Old Guard, essentially *La Migra* of academe, had so passionately insisted on sustaining. The first part explores the political essay, the genre that has ostensibly flourished *least* among those practiced by Latina/o writers. The second part zeroes in on autobiography, a key genre through which these writers have inserted themselves into the national discourse as accomplished and provocative commentators on a range of experiences, from tragedies and triumphs to timely political matters—also a major concern of essayists. When all segments of the US population have achieved the affirmation of belonging and the sense of full citizenship, the cultural playing field will have become more level. Readers will no longer regard characters with Spanish surnames as less denotative of the American experience than those with Anglo ones.

The Political Essay and Autobiography

The essay as literary form traces its roots back to Europe, beginning with the French sage Michel de Montaigne, who named his collection of nonfiction prose writings *Essais* (1580), a term that he coined from the verb *essayer* ("to attempt"), to convey the exploratory, provisional, and personal nature of the observations and analyses contained in his book. The essay has abounded in contemporary literature of the United States as well as Latin America and Spain. American writers who have excelled in the genre include Ralph Waldo

Emerson, W. E. B. Du Bois, T. S. Eliot, Edmund Wilson, James Baldwin, Adrienne Rich, Joan Didion, Susan Sontag, bell hooks, and Barry Lopez. A roster of distinguished essayists from Spain and Latin America could include the likes of José Martí, Juan Montalvo, José Ortega y Gasset, Luisa Capetillo, Rosario Castellanos, Alfonso Reyes, Pedro Henríquez Ureña, Jorge Luis Borges, and José Luis González. As conventionally understood in literary studies, the essay stands out for its structural looseness, concentrated commentary, limited length, and discursive integrity largely dependent on the author's keen and penetrating gaze. Essayists normally distinguish themselves by dint of the clarity of their diction, their stylistic simplicity, and the honesty of the speakerly voice (Torres-Saillant, "Essayists" 72–73; Good xix–xx).

Latino literature gained ascendancy at a time when nonfiction prose in the United States had become the domain of scholars, experts, or voices otherwise sanctioned or buttressed by institutional authority. Professional qualifications or demonstrated expertise, rather than insight, creativity, or enticing use of language, generally tend to serve as the basis of authority. We might think, for instance, of the author of any op-ed piece in one of the country's major newspapers. Nonfiction prose authored by Latina/os typically comes from the pens of scholars, not of writers in the literary sense of the term. Unlike the essayists, scholars depend on methodological rigor and sound conceptual paradigms to establish their intellectual authority. They attain credibility to the extent that they strive for quasi-scientific credentials by following established norms in gathering data, exercising sound judgment in the process of observation, and demonstrating theoretical proficiency in the task of interpretation. Owing to the relative marginality of the US Hispanic population in the United States, their share of the market of opinion on the national scene is not large. Entering the public sphere as wielders of words and world-changers would seem highly risky if done as individuals competing for attention and intellectual confidence in a field dominated by voices of the (Anglo) mainstream. Not surprisingly, perhaps, most educated Latina/os seeking a space within the thought economy tend to acquire the necessary credentials to channel their intellect, not as single voices within a fiercely competitive market, but as guild members operating under the mantle of academic authority. Consequently, scholars will greatly outnumber essayists among Latina/o authors of nonfiction prose, which also means that the body of "political" writings produced by them will more often consist of scholarly studies of "Latino politics" than of texts one might properly call "political essays."

The collection *Latino Politics: Identity, Mobilization, and Representation* (2007), coedited by Rodolfo Espino, David L. Leal, and Kenneth J. Meier, exemplifies the previous point. As the introduction notes, the volume brings together experts in the field to outline a twofold process: nonspecialists identifying the connection of Latino politics to their own respective areas, and specialists committing to "make the case for the relevance of Latino politics to the wider discipline" (12). Learned compilations of writings on various aspects of the Latino experience, such as *The Latino/a Condition: A Critical Reader* (1998), edited by Richard Delgado and Jean Stefancic, generally consist of excerpts or chapters that explicate the historical, political, cultural, or socioeconomic situation of the US Hispanic population. Rarely do they include authors who abandon the authoritative cloak of the scholar to take on the opinionated, interventionist guise of the political essayist. That characterization applies even to collections that name the subject of "politics" in their titles, such as the compilation *Latino/a Thought: Culture, Politics, and Society*, either the 2003 version, coedited by Francisco Hernández Vázquez and Rodolfo D. Torres, or the 2009 version, edited by Hernández Vázquez alone.

The sociohistorical circumstances surrounding the emergence of Latino literature, from the 1959 publication of the novel *Pocho*, by Jose Antonio Villareal, onward, appear to have fostered a preference for the genres most suited to the scrutiny of *collective* dramas. The literary exploration of personal predicaments through the speculative flair added by talented individuals seemed less urgent. Since Latino letters evolved as the cultural expression of a US ethnic minority in need of asserting its rightful belonging in American society, writers tended to veer toward the literary forms most closely associated with the act of bearing witness to, and documenting, the experience of "the community." As a result, autobiography became a predominant genre among Latina/o writers. Described by literary historian Nicolás Kanellos as "the melting pot genre par excellence," the autobiography has prevailed for over half a century of US Hispanic literary production (11). Many of the salient books tread a recognizable autobiographical terrain, whether or not they bear the label "memoir" or "fiction" on their back covers. Life writing surfaces predominantly in *City of Night* (1963) by John Rechy, *Down These Mean Streets* (1967) by Piri Thomas, *. . . y no se lo tragó la tierra* (1971) by Tomás Rivera, *Barrio Boy* (1971) by Ernesto Galarza, *Autobiography of a Brown Buffalo* (1972) by Oscar "Zeta" Acosta, *The House on Mango Street* (1984) by Sandra Cisneros, *Exiled Memories: A Cuban Childhood* (1990) by Pablo Medina, *How the García Girls Lost Their Accents* (1991) by Julia Alvarez, *The Line of the Sun* (1991) by Judith Ortiz Cofer, *Dreaming in Cuban* (1992) by Cristina García, *Drown* (1996) by Junot Díaz, *Canícula: Snapshots of a Girlhood in La Frontera* (1997) by Norma Cantú, and *We the Animals* (2011) by Justin Torres, among numerous others.

On key occasions, the political essay has been subsumed within texts otherwise recognized as autobiographies or as generically hybrid literary works.

One such instance is *Borderlands / La Frontera: The New Mestiza* (1987), by Gloria Anzaldúa, some of whose essayistic portions articulate questions of language, gender relations, intellectual traditions, and cross-cultural solidarities. The powerful political implications of such commentaries have resonated distinctly with readers. Similarly, Cherríe Moraga's *Loving in the War Years: Lo que nunca pasó por sus labios* (1983) includes poems, personal reflections, remembrances of things past, and sundry musings that politicize the sphere of family life in gripping ways. Owing to the force of the embedded essays that influence the poetry, memoir, and fictional pieces accompanying them, the volumes written by Anzaldúa and Moraga have earned their authors a place of distinction among theoretical voices in woman-of-color feminism, queer studies, and ethnic studies broadly.

The case of subsumed political essays notwithstanding, the form has failed within Latino writing to establish a presence primarily among liberal and progressive thinkers. One needs to look to the conservative milieu to find the bona fide political essay showing some measure of vitality. Understood as a discursive intervention in the public sphere bent on swaying collective opinion in a particular direction, the political essay has thrived mostly among conservatives. Richard Rodriguez started his literary career by launching a sharp critique of bilingual education and affirmative action, two spheres that Latino liberals have conventionally protected as mainstays of their political agenda. His claims and observations came infused with the story of his life, as he detailed it in *Hunger of Memory: The Education of Richard Rodriguez* (1982). The book's subtitle perhaps intentionally invites an association with *The Education of Henry Adams*, the nineteenth-century autobiography of a Boston aristocrat, to stress Rodriguez's view of having transcended minority status, despite his origins in a humble Mexican immigrant family. *Hunger of Memory*'s book cover carries the label "an autobiography," but the opening section, "Prologue: Middle Class Pastoral," includes a disclaimer that renames the genre of the text: "Essays impersonating an autobiography" (6). Rodriguez construes his book as "necessarily political, in the conventional sense, for public issues—editorials and ballot stubs, petitions and placards, faceless formulations of greater and lesser good by greater and lesser minds—have bisected my life and changed its course" (5). The author then proceeds to tell those parts of his life story that best enable him to substantiate his case against such public policies as affirmative action. A national bestseller, the book gave a sizeable boost to the opponents of those programs in Congress and educational sectors nationwide.

Similarly, Linda Chavez, a high-ranking White House official during the administration of Ronald Reagan, published a forceful volume that attacked Latino politicians and community leaders for interfering with the Hispanic population's move "out of the barrio" and into the American middle class by promoting cultural separatism through bilingual education. Titled *Out of the Barrio: Toward a New Politics of Hispanic Assimilation* (1991), the text became a bestseller. A year after the book by Chavez, Ruben Navarrette, Jr., emulated the precedent set by Rodriguez by deploying the autobiography as a political essay. Navarrette also drew on his university experiences to preach the value of self-reliance in the Hispanic population, thereby indicting public policies designed to respond to the needs of the community as a protected class. Navarrette's book *A Darker Shade of Crimson: Odyssey of a Harvard Chicano* (1992), also sought to articulate a locus of identity that conservative Latina/os could comfortably inhabit.

The best-known expression of Latino political conservatism in the first decade of the twenty-first century came via *One Nation, One Standard: An Ex-Liberal on How Hispanics Can Succeed Just Like Other Immigrant Groups* (2006) by Herman Badillo, a New York politician who holds the distinction of being the first Puerto Rican to have attained a seat in Congress. As chairman of the Board of Trustees of the City University of New York during the mayoralty of Rudolph Giuliani, Badillo oversaw the mayor's systematic elimination of open admissions and academic support services for minority student populations in the public higher education system. The message of Badillo's book largely corroborates his track record as a conservative hardliner who, since the 1990s, has declared his opposition to programs that seek to level the playing field for more students of color, including Hispanics. His book dismisses the existence of any systemic or social barriers to explain the lesser educational attainments of Hispanic students when compared to whites. He pinpoints dysfunctions in their families as the explanation for the social disparity.

Badillo's book, like those of the other conservative Latina/o essayists mentioned above, received considerable media coverage in news venues nationwide, including a C-SPAN book presentation and a CNN interview, among numerous other instances of favorable publicity. His unscholarly and clearly retrogressive views enjoyed an acclaim that liberal Latina/o thinkers, who tend to speak as scholars from the halls of academe, cannot dream of attaining. Utterances like Badillo's arguably benefit from a prevailing ideological climate in the media that privileges conservative rhetoric. The Spanish-language media replicates this tendency as the career of Univision anchorman Jorge Ramos can demonstrate. The author of *The Latino Wave: How Hispanics Will Elect the Next President* (2004), among other best-selling books of essays, this television newsman and columnist regularly espouses right-wing and counterrevolutionary views about political affairs in Latin America. During the presidency of George W. Bush, he quickly repurposed the epithet "Axis of Evil" (coined by the White House for Iran, Iraq, and North Korea) to designate Cuba, Venezuela, and Bolivia, among the countries declared inimical to the United States (Noticias La Paz). He thus capitalized on his influence as the darling of a powerful television network to cultivate disfavor among the US Hispanic public toward leftist or liberal-leaning Latin American governments. Assumed by others to be a credible voice of the Latina/o population, Ramos often lands public appearances in some of the most influential media venues. He speaks about "the community" while ushering forth his own best-selling books, which are typically compilations of opinion pieces written during his time as a syndicated columnist. No serious scholar active in the US academy today can match the widespread appeal and star power that Ramos appears to have cultivated with various engines of influence in the mainstream.

In the world of Latino writing, the likes of Badillo and Ramos possess the upper hand in the battle of ideas. They seem to benefit from the ideological leanings of the media that welcome them and from the celebrity they enjoy through long careers in public life or on network television. They most likely also benefit from the near absence of progressive voices among practitioners of the political essay. Essayists write to regular citizens in an accessible language. Conservative ideologues do precisely that, making savvy use of the opportunity of engaging the public to advance their beliefs. Most Latina/o academics tend to identify with a progressive stance on major issues, but, as scholars, they write to an audience of their peers through the sometimes-inaccessible language and platforms offered by scholarly journals and academic monographs. While many Latina/o scholars now circulate on social media, these traditional academic genres cater to university faculty members and advanced students with access to higher education. They curate their language to appeal to the intellectual expectations of readers with specialized academic training. One could argue that Latina/o progressive scholars have lacked the favor of the general public mostly because they do not talk principally to it. Conversely, the ideas of conservatives have prevailed because they have remained relatively unchallenged by progressive-minded competition. With the advent of an enhanced climate of responsibility in colleges and universities throughout the country that has proclaimed the importance of civic engagement for all levels of scholars, a new generation of Latina/o academics may feel encouraged to enter the battle of ideas as public intellectuals, hence speaking to increasingly large and diverse publics. A versatile cadre of Latina/o scholars who can engage the regular public without relinquishing rigor may perhaps remedy the ideological imbalance that at present sorely afflicts the political essay.

Autobiography

The autobiography, which is as loaded a genre in American writing as in any other branch of world literature, reveals key levels of complexity in the hands of Latina/o authors. For the purposes of this discussion, *autobiography* will encompass memoirs, *testimonios*, confessions, and other personal narratives that document the story of the self with the presumption of truth. The constituent etymological elements of the word that names the genre (*autos*: self; *bios*: life; *graphé*: writing) all point to areas of epistemic uncertainty. These elements seem to put forth no guarantee of truth, often causing scholars to raise such questions as "What do we mean by the self (*autos*)? What do we mean by life (*bios*)? What significance do we impute to the act of writing (*graphé*). . . . What is the significance and the effect of transforming life, or *a* life, into a text?" (Olney 6). Students of the Western autobiographical tradition, as practiced by writers from Jean-Jacques Rousseau to Malcolm X to Richard Rodriguez, have insisted on highlighting the multiple layers of psychological, cultural, and ideological complexity that catalyze the literary construction of the self.[1] The autobiography is, in the words of Roger Rosenblatt, "the least reliable of genres" (169). Several scholars have followed Paul de Man's lead in denying the form the status of a "genre or mode," conceiving it instead as "a figure of reading that occurs, to some degree, in all texts" (de Man 921). Consequently, some would favor Leigh Gilmore's contention that to construe the autobiography as a genre, one would have to engage in "domesticating its specific weirdness" (qtd. in Mostern 46). Since autobiographers produce their texts while the life being evoked is still in progress, they necessarily rely on the less than impeccable mechanism of memory and contend with the fact that the structure of a person's lived experience will not easily accord with the contours of a literary form. As such, their discursive task presents obstacles that many deem insurmountable at worst and challenging at best.

In addition to the epistemic indeterminacy that scholars regard as inherent to the practice of writing about the self, Latina/o autobiographers face complications stemming from the history of colonial domination that created US Hispanics as a segment of the American population. These authors will rarely escape the need to superimpose the private and the public in their texts. Writing the self thus becomes an act of collective representation. They find themselves compelled to represent the experience of their community through narratives of their own individual lives. Their texts thus adopt the dual task of accounting for personal dramas and analyzing their community's predicaments as the members wrestle with questions of identity, citizenship, and belonging. Latina/o autobiographers cannot help but serve as mediating voices with the power to assist in shaping the image of their people (however provisional or complex this designation may be) in the eyes of the larger society. In light of the multivalent and amorphous nature of the form, literary theory on autobiography has considered the difficulty of defining it as a genre, especially isolating fiction from purely biographical reportage, and establishing a firm separation between literary and non-literary instances of the form.

Latino Identity

Defining Latino autobiography presupposes the existence of a literary corpus bearing the same gentilitial (that is, ancestral) designation and a group of people to whom the name applies. A prefatory explanation, therefore, is in order. As mentioned earlier in this chapter, *Latina/o* specifically describes the Hispanic-descended segment of the US population. This group became part of American society through a combination of historical factors, chief among them US imperial expansion to the south and migratory flows triggered primarily by American involvement in Latin America. The 1846 invasion of Mexico, which culminated in the 1848 Treaty of Guadalupe Hildalgo, whereby the vanquished nation ceded to the victor the lands that now make up the US Southwest, and the 1898 Spanish-American War, which led to the takeover of Puerto Rico as well as to the establishment of a protectorate in Cuba, were key events that gave rise to migration north of the Rio Grande. Today Latina/os are a composite of diverse realities, national experiences, and collective existential traumas. Before emigration from Latin America, which for each distinct group corresponded to different sociohistorical and geopolitical events, no one was "Latina/o" or "Hispanic" but rather Puerto Rican, Cuban, Colombian, or Dominican, to name only a handful of the Latin American subgroups. Once in the United States, however, they become unified in significant ways. Latina/os share the experience of being uprooted by large socioeconomic forces from their original homelands. They come from societies with a history of unequal association with an imperial overseer that has influenced and often dictated political policy there. The habit of US policymakers to refer to Latin America as "the backyard of the United States" to signal geographical proximity metaphorically renders nations in the region as subordinates rather than partners or allies.

By the 1930s, a good many Latin American nations already had ascertained, through the incursion of US armed forces into their territories, the concrete inequality of their relationship with their North American neighbor. They had also become acquainted with the views that informed these military invasions. President Theodore Roosevelt publicly decried how Cubans,

Dominicans, Haitians, and Nicaraguans conducted themselves in political and economic matters. The famous "corollary to the Monroe Doctrine," in Roosevelt's 1904 annual message to Congress, enunciates the US sense of moral and political superiority over the peoples of Latin America:

> Chronic wrongdoing, or an impotence which results in a general loosening of the ties of civilized society, may in America, as elsewhere, ultimately require intervention by some civilized nation, and in the Western Hemisphere the adherence of the United States to the Monroe Doctrine may force the United States, however reluctantly, in flagrant cases of such wrongdoing or impotence, to the exercise of an international police power. (qtd. in Torres-Saillant, "Visions" 140)

Latino Literature

The foregoing scenario, which explains the emergence of a sense of community among US Hispanics, provides necessary context for understanding how they would have a distinct literary tradition. To recognize the boundaries of Latino literature, and the occurrence within it of the autobiography, it would help to draw a parallel. Readers will easily agree that African American literature is not African. Despite the shared blackness of the two authors, nobody would think of Harlem Renaissance poet Langston Hughes and Nigerian novelist Chinua Achebe as belonging in the same literary tradition. Similarly, Latino literature is not Latin American, nor is it Spanish. It would therefore seem inappropriate to group Chicano author Américo Paredes with Argentinian fiction writer Jorge Luis Borges, though they both have Spanish last names. Yet the reader will encounter readily available reference sources that do precisely that. One of them undertakes to map US Hispanic letters by surveying "a rich tapestry of Latino literary culture," from "the early poetry of Sor Juana Inés de la Cruz to the contemporary poetry of Jimmy Santiago Baca" (Magill v). Another source chaotically skims over Latin American authors such as Alejo Carpentier, Eduardo Mallea, Laura Esquivel, and Luis Rafael Sánchez, along with the likes of Latina/o authors Cristina García, Abraham Rodríguez, Luis Valdez, and Sandra Cisneros, without making any necessary distinctions. A reference volume entitled *Hispanic Writers*, consisting of sketches extracted from the series Contemporary Authors, provides information on "over 400 20th-century authors representing Hispanic literature and culture" (Ryan vii). The sketches included range from those born stateside (Oscar Zeta Acosta) to Latin Americans (César Vallejo) to peninsular writers (Federico García Lorca), exhibiting a planetary rather than a US-based ethnic understanding of the term *Hispanic*. Guided by a loose application of the terms *Latina/o* and *Hispanic*, and encompassing cultural histories that simply do not belong together, those reference texts end up muddying the concept of Latino literature. They proceed as if a shared Hispanic ancestry suffices to group writers together, irrespective of their different cultures, histories, languages, geographies, and birthplaces.

Ultimately, we cannot think of the nineteenth-century Dominican poet Salomé Ureña as a Latina in the way one uses the term when referring to Dominican American poet Rhina P. Espaillat. Nor can we think of the Mexican poet and playwright Rosario Castellanos as a Latina in the manner we do Mexican American poet Lorna Dee Cervantes. For as long as nation-states continue to exist, it will behoove readers to recognize the difference between an American writer of Latin American descent located in society as a member of a disempowered ethnic minority and a writer from Chile, for instance, who belongs there as a citizen, unencumbered by marginalized difference and ethnic constraints. Readers will simply find that these respective authors' texts require different reading practices. In Latin America or the Spanish-speaking Caribbean, Hispanic descent does not constitute a differentiated ethnic identity that merits naming. The naming of ethnicity normally occurs by reference to a normative, dominant group. Hispanic descent in the region is the norm. The misuse of the term *Latina*—with capital *L*—for a woman in Nicaragua has serious conceptual implications for our understanding of the contours of Latino identity and Latino literature. Latina/os exist as a component of an ethnoracial paradigm that makes sense only in the context of US history. There may be writers who, on account of their discrete circumstances, authentically occupy a sociocultural space where the dividing line between Latina/os to the north and Latin Americans to the south gets considerably blurred. Nor can we ignore the earnest desire of scholars who yearn for an eventual erasure of borders. Consistent with that spirit, Roman de la Campa opens his book *Latin Americanism* (1999) with a series of questions that occupy his attention throughout the volume. One of them is "Are Latino texts produced in the United States directly transferable to the study of Latin American literature?" (6). The question remains unanswered by the conclusion of the book, but those undertaking any serious inquiry into Latino literature, committed simultaneously to defining and heralding the tradition that US Hispanic texts have constituted, cannot afford to leave it unanswered. Enough information exists for scholars to affirm that Latino texts have borders. They speak primarily to interlocutors whose ears have been tuned by the sounds of the American experience. Even in those cases when the text occurs in Spanish, as with Tomás Rivera's . . . *y no se lo tragó la tierra* (1971), one can hardly think of its content and form as "directly transferable" to Latin American literature. The Spanish of Tomás Rivera, or the Spanish passages in the texts of Rudolfo Anaya or Denise Chávez, constitutes an American—not a Latin American—language.

Autobiographical Form

Autobiography may be regarded as the most important form in Latino literature since its practice epitomizes the main sociocultural compulsions that have fueled US Hispanic writing from the outset of the tradition. Like writers, literary scholars, and cultural critics from the other racialized minorities in the United States, Latina/o authors tend to display two dissimilar yet paradoxically complementary intents regarding American literature. They generally wish to assert their rightful place in the national corpus that bears the name "American literature," while at the same time challenging the sociocultural framework that informs traditional notions of Americanness. They seem to demand inclusion as legitimate members of the national community while simultaneously asserting their right to proudly display the trappings of their difference (Torres-Saillant, "Before the Diaspora" 10). Robert Sayre has persuasively envisioned autobiography as a vehicle by which citizens discursively travel the public sphere, assess the republic, and enter into the "House of America," which means that they participate in the country as an idea and a restorative project (150). While applying harmoniously to classic mainstream (Anglo) autobiographies, such as those of Benjamin Franklin and Henry Adams, the formulation needs adjustment to fit the situation of autobiographers from "communities not part of American success" (Sayre 162). Clearly this latter phrasing underscores the nation's inveterately racist, sexist, and classist histories and traditions.

No expression of the form exhibits a more forceful response to, or coming to terms with, that predicament than the Latino autobiography. Anyone approaching the US Hispanic literature section of a major bookstore or any student browsing a description for a Latino literature course at a fair-sized college or university will most likely notice the prominent place accorded to autobiographical texts. Consistent with the unstable generic constitution of the form, the selection would typically include memoirs, novels, and assorted works, all linked by their autobiographical texture. Some samples might include *Down These Mean Streets* (1967) by Piri Thomas, *Pocho* (1959) by José Antonio Villareal, *The Autobiography of a Brown Buffalo* (1972) by Oscar "Zeta" Acosta, *Barrio Boy* (1971) by Ernesto Galarza, *Hunger of Memory* (1984) by Richard Rodriguez, *Family Installments* (1982) by Edward Rivera, *How the García Girls Lost Their Accents* (1994) by Julia Alvarez, *Rain of Gold*

(1991) by Victor Villaseñor, *Silent Dancing* (1990) by Judith Ortiz Cofer, *When I was Puerto Rican* (1993) by Esmeralda Santiago, and *Drown* (1996) by Junot Díaz.

Certainly there are some Latina/o authors, such as the fiction writer Ed Vega, who steer clear of "wholly autobiographical" work, and even decry the practice of autobiography if it does not meet their criteria for linguistic sophistication and literary excellence (Augenbraum and Stavans xx–xxi). But, for the most part, autobiographical writing dominates Latino literature. This, no doubt, has to do with the importance of the immigrant story in the cultural history of the United States. Taking the form of "ethnic autobiography," this kind of writing accords neatly with the values American society uses to define itself (Kanellos 11). Needless to say, not all memoirs or autobiographies buy into the assimilationist ethos. It seems fair to assert that the cult of the individual in American society creates a favorable environment for publicly sharing private stories. Narratives of individual lives also tend to make the human experience more recognizable than the often-abstract plights of groups. When singly presented, material appears digestible to the consumer, who also comes to the story assured of its value because of its inherent lived truth. The pull of the market, therefore, plays a meaningful role in the production of autobiographies.

When the writer from a minority group has a social sensibility, the urgency to fight invisibility will surface strongly. Nicholasa Mohr recalled her desire early in her career to see both her people and herself framed in the text: "*Nilda*, my first novel, like so many writers' first books, contains a great deal of autobiographical material. . . . In American literature I, as a Puerto Rican child, did not exist . . . and I as a Puerto Rican woman do not exist" (qtd. in Rodríguez, "United States" 268). Some Latino texts that set out to write the self are thus milestones, providing key resources for understanding the formation and development of particular subsections of the overall population. The *Memoirs of Bernardo Vega* (1984), an engaging account of the life of a Puerto Rican labor organizer and political activist residing in New York during the first half of the twentieth century, provides invaluable ethnographic data for reconstructing the early years of the Puerto Rican community in the United States. Similarly, Evelio Grillo's memoir, *Black Cuban, Black American* (2000), shares the journey of a Cuban Tampa native who, split by Jim Crow segregation in the South, carved out a space of belonging in the African American community. The text contains a wealth of knowledge about race relations among US Cubans prior to the migratory flows that followed the 1959 Revolution.

Besides those works that are evidently autobiographical, in that the narrative *I* in the story being told corresponds to the person writing it, numerous

Latino publications exist that provoke the reader to connect the life of the author with that of the main character featured in the text. Readers of Villareal's *Pocho*, which tells of a young man growing up in California among farm laborers, will be tempted to identify the main character Richard Rubio's cultural ambivalence about Mexican and Anglo values with the author's own experience as a mixed-race youngster growing up between competing traditions. By the same token, when perusing Diaz's *Drown*, readers may find it hard to resist equating the incidents in the life of protagonist, Yunior, with those in the life of the author, especially since the two seem nearly identical at repeated instances broached in the writer's interviews. One could probably apply to Latino writing Rosenblatt's assessment of African American texts, namely that "fiction is often so close to autobiography in plot and theme that the study of the latter almost calls the existence of the former into question" (170). In some Latino texts, among them Rivera's *Family Installments* and Alvarez's *How the García Girls*, the line between the biographical and the fictional blurs to such a degree that publishers and librarians sometimes classify them as either "fiction" or "autobiography/nonfiction" interchangeably.

Key Contributions: Mexican Americans and Women Writers

Autobiography has reached the position of prominence it currently enjoys in Latino literature as a result of the community's need to assert, protect, and encourage itself through narrative art. The rise of the form corresponds to stages of collective self-affirmation running parallel to moments in history that vary for each of the subgroups that make up the US Hispanic population. Following their different moments of insertion in labor markets, the creation of ethnic enclaves on the margins of mainstream society, and the recognition of existing systemic barriers that would ignore or silence the group's voices, Latina/os began to brandish language as a tool to fight their way into the national discourse. The drive for the community to make its presence felt continues to trigger the need to speak up. Since Mexican Americans first became part of the US population through an act of military conquest and subsequent subjugation, their need to speak up, which Genaro Padilla calls a "discursive necessity," flows from an inherited awareness of historical traumas. He observes, "The rupture of everyday life experienced by some 75,000 people who inhabited the far northern provinces of Mexico in 1846 opened a terrain of discursive necessity in which fear and resentment found language in speeches and official documents warning fellow citizens to accommodate themselves to the new regime" ("Recovering" 153). Even at that early juncture, speaking up came from the contestatory imperative to argue "for justice and equality for Mexican Americans" under Anglo domination (153). Political traumas shake the pillars of memory, inducing amnesia or spurring the desire to remember. What ensues is a scenario that is hospitable to testimonial utterance and historical reckoning.

Though initially criticized for its assimilationist emphasis, Villareal's *Pocho* demonstrated a meaningful willingness to delve into the issues of identity that emerged from the clashing worldviews that Mexican Americans experienced on the eve of World War II. In that respect, it stands as a seminal text in the evolution of the form among Chicano authors. Galarza's *Barrio Boy*, which depicts a protagonist whose sense of identity and self-worth stems from a healthy affiliation with his community, also has a special place as a foundational autobiographical text. Contemporary Mexican American autobiographers such as Ruben Martínez, Ruben Navarrete, Luis J. Rodríguez, John Phillip Santos, Gary Soto, and Luis Alberto Urrea add further layers of complexity to the exploration of contemporary identity and the relationship between the individual and the collective.

Reconstructing the history of a former time can become an urgent need. As Padilla explains, such an impulse has given way "to an autobiographical formation in which the desire for historical presence" remains paramount ("Recovering" 153). Thus, the earliest Hispanic autobiographical narratives in the US Southwest—José Antonio Menchaca's "Reminiscences" (c. 1850) and Juan Nepomuceno Seguín's *Personal Memoirs* (1858)—share a common desire to bear witness to the authors' respective plights, as they each negotiated the delicate circumstances that caused them to shift loyalties more than once. Perhaps the most ambitious attempt to mark the community's historical presence from the perspective of the observing individual subject was the landowning Californio Mariano Guadalupe Vallejo's "Recuerdos históricos y personales tocante a la Alta California," a lengthy, unpublished manuscript housed in the Bancroft Library at the University of California, Berkeley. Examples of Mexican Americans who felt compelled to bear witness abound from Vallejo's time through the mid-twentieth century, with women playing a role that should not be ignored, as has been the case too often in literary history. Some fifteen women of Hispanic descent participated in the project conducted during the late 1870s by California bookseller and historian Hubert H. Bancroft, who had numerous autobiographies transcribed from oral dictation as part of his data-gathering for writing the state's history.

The stories told by several of the participants provided otherwise unavailable ethnic- and gender-inflected perspectives on society, culture, and politics. The documents they left, including the noteworthy personal accounts "Cosas de California" ("Things Californian") by María Inocenta Pico Ávila, "Narración de una californiana" ("A California Woman's Story") by Josefa Carrillo de Fitch, and "Recuerdos del pasado" ("Memories of the Past") by Felipa Osuna de Marrón, constitute invaluable glimpses of life in the state during a pivotal moment of cultural transition. Scholars often highlight "Memorias de la beata" ("Memoirs of a Pious Woman"), by Apolinaria Lorenzana, and "Una vieja y sus recuerdos" ("An Old Woman and Her Recollections"), by Eulalia Pérez, as meaningful portrayals of courageous women wrestling with multiple adversities in a suffocatingly patriarchal domain. Lorenzana, who became a teacher, nurse, and supervisor of the Indigenous seamstresses in a San Diego mission, had come as an orphan to Alta California to serve in various homes. A witness to the Anglo takeover of California, she rose to become owner of three ranches. Pérez, for her part, worked as housekeeper in the San Gabriel Mission, where she oversaw the distribution of all stock and supervised the Indigenous domestic workers.

Lodged in the archives of the Bancroft Library, these autobiographical interventions by Mexican American women still remain relatively unknown, as the project that instigated their collection did not contemplate their dissemination and restricted their value to enhancing the research resources of their Anglo collector. Ironically, *The Rebel* (1994), an autobiography written in Laredo, Texas, by Leonor Villegas de Magnón, a participant observer who wished to foreground the role of women on both sides of the border during the Mexican Revolution, did not make it to print until nearly a half century after the death of the author. This delay was despite her having tried hard to publish it either in Spanish or in English. She founded in 1913 the women's nursing corps La Cruz Blanca (the White Cross), made up mostly of women from the Texas side of the border who supported the insurgent leader Venustiano Carranza in Mexico. Her legacy as an activist and writer poignantly affirms the fundamentally transnational texture of political and social life on the border. Born in northern Mexico to an elite family, Villegas attended Catholic school in San Antonio and Austin and received her bachelor's degree and teaching certification in 1895 from the Academy of Mount St. Ursula in New York (Kanellos 382). Her involvement in the work of the Revolution, a political movement that would spur significant social transformations in Mexico, did not imply that she had much choice relating to her political commitments to either side of the border. On the night of her birth, her father had wondered, "My son born in American soil. My daughter in Mexican territory, and I, a Spanish subject. Who will be more powerful, he or she?" (Villegas 7). This was a question that her mother, holding the newborn daughter "in a warm embrace," settled by addressing the infant with these words: "A Mexican flag shall be yours. I will wrap it together with your brother's. His shall be an American flag, but they shall be like one to me" (7). A US citizen whose national loyalty would continually be questioned by Americans and Mexicans, she chose to embrace an agenda of "international social justice" that ignored juridical boundaries (Lomas xxxix).

In the generations that followed Villegas de Magnón, Nina Otero-Warren, author of *Old Spain and Our Southwest* (1936); Fabiola Cabeza de Baca, who wrote *The Good Life* (1949) and *We Fed Them Cactus* (1954); and Cleofas Jaramillo, author of *Romance of a Little Girl* (1955), stand out among the Mexican American women who had recourse to autobiographical writing to establish a legacy. A cadre of women authors who merit mention as founding mothers of Latina letters, Otero-Warren, Cabeza de Vaca, and Jaramillo, all natives of New Mexico, satisfy their discursive necessity in a manner that accentuates the significance of class in collective constructions of identity. Evincing an aristocratic mode of representation consistent with their own upper-class origins, their texts formulate claims to cultural resistance by stressing their association with a glorious past of their forebears, devoid of the oppression perpetrated by the Spanish conquistadors against the Indigenous population. As their evocations repress the vanquished Other and relegate them to the margins (as "savage" Indians, "lazy" Aztecs, and simple *peones*), their "autoethnographies" participate in a process that Sonja Z. Pérez terms "participatory resistance," meaning that they "simultaneously participated in and resisted Anglo-American domination" (288). Broadly speaking, these women deserve credit as subordinated writers from whose narratives we can unearth "a textual signal of embryonic consciousness, whispers of antecedent resistance" that contributed to clearer expressions of the Latino contestation that would come later (Padilla, "Imprisoned" 60).

Cuban American Variations

Cubans are the Latino subgroup with the deepest historical roots in the United States after Mexican Americans. The 1858 publication in New York of *El laúd del desterrado*, a compilation of patriotic Cuban verse by exiled poets, which includes compositions as early as the "Himno del desterrado" (1825), by José María Heredia, clearly illustrates the longevity of Cuban writing in the United States. Other important case studies include Cirilo Villaverde's *Cecilia Valdés* (1882), an abolitionist novel that has a central place in the national literary history of Cuba yet was published while the author lived as an exile stateside, and a sizable body of work that José Martí, the founding father of the Cuban nation, wrote while he resided in New York. Throughout the nineteenth century, American legislators and government officials sustained a set of undefined and ambiguous positions regarding US–Cuban relations, both providing a haven for rebels from the island, who sought the overthrow of the Spanish colonial regime, and exhibiting solidarity with Cuba's colonial rulers. US interest in annexing Cuba to the American territory, dating back to the time of Thomas Jefferson, largely modulated that inconsistent policy (Montes Huidobro x–xi). The ambivalence came to an end in the mid-1890s when the American government announced its support of the Cuban independence movement, culminating in the invasion of 1898 and the Spanish–American War that did away with the last remnants of an Iberian imperial presence in the hemisphere.

Of course, the interests of Cuban independence leaders did not prevail once US forces secured their defeat of Spain, which led to the American occupation of Puerto Rico, the Philippines, and other overseas territories. But in 1895, US imperial interests *did* benefit from autobiographical writing. William Randolph Hearst, the powerful and enigmatic publisher of the *New York Journal*, like his competitor Joseph Pulitzer, owner of the *New York World*, favored the invasion and passionately lobbied for it. Among Hearst's most successful advocacy stunts was the publicity campaign he orchestrated around the liberation of the patriot Evangelina Cossío y Cisneros, a sort of Cuban Joan of Arc whom the Spanish authorities had incarcerated in the women's prison of Las Recogidas. He sent his employee Karl Decker, then one of the paper's star correspondents, with the mission to free the young damsel from Havana. The plan to rescue Evangelina, which involved a clever stratagem, proved successful, and she escaped disguised as a man, ending her fifteen-month imprisonment. Evangelina and her American savior came to New York to a triumphant reception on Fifth Avenue, with President William McKinley in attendance (Fernández, "Crónica" 21).

Born in 1878 in Puerto Príncipe, the capital city of Camagüey province in Cuba, Evangelina was seventeen when Americans brought her out of captivity. Two years later, while she enjoyed her status as a media darling in New York, an English-language autobiography signed by her was published. *The Story of Evangelina Cisneros* (1897), which had the backing of the Hearst publicity machine, appealed directly to American women. "This is the story of my life," she remarks, adding pointedly, "American women may find it interesting" (Cossío y Cisneros 356). The author underlines the similarity between her birthplace and the host country ("Camagüey is said by Americans to be the Kentucky of Cuba"). The parallel subtly invokes the geopolitical logic of the Monroe Doctrine, thereby foreshadowing the imperial outlook that viewed the rest of the hemisphere as the United States' "backyard." Evangelina deemed it inconceivable "that some of the things which I must tell you could really happen so close to the free country of America" (356). Since it does not seem that a Spanish version of Evangelina's story really existed, we can speculate that both her writing in English and the ideological direction of her thought received considerable input from Hearst and his staff. In general, Evangelina's autobiography probably deserves credit for garnering allies to the cause that promoted the invasion of Cuba, which occurred the following year.

At the time of the Spanish–American War, whereby Cuba became a US protectorate, a large and vigorous émigré Cuban community thrived, especially in Florida, connected with the cigar industry. Since their presence in the United States preceded the US takeover of their ancestral island, they can be said to have escaped many of the traumas associated with being marginalized minorities "of color." Perhaps that may explain why the autobiography occurs less frequently among Cuban authors. We can speculate, in other words, that they suffered less of the existential impact from the negative forces that incite the need to speak up, especially when comparing the discursive necessity that Mexican Americans shouldered from the outset. A major work that we could list among Cuban autobiographies, *The Goodbye Land* (1967), by Tampa-born José Yglesias, lacks the markers of ethnic self-affirmation evinced, for instance, by Piri Thomas's *Down These Mean Streets*, which appeared the same year. Apart from offering some scintillating glimpses of the author's childhood at the start of the twentieth century, the book concentrates on the memory of his father, a native of the northern Spanish province of Galicia who, at the age of thirteen, arrived in Havana, where he learned the cigar trade. He eventually journeyed to Tampa to work in the cigar factories. But he fell ill with typhoid in 1920, and efforts to regain his health took him back to Havana, the first trip out of Tampa for the author's twenty-eight-year-old mother. From the Cuban capital, his father then had to go on a ship for Spain while the wife and the children, including José, returned to Tampa. Since his father eventually died in Spain and the family never saw him again, the story relates the author's quest to reconstruct his deceased parent's long trajectory. Already an adult, traveling with his own wife and children, Yglesias undertakes a sentimental journey in pursuit of meaning by tracing his family roots. The pathos in the narrative comes from frustrations stemming from his individual search rather than from ethnic constraints.

The autobiographical impulse in Cuban writing can be found in texts that are better known as fiction, such as the novel *Our House in the Last World* (1983), a tale by Oscar Hijuelos that spans three generations of a Cuban family in the United States. Subscribing to "the conventional norms of an immigrant memoir," with evident fictional elements, the text has been described by Jorge Duany as the author's "first autobiographical novel" (171). The same scholar refers to Cristina García's *Dreaming in Cuban* (1992) as a novel that tells "the partly autobiographical story of three generations of a Cuban family," namely, the children and grandchildren of Jorge and Celia del Pino (177). What causes the del Pino children to come to the United States, splitting from the branch of the family that chooses to stay on the island, is the Cuban Revolution, an event that had traumatic consequences for several contemporary Cuban memoirists. Their texts range from the moving narrative of Flor Fernandez Barrios in *Blessed by Thunder: Memoir of a Cuban Girlhood* (1999) to the personal drama of a gay Cuban physician dealing with AIDS patients, told by Rafael Campo in *The Desire to Heal: A Doctor's Education in Empathy, Identity, and Poetry* (1998). In *Life on the Hyphen: The Cuban-American Way* (1994), Gustavo Pérez Firmat extends analytical recollections of his life, therein developing his 1.5-generation thesis to describe the identity of those Cubans who came to the United States around the age of twelve or thirteen. Their exodus prompted by the Revolution, they were old enough to retain a cultural memory of the pre-Revolutionary past but too young to share the exilic mindset of their parents. That Cuban American autobiographers seldom address racial matters in narrating their lives, an issue other Latina/o authors cover almost invariably, may have to do with the great hold that the trauma of the Revolution has had on their imagination. Grupo Areito issued *Contra viento y marea* (1978), a collection of personal testimonials by young people who, by then, were already rethinking their relationship with post-1959 Cuba. The 1995 collection *Bridges to Cuba*, edited by Ruth Behar, revisits the project following the fall of the Berlin Wall. Both compilations present highly engaging texts on the existential implications for individuals of the geopolitics of US–Cuban relations.

Perhaps most illustrative of the way the Cuban American autobiography satisfies its discursive necessity differently compared to that of other Latinos is Pablo Medina's *Exiled Memories: A Cuban Childhood* (1990). This book chronicles the author's first twelve years, a period that ends at 5 a.m. on January 1, 1959, when his father rushes into the house shouting, "Batista fell!" Preparations to leave for the United States began immediately, starting their interminable exile (108). The 1990 edition of the autobiography ends on a sober note about the inevitability of departure and the loss of home. A second edition, published in 2002, adds a chapter in which Medina summarizes the deaths of several older relatives and records his experience of returning for a visit to Havana in January 1999, at the age of fifty, to reconnect with his past. Despite the indictment of the Cuban Revolution, what emerges is a more serene adult voice, one that seems to have reconciled himself to the losses inherent in growing up. What we do not derive is any inkling of the life the author has lived between the loss of his childhood world and his subsequent coming to terms with the loss. Interestingly, the omitted portion is precisely the one that would yield material for ethnic autobiography. Despite the political setting in which the story transpires, the text really belongs with *The Goodbye Land*, that is, among tales of personal questing devoid of the constraints that typically fuel the Latina/o autobiographer's desire to bear witness to historical upheaval.

Puerto Rican Autobiographers

Medina avoids the Bildüngsroman component that so characteristically emerges in Latino autobiographies, which are predominantly coming-of-age stories. The bulk of Esmeralda Santiago's *When I Was Puerto Rican* (1993) evokes nostalgically—even exotically—the author's childhood years in her rustic village of Macún. Less than a third of its pages go to her growing up as an immigrant in low-income Brooklyn tenements, which could perhaps merit comparison with Medina's *Exiled Memories*. Yet these texts differ significantly, in that Santiago's tale, more characteristic of the Latino autobiographic tradition, does not, like Medina's, seek to reconstruct a tragically lost world of comfort and solace. Rather, her book re-creates the transition from the discomfort of poverty in rural Puerto Rico to the discomfort of poverty in inner-city New York. What changes for her is internal, namely, her inevitable maturation. With the loss of the magical schemes of thought prevalent during childhood, she found herself less disposed to smile in the face of utter misery. Santiago's book, in this respect, behaves normally in relation to the texts of other US Puerto Rican authors, as well as the overall Latino autobiographical corpus. *Almost a Woman* (1998), the second installment of Santiago's autobiography, concentrates fully on the exploration of her American experience on the mainland.

Scholars often mention Pedro Juan Labarthe's *Son of Two Nations: The Private Life of a Columbia Student* (1931) as an exceptional panorama that glorifies the cultural and social options that Puerto Ricans faced after the US occupation of their land three decades earlier. Illustrating the benefits of the colonial condition, the book recounts an immigrant success story of the kind that "Americanization makes possible and which reflects the worldview of more privileged Puerto Ricans" (Acosta-Belén 18). Labarthe seems particularly atypical when juxtaposed with such contemporaries as Bernardo Vega, whose *Memorias*, though first published in 1977, was written in the 1940s, and Jesús Colón, whose 1961 collection *A Puerto Rican in New York and Other Sketches* gathered personal essays that he had published over the previous decades. Attuned to community dynamics, both writers came at a young age from the

Puerto Rican countryside town of Cayey to New York City, where they became cigar factory workers and involved themselves in political activism on behalf of working-class constituencies. Both wrote texts of a "compelling autobiographical and testimonial nature" that served as "invaluable historical sources" for the study of the Puerto Rican community and wider Hispanic community in the city during the first half of the twentieth century (Acosta-Belén 183).

As practiced by Santiago, Judith Ortiz Cofer, and others, contemporary Puerto Rican autobiography traces its social, political, and existential roots to Vega and Colón rather than to Labarthe. The reason for this genealogy is found in the socioeconomic profiles of the migratory flows that came from the island to the mainland during the first two-thirds of the twentieth century, when working-class arrivants predominated. Extreme poverty and racial discrimination provide the backdrop against which Piri Thomas sets his own story in *Down These Mean Streets* (1967). We learn about his dealing with self-hatred, gangs, drugs, crime, incarceration, and ultimate rehabilitation. The young man's inability to negotiate the racial codes of his Hispanic Caribbean household, alongside those in place on the streets of pre–Civil-Rights-era New York, largely accounts for the pain he endures. Issued by a major publisher and reviewed widely in the press, the book brought considerable celebrity to the author, making him an influential figure in Latino literature.

Also worthy of note is the pithy autobiographical essay "Halfway to Dick and Jane" (1971), by poet and translator Jack Agüeros, a New York–born Puerto Rican whose father, a teenager in 1920, ventured to the big city as a stowaway on a steamer from San Juan. Agüeros recalls how his father explained the main cause of migration for his community. Like birds, men take flight from hostile environments (104). The elder continues,

> When a Puerto Rican comes to America, he comes looking for a job. He takes the cold as one of a negative series of givens. The mad hustle, the filthy city, filthy air, filthy housing, sardine transportation, are in the series. He knows life will be tough and dangerous. But he thinks he can make a buck. And in his mind, there is only one tableau: himself retired, owner of his home in Puerto Rico, chickens cackling in the back yard. (104)

The parents, if fortune smiles on them, can return; the mainland-born children, if social marginality blocks their sense of belonging, cannot. According to Agüeros, "I am very much a migrant because I am still not quite at home in America. Always there are hills; on the other side—people inclined to throwing cabbages. I cannot 'earn and return'—there is no position for me in my father's tableau" (105).

The Puerto Rican pilgrimage that New York City–born Agüeros enacts in his moving autobiographical essay epitomizes the angst of the immigrant experience as it afflicts the US-born children. They realize they have already lost their ancestral homeland, without necessarily having gained one in their place of birth. The Latino autobiography in general, and its Puerto Rican segment in particular, characteristically captures that predicament. This is the case in straightforward accounts of individual lives in texts that explore the author's biography while deploying imaginative models of community, or in literary exercises resembling the "testimonial novel," such as Nicholasa Mohr's *Nilda* (1973) and Edward Rivera's *Family Installments* (Flores 65). Rivera's book entices the reader to take it for a biographical account. We observe its labeling as "memoir" on the back cover and its subtitle, "Memories of Growing Up Hispanic." Yet it asserts its fictional texture as well. The story begins prior to the protagonist's birth, and his name differs from that of the book's author. Partly a portrait of the artist as a young man, the narrative captures the formative experiences of a Puerto Rican youth who carves out his individual identity as a Latino in New York without treating his Boricua background with contempt or pastoralizing the promises of the American Dream. The ideological equanimity of Rivera's book, which can also be found in the title story of the collection *The Boy without a Flag: Tales of the South Bronx* (1992), by Abraham Rodriguez, Jr., largely captures the overall Puerto Rican contribution to the form. This is a body of writing that is far more substantial than this brief overview can attempt to encompass.

The Rise of Dominican Voices

When Dominican American writers emerged as bona fide members of the Latino literary family in the 1990s, they became known primarily for the autobiographical bent of their texts. The case has been made that it should not have taken so long for US Dominican writing to attain visibility, since its history is not as short as scholars of Latino literature seem to have assumed (Torres-Saillant, "Before the Diaspora" 250–251). Though belated, the recognition did come, ushered in by the remarkable success of *How the García Girls Lost Their Accents* (1991) by Julia Alvarez. Now a staple on reading lists for courses dealing with the immigrant experience or ethnic minorities in the United States, the book so much resembled the author's life that friends and relatives recognized themselves in it and occasionally objected. As a conciliatory gesture to these individuals who cross paths with the protagonist, Yolanda "Yo" García, Alvarez produced the ingenious novel *¡Yo!* (1997), which consists of a series of appraisals in which these characters "write back," sharing their own thoughts and representations of Yo. The product is a highly energetic meditation on both the self (*yo*) and others (*los otros*) who mutually create one another and the circumstances that shape their lives.

Born in 1950 to affluent immigrant parents from the Dominican Republic, Alvarez was taken to her parents' country only a few weeks after her birth in New York City. Her family lived in her ancestral homeland until 1960. Political problems would cause the couple to migrate again to the United States with all four daughters. Details about the writer's early childhood appear throughout her essays, especially in "An American Childhood in the Dominican Republic," which meditates on the extent of her continuous contact with US society during her ten years away. Her maternal grandfather, a long-standing cultural attaché to the United Nations, "spoke perfect English," having graduated from an American university, and kept an apartment in New York City (72). His children, in turn, attended boarding schools stateside, and the boys, especially, attended top American institutions of higher learning, among them "Cornell, Yale, [and] Brown." Alvarez recalls that back in the Dominican Republic, her family "subscribed to American magazines, received mail-order catalogues, and joined honorary societies," while she and her three sisters, along with their numerous cousins, played with US-made toys (80). Similarly, during her formative years, the would-be writer attended the Carol Morgan School, an institution founded by a diplomat's wife to serve the learning needs of the children of Americans who lived in the Dominican Republic. Alvarez recollects, "We began each day by pledging allegiance to the flag of the United States, which I much preferred to the Dominican one, for it had the lovely red-and-white stripes of the awning at the ice-cream parlor" (77). As the language of instruction at Carol Morgan, English was also the language of home. Alvarez has described her early linguistic experience in the 1992 essay "My English," which appears in her collection *Something to Declare* (1998). There, we learn that her parents spoke English strategically, for instance when the children did yet not know enough of the language and the elders wanted to keep a secret from them. Later, when everyone had become "a bilingual family," her parents stressed the use of English to make the young ones proficient (21). When her parents migrated north, the ten-year-old Julia's knowledge of English facilitated her (re-)settlement and comfort.

Alvarez reconstructs her feelings at the precise moment when her plane landed in New York from Santo Domingo: "All my life I had dressed like an American. . . . I had gone to an American school and spent most of the day speaking and reading English. . . . All my life I had longed for this moment of arrival. And here I was, an American girl, coming home at last" ("An American Childhood" 85). The author's yearning for the United States while in her parents' homeland resonates with the mood of the speaker in her autobiographical collection of poems *The Other Side / El Otro Lado* (1995). The section that gives this book its collective title includes a narrative poem made up of twenty-one parts that chronicle the speaker's adventures in a quasi-mystical *over there*. She, a "so-called writer working on her two-year writing block," goes to spend a "winter's residency" at an artist's colony on a mountain in the Dominican Republic (109–110). The speaker and her American boyfriend, Mike, "like two Brits—trekking through darkest Africa," hike down literally to the level of the common folk (111). During her momentous crossing of a Dominican vale that strikes one as a heart of darkness, the narrator stops to seek the counsel of a Haitian vodou priest to help her "make up" her "divided Dominican-American mind" and hopefully also help "lift" her from "middle-aged self, / empty of passion, empty of song" (131).

This traveler, stumbling "between the Scylla and the Charybdis / of two cultures," finally arrives at a point of revelation. During a private séance with Luisa the *santera*, a priestess communing with various Afro-diasporic gods, Julia succeeds at extracting from the spirit world a message that illuminates her path. She comes to the following blunt but crucial realization: "I know / I won't be coming back to live / in my ex-homeland" (147). She casts away "self-doubt," fending off the disorienting spirit that was "double-crossing my life with its homesickness" (148). Like Dante back from his descent into Hell or Galahad returning from successfully locating the Grail, the self-assured speaker migrates "steadily across the watery darkness / to the shore [she has] made up on the other side" (150). She has escaped from danger into safety, having distanced herself from what she might have become, namely, a captive woman "posed like a siren / on the barnacle-crusted cliffside," had she paid heed to the treacherous voice within, luring her back "from the self I toil over in the States" (150). The speaker triumphs over the deleterious forces that deceived her into imagining the possibility of defining and establishing a permanent place in the Dominican Republic. This vision accords with that which informs the ideas and choices of Yolanda, the main character in both the aforementioned autobiographical novels.

Another Dominican American author who enjoys considerable distinction, Junot Díaz, has spoken extensively about his personal life to readers and interviewers, who tend to see his texts as transcriptions of lived experience. He explains his relationship to autobiography as follows:

> I love to play with it. It's like a medium. I was saying in an interview before that, no matter how hard I try to be autobiographical, the demands of fiction transform the material. There was no possible way to be autobiographical. The same way a memoir is also a kind of fiction. And so, the same way I said my friends as audience have certain demands, the craft of fiction, as I know it, has rigorous demands which

transform what I think is autobiography into something entirely different. (Céspedes and Torres-Saillant 905–906)

But still, reviews of his work and interviews invariably privilege the sociological angle of his background, namely, experiences of abject poverty and living without a father at home.[2]

Díaz has had a remarkable literary career since he first broke into print with a short fiction piece titled "Ysrael," in the autumn 1995 issue of the magazine *Story*. He eventually earned inclusion in the Best American Short Stories series over the course of multiple years, serving also as guest editor of the anthology himself in 2016. When the short fiction collection *Drown* came out in 1996, it met with universal praise. While his stories might dabble in the scrutiny of contemporary Dominican history and "cross cultural experiences," David Gates, appraising *Drown* for *The New York Times*, confidently placed the book "smack-dab in the middle" of the American experience (9). With a clinical eye, Díaz pierces into the Dominican chapter of the human experience, revealing a field virtually unexplored by canonical American fiction. With its discrete history and geography, following the characters' whereabouts from the homeland in the Dominican Republic through their immigrant odyssey in the United States, the book shines a light on misery, uprooting, and endurance. Dominicans harbor the greatness, the baseness, the beauty, and the mediocrity of all humans seeking a better life at home and abroad.

The last and longest of *Drown*'s stories, "Negocios," reconstructs the adventures of Ramón, a father who leaves his wife and children behind to try to make it in the United States, from the vantage point of Yunior, his youngest son. In the host country, having survived the initial hurdles of a Herculean immigrant crossing, Ramón ends up married to Nilda, a concurrent second wife with whom he sires an additional set of children. The narrator's father and mother have names that coincide with those of the author's parents, Ramón and Virtudes, and the evocation of family life loosely resembles the biographical details the author has shared with interviewers. That resemblance between people or events in their books with people or events in the authors' lives occurs as well in *Geographies of Home* (1998) and *Soledad* (2001), novels authored respectively by Loida Maritza Pérez and Angie Cruz, two other contemporary Dominican American writers who have drawn discernibly from personal and family circumstances to compose their immigrant-focused narratives. Nelly Rosario's *Song of the Water Saints* (2002), a novel that links the drama of a family in New York City's Washington Heights neighborhood to a historical genesis traceable to the 1916 US military invasion of the Dominican Republic, is less clearly connected to the tradition of ethnic autobiography.

Besides those authors mentioned here, Dominicans writing in the United

States are linguistically heterogeneous, the majority producing their texts in Spanish. The autobiography does not seem to have surfaced as a prominent form among Hispanophone US Dominican writers. On the whole, the biographical engagement displayed in Dominican American fiction, like the greater Latino literary corpus to which it belongs, would seem to justify Paul de Man's recommendation to place the distinction between fiction and autobiography in the realm of the "undecidable" (921).

Amorphous Forms

The Chicana writer and scholar Norma Elia Cantú, herself a fine autobiographer, has drawn attention to autobiographies written in the late twentieth century by denizens of the border town of Laredo, Texas. Focusing on four such cases, she discusses *Infancia peregrina* (n.d.), by Belia Treviño; *Mis memorias* (1985), by Hilario Coronado; *Holidays and Heartstrings: Recuerdos de la casa de miel* (1995), by Norma Benavides; and *My Spanish-Speaking Left Foot* (1997) by José A. Cárdenas. These autobiographers, none of whom appears moved by the desire for widespread literary recognition, apparently wrote their texts to convey accounts of their experiences to family, friends, and community. Humbly presented, their writings constitute narrative attempts to preserve the cultural memory of the borderlands by regular people dealing with the challenges of living between two converging nation-states. In a presentation on the narratives, Cantú noted that these "homemade autobiographies" do not necessarily document the exploits of one person but tend to portray "a much wider protagonist, the community." On the matter of form, Cantú quotes the following disclaimer laid out by Benavides to introduce her own work: "Aside from liberties of content, there are those of form and style, mood, language, and punctuation. The text fluctuates from one style to another, never adhering to any definite pattern or fixed set of rules. Also, it drifts from formal to informal, from carefree to soulful, dramatic, or even philosophical at times, or from comical to tragic. After all, isn't life itself this way?" (Cantú, "Whose Story").

Curiously, though representing herself as a "non-writer," Benavides formulates a disclaimer that goes directly to the core of the theory and practice of Latino autobiography, an eminently amorphous form that has historically embraced all the deviations that she describes. The frequently cited definition of autobiography enunciated by essayist Philippe Lejeune would seem inapplicable to the manifestations of the form in the Latino literary tradition: "a retrospective prose narrative produced by a real person concerning his own existence, focusing on his individual life, in particular on the development of his personality" (193). Lejeune, of course, concurs with others in viewing the autobiography as "a way of reading" as much as "a kind of writing";

he accepts its very existence as an "historically variable contractual product" (220). Among Latina/os, the form is not circumscribed to prose narrative since examples abound that incorporate verse into the evocation of the protagonist's life. Examples include Ortiz Cofer's *Silent Dancing* and Moraga's *Loving in the War Years*. Cantu's *Canicula: Snapshots of a Girlhood en la Frontera* (1995) oscillates between the verbal and the visual by having the words converse with family photographs over the course of weaving her story. The author provokes the reader by offering a tantalizing explanation of her use of family pictures: "[A]lthough it may appear that these stories are my family's, they're not precisely, and yet they are. . . . I was calling the work fictional autobiography, until a friend suggested that they really are ethnographic and so if it must fit a genre, I guess it is fictional autoethnography" (xi).

While the veteran theorist Lejeune typically casts the autobiographer as a *he*, writing singly about his own existence and personality, in the Latino practice of the form, the *she* predominates, and the concerns of the texts transcend the mere self-study of an individual author. For example, *Getting Home Alive* (1986), a collection of verse and prose that now figures among the most notable autobiographies by Latinas, presents us with the peculiar collaboration of Aurora Levins Morales and her mother Rosario Morales (Torres 276). With *Borderlands / La Frontera: The New Mestiza*, the celebrated book by Anzaldúa that has also earned inclusion as a major autobiography in more than one literary canon, we have a volume that combines poetry with speculative thought and hardly any, *pace* Lejeune, "retrospective prose narrative." Code-switching occurs frequently in these texts as narrators move from English into Spanish and vice versa. Acosta's *Autobiography of a Brown Buffalo*, a fair portion of which we receive from a hallucinating narrator whose perception has been altered by the effects of heavy drugs, forces the reader to distinguish the real from the imagined. Finally, the best-known Latino autobiographer, Richard Rodriguez, deliberately structured his text as a series of essays despite the advice by his New York editor that he should exploit the "narrative" potential in his manuscript (Rodriguez 7).

A more exhaustive study than this one would consider the ways in which the autobiography manifests itself in the literary production of writers of Central and South American descent since US-based Colombian, Guatemalan, Nicaraguan, Peruvian, and Salvadoran communities, among others, have become increasingly visible. They are already a presence within Latino literature. The foregoing overview of authors from the four largest Latino subgroups would seem already to justify some preliminary generalizations. The Latino autobiography defies formal prescriptions; thus we observe a juxtaposition of vitality and power as well as potential pitfalls. Irrespective of its generically protean quality and the difficulty of guaranteeing the continuous stability of the self it contains, the form can command formidable authority to represent a particular community. Its precarious reliability will not negate its capacity to articulate the community's collective identity. A commercially successful autobiography will far outweigh the impact of politicians and activists on how to bridge gaps and negotiate fissures between the minority community and the cultural mainstream.

An autobiographical intervention can wield the power to represent an ethnic minority community, even if its author's ideologies clash with the overall political persuasion or cultural worldview of the group. The African American community received *The Autobiography of Malcolm X* (1965) as an unproblematic account of a completed self with a stable moral structure and an unchanged political creed. As such, the book went into high school and college curricula and has become a classic. But, consistent with the difficulty of leading an uncommon life and writing an autobiography about it, the Malcolm of biographical fact had diverged from the Malcolm of the text by the time Alex Haley completed the book. Haley even had to struggle to keep the civil rights leader from going back to reinterpret (on the basis of new revelations and disappointments) statements he had dictated before but no longer believed in (Eakin 189).

Similarly, the Latino community receives representations of itself with which it may disagree without being able to arrest their power to shape society's perceptions. The ideology of the Latina/o autobiographer will always be individual, but it will have repercussions at a collective level. These writers will champion a construction of identity informed by their individual subject positions. Anzaldúa, wielding the authority of the theorist and the license of the poet, describes a New Mestiza who simultaneously occupies multiple and disparate identity spaces while transcending all borders. Rodriguez endorses a view of citizenship and belonging that promotes ethnoracial and cultural self-effacement. Alvarez commits herself to a structure of belonging that celebrates hybridity while safely storing the trappings of her ancestral origins under the regulatory moral and political superiority of the Anglo tradition. Unable to cope with race outside the logic engendered by US history, Thomas overemphasizes race in his family interactions to the detriment of any positive rapport with his relatives. Moraga highlights the intersectional links between class, gender, and ethnoracial location alongside sexuality in the articulation of her social identity. In her words, "It wasn't until I acknowledged and confronted my own lesbianism in the flesh, that my heartfelt identification with and empathy for my mother's oppression—due to being poor, uneducated, and Chicana—was realized" (52).

The autobiography ultimately inhabits a site that is nearly beyond refutation. For even while its deployment of a particular ideological agenda may have implications for the image of the community, critics will find it hard to prove it wrong without having substantial incriminating evidence and the will to dispute the legitimacy of someone else's word. For instance, the foes of affirmative action and bilingual education have, on occasion, brandished the famous autobiography written by Rodriguez to make their case. Yet, the author will invariably have the option of mitigating criticism by reminding the "gullible reader" that far from modeling "the typical Hispanic-American life," he is himself the subject of his book: "I write about one life only. My own" (7). Whether the book consists of public-policy opinions, speculative articulations of community identity, or poetic musings on the lure of the author's ancestral homeland in Latin America, it will retain its status as a text about the self, making it inherently indisputable.

Autobiographers remain the ultimate authority on their material, provided it is verifiable and convincingly rendered, even though we cannot assume them to be in total command of their subject. As French philosopher Georges Gusdorf once argued, the historian of the self confronts a serious difficulty: "Returning to visit his own past, he takes the unity and identity of his being for granted, and he imagines himself able to merge what he was with what he has become" (40). This is a difficulty not easily overcome, since narrating one's past, rather than a simple recapitulation, involves a struggle to "reassemble himself in his own likeness at a certain moment of his history" (47). Gusdorf contemplates the potential of the writing to turn back on the life and affect it like "a kind of boomerang," as well as to take precedence over it. He concludes, "The great artist, the great writer lives, in a sense, for his autobiography" (47). At a time when readers seem to harbor a voracious appetite for personal stories that purport to be true, established Latina/o writers who are also autobiographers would do well to consider the ongoing whims of this market. Authors who have cultivated the multivolume life narrative, much like celebrated serial autobiographer Maya Angelou, may confront the temptation to choreograph their daily lives so as to produce usable material for the next installment of their forthcoming book. Their position remains one of latent power as well as intense vulnerability.

Notes

1. See, for instance, Gutman; Eakin.
2. See Stanton.

CHAPTER 6

INVENTING THE RACE

Latinos and the Ethnoracial Pentagon

This chapter wades into prevailing scholarly and popular paradigms of race, ethnicity, panethnicity, solidarity, and community, including the "ethnoracial pentagon," the term used by historian David Hollinger to refer to the five subsections of the population adopted by the US Census since 1977. Torres-Saillant contemplates the most effective means of defining and centering the unique position inhabited by people of Hispanic descent in the United States. Citing several key theories and choice examples from the twentieth century, he addresses the "aggravated anxiety" of Latina/os regarding the limiting and unsatisfactory identity labels and ethnoracial groupings from which they are asked to choose. He grants that the current racial classifications have utility because they emanate from a particular national history of racism, inequality, and resistance and serve the goal—initiated by the Civil Rights Movement—of redressing the political and economic imbalances to which white supremacy had subjected racialized minorities for several centuries. The author concedes that "ethnoracial ontology lies firmly at the core of the construction of Americanness," and that Latina/os have not achieved much progress in the quest for equality because of their ambivalence about their relationship to the dominant white population. He critiques as "politically debilitating" those who do not "assert their ethnoracial alterity" vis-à-vis whiteness. Likewise, the adoption and perpetuation of white supremacist ideas, often but not always unconsciously, hinder Latina/os from contributing meaningfully to dismantling racist structures.

Torres-Saillant proposes that we adopt greater flexibility in conceptualizing categories of race and ethnicity, and even that we fuse them, as they are both abstractions. Doing so may lead Latina/os and other communities of color "out of [their] epistemic and political dead end." Furthermore, he asserts the ongoing need for conscientious self-scrutiny by Latina/os to yield transformative change in the sphere of social relations. The "community" is undeniably heterogeneous but still capable of envisioning and achieving shared goals, particularly of political and social empowerment—both for themselves and for other historically marginalized groups.

Introduction

Race is no longer the "relatively intelligible," stable, natural phenomenon that it was generally taken to be in the years preceding World War II, according to sociologist Howard Winant. He contends that theories on the subject must focus on "the continuing significance and changing meaning of race" (181–182). As he muses on the likelihood of our depending on "familiar ways of thinking about race," Winant finds "some occasion for delight" in the conceivable advent of "yet another view of race, in which the concept operates neither as a signifier of comprehensive identity nor of fundamental difference . . . but rather as a marker of the infinity of variations we humans hold as a common heritage and hope for the future" (188). For David López and Yến Lê Espiritu, the construction of panethnicity, while it assumes a specific concept of race, has the potential for "supplanting both assimilation and ethnic particularism as the direction of change for racial/ethnic minorities" (198). In the pages that follow, I entertain these ideas as a sound approach to the ethnoracial predicament of Latina/os. It strikes me as rather mundane to speak of them as a panethnicity, insofar as the "subgroups of ethnic collectivities" that constitute the US Hispanic population are "often regarded as homogenous by outsiders," encouraging among them the development of internal structures of solidarity (López and Espiritu 198).

As a "hybrid category" that entered "the ethnoracial imagination of American social life" in the 1970s, the classification *Hispanic* remains as pliable as the very texture of race has proven to be (Goldberg 64). Considering this pliability, in the current discursive atmosphere surrounding the debate on race and ethnicity, no existing ethnoracial label commands such authority that it can categorically prohibit the proposal of a fusion of race and ethnicity as units of analysis. David Theo Goldberg has highlighted the extent to which *Hispanic* as a term "problematizes certain prevailing assumptions about racial definition and formation," serving "not so much as a third race, a category of mixed race—black and white melding into brown—as an evidencing that race is politically fabricated and contested, that the very conception is elastic and transformable" (65–66). His useful formulation, despite his inability to see Indigenous and Asian people as also inhabiting the sphere of the *Hispanic*, envisions no conceptual impediment for the further manipulation of *race* to become one with *ethnicity*.

I believe such a fusion can help Latina/o scholars overcome what appears to be an aggravated anxiety over the official classifications of the US population into differentiated ethnoracial groupings. Current theoretical developments in the human sciences have no doubt interrogated the conventional paradigms used to classify the human family into distinct racial branches. I sense that American society still needs the existing racial classifications to implement programs of compensatory justice. Seeking to disband the only classification system that the society has at its disposal, before it has developed the necessary proficiency in the handling of a replacement, might have grave consequences. I dread the possible outcomes of a deracializing of the field that is not preceded by some leveling of the playing field in American society. I fear the unintentional collusion of Latina/o spokespersons with the backlash unleashed by affirmative action programs and the widespread efforts of those conservatives who seek to reverse the gains that historically underserved minorities have made in the wake of the Civil Rights Movement. By the mid-1990s, several attempts to dismantle affirmative action programs had encountered success. California governor Pete Wilson's Executive Order to End Preferential Treatment and to Promote Individual Opportunity Based on Merit sizably curtailed state affirmative action programs in 1995, the same year that the University of California Board of Regents voted to end affirmative action in admissions, hiring, and contracting (Anthony 26). Unless Latina/o scholars can devise a way of abandoning the thinking bequeathed by the Civil Rights Movement to address this country's history of racial wrongs without simultaneously playing into conservative agendas in public policy, prudence would advise that we think twice before tampering with generally effective precedents.

Salient among the subsidiary claims of my argument is the understanding that ethnoracial ontology lies firmly at the core of the construction of Americanness. In their foundational statements, the early ruling elites imagined the United States as a white European-descended monolingual nation, leaving outside the contours of Americanness those segments of the population that diverged from this exclusionary profile. The excluded, in time, came to wield the banner of their difference to demand inclusion. Thus, racialized collectivities turned the affirmation of their otherness into a tool to challenge their othering. Paradoxically, they embraced (and even flaunted) their racial difference to combat racism. Over time, out of that effort to self-differentiate came the Civil Rights Movement and the subsequent classification of the US population into five distinct lines of descent, namely whites, blacks, Native Americans, Asian Americans, and Hispanics, a taxonomy that David Hollinger has called "the ethnoracial pentagon" (*Postethnic America* 8, 13). The gains of the Civil Rights Movement—the Voting Rights Act, affirmative action, open admissions in public schools, and other legislative measures devised to address discrimination and social inequity—speak volumes to the success of the strategy of self-differentiation that cohered in the ethnoracial pentagon. The success, however, tended to be less discernible for those communities who, relatively speaking, did not fashion and assert their alterity as vigorously as other groups vis-à-vis the dominant white core.

I contend that Latina/os have made insufficient strides in the quest for full citizenship in American society largely because of their ambivalence regarding their difference from the white majority. By *full citizenship* I mean merely having socially unobstructed possibilities to use their talent and energy to lead productive lives in the present and build a safety net for the future. In the language of the New Deal, achieving full citizenship meant people would become free "from fear" as well as "from want" while having their "economic rights" acknowledged (Roosevelt 32–44). More recent language, according to such scholars as William Vincent Flores and Rina Benmayor in their collection *Latino Cultural Citizenship: Claiming Identity, Space, and Rights* (1997), requires a larger coverage of well-being, encompassing the right to one's difference or "cultural citizenship." I contend further that the hesitation of Latina/os to assert their ethnoracial alterity in contradistinction to the dominant white core is politically debilitating to the larger US Hispanic population. Furthermore, it leaves unaddressed the white supremacist legacy that the community inherits from its tributary cultures on both sides of the Rio Grande. Harboring white supremacist assumptions renders Latina/os less able to contribute to the goal of dismantling racism, a goal without which no project of major social transformation deserves to be taken seriously in the United States.

Even when mediated by an awareness of mestizaje, white supremacist practices stifle the aspirations of the darker segments of the Latino population. They allow the existence and continuation of intra-group injustices. At the same time, they interfere with the emergence of a viable, integrated image of "the community" by which all subsections of the US Hispanic population can feel adequately represented. Panethnic instruments of representation matter because they permit Latino political and intellectual leaderships to forge agendas of ethnic uplift aimed at benefiting the population across the board. If the desirability of galvanizing the energies of millions of people toward common objectives of sociopolitical advancement does not seem self-evident, one could think of pan-Latino cohesion as an antidote to the deleterious consequences of intra-Latino friction. We might take, for instance, the stifling inability of Cornell University's Chicana/o and Puerto Rican faculty and students some decades ago to agree on a shared vision for the Latino studies program. Likewise, the Puerto Rican community in New York City's Spanish Harlem tenaciously advocated for the preservation of a Boricua focus for Museo del Barrio in the face of forces apparently wishing to "Latin-Americanize" it. In the religious realm, journalist Juan González evoked what he called the "battle of the virgins" to highlight clashes in churches of the Lower East Side over whether to house a virgin revered by Chicanos over one venerated by Puerto Ricans (xvi–xvii). On June 7, 2002, the Latino Network brought me to Lawrence, Massachusetts, to join an effort aimed at addressing the political disunity that was keeping the various Latino subgroups there from bringing a Latina/o representative to local office, despite their having the numbers to do so.

During the panel "The Changing Roles of Latinos in the United States" in September 2002, part of the seventh triennial Coming Back Together reunion of black and Latina/o alumnae/i at Syracuse University, the students, faculty, staff, and visitors participating had little to celebrate. They grieved the insufficient gains Latina/os had made over the previous three decades, even as compared with African Americans. A column had appeared a few days prior in the *Detroit Free Press* in which Alejandro García, a Syracuse University faculty member, urged Latina/os to beware of civic leaders wearing sombreros and brandishing their "smattering of Spanish." García exhorted Latina/o readers to "demand more than symbolic attention from politicians." US census data from the early 2000s show Hispanics earning considerably less, suffering greater rates of unemployment, falling below the poverty line in larger numbers, and having poorer educational attainments than the rest of the national population (Suárez-Orozco and Páez, "Research Agenda" 25). Such a scenario gave the panel participants the shared sense that Latina/os could boast meaningful advancement mostly, if not solely, in the symbolic realm. Aware of the "Latinization" of New York City and other culturally transformative dynamics brought about by globalization and transnational relations—a development well mapped in Agustín Laó-Montes and Arlene Dávila's collection *Mambo Montage* (2001), which describes "archaeologies of latinidad and the genealogies of latinization" (Laó-Montes 5)—the speakers still voiced their yearning for concrete indicators of improvement in the community's material conditions.

While valuing the achievements of now-veteran celebrities such as Andy García, Gloria and Emilio Estefan, Jennifer Lopez, Sammy Sosa, Alex Rodríguez, Shakira, Oscar de la Hoya, and other Hispanics who, at the time, enjoyed recognition as household names on the national front, the Syracuse panelists spoke cautiously about the enhanced visibility of Latina/os. They recognized the risk of mistaking increased visibility in the media and the entertainment industry for community empowerment. They noted the disparity of place assigned to Hispanics in the August 2000 Republican National Convention, where keynote speeches by African Americans Colin Powell and Condoleeza Rice voiced their party's vision of the future of the nation while, in contrast, Ricky Martin's "La Vida Loca" merely made the ambience festive for the arrival of George W. Bush onstage to deliver the party's presidential nomination acceptance speech. One could interpret that disparity as the assumption that while black voters required concrete inclusion in the political agenda, symbolic inclusion by means of entertainment sufficed for Latina/os.

An undergraduate student finally encapsulated the Syracuse panel's collective plaint by stating that "we" have lacked a major leader "like a Martin Luther King or a Malcolm X who could help us advance our cause." Another speaker added the name of Jesse Jackson. Having only the week before been moved by the continued vitality of Dolores Huerta, during the Fourth Conference of the National Association of Latino Arts and Culture in Austin, Texas, I invoked Huerta's leadership and that of Cesar Chavez. But I immediately realized that the comparison did not hold. Except for the learned and the politically engaged, Chavez and Huerta belong on the West Coast and they matter primarily to Chicana/os and Mexicans. The naming of a street in homage to Chavez in Washington Heights or El Barrio would seem as unlikely as the hiring of a Dominican or a Puerto Rican to head a Latino studies program at a major university in California or Texas.[1] Reformulating the Syracuse student's claim, I would contend that lacking a collective voice points to the failure to articulate agendas that matter equally across the various subsections of the US Hispanic population.

There are several reasons for that failure, including the differing histories and lengths of presence of each subgroup in what is now the United States. Comparing the plight of a Latina/o whose ancestors came to New Mexico over four centuries ago, as part of the Spanish entourage of Juan de Oñate, with that of a New York City Latina born in 1970 to recent Dominican immigrant parents, or a Chicana whose Indigenous roots in the Texan soil stretch back fifteen thousand years, might require a somersault of the imagination. The subgroups have distinct stories, and their ancestral homelands may have interacted differently with the United States. The list can continue, but to return to my argument, I will privilege the ethnoracial reason, the most abstract variable, hence the most susceptible to productive manipulation. The Latino reticence about embracing a distinct ethnoracial identity in contradistinction to whites diminishes the group's power of negotiation with the dominant core and fails to combat the community's own white supremacist legacies. Latina/os often boast of their comfort with hybridity, proclaiming their potential to liberate the United States from the conceptual throes of the racial binarism reflected in the normalized black/white paradigm. At the same time, the 2000 US Census showed Latina/os hesitating to distinguish themselves racially from whites. I fear that such hesitation might presage the triumph of a sort of ethnoracial self-sabotage, effectuated by the ideology of amalgamation.

Perspective, Method, and Language

I tread the territory of race and ethnic identity in relation to Latina/os fully aware of the futility of speaking with authority on the matter. Hardly fathomable units of analysis, the floating signifier of race and the construction of identity seem to resist containment by the resources of any individual discipline. I approach the subject as a humanist; as such, my inquiry will lack a display of massive quantitative data. I will not shun the possibility of extracting insights from a literary passage, a political speech, a televised image, or an empirical observation of my own. Noting the hazy boundaries of the evasive subject at hand, we must cope with inevitable epistemic discomfort. Most scientists can verify or falsify a truth claim by means of an experiment or series thereof. Humanities scholars, however, must often rely more on the goodwill and wisdom of their peers in keeping with the established state of knowledge. A chameleon-like entity susceptible to external stimuli, ethnoracial identity, especially as applied to Latina/os who view it ambiguously, is contextual and situational. As the subject defies measure, the knowability of Latino ethnoracial identity must remain unsettled and unsettling. The scholar treading this indeterminate territory must therefore dispense with the assurance that familiarity with the latest research in the field will entail access to the most accurate findings, the current data having indisputably falsified previous knowledge.

Following Gayatri Chakravorty Spivak's recommendation that scholars mark their own positionality as investigating subjects (92), I should disclose my compulsions regarding intellectual authority and language. I will not attempt to comb the field for every related publication to date, given precisely the difficulty of discerning the outermost bounds delimiting the territory of our inquiry. Less mindful of the respectability or currency of authors in "the field," I have allowed the logic of my reflections to determine which scholarly interventions to reference. Similarly, I must admit my own reticence to parrot the received lexicons that have become staples in contemporary discourse in the humanities and social sciences. I draw insight from Mikhail M. Bakhtin's refusal to use *scientizing* terminologies wherein he rejected the tendency of specialized terms to stabilize the meanings of words, diminishing their metaphoric potential, sacrificing polysemy and the overall play of significations. He decried "the extreme monotonality" of such terms, recalling that "ancient Greek philosophical and scientific thought" shunned words that could not participate "with the same meaning in ordinary speech" (Bubnova xv).

As someone initially trained as a literary scholar, I cannot approach language without a measure of suspicion. In the linguistic demeanor that I display here, I do not mean to dismiss the discursive protocols that obtain in the profession. Rather, I wish to safeguard the clarity of my meanings and to make evident my own subject position. By the same token, while insisting that race matters, I will take as a given its social constructedness. I embrace an understanding of race closely resembling the definition forwarded by Ian F. Haney López, an articulate proponent of critical race theory. He defines the term as "a vast group of people loosely bound together by historically contingent, socially significant elements of their morphology and/or ancestry" (193). I argue that race must be understood as a sui generis social phenomenon in which contested systems of meaning serve as the connections between physical features, personal characteristics, and collective dynamics. In other words, social meanings connect our faces to our souls. Race is neither an essence nor an illusion, but rather an ongoing, contradictory, self-reinforcing, plastic process subject to the macro forces of social and political struggle and the micro effects of daily decisions. As used here, such referents as black and white are "social groups, not genetically distinct branches of humankind" (Haney López 193).

Racial Americanness

Latina/os cannot escape the preponderance of race and racial discourses in the United States. The history of the discourse on Americanness and national belonging consists largely of episodes that feature the dominant white core racializing marginal groups and the latter responding in varied ways. The rise of what Hollinger calls the ethnoracial pentagon marked a pivotal moment in that history. In the second quarter of the twenty-first century, it still seems too soon to move beyond the pentagonal model, as Hollinger himself does. He would wish us to expand the epistemic "we" beyond racial classifications. In *Postethnic America*, he recalls the enlightened antiracist concerns that led to the "manufacturing of today's ethnoracial pentagon out of the old, racist materials": in other words, the issuing in 1977 of the Office of Management and Budget's Statistical Directive 15, which classifies people racially, came to address the need for reliable statistics that could enable the government to enforce the mandates of the Voting Rights Act of 1965 and Title VII of the Civil Rights Act (Hollinger, *Postethnic America* 33). It saddens Hollinger, however, that the racial thinking of the original initiative has fostered in the country's imagination a "transition from species to ethnos" (65). Though one might accept his concern that the stress on ethnos eschews the essential humanity we all share, irrespective of pigmentation, phenotype, and ancestry, he naively posits that this country's "national ideology is non-ethnic by virtue of the universalist commitment—proclaimed in the Constitution and the prevailing political discourse—to provide the benefits of citizenship irrespective of any ascribed or asserted ancestry affiliations" (19). Some historical references come in handy here.

The Founding Fathers did not transcend the racial imaginary. Witness a 1751 article by Benjamin Franklin in which the sage decried the increasing presence of Germans in the colonies and expressed anxiety over the disruptive effect of their influence on the nation. Franklin feared that they would not learn English and that they would impose their ethnic traits on the population, Germanizing "us" rather than "our Anglifying them," since they could not change their culture any more than they could shed their "Complexion" (234). His attribution of an "alien" complexion to German immigrants suggests not only that, from the outset, whiteness stood out as a fundamental prerequisite to national belonging, but also that European descent alone did not constitute sufficient basis for attaining whiteness. Franklin mourned the "proportionably very small" number of "purely white People in the World," with "black or tawny" folks inhabiting Africa and Asia while people with "a swarthy Complexion" predominated throughout Europe. Only the Saxons and the English made up the "principal Body of White People on the Face of the Earth," asserted Franklin, and he voiced the belief that this country had "so fair an Opportunity, by excluding all Blacks and Tawnys, of increasing the lovely White and Red" (234). European immigrants had to conform to the demands of the normative Anglo model. In a letter from June 4, 1819, John Quincy Adams tellingly described the attitude he judged advisable for prospective German immigrants, namely that "they must cast off the European skin, never to resume it. They must look forward to their posterity rather than backward to their ancestors," meaning that they had to embrace Anglo ways (qtd. in Sollors 4).

The 1790 Naturalization Act restricted citizenship to white male landowners. When they ceased to be property, blacks became a problem in the United States. Public policy condemned the vast majority to generations of poverty and excluded them from "the industrial activity taking place in the rapidly growing cities of the North and West in the aftermath of the Civil War," even while European immigrants found here a land of opportunity (Steinberg 198). For so-called persons of color, to speak about race in the United States has meant necessarily to locate oneself in relation to normative whiteness. We might recall the two Frenchmen who famously evoked the harmony that this country had attained, despite the diverse origins of the population. J. Hector St. John de Crèvecoeur in his *Letters from an American Farmer* (1782) marveled at the "strange mixture of blood" that made "this new man," the American (Hollinger 87). The vision of the United States as a venue suitable for a new amalgamated people dates back to the Revolutionary era. The other Frenchman, Alexis de Tocqueville, could attest in his 1835 book *Democracy in America* to a proliferation of "voluntary associations" that since then would become "a staple of commentary on American society" (Hollinger 155). Significantly, while both noted the conditions of Indigenous peoples and blacks, who clearly did not go into the mix of origins they admired, they somehow did not allow that contradictory empirical reality to alter their image of the harmonious fusion of difference in America.

The official definition of Americanness did not intend to cover everybody. The foundational discourse rested largely on protocols of exclusion. The nation was imagined not only white, but also monolingual, despite what Venezuelan revolutionary Francisco de Miranda observed when he visited in 1783–1784, nearly fifty years prior to the better-remembered visit by de Tocqueville and Gustave Baumont (1831–1832). When Miranda set foot in Central New York, he found it curious that women walked around without shoes, that the number of blacks was high, and that the predominant language was Dutch among blacks and whites alike (70). The nation continued to regard itself as monolingual even after the 1848 takeover of what we now call the American Southwest. The French of Louisiana, the German of other places, and the Spanish of Texas, to say nothing of the myriad languages spoken by more than five hundred Indigenous nations that had forged long histories here prior to the arrival of the Europeans, did not earn consideration in the minds of the architects of Americanness. When they imagined the United States, they saw linguistic and racial homogeneity, despite glaring evidence to the contrary.

Israel Zangwill (1864–1926), the author of the play *The Melting-Pot* (1905), spoke ardently about interethnic fusion, and his work provided the lasting image that describes the country's assimilationist ideal. However, he did favor America's "scrupulous" and "justifiable" avoidance of physical "inter marriage with the Negro," preferring to limit the mixture to what he called "spiritual miscegenation" (207). Though Zangwill advocated interracial understanding and felt negrophobia had reached a "barbarous pitch," he nonetheless accepted as true that "the prognathous face is an ugly and undesirable type of countenance" and that it "connotes a lower average of intellect and ethics" (206). He suggested further that "Melanophobia, or fear of the black, may be pragmatically as valuable a racial defense for the white as the counter-instinct of philoleucosis, or love of the white, is a force of racial uplifting for the black" (206). A British Jew, the writer embodied the contradiction inherent in a racist cultural regime that preached the ideal expressed in the integrationist motto *e pluribus unum*. Not all European observers, however, failed to see the gravity of the problem. Prolific English writer H. G. Wells noted the explosive nature of the race question in America (186). French philosopher Jacques Maritain, for his part, pointed out that the contradiction made for "the spectacle of a nation struggling obstinately against itself" (my trans.; 57). The foregoing scenario highlights as "the central drama of American culture" the stark contrasts "between contractual and hereditary, self-made and ancestral, definitions of American identity—between consent and descent" (Sollors 6). It also underscores the resilience of race as part of the conceptual arsenal deployed by the bureaucratic architects of the official discourse that delimits the contours of the nation.

Racial Reticence and the Nation

With the advent of postmodernism and the rise of such derivations as postcolonial and cultural studies, demands for specifics as related to racial or ethnic identity have often been seen as suspect in academe. Concomitantly, approaches that seem to validate the nation-state as a social field within which to understand human agency and interaction have faced challenges from proponents of transnationalism. The current disfavor of the nation as a unit of analysis accords with a prevailing suspicion about race and ethnicity because these categories are largely intertwined. The black British scholar Paul Gilroy owes his celebrity to his critiques of both the nation and ethnic identity. He has denounced African American cultural projects that embrace "narrow nationalist perspectives," which he characterizes as incurably committed to "the spurious invocation of ethnic particularity" (29). Gilroy proposes as an alternative to those projects the "image of the ships in motion across the spaces between Europe, America, Africa, and the Caribbean" as an organizing principle of the "rhizomorphic, fractal structure of the transcultural, international formation" that he calls "the Black Atlantic" (4). This formulation, in his view, transcends "both the structures of the nation state and the constraints of ethnicity and national particularity" (19). The Latino counterpart of the scholarly climate that Gilroy exemplifies is perhaps well summarized by Antonia Darder and Rodolfo D. Torres's description of the emergence of "an unproblematized 'common sense' acceptance" of race in a way that appears to veil its social constructedness (7).

I believe, however, that the yearning for a paradigm that would help us escape the throes of race, ethnic particularity, and nation-state formations stems from an academic desire to reach an elusive cutting edge rather than from a down-to-earth assessment of what has worked in the overall effort to elevate the condition of historically underserved ethnic minority groups in the United States. Having endured such duress on account of their ethnic and racial difference vis-à-vis a cultural and political center of power, marginalized minorities have little chance of asserting their human dignity outside the ethnoracial and national frameworks wherein their disempowerment has occurred. Ultimately, the objective of their struggle has been no other than to have their ethnoracial difference accepted as well as respected and to carve a space of stability inside the entity called the American nation. Only the nation at this point provides ethnic minorities with the platform on which to fight for material improvement, equality, and justice.

Communities of color in the United States have long fought to attain full citizenship. The fruits of that labor should not be forgotten. Lynchings and Jim Crow segregation no longer predominate among the sorrows and indignities that blacks in this country endure. The overall society no longer condones public aggression against minority groups to the degree that it did decades ago, but not every group is treated with the same solicitude. For instance, the La Follette Civil Liberties Committee (Committee on Education and Labor, Subcommittee Investigating Violations of Free Speech and the Rights of Labor [1936–1941]) was chaired by Sen. Robert M. La Follette, Jr. Today a police spokesperson might feel compelled to repress in public the expression of contempt evinced in the testimony of the officer who appeared before the La Follette Committee in the 1930s with these words: "We protect our farmers here in Kern County. . . . They are our best people. . . . They keep the country going. . . . But the Mexicans are trash. They have no standard of living. We herd them like pigs" (qtd. in Trumpbour and Bernard 128). Likewise, property managers nowadays might anticipate lawsuits were they to post signs that declare "No Pets, No Kids, No Cubans," the likes of which appeared in the 1960s in Miami Dade County (Stepick and Stepick 81).

The nation has indubitably come closer to living up to the true meaning of its creed. We still have serious challenges that cry for urgent redress: alarming incarceration rates among black and Latino populations; overrepresentation of children of color among the unschooled, the underfed, and the hopeless; and continuing underrepresentation of people of color beyond blacks and Latina/os in centers of knowledge production and policymaking. However, at this point, there is no postnational, transracial, cross-cultural, or postethnic structure that can help racialized minorities correct their residual social ills more efficiently than the policies that enabled them to make any progress in the first place. Rather than wrestling with the anxiety of finding a way out of race, we might do better to strategize the artifice of race to enhance its political utility. By strategically manipulating the concept, we ought to perfect the construction of Latino ethnoracial identity to make it less complicit with white supremacist paradigms, more inclusive of intra-Latino diversity, and consequently, more suitable as a vehicle of empowerment.

Assertion and Citizenship

We continue to live in a racial world. Though Hispanics have inhabited North America since before the first English settlement at Jamestown, Americans with Spanish surnames will be taken as foreigners a lot more frequently than citizens of German, Irish, or Italian ancestry. The US publishing industry still wonders whether the number of Dominican, Puerto Rican, or Colombian readers is large enough to make the publication of a book authored by a member of one of these communities worth the investment. Publishers remain persuaded that such a book may not automatically elicit the interest of the general reader. Certainly, we should have the vision and willpower needed to help reconfigure and liberate us from the prevailing schemes of thought. Promoting a deracialization of the collective imaginary might be an ideal. But such a project will not thrive before the advent of racial equality, before the leveling of the racial playing field, before the equitable sharing of power by each of the groups that make up the "ethnoracial pentagon." We do not dismantle racism simply by renouncing the identity labels born of the Civil Rights Movement or by replacing them with more recent social justice–oriented mobilizations, terms, and mass media campaigns.

African Americans have made the political gains they currently enjoy because of a racial self-assertion that galvanizes the community, lending them a sense of wholeness. Their impression of a common history and a shared destiny often extends to black immigrants whose ancestors experienced their slave past elsewhere. Sociologist Nancy Foner has shed light on the extent to which West Indians in Brooklyn, from the start of the 1990s, saw their political power increase by their strategically embracing racial (black) or ethnic (Caribbean) modes of belonging interchangeably, depending on whether an immediate agenda called for unity with African American New Yorkers or with coethnics from among the various other West Indian nationalities (182–183). The most difficult component of that act of vision will be making conceptual room to accommodate the great internal diversity represented in the more than sixty-five million members of the US Hispanic population without falling under the equalizing spell cast by mestizaje. The operative concept of race could follow the model suggested by philosopher Jorge J. E. Gracia, wherein he regards Hispanics as "a group of people who have no common elements considered as a whole"; as such, he envisions their coming together as "not a unity of commonality" but "a historical unity founded on relations" (50). Only by coming together and confronting the discomfort of their internal difference, the negrophobia and anti-Indigenous feelings in their midst, might Latina/os be in a position to fight external racism while empowering themselves holistically in relation to the Anglo majority.

At this point, we might invoke the night of February 29, 1940, when the Academy Award for the Best Supporting Actress went to Hattie McDaniel, who had played Mammy in the epic *Gone with the Wind* (1939). This momentous evening made McDaniel the first African American ever to win an Oscar. Tears pooled in the performer's eyes as she approached the stage to accept the distinction. She thanked her audience in a speech that included this remark about the recognition she had just received: "I shall always hold it as a beacon for anything that I may be able to do in the future. I sincerely hope that I shall always be a credit to my race and to the motion picture industry" (Jackson 52). Today, McDaniel's words may strike something of an odd chord. They smack of self-effacement, a willingness to cast her personal achievement into a form of quantified worth that gets automatically computed into her racial group's aggregate value. Implicit in this notion is the understanding that just as individual accomplishments will add to the racial collective's "bank," as it were, individual failures and misbehaviors will subtract from this selfsame account.

On the night of the event at the Coconut Grove in Los Angeles's Ambassador Hotel, McDaniel became not only "the first of her race" to receive an Oscar, but also "the first Negro ever to sit at an Academy Banquet" (Jackson 104 et passim). Socially, economically, and culturally, African Americans in the 1940s had little say in regulating the contours of their public identity. Jim Crow segregation reigned supreme, and just as blacks in the South could not vote, their counterparts in the North knew they had little for which to vote.[2] They endured a condition of collective marginality with respect to white America, thereby regarding themselves in stark contradistinction to the dominant population. They had solid grounds for believing that their virtues or shortcomings mattered less to their individual subjectivities than to their status as a group. It would, therefore, have been ludicrous for McDaniel to think of herself strictly as an individual talent whose success had implications only for her craft. She simply lacked the unproblematic claim to unencumbered individuality that power confers in the relationship between groups holding unequal positions in society.[3]

We cannot assume, of course, that African Americans achieved their sense of racial wholeness without contention. Certainly, the Civil Rights agenda did not spring from a "spontaneous" mass mobilization, stemming rather from smaller gains catalyzed by "the deliberate efforts of organizers" (Morris 66). One scholar, Harvard Sitkoff, looking at the early twentieth century, observed that organizations advocating for civil rights then lacked "the support of most blacks" (11). Another examines a scenario wherein some communities and individuals harbored doubts as to whether their situation resembled the life experiences of others closely enough "to warrant collective political action" (Crenshaw 556). We can conjecture that history has conspired to give credence to a discourse of oneness, from the time of the abolitionists through to the key pronouncements of such nineteenth-century black luminaries as Frederick Douglass and Frances Ellen Watkins Harper. As a result, W. E. B. Du Bois would invoke "the Negro" with the same all-inclusive assumption displayed later by Martin Luther King, Jr.

Latina/os in the 1940s did not have (nor have they had since) the kind of historical experience that would have enabled them to invoke as clear a frame of reference as McDaniel had, when she expressed the hope of being a credit to her race. Latina/os have too inconsistently articulated their alterity vis-à-vis the dominant white population, which is arguably the ultimate source of racial meaning, since it is primarily in relation to this population that the other segments of this country's inhabitants attain their racialized differentiation. While watching the Republican National Convention on August 3, 2000, on CNN, I was taken aback by a brief offstage interview with Colorado state senator Bob Martinez, a native of New Mexico who represented the Colorado delegation. A successful businessman and flag-waving patriot, Martinez used the moment of his appearance on national TV to vaunt his Americanness and pay tribute to the greatness of "what we have accomplished in only two hundred years." It followed from the rest of his words that "we" referred not to Hispanics but more abstractly to "Americans." His enthusiastic utterance also looked forward to the future, though saying nothing about the place Latina/os would occupy in the America imagined by Republicans. Phenotypically as white as the Anglos surrounding him, Martinez probably felt no compulsion to stress ethnoracial difference. Nor did the speaker who introduced George W. Bush, his nephew George Prescott Bush, the son of Jeb Bush and his Mexican-born wife, Columba. George Prescott referred to his pride about coming from a "diverse" background, but he never explicitly named the non-Anglo heritage that accounted for his "diversity." I will not attempt to flesh out the myriad implications of the young man's reticence to call the Hispanic component of his background by name. I will simply present his case and that of Martinez, atypical though they might appear, as instances of US Hispanic ethnoracial indecision.

The ambivalent rapport of Latina/os with this country's existing racial categories, though often grounded in earnest epistemic preoccupations, hints at the idea of themselves as somehow *nonracial*. Among other likely consequences, such a hesitant self-definition has the potential for nurturing the white supremacist ideals that have historically influenced the ways Latina/os construct identity broadly. I would reiterate that white supremacist leanings have a debilitating impact on the chances of the various subsections of the US Hispanic community to achieve a politically salutary sense of panethnic wholeness. By the same token, one could conjecture that their insufficient delinking from white supremacist reflexes diminishes their ability to advance programs of social transformation in American society. As such, they are less equipped to assist in the necessary goal of forging a nation where we all can realistically expect to have our full citizenship honored. Considering their growing numbers and undeniable diversity, Latina/os face the challenge of devising a composite ethnoracial identity that convincingly includes every Hispanic subgroup. While helping to address in-group prejudices, such a construct could bring about transformative change and representational tools permitting "the community" to speak as a solid bloc with the other differentiated segments of the US population.

Formulations of their community's ethnoracial identity by Latina/o spokespersons often boast a superior understanding of the complexity of racial codification, emphasizing the extent to which *our* historical experience challenges the black-white binary that has informed thinking on race in this country. Latina/o scholars often claim that "while 'race' distinctions and prejudice exist in Spanish America, they do not, nor ever have they, taken the form of institutionalized discrimination as in the United States" (Kanellos, "Hispanics and Race" 178). At the same time, the elevation of mestizaje as a third space of ethnoracial identity—a presumably more enlightened site that Latina/o voices often seem to ascribe exclusively to themselves as a special feature of the Hispanic condition—often appears as a potential solution to the race problem in American society. The conceptual panacea of mestizaje has insufficiently addressed its own white supremacist bias. Nor has it confronted the tensions in de facto assumptions about the US Hispanic population as one undifferentiated group, despite its heterogeneity.

The history of US Hispanics does not lack pivotal moments of sociocultural and political conflict that have resulted in polarization, causing individuals and groups to situate themselves in stark opposition to white Anglos. The takeover of Texas by Anglos, with the backing of the US government, in the 1830s brought about a climate of reciprocal hostility. The 1846 invasion of Mexico by the US Army culminated in a treaty whereby the old Hispano landed gentry in the Southwest had to make way for Anglo power, descending to the rank of the subaltern. Not too dissimilarly, the outcome of the Spanish-American War of 1898 created conditions that would shape the entrance of Puerto Ricans, Cubans, and Dominicans into the US domain as scions of a conquered people. That general context explains the oppositional stance that characterizes a good deal of the folk tradition, exemplified by the anonymous corrido "The Ballad of Gregorio Cortez," which writer Américo Paredes studied in his classic monograph *With His Pistol in His Hand: A Border Ballad and Its Hero* (1958). The polarization manifests itself most graphically in the Texas Mexican rebellion of 1915 known as the *El Plan de San Diego*. Led by political activists Aniceto Pizaña and Luis de la Rosa, the separatist movement envisioned the utopian creation of the Republic of the Southwest. Its ranks included rebels of Hispanic, Asian, African, and Indigenous descent advancing an entirely nonwhite agenda. The Chicano Movement drew substantially from the foregoing oppositional climate in their formulation of a Latina/o "us" versus a gringo "them," hence the reference to the "foreign Europeans" and the affirmation of the Indigenous heritage in *El Plan Espiritual de Aztlán*, the "cultural nationalist manifesto" written by the poet Alurista for the 1969 Chicano Youth Liberation Conference in Denver (Arteaga 12–13).

By the same token, the New York–based Puerto Rican leadership that in the 1960s launched the Young Lords Party constructed Latino subjectivity based on a very deep sense of self-differentiation with respect to American society's dominant white Anglo core. The language of their thirteen-point platform accentuates the contradistinction of Latina/os to "amerikkkan business" as well as their joining the war "against imperialism" (Luis, *Dance* 279). In its conclusion, the text hails "La Raza," leaving little doubt as to the ethnoracial difference implicit in their cause, one that aligned with the West Coast–based Chicano Movement. The Young Lords identified with the political precedent demonstrated by Colorado native Rodolfo "Corky" Gonzales's poem "I Am Joaquín" (1967). This text embodies the persona of the outlaw Joaquín Murrieta, singing the plight of "La Raza" ("Mejicano! / Español! / Latino! / Hispano! / Chicano!"), caught in the inhospitable "whirl of a / gringo society" (Gonzales 266, 279).

Yet the cultural and political history that the foregoing moments illustrate does not prevail in the discourses on Latino identity that have come down to us. No pervasive oppositional stance has thrived. Latina/os lack a clear frame of reference with which to invoke a distinct, recognizable, and useful ethnoracial space. Besides impeding the rise of voices that might speak compellingly about the condition of the overall community, thereby helping in the multiethnic fight against racism in this country, the vagueness and hesitation may disarm us in yet another way. Latina/os may fail to curtail corporate and government schemes, orchestrated by transnational partners, interested in controlling US Hispanic agendas on both sides of the Rio Grande.

Identity and Its Discontents

Scholarly conversations on racial dynamics too often satisfy themselves by merely problematizing the issue of Latino identity and then questioning the validity of race as a category of classification, in light of its lack of objective correspondence in the empirical world. Often informed by the phraseologies of postmodern critical theory, they seem to relish the notion of a decentered and epistemically unstable self. A person's identity is thus "relative and is constantly negotiated through relationships and situational contexts. Instead of a core of identity, or self, one has a plurality of selves, each of which surfaces in a particular situation. Thus, an individual is not committed to only one identity, and similarly, one's ethnic identity is variable and subject to construction of the individual" (C. Rodríguez, *Changing Race* xxi). Probably the most radical feminist-of-color intervention is that of Gloria Anzaldúa, who has become an obligatory reference since the 1980s, along with the likes of postcolonial theorist Homi K. Bhabha. In discussions of identity, Anzaldúa trades mostly in metaphor, combining the discursive authority of the theorist with the poetic license of the artist. She claims to inhabit the space she famously termed "the borderlands," which means the speaker is "neither *hispana India negra Española / ni gabacha, eres mestiza, mulata,* half-breed / caught in the crossfire between camps / while carrying all the five races on your back" (217). Also, occupying that locus articulated by Anzaldúa "means knowing / that the *india* in you, betrayed for 500 years, / is no longer speaking to you," hence the speaker's conclusive recommendation to "live *sin fronteras* / be a crossroads." Survival entails transcending the crossfire of multiple identities (216–217).

In upholding the radical porosity of Latino identity—assuming that Anzaldúa approves of our extending the explanatory value of her borderlands paradigm beyond the Chicana sphere—one is also recognizing a certain futility to the sociopolitical and cultural project of promoting a Latino agenda to advance the interests of the population conventionally thought of as constituting "the community." We cannot persuasively advocate on behalf of a group we cannot identify clearly. Nearly 50 percent of all US Hispanics who answered the 2000 Census chose to call themselves "white," thus declining to classify themselves in a manner that would distinguish them from the dominant majority (Suárez-Orozco and Páez, Introduction 21). As the population grows, this self-definition will likely undergo stress and metamorphosis. The reticence of Hispanics to situate themselves outside the sphere of whiteness has a long history. One must not forget that in the nineteenth century, putative whiteness made Mexicans eligible for US citizenship, conferring to them a benefit seldom extended to African Americans. Similarly, in the twentieth century, some Mexican American civil rights organizations "evaded segregation with blacks by claiming whiteness under the law" (Kanellos 182–183). The pervasive Hispanic predilection for whiteness as self-identification often coexists with a certain reticence to specify or affirm one's ethnoracial location. The words of early Dominican immigrant Frank Rebajes, who came from Puerto Plata to New York in 1923, epitomize a dismissal of ethnic loyalty as "a mistake of Latin Americans." He complained that they "settle in quarters only among themselves, neglecting to get to know the real native-born Americans", (qtd. in Alig 8, 43). Speaking in the 1950s, having succeeded in business and married into a white family, Rebajes most likely used the word "Americans" as a synonym for "whites."

Even among Dominicans, one of the Latino subgroups displaying the darkest skin hues, the 2000 US Census reveals 80.2 percent of the community choosing the classification "white" against 18.3 percent that opted for the classification "black." The scholars who present these data would warn us, however, that the above breakdown reflects Dominican and Latino racial categories, not the more rigid US racial concepts (Castro and Boswell 10). A question that lingers, of course, is whether dissimilar racial paradigms can subsist in the American public sphere and, if so, to what end? We live in a country that came to divide people into five differentiated lines of descent to resolve the injustices that racist public policies had committed against the racialized non-white subsections of the population. I fail to see how one can, on the one hand, contend that ethnoracial identity is socially constructed, while, on the other hand, seek a formulation that describes the community with greater ethnoracial accuracy than we have now. From the recognition of the social constructedness of race, it should follow that insofar as none can attain ideal precision, any classification would do, especially one that already exists and has proven fairly useful.

We hardly need to make the case that, despite its social constructedness, race has played a key role in the marginalization that Latina/os of various national origins have suffered. In that respect, race has mattered; it has been real. One need not attribute to it an objective constitution to see its power.

One may just call it, as does the character Tshembe in Lorraine Hansberry's play *Les Blancs*, "a device. No more. No less. It explains nothing at all" (92). When asked by his interlocutor, Charlie, for elaboration, Tshembe describes it as "a means. An invention to justify the rule of some over others." He then has to go on to dispel Charlie's hurried conclusion, from the words the latter has just heard, that race doesn't matter:

> I am simply saying that a device *is* a device, but that it also has consequences: once invented it takes on a life, a reality of its own. . . . I may recognize the fraudulence of the device, but . . . a man . . . who is shot in Zatembe or Mississippi because he is black—is suffering the utter *reality* of the device. And it is pointless to pretend that it doesn't *exist*—merely because it is a *lie*! (92)

The dissatisfaction one might feel about the current pentagonal paradigm has its roots in the contradiction inherent in the juxtaposition of *reality* and *lie* vis-à-vis the "device" of race. I propose that pursuing a way out of the contradiction will only result in disappointment. Nor is the intrinsically contradictory nature of the device of concern solely to Latina/os.

On Being Racially Exceptional

Latina/os face a troubling dilemma. While this country's white core has constructed its subjectivity by relegating other components of the population to a space of marginal alterity, Latina/os have resisted asserting their identity in opposition to whiteness. This resistance, of course, has complexities of its own. For one thing, Latina/os often partake of the territory of whiteness via phenotype and in shared prejudices. When young Richard Henry Dana took a break from Harvard in 1835 to undertake the travels he chronicled in *Two Years Before the Mast*, he crossed over to Mexican California and found that many Anglo males had married into Mexican families to qualify for land ownership and to do business there. While he at times evinces a clear conviction of the cultural superiority of the Anglos over the Hispanics of California, as when he observes that "nothing but the character of the people prevents Monterey from becoming a great town," Dana's narrative generally lacks explicit expressions of racial aversion (81). He remarks that in Monterey, "there are a number of English and Americans, who have married Californians, become united to the Catholic Church, and acquired considerable property. Having more industry, frugality, and enterprise than the natives, they soon get nearly all the trade into their hands" (80). One assumes that rabid racism would deter the practice of marrying one's inferior or converting to their religion, even when doing so would yield economic and social advantages.

The cultural offspring of European colonial formations, Latina/os have received no less of a negrophobic, anti-Indigenous, and anti-Asian education than their white Anglo counterparts. Some foundational texts of Latino literature might come in handy here. In the 1885 novel *The Squatter and the Don*, by California native María Amparo Ruiz de Burton, the Hispano landowner Don Mariano Alamar has no greater appreciation for non-whites than does his encroaching Anglo nemesis, William Darrell. When the Don looks back nostalgically to his lineage, namely the landlords who settled California on territories granted by "the Spanish Government or the viceroys of Mexico," he highlights their service as faithful collaborators in the founding of missions. He emphasizes their efforts to attract "population by employing white labor," as well as their hiring Indigenous workers so as to make them "less wild" and to assist in the defense of the country "threatened by the savages" (176). Latin American societies and the United States were both founded on the sweat and blood of racialized populations for the benefit of white or light-skinned elites. The entire hemisphere, in that sense, bought into the paradigm that Roberto Márquez has called the "*Society of Race* and racial castes" as the one principle "by which the Americas all have been historically shaped and socially articulated" (13). I can find, therefore, little justification in the wisdom that would insist solely on a more "civil" understanding of race.

While we may agree that some basic differences exist "between the way that Latinos view race and the way that race is viewed overall in the United States," we might fail to detect any positive implications in sociologist Clara E. Rodríguez's claim that the construction of race in Latin American countries "has been more fluid," transcending "the binary division adopted in the United States" (*Changing Race* 9, 123). Racial paradigms in Latin America, we are told, follow "a continuum with no fixed demarcation between categories," and US Hispanics, coming "from a culturally and generally mixed racial background," had to enter "a biologically based biracial structure" that featured European Americans at one end of the pole and African Americans at the other, with Native Americans and Asian Americans occupying "ambiguous gray positions vis-à-vis the dichotomy" (C. Rodríguez, "Challenging Racial Hegemony" 131–132). One gathers from the distinction detailed above a marked interest in stressing the exceptionality of Hispanic racial thought. However meaningful we may find the distinction for inquiries into the epistemology of racial classifications, it will not lessen the gravity of racial aggression south of the Rio Grande. Prior to the arrival of José Martí and Antonio Maceo on the political scene, the ideologues of Cuban nationalism invariably articulated their burning desire to extirpate the black element from the body of the nation. Likewise, for nearly five decades—until well into the twentieth century—the Mexican state invested itself ardently in a caste war that sought to erase the Mayan presence from any position of social relevance in the Yucatán Peninsula.

Latina/os are, by no means, the sole group in the United States that has reason to feel dissatisfied with the rigid racial codifications that American society has espoused. Sociologist Mary Waters, while commenting on multiethnic identities, has described the situation at the end of the twentieth century as one "where growing numbers of Americans no longer fit the categories we currently use to define Americans" (44). Nor should we think of blood mixing or other supposed transgressions of racial borders as unique to any subsection of the American population. Even the Founding Fathers, when confronted with the inexorability of the racial divide, had occasion to ponder the implications of blended bloodlines. In 1803 Thomas Jefferson envisioned amalgamation as a solution to the plight of Native Americans: "to let our settlements and theirs meet and blend together, to intermix, and become one people. Incorporating themselves with us as citizens of the United States, this is what the natural progress of things will, of course, bring on, and it will be better to promote than to retard it" (qtd. in Hilden 149). During the mid-nineteenth century, Lewis Henry Morgan, the renowned anthropologist whose research Marx and Engels so greatly admired, claimed to have witnessed the desirable outcomes of such Indigenous–white cross-fertilization: "The color of the Indian women is quite uniform, and is light. It shows that the white blood infused into them in the East has been well diffused throughout. The next cross will make a pretty white child" (qtd. in Hilden 149–150). Morgan welcomed the absorption of so-called Indian blood into Anglo veins because the genetic transaction would benefit whites, given the numerical advantage of European-descended Americans in the 1850s. He believed the mixture would "improve and toughen our race," and that the immiscible among the Indigenous populations ("the residue") would be "run out or forced into the regions of the mountains" (150). He articulated a sort of benevolent eradication of the American Indian, in other words.

By 1900, when African American writer Charles W. Chesnutt published "The Future American," the idea of amalgamation had captured the imagination even of non-whites. A distinguished mulatto essayist and fiction writer, Chesnutt conceived of a process whereby the "one-eighth Negro" population would dissolve into the majority white citizenry. As a result of that fusion, "there would be no inferior race to domineer over; there would be no superior race to oppress those who differed from them in racial externals" (21). Amalgamation presaged the end of racism through the disappearance of discrete races. Chesnutt's conceptualization, of course, empowers Caucasian blood alone with the ability to provide the matrix into which all the other races would dissolve. Twenty-five years later, the Mexican thinker José Vasconcelos would imagine the advent of the "synthetic race," born of the absorption of "the inferior races"—blacks and Indigenous people redeeming themselves "step by step, by voluntary extinction"—into the superior white, with the final product constituting a "fifth universal race" that he called "the cosmic race" (32). Strangely enough, Anzaldúa embraced this idea of amalgamation as one that champions "inclusivity" and proposed an alternative to the often deluded "racial purity that white America practices" (99). For all their stress on crossing racial boundaries, Chesnutt and Vasconcelos remain in thrall to white supremacist paradigms. The two thinkers imagine a scenario in which the subordinate racial groups—ethnic rivulets formerly pooled at the margins—disperse and dissolve within the vast sea of superordinate whiteness.

As we can see, Hispanics cannot claim a monopoly over the phenomenon of mestizaje. Native Americans, for instance, have had to contend with vexing questions stemming from the legitimacy of mixed-bloods or cross-bloods in matters of cultural and communal belonging. At one end, Minnesota Chippewa thinker Gerald Vizenor affirms that "mixed-bloods are not incomplete," not "half of something" but "whole people" (158). Conversely, Spokane–Coeur d'Alene writer Sherman Alexie speaks very unflatteringly of mixed-bloods, in whom he detects the same inauthentic affectation that he criticizes in non-Indian commentators on Indian life (10–11). Native Americans have also had to deal with issues of blood quanta to establish reservation membership eligibility and related matters of legitimacy and citizenship. The reservation system bifurcated the integrity of the Tohono O'odham, the tribe also known as the Papago, whose traditional territory extended beyond the international boundary created by the advent of the Mexico-US border. The family of writer Ofelia Zepeda, a Tohono O'odham who traces her roots to Sonora, Mexico, did not qualify for admission into the reservation, on account of the family's location on the Mexican side of the border, despite its blood ties to the other half of the tribe on the US side (Zepeda 408). The case of her family's struggle alerts us to the existence of several "invisible" Latina/os who, like her, occupy non-Hispanic ethnoracial identity spaces, despite their important ties, including lived experience, to Latin American ancestry and heritage.

Exiting the Ethnoracial Impasse

The intellectual conversation on the ethnoracial location of Latina/os appears to have reached an ideological cul-de-sac. Skidding down the slippery slope of accurate definability, the debates tend to go two ways simultaneously. Generated primarily by activists and scholars from communities of color, they try to serve competing needs: to voice the interests of racialized constituencies and to underscore the scholarly community's contention about the untruths of race. Compounding the precariousness of these discourses is the emergence of novel ways of self-fashioning. We observe as a trend that many members of ethnic minorities now shun the traditional language of self-affirmation. They often choose to configure their subject positions by destabilizing the logic of self-differentiation upheld by their elders. No longer compelled to brandish their ethnic or racial selves as a political banner, many Latina/os now seem less willing to assert their otherness in contradistinction to a dominant white core. It has become customary for them to regard themselves as biracial or bicultural, stressing individual subjectivities that partake of multiple identity spaces rather than obediently embracing the imperative of communal identities that informed standard ethnoracial agendas during the Civil Rights era. The frequency with which ethnic minority respondents chose several categories of self-representation at the same time in the 2000 US Census attests to the prevailing mood. In the twenty-first century, when speaking about themselves, many people of color wish to privilege their ontological complexity, thereby endorsing the idea that such definitions can and will remain in flux and negotiable.

I do not wish to belittle the philosophical seriousness behind the widespread fear of definitions. Concerns over the metaphysics of naming do have a rightful place in the public sphere, the academy included. However, we might derive much enlightenment from research that would examine whether a similar uneasiness about the existing ethnoracial labels can be discerned among white Americans. I would conjecture that if ethnic minority communities alone appear committed to expanding the conceptual paradigms of self-representation and pursuing greater epistemological flexibility in delimiting the boundaries of their ethnoracial selves, we might have reason to worry. We might also be witnessing the final triumph of the logic of amalgamation wherein the subordinate groups accept the idea of "diluting" themselves with the hope of erasing the distance that separates them from normative whiteness. I fear further that if millions of Latina/os do not define themselves *for themselves*, corporate and government interests will do it instead. Considering the corporate tendency to construe Hispanics in panhemispheric terms, superseding the focus on Latina/os as a specific US ethnicity, the external definitions may involve political and economic partners from both sides of the Rio Grande. A time may come when a shrewd Mexican president commands greater influence in dictating policy for the Mexican American community than Chicana/o intellectuals, Mexican American legislators, or the National Council of La Raza, for instance.

Part of the impasse displayed by current conversations about difference, identity, and belonging in the United States emanates from the difficulty of harmonizing the rapport between race and ethnicity. As African American scholar Manning Marable contends, these paradigms have undergone considerable scrutiny by scholars, but "too often the discussion has been mired in old debates and definitions." He thus calls for "a new and critical study of the increasingly complicated relationship between race and ethnicity." The position advanced by Michael Omi and Harold Winant contending that race has, in effect, superseded ethnicity as a social identification among blacks and other historically underrepresented minorities has found much favor in the academy since it appeared in print during the 1980s (20). I find it telling that sociologists Richard Alba and Victor Nee concluded that assimilation had indeed taken place among Latina/os, despite the aversion of scholars within that population to conceiving of such a possibility in their midst, deeming it unlikely. Alba and Nee even settled for a usage whereby "racial" distinctions presuppose the "ethnic" and vice versa.[4]

It is not clear which identity paradigm between these two can prove more salutary for those hoping to inhabit the field of social relations productively, irrespective of ancestral difference in a country like the United States, whose exclusionary instincts have thrived for over four hundred years. After all, nations, which tend to provide the contours within which ethnoracial identities typically form, are fractious in and of themselves, just as race has fallen from grace as a reliable mode of classifying the human population into differentiated segments. Since the latter half of the twentieth century, geneticists, except when they are consummate racists themselves, have disavowed race as a legitimate biological taxonomy. Racialized denizens throughout the nations of the Western Hemisphere suffer their exclusions primarily from European-descended compatriots who can wield the power to assert themselves as members of the race most qualified to rule the destiny of their heterogenous nation. In view of this scenario, there would seem to be little justification for hoping that a sustained exploration of the precise relationship between race and ethnicity will break new and productive ground. The time has come for us to refrain from distinguishing between the two and to accept their conceptual fusion.

Using race and ethnicity synonymously may lead us out of the epistemic and political dead end. When it comes to oppressed communities of color, we do not need to know the difference between the terms if they both translate into a common exclusion and disempowerment. Both come from a similar effort to imagine a collective internally or externally. Their reality occurs only as they translate into social, political, and economic advancement or regression. I would venture to say that we have little to gain from subverting the pentagonal paradigm bequeathed by the Civil Rights Movement. Our mental energies could be better invested in efforts aimed at fashioning a Latino ethnoracial identity-space devoid of white supremacist assumptions. That way, members of the US Hispanic population with African, Indigenous, Asian, and European ancestry from coast to coast might truly identify with statements that speak about "the community." This would be a necessary step to galvanizing voices that can effectively advocate for more inclusive Latino future.

Notes

1. This observation may no longer be valid, especially after a couple of decades of a Hispanic Caribbean presence on the West Coast.

2. I am, of course, echoing Martin Luther King, Jr.'s "I Have a Dream" speech here. See King on *NPR* ("Read").

3. Dominican American poet Rhina P. Espaillat's poem "Two Cameos" meditates on McDaniel's experience alongside that of Rita Hayworth. See, for instance, Kang and Torres-Saillant's *The Once and Future Muse*, chapter 3.

4. See, for instance, "Rethinking Assimilation."

CHAPTER 7

PROBLEMATIC PARADIGMS

Racial Diversity and Corporate Identity in the Latino Community

This chapter ponders the nature of Latino panethnicity, weighing both the utility and the inherent limitations of homogenizing discourses related to US Hispanic identity in the late twentieth and early twenty-first centuries. Torres-Saillant wrestles with the question of whether unity is indeed possible across so many planes of difference, with Latino subgroups having their own unique historical trajectory, levels of empowerment, and visibility—as well as divergent experiences with racism, economic disenfranchisement, and political crises back in their ancestral homelands. The writer calls for a "measure of caution" any time "overly broad claims" emerge about Latina/os, casting doubt on the impression that everyone stands as "one big happy family." He asserts that keeping the Latino community uniform for marketing purposes serves the corporate bottom line. Additionally, the overrepresentation of fair-skinned Latina/os in prominent Hispanic media roles may facilitate acceptance by an Anglo population not particularly interested in confronting race, class, and other key sites of inequality. What appears profitable to executives at major corporations may be shot through with white supremacist assumptions about what the ideal televised Latina/o should look like. A spectrum of phenotypes remains lacking even while the corporate leadership is aware of the problem and a good many voices have brought the exclusion to light.

Torres-Saillant also offers some targeted insights on Dominican Americans as a subsection of the whole that is too often relegated to the periphery in scholarly studies. The relative erasure of the group occurs despite its key contributions, its growing numbers, and its complex concerns as a diasporic population. In light of this and other examples, Torres-Saillant underscores the need to differentiate the various ethnic, racial, and regional subgroups within the US Hispanic population, with a special emphasis on internecine competition and injustices, the specific histories and struggles of each collective, and consideration of the varied impact of compounded intersectional concerns on those in "the community." He ends by encouraging greater engagement with those whose identity straddles traditional ethnoracial categories, among them Afro-Latina/os, Asian Latina/os, and Indigenous Latina/os. Problematizing received paradigms of Hispanic ancestry avoids monolithic narratives about Latino identity, introduces greater flexibility in conceptualizing the inherently diverse Latino population, and ultimately empowers everyone.

Borders That Exist

Presuming a seamless, unproblematic Latino identity militates against the unity that US Hispanic communities could and should forge in order to increase their levels of empowerment in American society. The potential for building coalitions, fashioning collaborative agendas, and joining forces in common causes can become a reality only through serious reflection, inclusive dialogue, and tactful planning. Simply assuming that Latino unity exists is to eschew the hard work, time, and deep thought that realizing its existence requires. Numerous thinkers have warned against uncritically embracing homogenizing discourses when defining the Hispanic subsection of the American population.[1] Juan Flores and George Yúdice cast Hispanics in the United States as a "very heterogeneous medley of races and nationalities," constituting not even "a relatively homogeneous 'ethnicity'" (Flores, "Living Borders" 199). These authors and many others have abundantly shown that promoting totalizing representations of the Latino "community" overlooks the differentiated cultural contributions and particular social legacies that each individual subgroup has brought to American society. The disadvantages have thus far been articulated in terms of how Hispanics can lose material or symbolic power through homogenizing representations vis-à-vis the non-Latino political and economic mainstream. But not enough voices have alerted us to what is perhaps an even graver danger: the debilitating impact that such representations can have on the ability of individual subgroups to fend off intra-Latino injustices.

When we consider the unique circumstances under which various subgroups have entered the United States, as well as the differing lengths of their relationships with the country, it is not surprising to see how economic and political leadership varies in terms of national visibility, access to resources, and levels of empowerment. Differing levels of empowerment imply, of course, unequal degrees of vulnerability. Divides exist even among Latina/os of the same national origin, when intersectional factors such as race and class intervene. Narrating his experiences in Tampa, Florida, in the 1930s, the US-born black Cuban Evelio Grillo recalls that "black Cubans and white Cubans lived apart from one another in Ybor City" (9). Grillo does not remember "playing with a single white Cuban child" when he was a kid, but he, unlike his white Cuban compatriots, also had doors of opportunity slammed on him by Jim Crow America because of his phenotype. He comments, "I don't know any black Cuban college graduate of my generation, and of all the generations preceding desegregation, who is not a graduate of a historically black college" (11–12). He notes that even in matters of romance, the racially driven experiences among black Cubans and white Cubans outweighed their shared national origin. Thus, for black Cubans, dating almost exclusively involved "eligible black American counterparts" (12). Kenya Dworkin y Méndez, a Cuban American scholar who has studied the cultural history of south Florida, notes the irony inherent in the fact that Círculo Cubano and La Unión Martí-Maceo, the mutual aid societies that serve Tampa's white and black Cubans, respectively, both engaged in centennial celebrations in 1999–2000. The clubs approached the anniversary events in "significantly different ways" (Dworkin y Méndez xii). That is, they reflected their unequal conditions, an enduring legacy of the fact that one group bore the historical burdens of Jim Crow policies while the other did not. Clearly, these examples of inter- and intra-group divisions among the multiple segments that the Latino community comprises place in stark relief the need to exercise caution when formulating overly broad claims about Latino identity.

With this background in mind, I would like to suggest that current assertions of a harmonious panethnic Latino selfhood can perpetuate intra-Latino exclusions and injustices, thus preventing the emergence of a genuinely inclusive sense of community among the various Hispanic groups that constitute such a vital part of the US population. A corollary to this critique would be an argument against locating Latino identity in the obtuse vastness of panhemispheric or intercontinental cultural spheres. I argue that borders exist, the global economy notwithstanding, and these demarcations obtain despite the transnational dynamics that self-proclaimed postmodernists point to as indicative of the demise of the nation-state. I insist on the need to separate Latin American from Latino identity, given the legacies of racial inequality in countries south of the Rio Grande. In so doing, I reject the seductive fusion of the Latin American South and the Latino North encouraged by the Hispanic subsection of corporate America.

Imperial Contiguity, Latino Unity, and Levels of Marginality

Like any other minority group, Latina/os generally lack the freedom to choose the way the larger society configures their ethnic selfhoods. Richard Delgado is not far off the mark when he insists that "membership in a racial minority can be considered neither self-induced, like alcoholism or prostitution, nor alterable" (159). We do not need to repeat the work of documenting the process whereby people with disparate Latin American origins gradually dissolve under the single homogenizing label of "Hispanic" or "Latina/o." But preceding the nomenclature that scholars like Suzanne Oboler have mapped is an earlier imperial history that describes the expansionist impulse of the United States. The logic of US geopolitical self-defense sounded by President James Monroe in his famous 1823 speech evolved into a self-assured affirmation of the United States' right to expand by virtue of what became known as its Manifest Destiny. The 1846 US invasion of Mexico, under President James Polk, led to the takeover of the Mexican territories of Arizona, California, Colorado, Nevada, New Mexico, and Utah, ratified by the Treaty of Guadalupe Hidalgo, signed between the victors and the vanquished two years later. The outcome doubled the size of the United States' territory. With American military might having proved its dexterity at gliding over contiguous nation-states, within fifty years the country had readied itself to bring this might across the oceans to become a world power. The 1898 US defeat of the Spanish Empire in what US textbooks call the Spanish-American War, a conflict that Washington had entered ostensibly to support Cuba's independence from Spain, yielded enormous profit geopolitically and gave the younger empire a firm footing in the Caribbean and the Asia Pacific region, with Cuba, Puerto Rico, the Pacific Islands, Guam, and the Philippines coming under US dominion. From that point on, the irresistible power of the United States would know no bounds, as military might could overcome the inconvenience of great distances across large bodies of water. With the enthusiasm awakened by the awareness of the country's imperial possibilities, on September 16, 1898, Indiana senator Albert J. Beveridge re-signified the idea of contiguity, proclaiming,

> The ocean does not separate us from lands of our duty and desire—the oceans join us, a river never to be dredged, a canal never to be repaired. Steam joins us; electricity joins us—the very elements are in league with our destiny. Cuba not contiguous! Puerto Rico not contiguous! Hawaii and the Philippines not contiguous! Our navy will make them contiguous. . . . American speed, American guns, American heart and brain and nerve will keep them contiguous forever. (Beveridge 333)

The contiguity created by its imperial expansion elevated the United States to the rank of ideological overseer of the Western Hemisphere, with the capacity and will to interfere economically or intervene militarily in any country that attempted to implement a form of government or an economic system outside the strictures and logic of capitalism.

US hegemony in Latin America and the Caribbean created the historical grounds for the presence of Hispanic communities in the United States today. The awareness that one is in the United States as a result of the defeat suffered by one's forbears, or the understanding that one's original homeland has existed for over a century in a position of subservience vis-à-vis American power in the hemisphere, does seem sufficient to create a sense of commonality. Such a commonality may be understood as stemming from a composite of diverse historical realities, national experiences, and collective existential traumas. The historical, contingent nature of presumed Latino unity seems to suggest that the need for unitary political practices cannot be viewed as resulting automatically or unproblematically from some sort of ontological sameness. The distinct subgroups that make up the segment of the US population that is called Hispanic are neither identical nor equal. Let us, for argument's sake, concentrate on the epistemic inequalities among the various subgroups. Dominicans provide an illustrative case. Until not long ago, a disdain for the Dominican experience was evident in several of the overviews, surveys, and compilations that aimed to cover the history, culture, and contributions of Latina/os in American society. Because such panoramic vistas are normally penned or coordinated by authors who belong to the Latino subgroups that enjoy greater socioeconomic and political empowerment, it makes sense that they should either omit any mention of the Dominican portion of the Latino experience or dispatch it briefly, if not also superficially. The same logic applies here regarding the rapport between dominant and dependent nation-states. Studying the experiences of the larger, better-positioned portions of the Latino population—the "meaningful" parts that can stand for the whole—seems to lessen the need for complex and in-depth coverage of the smaller and apparently weaker portions.

We could take up, for instance, the case of Antonia Darder and Rodolfo D. Torres's collection *The Latino Reader: Culture, Economy, and Society* (1998). The book includes no chapter on, and no extended consideration of, the Dominican experience. The editors proceed as though they deemed knowledge about the life of that subgroup unnecessary to understanding the Latino community as a whole. The exclusion of Dominicans, as authors and as subject matter, from the ninety-four-chapter anthology *The Latino/a Condition: A Critical Reader* (1998), edited by Richard Delgado and Jean Stefancic, seems to say no less. From the perspective of the major Latino subgroups, then, the experience of the lesser groups does not promise to yield information capable of transcending the limits of such a community. We see here a case of what could be called *intracolonial epistemic inequality* that leaves Dominicans out of the master narrative of the Latino experience. In addition to omitting Dominicans, the dynamic manifests itself as a casual treatment of the lesser group. In *Washington Post* journalist Roberto Suro's book *Strangers among US: Latino Lives in a Changing America*, the chapter on Dominicans rebukes community leaders for not attacking with sufficient energy the drug problem in their midst and for not being proactive in circumventing the limits of the enclave economy (197, 202–203). Exhibiting a similar sense of superiority, Univision anchorman Jorge Ramos assigns himself the poetic license to coin his own gentilitial labels for those of Dominican ancestry: "portodominicanos" for those living in Puerto Rico and "neodominicanos" for those living in New York (179–185). I cannot help but conjecture that if this Mexican brother had been writing about a group with a greater degree of power vis-à-vis the other Latino subgroups, he would have consulted appropriate sources to find out the terms that the members of the community use to name themselves, instead of inflicting on them his own neologistic acrobatics.

By the same token, *New York Daily News* journalist Juan González, the author of *Harvest of Empire: A History of Latinos in America* (2000), does not invest in Dominicans anywhere near the intellectual labor apparent in his coverage of Chicanos and Puerto Ricans. For these two groups, he draws amply from the existing scholarship. As a result, he writes competently about them. In the case of Dominicans, however, he seems to have felt no compulsion to consult the bibliography that US Dominicans have generated, a great portion of which had already been annotated in *Dominican Migration* by librarian Sarah Aponte. Apparently confident that he could discern the intricacies of the Dominican experience without the aid of extant work by Dominican American scholars, and disdaining the archival resources of the City University of New York's Dominican Studies Institute, González proceeds to create his description of the community ex nihilo, basing his account largely on scant readings and several interviews with Dominican New Yorkers. Not surprisingly, his Dominican chapter proves threadbare. A Dominican reader would indeed find it very hard to concur with Juan Flores's assessment of *Harvest of Empire* as "no doubt the most wide-ranging, engaging, and critically reflective book about Latinos to date" (Review 43). A bit of irony resonates well here: *Magical Urbanism* (2000), written by notable Anglo scholar-activist Mike Davis, is remarkable in that a non-Latina/o sheds light on Latina/os by centering knowledge produced by Dominican-descended scholars, integrating it seamlessly into the larger panethnic conversation. Perhaps this is an instance where non-Latino colleagues, unencumbered by membership in, or allegiance to, any of the individual subgroups, inhabit a position that allows them to look panoptically (and with less bias) at Latina/os, making it less likely for individual subgroups to be left out of the picture.

White Supremacist Hybridity

The repetitive musings about borderlessness, hybridity, and transnational dynamics that pervade recent scholarly production on the Latino experience have tended to celebrate diversity and champion inclusivity. Yet the exclusionary ideological structures that lie at the core of corporate identity formulations in the community remain virtually unchallenged. The academy, the media, and the consumer market, for the most part, have rallied around the consensus that US Hispanics constitute a seamless unit. Few have stopped to consider the resonance of that view with the elitist, Eurocentric, and white supremacist ideas on *Hispanidad* that cohered in the minds of the Latin American intelligentsia of the generation that witnessed and mourned the change of imperial guard that took place in 1898 in the Western Hemisphere. Although they paid lip service to the virtues of mestizaje, the celebrants of *Hispanidad* (or *Latinidad*) in practice embraced negrophobic and anti-Indigenous regimes. José Martí denied the existence of "races" in his April 16, 1893, essay, "My Race," arguing for the essential, unquestionable humanity of all peoples. His opening paragraph affirms, "No man has any special rights because he belongs to one race or another: say 'man' and all rights have been stated. The black man is not inferior or superior to any other man" (318). But to take Martí's disavowal of racism as somehow common to many Latin American intellectuals at the time would be erroneous.

This warning matters in the present context, in which many Latina/o scholars find it natural to proclaim their intellectual kinship to a history of ideas rooted in the Iberian side of the hemisphere. They are spurred on by the recognition of a certain geopolitical and economic interdependence between the United States and Latin America. The distinguished scholar Frank Bonilla, who invested enormous amounts of energy in creating bridges of intellectual communication between Latin Americans to the south and Latina/os to the north, has borne witness to serious obstacles that have emerged at particular moments, sometimes even stemming from our lack of a shared understanding of such concepts as ethnicity, culture, and racism ("Rethinking" 224). Many colleagues accept too quickly the view that the Spanish-speaking world has a less racialized and more humane understanding of the differences among human beings. A 1996 conversation, on the topic of race relations, between Latino scholar Jorge Klor de Alva and African American public intellectual Cornel West, moderated by Earl Shorris, left little doubt that Klor de Alva felt that his privileging of linguistic background and culture to define US Hispanics constituted a more accurate rendition of social identity than his African American colleague's focus on blackness (Klor de Alva, West, and Shorris 55). Latina/o colleagues at times can hardly conceal their pride at the thought that their culture is less racist than that of the Anglos. As Nicolás Kanellos has put it, "[Although] 'race' distinctions and prejudice exist in Spanish America, they do not take, nor ever have they taken, the form of institutionalized discrimination as in the United States; they are more subtly expressed (some glaring exceptions are to be found in the history of Cuba and Puerto Rico under US domination)" ("Hispanics" 178).

I would be less sanguine about exonerating Latin America from official, institutionalized racism, especially in view of the many countries in the region that specified a preference for whites in their immigration policies at given points in the nineteenth and twentieth centuries. Jorge Cañizares Esguerra has even advanced the idea that modern racism originated in Latin America. He contends that "the science of race, with its emphasis on behavioral-cultural variations, and its obsession with creating homogenizing and essentializing categories, was first articulated in colonial Spanish America in the seventeenth century, not in nineteenth-century Europe" (35). At any rate, without clear, tangible institutional barriers exacerbating the subjugation of particular racial communities, one would be hard-pressed to explain most of the violent racial clashes that Latin America has witnessed, with the 1912 protest led by members of Cuba's Partido de Color and their subsequent mass killing by the country's armed forces standing out as a particularly glaring example.

The following incident also comes to mind. During the evening of February 24, 2000, a Haitian Dominican woman activist named Sonia Pierre suffered abuse upon entering the United States through JFK Airport in New York City. She had traveled in her capacity as head of the Santo Domingo–based Dominican–Haitian Women's Movement. Pierre was a guest at a national conference, organized by a Dominican youth group called Dominicans 2000, to be held at the City College of New York on February 25–27, 2000. The dynamic outreach of the young organizers was clear from the impressive roster of speakers and performers who appeared on their program, including the merengue superstar Johnny Ventura and First Lady Hillary Rodham Clinton, among other well-known speakers. Pierre had come to share with the audience the plight of Dominican-born children of Haitian parents, whom Dominican government authorities typically refused to recognize as citizens. The administrative tactic was simply for hospitals to decline issuing a birth certificate to the children of Haitian immigrant mothers. Pierre brought data to the conference to show the extent to which the intellectual heirs of the Trujillo dictatorship would go to declare Haitian ancestry incompatible with the very concept of Dominicanness, despite the principle of jus soli (birthright citizenship), which the Dominican Republic's constitution had long embraced. She could not possibly have imagined that the affronts she suffered daily as a member of a despised minority in her birthplace would follow her all the way to this international airport. After all, what does mainstream America know about ethnic tensions in the Caribbean island of Hispaniola? By her account, offered as prefatory remarks to her presentation at the conference, Pierre had the misfortune to be received at the immigration checkpoint by a Latina INS (Immigration and Naturalization Service) agent, a Dominican-descended US citizen with the surname Goico on her nametag. When Pierre presented her passport and other qualifying papers, the official challenged their authenticity and accused her of forgery. Officer Goico looked at Pierre's "Haitian appearance" (that is, her coarse hair, untamed by relaxers, and her Negroid facial features) and concluded that the traveler was trying to pass for Dominican. The French surname Pierre did not help her case either. The letter of invitation from the conference organizers proved insufficient. A close examination of the suspected forged papers and lengthy interviews with several INS officers ensued before Pierre, after nearly two hours of difficult and humiliating detention, was allowed to proceed without a word of apology from Officer Goico.

What Pierre saw as Goico's anti-Haitian antipathy corresponds to a prediasporic experience of Dominicans in their homeland, dating back to a national milieu that fueled distrust for people ancestrally linked to the Haitian side of Hispaniola. Dominican anti-Haitianism tends to fade gradually in the diaspora, especially among people with some community involvement. Collective activism tends to bring Haitians and Dominicans together in diasporic sites where they share space. Free from the supervision of the state that fueled their ethnic antipathy, they often learn to recognize each other as allies in a common struggle for survival as racialized minorities in the United States. An affirmation of Pierre's difference as a person of color and her presumptive otherness, vis-à-vis the Anglo majority, would have ideally fostered in the examining officer a sense of kinship with Caribbean people and other non-white ethnic groups. Such solidarity, of course, cannot be deemed automatic.

If Pierre's understanding of the agent's behavior was correct, Officer Goico probably displayed allegiance to the exclusionary view of Dominicanness received from her elders, who may have brought to the United States the ethnoracial antipathies operative in their land of birth. If these elders were part of the great Dominican exodus that began in the mid-1960s and did not abate until the late 1980s, they may have learned their patriotism at a time when the official discourse appeared most fanatically invested in tying Dominican national identity to derision of all things Haitian. This possibility lends plausibility to Pierre's understanding that what she experienced at JFK airport in February 2000 was anti-Haitian abuse of the kind she had long endured in Santo Domingo at the hands of self-declared "patriotic" Dominican nationalists. To continue this line of conjecture, we could be seeing here a psychosocial phenomenon worthy of note, that is, the case of a Dominican American, entrusted with safeguarding a concrete US border from unauthorized entry by foreigners, who has been unduly swayed by the need to protect the abstract identity border of her elders from someone of Haitian ancestry, an ethnicity she had learned to recognize as antithetical to Dominicanness. Suspecting Pierre of being a Haitian, perhaps unable to imagine such a thing as a *Haitian Dominican*, Goico set out to establish that the traveler was seeking to pass for Dominican using forged papers. Her INS job expected her, on behalf of the state, to patrol a US border against illegal entry by foreigners, yet the Haitian ancestry of Pierre caused Goico to forget her most immediate self, becoming absorbed instead by the need to patrol the borders of her ancestral Dominicanness on behalf of her elders.

I believe this uncomfortable, indeed, traumatizing, incident illustrates the extent to which blurring the boundaries between the Latin American South and the Latino North can complicate the process of cultural and political self-definition of US Hispanics. Should that blurring become endemic, the Latino community would abdicate its position as a vanguard committed to furthering democratic inclusion in the United States while helping to promote a greater climate of equality and justice in their ancestral homelands to the south. For we can play that role credibly only if we free ourselves from the influence of those aspects of our Latin American origins that still normalize inequality and injustice. I do not see the Goico incident as a unique or isolated case; nor is the officer alone in importing to the Latino North, and internalizing, hatreds that belong to a specific part of the Latin American South. I see a parallel in the racial misconduct of the business executives who control the TV programs that Spanish-speaking Hispanics watch. Some of the US corporate heads behind Univision and Telemundo still prevent Indigenous or black faces from appearing before the cameras. One could surmise that in an applicant's effort to land a job as a newscaster on a Spanish-speaking TV station or network, Nordic features would prove quite helpful. Conversely, displaying the typically Indigenous features of nineteenth-century Mexican president Benito Juárez or the black features of Cuban independence leader Antonio Maceo would seriously reduce the applicant's chances of being a frontrunner and eventually a headliner. Anyone who watches Hispanic TV in the United States will easily recognize the white supremacist value system that governs the way mass media corporations promote the collective visage of the Latino community. It is through the disproportionally white faces of our anchors that Hispanic TV networks choose to represent the homogeneity that our corporate identity is supposed to embody.

I argue against uncritically embracing the notion that US Hispanics are unified by the bond of a shared linguistic heritage and a common culture. Unless we subvert the impulse to assume the linguistic heritage to be Spanish and the culture to be the legacy of Christian Europe imported by the conquerors, adventurers, and settlers who began to arrive on Caribbean shores in 1492, the notion of such a bond impairs our ability to combat the anti-Indigenous and negrophobic traditions we inherit from Latin America. The claim that Latina/os constitute one big happy family conceals the tensions, inequities, and injustices in our midst, contributing to an environment that legitimizes the absence of black, Indigenous, and Asian voices and faces from Latino public fora. The operating logic seems to be that because everyone in our polychromatic community is really the same, everyone is inherently represented even when only one phenotype continues to peer out at us from mass media screens with any regularity. A case in point: individuals with conventionally identifiable Indigenous features seldom appear in Latino academic forums to speak as producers of knowledge or as the intellectual equals of their non-Indigenous peers. Enjoying such privilege would come to an Indigenous person if they achieved a distinction comparable to that of Nobel Prize winner Rigoberta Menchú. The Mexican American essayist Richard Rodriguez, one Latino thinker with perceptible "Indian" features who has enjoyed intellectual prominence, attained his celebrity through Anglophone mainstream media venues such as PBS, not through Hispanic venues such as Univision or Telemundo. Evocative, in that regard, is Rodriguez's reflection on his phenotype as he opens the first chapter of his memoir *Days of Obligation*:

> I used to stare at the Indian in the mirror. His wide nostrils, thick lips. Starring Paul Muni as Benito Juárez. Such a long face—such a long nose—sculpted by indifferent, blunt thumbs, and of such common clay. No one in my family had a face as dark or as Indian as mine. My face could not portray the ambition I brought to it. . . . I remember reading the ponderous conclusion of the Kerner Report in the sixties: two Americas—one white, one black—the prophesy of an eclipse too simple to account for the complexity of my face. (1)[2]

Channel 41, the Univision TV station serving New York, New Jersey, Pennsylvania, and Connecticut, in the 1990s aired a well-orchestrated publicity campaign that sang the praises of our common Hispanidad. The campaign featured many popular entertainers from the music industry. Their song insistently dwelt on the language, the culture, and the traditions that make us *una sola familia* (one single family). Although I have long viewed the corporate media with suspicion on identity matters, I remember reacting most viscerally to the one spot that, in my view, most abusively mocked historical truth and scoffed at the suffering of the conquered. The spot I recall showed an Andean band made up of *indios* who enthusiastically sing the praises of Hispanidad and our shared Spanish heritage. The spot displays utter disregard for the grief of the Indigenous populations of South America and the rest of the hemisphere, who fell under the genocidal hand of the old Spanish Empire that invaded their land. Such historical amnesia also has the effect of completely exculpating the Latin American ruling elites responsible for perpetrating great evils against Indigenous peoples after their independence from Spain. At least from the time of Argentinean statesman Domingo Faustino Sarmiento onward, anti-Indigenous rhetoric has too often entered the official discourse of Latin American nations and influenced public policy, with dire consequences for members of these subject populations. The moving story told by the 1983 film *El Norte*, which dramatizes the plight of native peasants who escape their Guatemalan home to save themselves from imminent demise, testifies to the longevity and pervasiveness of anti-Indigenous violence in contemporary Latin America.

When we gleefully invoke Spanish as the language of our identity and our culture, we recklessly insult the rich linguistic history of the Latin American region whose civilizations were cut short by the heavily armed fortune seekers who followed Christopher Columbus to these lands. There was the genocidal onslaught against the physical bodies of Indigenous people whose warfare technology could by no means match the weapons of mass destruction deployed against them by the Christian invaders. The assault extended also to the bodies of knowledge that native civilizations had amassed over the centuries, including their languages, which depend on living speakers to survive. Indeed, many languages perished in the decivilizing violence of the conquest and colonization of the Americas; but that is no excuse for speaking as if Spanish were the only language of Latin America. Even if their monolingual imagination often causes Hispanic Latin Americans to omit mention of Portuguese, the imperial tongue spoken by over two hundred million people in Brazil, the fact remains that Indigenous languages did not vanish, despite the horrors of conquest and colonization. Indeed, in the first decade of the twenty-first century, a creditable sociolinguistic map of Latin America's aboriginal languages found as many as 420 of them still actively spoken in the region, with more than 100 of them enjoying a cross-border existence (*Atlas sociolingüístico*).

For Univision to have Indigenous people appear on TV praising the glory of our "shared" Spanish heritage is to mock the victims of a continuous five-century-long abuse in Latin America. By the same token, when the Channel 41 TV publicity campaign brought in the Afro-Cuban musical phenomenon Celia Cruz, adding her voice to the praise of the common culture, traditions, and Spanish language that make all Hispanics "una sola familia," one wonders whether she was aware of the negrophobic and anti-Indigenous project she indirectly legitimized. As journalist Michael A. Fletcher has observed, Afro-Latina/os and Indigenous people are rarely cast in Spanish-language television shows in the United States, and the few who are "most often play demeaning roles." In the widely popular *telenovelas* (soap operas), "darker skinned people most often play maids, gardeners, chauffeurs or dabblers in witchcraft" (Fletcher, "Latino Actors"). Because of her blackness, the popular New York–based radio personality Malín Falú, producer of a long-running talk show on Radio WADO, confronted insurmountable barriers in her attempt to land jobs in Spanish-language television in the United States. The Tomás Rivera Policy Institute surveyed four thousand Latina/o members of the Screen Actors Guild to learn that most of the respondents thought dark skin was a liability for any performer who hoped to win opportunities in Spanish-language television productions (Fletcher, "Latino Actors").

I had occasion to raise the issue of race on Hispanic network TV publicly with Henry G. Cisneros, when he, as President and CEO of Univision, delivered the keynote at the conference Latinos in the 21st Century: Mapping the Research Agenda, held at Harvard University on April 6–8, 2000. Having first gained national visibility as the successful mayor of San Antonio, Texas, from 1981 to 1989—the first Latino to hold that post since the annexation of Texas—Cisneros then went on to serve as the first US Secretary of Housing and Urban Development during Bill Clinton's first presidential term (1993–1997). His years on the campaign trail and in political life must have given Cisneros the opportunity to realize that ethnoracial difference matters in this country's public sphere. At the close of Cisneros's keynote address at the conference, I courteously asked him whether, from his position at the head of his TV network, he "envisioned a time in the near future when one would not have to be *güero* [blond] to serve as an anchorperson with Univision." After much circumlocution, Cisneros did not really commit himself to an answer, but he did reassure his audience that network managers had been looking seriously into the issue of representation. He urged us to find evidence of their concern in the composition of the live audience that appears in the very successful *Show de Cristina*, which was hosted by Cuban Cristina Saralegui, the author of a memoir significantly entitled *Cristina! Confidencias de una rubia* (1998; *Confessions of a Blonde*).[3] Cisneros also commented that the cast of the early morning variety show *Despierta América* reflected a concern for diversity, a clear allusion to Rafael José, a Puerto Rican mulatto featured among the hosts at the time. Clearly, I had posed a difficult question, and the answer Cisneros gave was no more satisfactory than that of Telemundo spokesperson Ted Guefen, who, fumbling for evidence to show his network's concern for racial inclusiveness, cited the case of the successful show *Xica*, a late-1990s-era soap opera based on the life of a nineteenth-century Afro-Brazilian slave who used her sexual allure and lovemaking skills to earn her freedom and ascend the social ladder. The Brazilian program, noted for risqué love scenes, featured the hypersexualized young actress Taís Araújo, reportedly the first black actress to land a leading role in a Latin American soap opera.

Cisneros tread on firmer rhetorical ground when answering the second part of my question, wherein I inquired whether Univision was planning to change the objectionable scenario depicted by the telenovelas, which invariably present blacks and Indigenous people as housemaids or servants. He immediately absolved his network of any responsibility for those portrayals by responding, "We have no control over what goes into the telenovelas because they are made in Mexico." A natural follow-up question would have demanded further satisfaction. One would suppose that as the telenovela producers' client, the network ought to have the power to influence the material it purchases. But the follow-up became unnecessary, as Cisneros proceeded to expound on the importance of the telenovelas as the network's number-one revenue-producing venture. Thanks to the genre, Univision has often enjoyed a greater share of the national market than the major English-language television networks. "Without them," the former HUD secretary insisted, "we would be out of business." He was emphasizing how Univision had to see itself first and foremost as a profit-making enterprise. Cisneros unambiguously pointed out that because the telenovelas bring in such great profits the way they are currently made, the network could not take any chances by altering the genre or the mainstay ingredients of the shows. His answer also communicated that Mexican society is less preoccupied with matters related to racial sensitivity and the politics of representation than are racialized minorities (including Latina/os) in the United States.

Latino Identity and the Corporations

Whether scholars and artists from the group know it or not, fidelity to a homogenized view of Latino identity perfectly serves the economic interests of the Latino segment of corporate America. When this vast number of people can see themselves as a unit, sharing values, language, culture, and aspirations, corporate capital can accumulate more rapidly. Businesses can target their publicity campaigns and marketing strategies with greater precision. The Spanish-speaking Hispanics willing and able to watch television, listen to the radio, and read newspapers in print or online are a gold mine that businesses are eager to tap into by any means possible. The Spanish-speaking population outnumbers all other "foreign"-language users in the United States. Hispanic buying power by 1999 had reached $348 billion a year, up 65 percent since 1990, according to the Selig Center for Economic Growth at the University of Georgia (Sleeper 10). One can therefore understand the insistence with which Univision and Telemundo promoted the idea of US Hispanics as an ethnically and culturally homogeneous people. The premise clearly informed Univision's extremely successful weekly variety show *Sábado Gigante* (1962–2015), hosted by the Chilean TV announcer Mario Kreuzberger, popularly known as Don Francisco. The same applies to the talk show *El Show de Cristina* (1989–2011), hosted by the aforementioned Saralegui. Vigorously embracing the view that US Hispanics have a common heritage that makes them one people, these shows exhibit the all-encompassing hemispheric notion that Hispanics north and south share one worldview. The most successful of the shows air in almost every Latin American city, as well as in the United States, and some, such as *Sábado Gigante*, were produced collaboratively in Latin America and the United States (Fox 47–49).

Media executives have a major stake in ensuring that US Hispanics see themselves as one, for these executives can use their power over the community's perceptions and opinions as a bargaining tool in their competition with corporate counterparts. Raúl Alarcón, president of the Spanish Broadcasting System, and Jesús Chavarría, publisher of *Hispanic Business Magazine*, have complained about major advertisers who, in their view, distribute advertising dollars unfairly to the advantage of Anglo companies. They cite such examples as the Miami Univision TV station, Channel 23, "which is ranked number one in terms of ratings but receives considerably less advertising revenue than other TV stations in its market" (Dougherty 26). In response to that perceived unfairness, Hispanic media executives have joined their African American counterparts, with the support of political leaders and legislators, in creating the Madison Avenue Initiative to advance the interests of minority-owned media companies. They can wield no greater weapon, however, than the assurance that they have a unified Hispanic community behind them. The leadership gains a competitive edge when Latina/os subscribe to a corporate identity. Counting on a homogeneous community supportive of their business interests, the Hispanic media executives can then exert greater pressure as they step up their demand for a larger piece of the economic pie. They can invoke "the community" to advance their bottom line. They have even gone as far as threatening to engage in boycotts, as was made clear by a New York Latino legislator who, siding with the Hispanic media executives, asserted that advertisers that "continue to ignore" the community "can suffer economic casualties" (Dougherty 28). Nor do these Hispanic media executives have any doubt about their own ability to forge a sense of pan-Latino identity; in the words of Alberto Ibargüen, the publisher of *The Miami Herald* and *El Nuevo Herald*, "technology and economic forces" have the power to define and shape the contours of collective identity, thereby impacting the community's direction (qtd. in Sleeper 3). Also, for them, insofar as the North and South have fused into one market, it is in their best interest to promote panhemispheric visions of Latino identity. As Ibargüen reminds us, "Miami is the central communication point for all of the Caribbean and much of South America. . . . Television, ad agencies, banks, music recording companies all have their Latin American headquarters here" (qtd. in Sleeper 3).

Restoring Borders (Temporarily)

I hope the foregoing discussion makes clear that both the homogenizing views of Latino identity and the panhemispheric compulsion to erase the dividing line between Latin Americans in the southern portions of the Western Hemisphere and the Latino segment of the US population coincide with the figurations promoted by powerful economic interests in mass media and other market forces. Latin American governments and corporate leaders are cognizant of the growing economic value of keeping their diasporas loyal to their lands of origin to preserve the constant flow of capital via monetary remittances and direct investment in business ventures in the ancestral homeland. They may also hope for voices in the diaspora to advocate in support of US foreign policy measures that favor the interests of their countries of origin. Those governments and corporate sectors will certainly encourage consolidation of panhemispheric Latino and Hispanic identity. These governments, along with corporations on both sides of the Rio Grande, are likely to relish an idea of Hispanic/Latino identity akin to that proposed by Cuban-born philosophy scholar Jorge J. E. Gracia, which is not only panhemispheric, spanning both north and south, but also transatlantic, covering practically the entire globe. Gracia describes Hispanics as "the people of Iberia, Latin America, and some segments of the population in the United States, after 1492, and the descendants of these peoples anywhere in the world as long as they preserve close ties to them" (52). I believe that this formulation confounds rather than clarifies the issues involved in the debate on Latino identity. Gracia concerns himself with what he calls "the total Hispanic/Latino population in the world," as well as shared "origin, culture, and values" in the context of a long history of mestizaje (ix, 128–129). Yet the debate in the US academy has been predicated on an understanding of Latina/os as a US ethnic minority, the only conceptual location where it could possibly make sense. It is only in the United States that Dominicans and Guatemalans can come to see themselves as Hispanics or Latina/os. In that respect, we can say, as political scientist Jorge Domínguez stated at a Latino studies conference I attended at Harvard University in April 2000, that "Latinos are a *problematique* of Americanness." This is a thought that did not survive the conversion of the (now disgraced) speaker's oral presentation into the formal text that appeared in the edited volume based on the conference titled *Latinos: Remaking America* (2002).

Despite his unfortunate thesis, Gracia insightfully construes the notion of Hispanicity as one that refers to "a group of people who have no common elements considered as a whole" and justifies their unity as "not a unity of commonality" but "a historical unity founded on relations" (50). Similarly, although he describes Hispanic unity as resembling that of a family, a trope that he draws from Ludwig Wittgenstein's notion of "family resemblances," he cautiously explains that "the metaphor of the family must be taken broadly to avoid any understanding of it as requiring genetic ties. . . . Indeed, the very foundation of a family, marriage, takes place between people who are added to a family through contract, not genesis" (50). Here, Gracia allies himself with what is arguably the most sober approach to defining the nature of ethnic identification. Many scholars today would agree with Max Weber that "it is primarily the political community, no matter how artificial, that inspires the belief in common ethnicity" (306–307). This understanding of ethnic identification corresponds almost entirely with the idea of a minority group, which, one might recall, does not necessarily depend on numbers. As Louis Wirth posited in the mid-twentieth century, a group may outnumber another and yet remain a minority by virtue of its social, political, and economic subordination (310). A minority defines itself by its unequal status vis-à-vis "a corresponding dominant group enjoying higher social status and greater privilege" as well as by its "exclusion from full participation in the life of society" (309).

In keeping with Gracia's useful caveat and focusing strictly on historical relations—that is, the material conditions, the social forces, and the political dynamics that frame the experience of Latina/os—one might perhaps explore ways of speaking about US Hispanics holistically without imposing a priori notions of homogeneity. As in the case of Dominicans broached earlier, essentialist claims will not take us very far. Definers of the essential features "shared by most Hispanics independent of their national background, birthplace, dominant language, or any other sociodemographic characteristic" have placed too great a demand on our imagination (Marín and Marín 2). According to scholars Gerardo Marín and Barbara VanOss Marín, to claim that Rosa, a descendant of Spanish settlers in New Mexico, who no longer speaks Spanish, is ontologically indistinguishable from José, an undocumented Nicaraguan who has just arrived in the United States, is to rely unduly on the power of so-called cultural values (2). Marín and Marín speak unambiguously of "the common cultural values that remain strong and personally significant across generations and that may lead both Rosa and José to think of themselves as sharing 'something' that they do not share with non-Hispanic residents of the United States" (2). These theorists attribute to Latina/os the quality of "familism," a "strong identification with and attachment to their nuclear and extended family" which they regard as one of the most-treasured culture-specific values of Hispanics (13). Such a claim would be stronger if the authors substantiated it by adducing comparative data that indeed showed whether Latina/os cherish their relatives appreciably more than other groups, such as Asian Americans, Italian Americans, Arab Americans, and Jewish Americans. Indeed, several scholars have insisted that immigration and displacement are highly stressful to Latino families (Falicov; Ainslie). David Abalos, for example, proposes that the disquieting levels of disruption affecting the Latino family are a consequence of migration, displacement, and the trauma that ensues from these events (54). Most disconcerting among the sources of familial stress is a variable that one could describe as cultural, because it is grounded in the place of male authority in the traditional Hispanic family (Falicov 280). Abalos, among other scholars, highlights male privilege and the patriarchal norms influencing how Latino families have functioned, with sexist and dehumanizing consequences for both men and women (53). Given this scenario, rather than highlighting familism as a special quality of the community, we might more convincingly assert that the institution of the family may be in no better shape among Latina/os than among any other subsection of the country's population.

The Tenuous Ties That Bind

We can rest assured that whatever its problems, the idea of a pan-Latino community with a claim to some kind of wholeness is not likely to vanish any time soon. We therefore face the challenge of articulating an all-encompassing narrative that might historicize the US Hispanic experience with all national groups and ethnic constituencies included. But we must remain acutely aware of the problematic paradigms that inform our effort to do so. Perhaps we ought to start by avoiding any query that might point to the distinctness of the "Latino soul." Essentialist claims will take us nowhere, as Jorge Klor de Alva warned many years ago, urging us to reflect on the importance of class differences within the Latino community. Equating "class" with "culture," he questioned the very existence of "such a thing as *the* Hispanic family" because family, kinship, and gender roles all vary along socioeconomic and generational lines (116, 122). It follows, then, that "the poor inhabit a different cultural and socioeconomic world" from other strata of society among Latina/os, as among any other segment of the US population (116). Along with many other colleagues from postsecondary institutions throughout the United States, I joined the Recovering the US Hispanic Literary Heritage project, an effort spearheaded by Nicolás Kanellos at the University of Houston that seeks to map the literary and intellectual presence of Hispanics in this country, from the beginning of the conquest in the early 1500s to 1960. But I would caution against letting white supremacist instincts shape the contours of the totalizing narrative(s) we construct.

There is no doubt we could all benefit from devising a historiographic model that enables us to claim a North American heritage that goes back to the colonial period, spanning the exploits of such fortune seekers as Juan Ponce de León and Hernando de Soto, along with literary and historical texts produced by the likes of Álvar Núñez Cabeza de Vaca and Gaspar Pérez de Villagrá. But we might wish to think twice before concurring with Carlos G. Vélez-Ibáñez in accepting Cabeza de Vaca as "the first" Chicano writer (213). The basis for this rather precipitous pronouncement is the author's understanding of the sociocultural sameness of the conqueror and the conquered. He asserts, for instance, that the "Hispanos/Mexicans who migrated north from New Spain after the post-Pueblo Revolt [sic] of 1680 were primarily craftspeople and agropastoralists who had more in common with the Pueblo peoples than they did with the upper reaches of the peninsular caste/class sector" (266). One wonders whether such a view of the fundamental similarity between the Indigenous peoples and the invaders during the colonial transaction in the present-day US Southwest might not epitomize the practice of erasing difference when imagining Latino history. Harold J. Alford's overview *The Proud Peoples: The Heritage and Culture of Spanish-Speaking Peoples in the United States* (1972) is a case in point. Among sixty biographical sketches of Hispanic individuals from Juan de Oñate to Herman Badillo, no Indigenous or black person made it into the compendium. Apparently not even Estevanico, the black Moor who accompanied the expedition that brought Cabeza de Vaca, author of *La relación de Alvar Núñez Cabeza de Vaca* (1542), to the North, merited mention.[4]

Clearly, we must come to terms with our collective traumatic past. We must also acknowledge as cultural progenitors the Indigenous populations who suffered the consequences of that early Hispanic presence in what is now the United States. We inherit a racist imaginary from both Latin and Anglo America, and we must try to keep it from dictating the logic of our remembering as we construct a Latino history. I propose that we protect ourselves from that pervasive and pernicious imaginary by instituting analytic safeguards in our models. Specifically, I recommend that we admit the utility of borders—those confines that, initially at least, enable people to recognize one another in light of their differences—once and for all. I would urge us to erect intra-Latino borders, at least temporarily, so that the differentiated experiences of specific national groups can come to the fore. I believe it is as wrong to demonize borders as it is to pastoralize the common linguistic heritage that, by dint of some unexplained mutation, turns all our disparate national and ethnic groups into one big happy family. We need to pause for a moment and begin to train our eyes to unveil the distinct histories and lived experience of all the Latino subgroups that make up the US Hispanic population, going beyond the exclusive focus on Chicanos, Puerto Ricans, and Cubans. A serious effort also needs to be made to determine the exact location of Brazilians within the larger spectrum of US communities sharing Latin American heritage. Even if the term *Hispanic* would tend to leave Brazilians out, the term *Latino* would seem to allow for their inclusion (Margolis 103–104).

Finally, I can see great utility in isolating those ethnic identity zones that supersede the boundaries of what David A. Hollinger calls "the ethnoracial pentagon," the five communities of descent into which the US population is divided for national census purposes (8). I think we can learn a great deal by looking closely at the differentiated experiences of white Latina/os, Indigenous Latina/os, Asian Latina/os, and Afro-Latina/os. I find no mere coincidence in the fact that the darker-skinned components of the US Hispanic population have become more visible in Latino forums as initiatives have emerged explicitly highlighting the Afro-Latino experience. In mid-September 1999, the White House hosted a program aimed at addressing the concerns of the

African-descended portion of the Latino community. Concurrent with the White House activities, extending through October 12, the Smithsonian Institution's National Portrait Gallery also devoted its Latino Festival Program to the differentiated experience of Afro-Latina/os. As a result, Dominicans, who seldom found themselves invited to national conversations about the Latino agenda, enjoyed inclusion in panels, roundtables, and discussions. This example suggests to me that by creating structures designed to examine intra-Latino difference, we can achieve greater inclusiveness than we have at present. Such structures counteract the omnipresence of a white supremacist education. I believe that temporarily erecting intra-Latino borders can lead to our self-recognition amidst our complex diversity. These borders help us discern our own internal oppressions and biases, making us accountable for the same principles of equality and justice by which we purport to judge the behavior of Anglo society. Recognizing our differences and understanding the tensions that often mark our rapport, we might develop the skill to see one another clearly, protect ourselves from too facile an identification with one another, rectify our tendency to stand in the way of one another's progress, and come to respect one another. With these goals securely achieved, it will then be realistic for us to aspire to federate our distinct constituencies and communities with the purpose of becoming that one big family, striving together in pursuit of common happiness.

Notes

1. See, for instance, Oboler; Davis.
2. See also Rodriguez's "Mixed Blood."
3. It would be worthwhile to consider the applicability of the comparison between Saralegui and African American talk-show host and entrepreneur Oprah Winfrey, to whom the former has been compared, albeit as a "Hispanic" version. See Saralegui.
4. *La relación de Alvar Núñez Cabeza de Vaca* appeared 1542 in Zamora, Spain, following the author's return to Iberia from his North American colonial misadventure. Its title has often varied from one edition to another, an inconsistency resulting from the predilections of publishers wishing to highlight certain aspects of Cabeza de Vaca's story. English translations of the Spanish original have generally reflected the versions of the Spanish title to be found in print, including *Naufragios* (*Castaways*). As to our own citations, they refer to the English rendition of the text published in 1993 by Arte Público Press.

PART III

CRITICAL READINGS OF RACIAL POLITICS AND AFRO-LATINIDADES

CHAPTER 8

AFRO-LATINIDAD

Phoenix Rising from Hemispheric Ashes

This chapter gathers anecdotes, observations, and examples from headlines as well as social and intellectual history, combining them into a cross-cultural analysis of Afro-Latino identity, a comparatively underexamined subject in academe at the time of its writing. As suggested by Torres-Saillant's titular metaphor and pursued throughout the text, the constant accelerant to the racial bonfire—whether discussing the 2013 denationalization of Dominicans of Haitian ancestry in the Dominican Republic or instances of antiblack racism endemic to the Caribbean, Latin America, and the US mainland—is white supremacy. Dehumanizing attitudes and exclusionary policies toward African-descended peoples have remained remarkably persistent for several centuries. Themselves diverse, Afrodescendientes, *or Latina/os of African descent, across the Americas have endured charges of deficiency in beauty, intellect, and morality, despite their key contributions to the development of societies throughout the Western Hemisphere. As Torres-Saillant sets forth, the study of blackness within the Latino panethnicity adds necessary complexity to the binary model of US race relations. Laying bare the ubiquity of negrophobic racism, Afro-Latinidad defies the monolithic views of collective identity often stemming from the homogenization of US Hispanics as an internally coherent demographic formation.*

The writer understands racism as the default ideology of the hemisphere, accounting for the seeming contradiction of racial antipathy toward people of other ancestries by individuals who are themselves racialized. The "additional layer of difference" conferred by African ancestry constantly forces Afro-Latina/os to advocate for themselves, negotiating a precarious belonging between self-affirming "celebrations of ancestry" on the one side and the threat of pernicious "ethnoracial self-hatred" on the other. In addition to reasserting that an Afro-Hispanic presence preceded *the very formation of the United States, Torres-Saillant claims that no nuanced conversation on race in the United States, or anywhere in the Americas, would be complete without underlining the core contributions of these racialized populations.*

The Dark Side of Self-Affirmation

Professional basketball player Charlie Villanueva, a native New Yorker who enjoyed an ascendant career after first joining the National Basketball Association (NBA) in 2005, remembers a high school photo shoot that occasioned his first serious encounter with racism. As he posed for the camera of the woman photographer, he recalls a man intruding: "There comes this gentleman, and he says to the lady, right in front of me, 'Why are you taking pictures of this . . . ?' And he said the 'N' word!" The athlete remembers the shock and the fear triggered by this act of verbal aggression, which distressed him to such a degree that he even considered leaving the school. To his credit, before further nurturing that thought, he picked up the phone and called his mother, a Dominican immigrant who had a very simple message to convey. She told him that if he harbored any hopes of getting anywhere in life, he could not afford to let insults make him change his course. Villanueva's account forms part of "One Nación: Afro-Latinos," a five-minute ESPN video aired on October 8, 2015, that sets out to make viewers aware of black people of Hispanic descent and the challenges they face as a demographically distinct part of the US population. Also featured in the segment is Victoria Benítez of the Office of Communications and Public Affairs at Columbia University, who remembers the disappointment she once caused her fair-skinned Puerto Rican mother by describing herself as black.

The last Afro-Latina/o[1] interviewed in the video, journalist and author Ed Morales, a faculty member at Columbia University's Center for Ethnicity and Race, explained that in Latin America, both racism and affirmations of black identity developed distinct traits vis-à-vis their equivalents in the United States. In a review of the ESPN production, Los Angeles–based writer and photographer Walter Thompson-Hernández commended the production's "attempt to package the Afro-Latino experience" in such a brief format, forgiving its inevitable elisions. Fortunately, the short film does not commit to answering explicitly the implicit question about the meaning of the term *Afro-Latinidad*. Thompson-Hernández prudently worries about the pervasive presence of music, dance, and sports that visually and sonically frame the piece. Such a frame seems to suggest artistic performance and athletics as constitutive elements of the identity of the group in question, inadvertently validating persistent stereotypes that still plague media coverage of Latina/os. Even so, both Benítez and Villanueva identify bilingualism as an aspect of their heritage that they treasure, while expressing perhaps *inordinate* pride in their respective ancestries. The former praises Puerto Rican music, and the latter extols Dominican food, just as they characterize their backgrounds, respectively, as a "blessing" and "a beautiful thing."

Celebrations of ancestry by people belonging to less empowered sectors of the US population—or their marginalized counterparts in other societies in the hemisphere—share the same space as ethnoracial self-hatred or alienation from one's heritage. These feelings stem from a history that deprived certain segments of the human family of the ability to take their ancestry for granted, requiring them to assume an ideological position on it and to politicize its significance. The "Black Is Beautiful" mantra of the 1960s in the United States emerged to offset the self-loathing that had plagued many African Americans after centuries of racist conditioning. The pernicious white supremacist creed aimed to dehumanize them systematically, and many people of African descent came to see themselves through the eyes of their detractors. Throughout the hemisphere, the vilification of blackness and the concomitant glorification of whiteness proved effective, damaging the self-concept of those in the African-descended population who lacked vigorous defenses to inoculate themselves from ongoing psychological aggression and related forms of trauma.

The famous Doll Test experiment, conducted by psychologists Kenneth and Mamie Clark in the 1940s, laid bare the detrimental impact that a racist environment can have on the minds of black children. The psychologists presented black children with a choice between a white and a black doll in various scenarios to test their preference. When asked to point to the doll fitting a pejorative term such as "ugly" or "bad," the children in the sample group would overwhelmingly select the black doll, just as they would point to the white one when asked to match the doll with a positive term such as "good" or "smart." Malcolm X, in his famous 1963 speech "Message to the Grassroots," berated those African Americans who looked at Africa with contempt or who boasted about being the only blacks living in a white neighborhood. Similarly, Maya Angelou's first installment in her serial autobiography, *I Know Why the Caged Bird Sings* (1969), captures a glimpse of the problem in a scene describing the trepidation many black patients felt when putting their health in the hands of a black doctor, having previously learned to associate medical skill exclusively with white practitioners. Indeed, the prominent nineteenth-century narratives of former slaves, such as those by Frederick Douglass (*Narrative of the Life of Frederick Douglass*, 1845) and Harriet Jacobs (*Incidents in the Life of a Slave Girl*, 1861), as well as militant antislavery orations like David Walker's *Appeal* (1829), tended to devote several pages to condemning the psychology of some blacks—enslaved as well as free—who identified with their white masters more deeply than they did with their black brethren and sistren. In chapter 3 of his *Narrative*, Douglass recalls fellow captives looking down on the slaves of another master who owned fewer bondspeople or had lesser power than their own master: "They seemed to think that the greatness of their masters was transferrable to themselves. It was considered as being bad enough to be a slave; but to be a poor man's slave was deemed a disgrace indeed!" (33).

Black affirmation in the United States, as in Latin America, has no greater raison d'être than to provide an antidote to the inferiority complex that the architects of the colonial transaction inculcated in the descendants of enslaved Africans, following the conquest of the Americas. It works to combat the enduring effects of the negrophobia that for centuries informed thinking about race and ethnic difference throughout our hemisphere. In that respect, while allowing Villanueva and Benítez to convey their joy at being Afro-Latina/os through references to the musical, linguistic, and culinary virtues of their ancestry, ESPN producers, again, deserve recognition for avoiding the folly of explaining (or glorifying) Afro-Latinidad. The best thing a person of African and Hispanic descent can do for their identity is to leave it undefined to avoid unleashing the epistemic pandemonium that might otherwise ensue.

The Afro-Latino label emerges as a reactive identity. It reacts to the racist regimes generated by the unique manifestations of imperialism and slavery in North and South America. These forms of domination distinguished themselves from previous chapters in the history of enslavement by the central role they assigned to ancestry when measuring a person's worth. That distinction culminated in the birth of societies whose cultural logic structured social relations according to a dogma that upheld inherent ontological inequalities among the various branches of the human species. The material conditions that brought this new ethnoracial reality into being, rather than any metaphysics of identity, ought to take precedence when attempting to explain or understand its meaning. That inquiry, which I and others have taken up elsewhere, lies outside the scope of this chapter. To call oneself an Afro-Latina/o, Asian Latina/o, or Indigenous Latina/o is to expose the Eurocentric bias at the core of Latinidad. Hispanics of African, Asian, or Indigenous heritage find it tempting to uphold a label that marks their distinct segment within the Latino panethnicity. It is a way to demand recognition and render themselves visible and legible before the eyes of both the Hispanic and Anglo worlds.

Before moving on to invoke the panhemispheric history that produced

Afro-Latinidad as a distinct identity location that a black person from the Hispanic world might embrace, a note on the currency of the label may come in handy. I use the term *Afro-Latina/o* in this chapter to name the African-descended portion of the US Hispanic population, while referring to their counterparts in societies south of the Rio Grande as *Afro-Latin Americans*. Similarly, the term *Afro-Hispanic* speaks of black people anywhere in the hemisphere, Spain, or elsewhere in the vast geographical space where the Spanish Empire once held sway, irrespective of chronology. While the chronology evoked in this chapter will correspond to the rise of Latina/os as an ethnically differentiated segment of the US population in the twentieth century, it behooves us to acknowledge the early presence of Afro-Hispanics in North America several centuries prior to the emergence of the United States. That presence started with Juan Ponce de León's 1513 exploratory expedition to Florida. His crew included the converted Christian and enslaved African Juan Garrido, who had previously accompanied the conquistador in the invasion of Puerto Rico.[2] Also, a North African black servant named Estevanico (referred to in various historical sources as Estevan or Esteban) formed part of the ill-fated 1527 voyage to Florida led by Pánfilo de Narváez. Estevanico figures as one of only four crew members who survived along with Alvar Núñez Cabeza de Vaca, the treasurer who told the story of the failed expedition in his 1542 memoir *Relación*.[3] In 1539, Estevanico appears as the official guide to a reconnaissance mission led by Fray Marcos de Niza from Mexico City into the Zuni territory in western New Mexico, where the missionary thought he would find the legendary Seven Cities of Cibola.[4] After this collaboration, the guide falls off the historical record, with Father Marcos going back to Mexico City before venturing to reconnect with Estevanico in Zuni territory. The following year, a mission sponsored by conquistador Francisco Vázquez de Coronado and Viceroy Antonio de Mendoza would explore the same region, but the sequence of events places Estevanico as the first non-Indigenous explorer of Zuni territory. Concomitantly, on the east coast in 1613, "a free mulatto from Santo Domingo" named Juan Rodriguez would settle on the land that subsequently became New York City, preceding the Dutch settlement that would start there nearly a decade later (Torres-Saillant and Hernández, "Community" 226).

Insofar as these instances of an Afro-Hispanic presence in the colonial period occurred as individual undertakings, they contribute little to a genealogy of Afro-Latinidad as a social identity with relevance for us today. Social identities, by definition, have little to do with individuals. When applied to those occupying a lesser rank in the structure of power, they operate as stigmas that brand groups, with individuals serving merely as illustrative samples of the character of the groups. Individuality must step out the moment racializing or ethnic othering comes in. Afro-Latinidad emerges as an option for a collective to embrace when historical circumstances enable it, which did not happen until quite recently. The dark-skinned Dominican women who in the 1940s came to Washington, DC, as maids of the light-skinned diplomats of Rafael Leónidas Trujillo's dictatorship had their ethnoracial allegiance determined by Jim Crow segregation, which barred them from seeking residence in the areas that their light-skinned employers could legally inhabit. As sociologist Ginetta Candelario has shown in *Black behind the Ears: Dominican Racial Identity from Museums to Beauty Shops*, these Afro-Dominicans went to live in mostly African American—or, in keeping with the parlance of the day, "Negro"—neighborhoods, often embracing the ethnoracial identity of their neighbors. The United States did not offer a site of belonging designed for piecing together the Hispanic and the black components of their ancestry without considerable stress. Perhaps the Afro-Puerto Rican Arturo (Arthur) Schomburg, a full-fledged member of the Harlem Renaissance intelligentsia, deserves credit for articulating via his lifelong praxis the search for an Afro-Latino site of identity that he clearly deemed wanting, as we gather from the work of such historians as Jesse Hoffnung-Garskoff (37–38).

The racial dramas endured by Afro-Cuban Evelio Grillo and the Afro–Puerto Rican Piri Thomas merit mention, insofar as they set forth telling glimpses of the difficult location that Afro-Hispanics inhabited in the decades before Afro-Latinidad became a readily available site of ethnoracial identification. On the one hand, Grillo's *Black Cuban, Black American: A Memoir* (2000) tells the story of a Cuban of African ancestry who became African American by virtue of his inability to find a space of belonging among the predominantly white Cuban community of Tampa. Thomas's *Down These Mean Streets*, on the other hand, dramatizes the existential plight of a New York–born Puerto Rican, the son of a black Cuban father and white Boricua mother, who finds it hard to navigate the complexity of a racially mixed ancestry in a society dominated by the ideology of racial purity. Grillo contends with negrophobia, as manifested publicly in Jim Crow segregation, which coincided smoothly with the racial mores of white Cubans in Tampa. Thomas confronts the existential discomfort produced by the two distinct legacies of racism that assail him in his Manhattan neighborhood and even in his household. He deals with the island-grown bias of the Hispanic world, transmitted to him via his mother's negrophobic expressions of parental love. She treats him to words of endearment encased in disparaging terms: "I have to love you because only your mother could love you, *un negrito* and ugly" (19). Outside of the home, he must ward off racial insults from members of rival gangs vying for ownership of the streets. He tastes the sour reality of antiblackness cultivated on the US mainland over two centuries. Like Schomburg, Piri tries to defect from the Hispanic side of his ancestry in order to seek racial refuge in the African American experience, but like Schomburg again, he fails to attain a harmonious identity there, reflecting, "I was a Puerto Rican trying to make a Negro" (Thomas 177).

The foregoing examples lend credence to the claim that Afro-Latino identity springs from the difficulty of achieving a comfortable sense of belonging among regular Latina/os, who themselves, irrespective of phenotype, have had their perception and desires molded by the Caucasian ideal. Heirs of both Anglo and Iberian histories of white worshipping and concomitant vilification of blackness, white and mestizo Latina/os rarely display a predisposition to embrace Afro-Latina/os without pause. The Hispanic/Latino label officially recognized a panethnicity as one of the five ethnoracially differentiated segments of the US population. This naming created the necessary conditions for US Hispanics of African ancestry to conceptualize for themselves a further segmentation. In that respect, Afro-Latinidad as a social identity comes into being on the heels of the widespread circulation of the Hispanic/Latino label to acknowledge Americans who traced their origins to the Iberian world as one of the country's minority populations.

The emergence of this identity category occurred, of course, amid the social movements that swept US society from the 1950s through the 1970s. With the African American–led Civil Rights Movement at its center, these instances of massive civic engagement catalyzed an increased urgency on the part of marginalized groups to assert the right to their difference vis-à-vis the prevailing homogenized ideal of American national identity. US Hispanics, no less than African Americans, Native Americans, and Asian Americans, sought to subvert the dogma of assimilation, which for at least a century had upheld a doctrine of Americanness that required citizens, irrespective of ancestry, to refashion themselves by shedding the trappings of their origins. As asserting the right to one's difference became a viable, even desirable cause, one that US Hispanics themselves had embraced, it did not take long for Afro-Hispanics to realize that they had their own additional layer of difference for which to advocate. Because Latinidad alone did not suffice to grant them access to an identity space free of misrecognition and exclusion, Afro-Hispanics in the United States have increasingly endeavored to articulate their further differentiated sites of belonging within the larger Latino panethnicity.

Over the last few decades the field of Latino studies has sought to map the conditions of Afro-Latina/os and Afro-Latin Americans vis-à-vis their counterparts in the larger non-black US Hispanic panethnicity or the non-black national population in one Latin American country or another. A few of the milestone publications merit mention for their immediate relevance, beginning with the 1995 collection *No Longer Invisible: Afro-Latin Americans Today*, edited by the human-rights advocacy organization Minority Rights Group. Consisting of scholarly overviews of the history and present conditions of people of African descent in sixteen Latin American countries, the volume ends with a comprehensive commentary by Brown University anthropologist Anani Dzidzienyo, who invites readers to consider whether Afro-Latin Americans can retain their sense of national identity unaltered when they cross over to the United States, where a recognition of one's "race" often trumps (or at least competes with) one's allegiance to the nationality of a home country. Dzidzienyo presciently asked, "Do Dominicans in the United States hold steadfastly to the single commonality of Dominicanness, irrespective of race or colour?" (353). By means of queries of this kind, he posited a panhemispheric framework for the study of issues surrounding black Hispanic heritage.

A decade later, Dzidzienyo paired up with literary scholar Suzanne Oboler in assembling *Neither Enemies nor Friends: Latinos, Blacks, Afro-Latinos* (2005), a volume whose fifteen chapters encompass experiences of racialization by Afro-Hispanics in the United States, as well as in Latin America. The collection includes the exploration of telling moments in the history of African American and Latino relations in US society, and the overall emergence of Afro-Latinidad. For example, in his solid overview of political collaboration and coalition building, Mark Sawyer places particular emphasis on the potential of such "diaspora research" to shed light on the political conundrums that draw such groups together, as well as the goal "to expand identities and create new political possibilities" (276). To cite only one more contribution to the volume, one might highlight a piece by anthropologist Mark Anderson that considers "the intricacies and ironies of the transnational dimension" in the lives of Garifuna in both Honduras and the United States (112). Anderson finds that Garifuna assert their identification with being "black" in Honduras more than they do in the United States, where they seem to find use in accentuating the Hispanic component of their heritage in order to distinguish themselves from African Americans (112). In other words, while assertive of their blackness, Garifuna seem no less intent on affirming the distinct culture their ancestors created as African-descended Hondurans.

While inherently valuable as a compilation of unique materials pertinent to the black experience in the Iberian world from the sixteenth to the nineteenth centuries, the collection *Afro-Latino Voices: Narratives from the Early Modern Ibero-Atlantic World, 1550–1812* (2009), edited by literary scholar Kathryn Joy McKnight and historian Leo J. Garofalo, illustrates the changing face of the academic field where one would place the study of Afro-Latina/os. The editors have no qualms about using the term *Afro-Latina/os* to name the groups and individuals whose experiences their anthology covers, which clearly take place outside the geography of knowledge of Latino studies, as a subsection of ethnic studies in the United States. At this point it would seem fruitless to wish to cordon off the territory of Latino studies, or to wish to control the nomenclature produced by scholars in the field to denote the regions and demography of their inquiries. Already by 2000, in a study titled *Hispanic/Latino Identity: A Philosophical Perspective*, Jorge J. E. Gracia surveyed the ontology of the Iberian world by means of a wide lens that encompassed US Hispanics, Iberian-descended Latin Americans, Spaniards, Amerindians (Indigenous people), and Africans (61). Gracia reads *Latinidad* as a fluid, expansive, and inclusive site of ethnoracial identity that exists along a panethnic, transnational, and multicultural plane of signification.

Latino Studies Transcending the Ethnic Contours of the US

According to Benita Heiskanen, the field of "transnational Latino studies" that some scholars now embrace covers a geography of knowledge that can conceivably bring ethnic and area studies together while straddling the cultural histories of the old and new worlds. To add to this selective chronology, we can view the collection *The Afro-Latin@ Reader* (2010), edited by Miriam Jiménez Román and Juan Flores, as the natural outcome of a quarter-century of scholarship and activism by multiple authors on the black experience in the Americas. Jiménez Román had long occupied herself with the subject of panhemispheric Afro-Hispanic identity as a researcher and curator of sociohistorical exhibitions at the New York Public Library's Schomburg Center for Research in Black Culture. She also served as managing editor of *Centro Journal* of the Center for Puerto Rican Studies at Hunter College, City University of New York (CUNY). Flores, who was director of the Centro de Estudios Puertorriqueños at one point, had achieved distinction as a scholar who excelled in the study of Puerto Rican and pan-Latino cultural discourse, including literature, music, and the arts. In 2006 the couple collaborated with George Priestly, a noted Afro-Panamanian political scientist who headed the Latin American and Latino Studies Program at Queens College, CUNY, in a project that sought to disseminate knowledge and foster dialogue about the conditions of Afro-Hispanics in the United States. With support from the Ford Foundation, they launched an ambitious undertaking that convened scholars as well as civil-rights activists and cultural advocates. If not to articulate a shared vision, they would at least come together in a productive conversation.

Their collaboration bifurcated shortly thereafter, resulting in the Afro-Latino Project, headed by Priestly in Queens, and the Afro-Latin@ Forum led by Jiménez Román and Flores in Manhattan.

Not unlike their counterparts in Queens, Jiménez Román and Flores convened many fruitful conversations on various facets of the Afro-Latino experience, but their *Afro-Latin@ Reader* stands as their most tangible contribution. As editors, they used to great advantage the legacy inherited from previous scholars, judiciously selecting nearly seventy pieces of moderate length, the majority previously published. The manageable size of the texts included, as well as the diversity of topics and approaches, rendered the volume superbly suited for use in an undergraduate classroom setting. One of the most comprehensive compilations available on the academic market thus far, the anthology stands as an eloquent testimony to the remarkable quantity of data, resources, and analyses available to scholars and educators exploring questions related to the Afro-Latino experience. This subject has lately elicited greater attention and continues to show signs of emerging as a discrete field of ethnoracial inquiry.

Two-Way Negrophobia

As a conglomerate of national and ancestral origins, the Hispanic or Latino label names a panethnic designation encompassing (at the time of this writing) over fifty million members of the US population. With its formal genesis in the 1977 Office of Management and Budget's Statistical Directive 15, which came about to address a need for reliable data that would enable the government to implement the mandates of the Voting Rights Act of 1965 and Title VII of the Civil Rights Act, the label survives as a joust between competing desires (Hollinger 33). On the one hand, in view of political expediency, affiliation to the panethnic Hispanic or Latino heritage attests to an in-group longing for the greater empowerment that the strength of numbers presumably promises. On the other hand, members still seem to wish for acknowledgment of the multiple national origins that make up their composite panethnicity, to account for differences in culture, language, region, religion, and political memory. In other words, they wish to promote a sense of the oneness of their impressive demographic force, while simultaneously seeking to fend off the media images and voices of public discourse that would too easily reduce them to a homogeneous mass.

In her highly acclaimed chick lit novel *The Dirty Girls Social Club* (2004), Alisa Valdés-Rodríguez sets forth a poignant critique of the homogenizing compulsion that plagues American society in matters of race and ethnicity.

Her main character, Lauren Fernández, who claims Hispanic heritage on account of her white Cuban father, but who is also "half white trash, born and raised in New Orleans," describes herself as "a pretty good journalist" but "not a good Latina," as judged by her bosses at the *Boston Gazette*, the newspaper for which she writes the weekly column My Life. She constantly has to check her temper and formulate noncombative ways of answering or deflecting odd questions about Latino life. When her Anglo editor, Chuck Spring, asks her about the position of Latina/os on current events, she tells him she does not know but would find out shortly as she has scheduled a conference call "with them" later in the afternoon. He takes her facetious response seriously. To avoid succumbing to angry outbursts, Lauren takes time off to cool down after Chuck finds fault with her column for not being "Latina" enough (5, 7, 164).

Dirty Girls intimates that the expectation for Latinas and Latinos to look, think, and behave in keeping with a panethnically preordained script operates internally no less than externally, bringing along arbitrary demands that impact lives negatively. The novel features a television news anchor named Elizabeth Cruz, a stunning, dark-complexioned black woman who migrated from Colombia. Elizabeth "has a hard time" attracting dates due to the misrecognition and stigma that her skin color elicits (37). Neither black nor white men can figure her out, apparently; nor does her appearance fare particularly well among Latina/os. The narrator tells us that, irrespective of their own color, Hispanic men "want a light girl. You can see it in our soap operas and magazines" (38). As a mixed but white-presenting person, Lauren shares the phenotype of her bosses at the paper. She discovers to her astonishment that the Promotions Department has doctored her face in the publicity photos, making her darker to accentuate her "Latina" appearance (10). The realization that she could look too white to be Latina while her Afro-Colombian friend would not qualify for the same category on account of a "deep dark" hue (38) shakes up Lauren's understanding about the delusional racial imaginaries operative on both sides of the Rio Grande. She poignantly observes that in the United States "Hollywood pretends that we all look like Penelope Cruz and JLo," whereas representations in the Latin American media seem to emerge out of the belief "that we all look like a Swedish exchange student or Pamela Anderson" (38). Through the chick lit genre, a type of popular fiction that generally promises readers light and digestible fare, *Dirty Girls* treads some daring ground as it explores the unsettling issues of identity that are showcased in the plights of both Lauren and Elizabeth.

Perhaps nothing distinguishes Afro-Latina/os from other segments of the US population more manifestly than the double-pronged structure of the racist legacy they must navigate. As people with African ancestry who trace their origins to Latin America, the Caribbean, and other sites of the Hispanic world, they exist at the existential crossroads of two traditions of ethnoracial disparagement: the Iberian on one side of the Western hemisphere, and the Anglo on the other. Intra-Latino hyphenation becomes a serious option for people of Hispanic origin whose phenotype, by virtue of ancestral origins outside of Europe or the Middle East, does not match the ideal type that the prevailing image of Latina/os summons to mind. Intra-Latino hyphenation offers them refuge in alternative locations of identity even while they may feel no need to delink from their affiliation to the panethnicity, as the case of the Honduran American Garifuna would illustrate. Overall, an intra-Latino hyphenation such as *Afro-Latinidad* becomes a useful identity marker to help Hispanics of African descent overcome the barrier that obstructs their visibility and recognition as "regular" Latina/os in the United States or "regular" Latin Americans in countries south of the Rio Grande. This is precisely the plight that afflicts the Afro-Colombian Elizabeth in the novel by Valdés-Rodríguez. When they look at social and historical phenomena across the hemispheric geography of their heritage, Afro-Latina/os cannot avoid encountering negrophobia embedded as a national patrimony in their ancestral homelands, no less than in their country of civic belonging. They will recognize this inheritance in official state practices, rules governing social relations, differential access to material well-being, cultural biases, and bodies of discourse developed with the purpose of impeding or conditioning their belonging to the citizenry and community. The two traditions of othering may coalesce into composite instances of disqualification from ready recognition within the panethnic group, much to the detriment of black Hispanics in the United States.

We can read the coming together of the Hispanic and Anglo negrophobic traditions in an episode experienced at the start of the 1960s by an eighteen-year-old Afro-Puerto Rican soldier named Rubén Díaz, who became a vocal New York state senator, known for a mixture of progressive and conservative positions that distinguished his legislative platform. His story, in a nutshell, describes the experience of a young man who, at one point, found himself assailed jointly by two types of Jim Crow law, one in effect legally in the US mainland and the other a de facto social practice in his place of birth. Senator Díaz evoked the racial episode in question on January 22, 2014, during the discussion of a motion to honor the legacy of Martin Luther King, Jr. The senator, seventy-one at the time, used his turn in the deliberations to support the motion by settling accounts with current public servants whom he viewed as failing to uphold the values preached by Dr. King. Díaz criticized a fellow state senator, a younger, fair-skinned colleague named Gustavo Rivera, who, like Díaz, was born in Puerto Rico. Díaz accused Rivera of mocking his strongly accented English. At this point in his harangue, Díaz used the occasion to share with fellow legislators his painful encounter with Hispanic and Anglo racism nearly sixty years earlier. A recent recruit in the US Army, stationed at Fort Buchanan, a military installation located in the metropolitan area of San Juan, Díaz formed part of a detachment sent from Puerto Rico to Fort Jackson in South Carolina. A YouTube video of the exchange on the Senate floor exposes the level of emotion and lingering bitterness with which Díaz recalled a day when he and his white Puerto Rican comrades went to have a drink at a bar in Columbia. A waiter came and promptly served his companions, but when it was time to take his order, his blackness presented a problem. The waiter stood behind him and said plainly, "Whatever you're looking for, we don't got it here."

The few details given by Díaz would set the story in 1961, the year when the Confederate battle flag went up on the South Carolina State House. During the flag-hoisting ceremony, among the messages conveyed by dignitaries addressing the whites-only crowd on the state grounds, two stand out as particularly memorable. South Carolina State Senator John D. Long invoked the heroic contributions of the Ku Klux Klan and the Red Shirts, two white supremacist organizations that had terrorized African Americans since the late nineteenth century, in helping restore the "dignity" of the South from its earlier humiliation. By "humiliation," Senator Long was referring to the "dishonor" the South had supposedly endured during the Reconstruction Era. This was the time from 1865 to 1877 when the US Civil War's victorious Northern troops occupied the South in order to help implement the terms of the Emancipation Proclamation that gave formerly enslaved blacks their freedom, legally speaking. After the state legislator, the other speaker, US Senator Strom Thurmond, was no less disdainful of the idea that blacks deserved treatment as the equals of whites. At that time, in the fifth year of forty-eight he would spend in that office, having previously served in the South Carolina legislature and as governor of the state, Thurmond expressed nothing but contempt for the doctrine of racial equality. He cheered his segregationist listeners with the assurance that the US Constitution did not anywhere "hint a purpose to ensure equality of man or things" and that the founders meant the country as a republic, not a democracy "where everyone rules and majority rule is absolute" (Bursey). Thurmond construed equality and inclusion, the goals behind desegregation, as threats to the very survival of the United States, characterizing the goal of "social equality among diverse races" as "the surest method" to destroy "free governments" (Bursey).

Thinking back to South Carolina in 1961, the waiter could not even have imagined breaking the segregation law by welcoming and serving the young

Díaz. US soldier or not, the customer was still a "Negro." Probably for that reason, Díaz did not focus on the waiter when recounting the story in 2014. Instead, he concentrated on his compatriots and fellow soldiers, who, in his view, "should have left that place with me, but no, they stayed." Perhaps his fellow soldiers had impediments of their own that kept them from displaying the solidarity that Díaz would have liked to see. While the island of Puerto Rico did not have Jim Crow laws that officially kept the "races" apart, it was not devoid of the long legacy of postplantation racism that had weakened ties of solidarity across ancestral differences. In a pathbreaking study entitled *Narciso descubre su trasero: El negro en la cultura puertorriqueña* (1974), the Afro–Puerto Rican scholar Isabelo Zenón Cruz captured the pervasive disparagement of African ancestry in his homeland and the normalizing of whiteness as a core element of Puerto Rican identity and cultural history. The author observes that black Puerto Ricans look at their likeness "in the distorted mirror" constructed by the commissar of national identity: "the white man." Thus "alienated" from "the image of Puerto-Ricanness" and effectively "injured, ill-treated, and repulsed *ad nauseam*," black inhabitants of the island have "learned to despise themselves" (Zenón Cruz 17).

Indeed, Puerto Rican leaders advocating statehood following the 1898 US takeover emphasized the visage of their people as whiter and more sophisticated than those in neighboring islands in the Hispanic Caribbean. The physician and political thinker José Celso Barbosa, himself of African ancestry, advanced the view that the island would lose out by aligning itself with other Caribbean nations in an "Antillean Confederation" and should seek instead an association with "a powerful and well-organized nation," namely, the US (qtd. in Ramos 29–30). More pointedly, in 1900, as Congress deliberated on the island's suitability for membership in the Union, the politician José Julio Henna wrote an open letter addressed "To the American People" seeking to dispel the doubts he suspected the mainlanders harbored about his people's ancestry. He described the island's population as "a million inhabitants, people of white race and Christian faith, with the refinement, culture, and intelligence of an ancient civilization" (qtd. in Ramos 69).

Perhaps the future Senator Díaz, as a naive US soldier entering Jim Crow country in South Carolina, was in no position to consider that the light-skinned recruits who traveled with him may have had their consciousness trained by a sort of island-based color line. Their homegrown color consciousness, while less clearly codified by means of overt segregation laws like those followed by the waiter at the bar, may have had a numbing effect on the soldiers' sense of solidarity. Conceivably, at that moment, the phenotype of the fellow soldier being denied service may have made the affront easier to stomach, since his blackness perhaps impeded immediate empathy. His features did not accord with the white Puerto Rican model vaunted by Henna in 1900 or other influential voices of later generations. Nor did they accord with the features discernible in the profile of the *jíbaro*, the rustic farmer of European descent who, from the 1930s onward, gained prominence as an embodiment of the ideal Puerto Rican, becoming the mascot of the Popular Democratic Party founded by Luis Muñoz Marín in 1938. In her study of Puerto Rican women writers in Borinquen and the US mainland, literary scholar Marisel C. Moreno argues convincingly for this complex engagement. When discussing Esmeralda Santiago's *When I Was Puerto Rican* (1993), for instance, she points out how the text endeavors to embrace "*el muñocismo*'s quest to cement the jíbaro as the foundation of *puertorriqueñidad*" while also breaking with the tenets of "the jíbarista discourse" by seeming to make room for a sort of "Afra-jíbara experience," thereby better accommodating the diverse appearances of Puerto Ricans in the diaspora (Moreno 119–122 et passim).[5]

In 1960s Puerto Rico, as elsewhere in the Hispanophone and Lusophone parts of the Americas, blackness remained outside official depictions of the face of the nation. The citizenry had learned to recognize blackness as relegated to certain differentiated sites of the national experience, such as athletics, performing arts, folklore and other forms of expressive culture, domestic labor, and unlawful activity. Blackness, in fact, did inhabit other core sites of the national experience. It did so, however, without being an exemplar of the collective Puerto Rican family. It inhabited those sites in a state of alterity vis-à-vis the norm, one that insisted upon its whiteness, irrespective of the diverse phenotypes prevalent in the population. A pattern had thereby emerged that caused African-descended peoples to attain visibility only in those spaces where the national imaginary had learned to notice them, thanks to the racial literacy imparted to the citizenry during the period of Spanish colonial domination and its sequel in the period of US hegemony. That the social psychology involved continued to influence the climate of human relations across the generations can be deduced from the present-day practice of law enforcement, which tends to approach the less-valued segments of the population with a predisposition to find them deserving of punishment, violent handling, or summary killing. As a result, in Puerto Rico, for instance, low-income populations and those of African descent, along with Dominican immigrants (who stand out in the national Puerto Rican imaginary for their blackness), have long suffered abuse at the hands of the police, who benefit from a prevailing culture of impunity.[6]

The ethnoracial drama that emerges from the foregoing scattered bits of social and intellectual history gains layers of complexity when Puerto Ricans come to inhabit the social margins of the US mainland, their US citizenship notwithstanding. A long history of contact with US blackness, consisting of collaboration, competition, harmony, and acrimony with African Americans after the great exodus from the island in the 1940s, has offered mainland Puerto Ricans an array of identity locations to inhabit the intersection of black and Boricua. The speaker in Willie Perdomo's poem "Nigger-Reecan Blues" wrestles with how best to answer the either/or question of belonging: "Hey, Willie. What are you, man? Boricua? Moreno? Que? Are you / Black? Puerto Rican?" (Perdomo 19). The poem's closing stanza settles for an answer that draws not on a metaphysics of identity but on a historical memory of shared disdain: the Madison Avenue lady who would tighten the grip on her purse as he approaches her, the cab driver who would switch the Off Duty sign on to avoid him as a passenger, or the media venues that would represent him only in association with violence, whether as victim or perpetrator. Thus, his answer to the question simply dismantles the either/or formulation:

> I'm a spic! I'm a nigger!
> Spic! Spic! Just like a nigger!
> Neglected, rejected, oppressed and dispossessed
> From banana boats to tenements
> Street gangs to regiments
> Spic, spic, spic. I ain't nooooo different than a nigger! (20–21)

An overview of racist pronouncements by the most revered intellects of the Northern and Southern Hemispheres—a task well beyond the scope of this chapter—could easily dispel any lingering view of negrophobia as somehow less widespread or virulent in Hispanic America than in Anglo America. Let us, for the sake of concision, simply draw a parallel between two figures whose legacies have had a comparable influence on the political and intellectual histories of Latin America and the United States, respectively. The venerated General Simón Bolívar, one of the most enlightened of the Ibero-American leaders heading the nineteenth-century independence movement from Imperial Spain, conceived of an emancipation scheme that entailed the decimation of the enslaved black population by the time military victory over the Spanish forces was achieved. In an April 20, 1820, memorandum to his comrade General Francisco de Paula Santander, he explained his order to free "all slaves available for bearing arms" and suitable for enlisting in the independence forces (Bolivar 222). Understanding that for the slaves there was no "more fitting or proper means by which to win freedom than to fight for it," and thinking it unfair for "free men" to "die for the liberation of the slaves," Bolívar posed this chilling rhetorical question: "Is it not proper that the slaves should acquire their rights on the battlefield and that their dangerous numbers should be lessened by a process both just and effective?" (223). As he envisioned upcoming clashes with the Spanish Army in Cundinamarca, the seat of power of New Granada (present-day Colombia), Bolívar went on to note that Venezuela had already experienced the undesirable outcome of the free population dying and the unfree surviving: "I know not whether or not this is prudent, but I do know that, unless we employ the slaves in Cundinamarca, they will outlive us again" (223). He could simply not bring himself to conceive of free blacks moving about in large numbers as citizens of the new republics that would emerge from the independence effort.

When it came to racial thought, then, Bolívar revealed a clear ideological kinship to the no-less-enlightened Anglo statesman Thomas Jefferson. Decades earlier, Jefferson had voiced his strong belief that free blacks could not become integrated into US society as citizens due to their moral, intellectual, and spiritual inferiority, not to mention their incapacity for improvement and their unsightly phenotype (Jefferson 264–270). The leader did not conceive of schemes to decimate the bondspeople, as would Bolívar, mostly because the greater success of the slave economy in the United States rendered them highly valuable as producers of wealth and as commodities themselves. To his credit, he had enough foresight to realize that one day bondspeople would become free; he could not, however, fathom their peaceful coexistence with whites. Perhaps more than the possibility of friction due to any rancor the free blacks might harbor against whites as their former masters, Jefferson found the likelihood that the two populations might interbreed especially unsettling, hence his conviction that upon emancipation, the country would simply have to coordinate the emigration of the former slaves "to such place as the circumstances of the time should render most proper" (264). Because he spent several pages of his only book, *Notes on the State of Virginia* (1785), conceptualizing the inferiority of blacks and fervently advancing his case (the poor quality of his reasoning and the odd handling of what he took for data notwithstanding), he stands among the intellectual founding fathers of US negrophobia; John C. Calhoun, Woodrow Wilson, and George C. Wallace, to name only three of the most virulent negrophobes in US history, may be thought of as Jefferson's heirs in this regard.

It would not work, however, to pursue the parallel further by presenting the likes of José Antonio Saco (1797–1879), Juan Bautista Alberdi (1810–1884), Domingo Faustino Sarmiento (1811–1888), José Vasconcelos (1882–1959), and José Carlos Mariátegui (1894–1930), among other prominent racist thinkers of Latin America, as Bolívar's intellectual heirs. Because the Spanish conquest and colonization of the Americas pioneered the construction of discourses of dehumanization, Iberian American authors have had an older and richer selection of intellectual ancestors to draw their racist dogma from, dating back to the first decades of the conquest. Readers will find, for instance, that the aspersions cast by Juan Ginés de Sepúlveda in his *Democrates Secundus* (1554) against the Indigenous peoples of the Americas, as a way to portray them unworthy of Christian piety and deserving of the bondage and destitution to which the Spanish invaders had subjected them, remained unmatched even by the most-acerbic negrophobic tirades produced by the apologists of plantation slavery in the US South during the nineteenth century.

Racism by Default

Although necessarily schematic, the preceding references to the racial views of leading social theorists, political thinkers, statesmen, literary scholars, and creative writers from both sides of the Rio Grande should buttress the claim that racism in the Americas operates as a default ideology. For countless generations, respect across ancestral and phenotypical difference in the region resulted from personal revelations. One thinks of Cuban ethnologist and sociologist Fernando Ortiz, who delinked from racist paradigms after having started his scholarly career under their powerful spell. His first books, *Los negros brujos* (1906) and *Los negros esclavos* (1916), were written while under the influence of theories suggesting heredity as the cause of a person's proclivity to bad behavior. These ideas, derived from the teachings of nineteenth-century Italian criminologist Cesare Lombroso, attributed to blacks the most criminal and immoral behavior on the island. He subsequently learned to recognize the humanity and creativity of the African-descended Cuban population. After his transformation, he became one of the leading scholars of the black experience in the Americas. His classic monograph *Contrapunteo cubano del tabaco y el azúcar* (1940) grants center stage to the defining role of the black experience in any credible account of Cuban culture. His essay *El engaño de las razas* (1946) sets out to dismantle the phony science and precarious arguments that until then had served as foundation for racist dogma. Ortiz mustered the foresight to remove the veil that had blurred his vision when looking at the value of the racially differentiated segments of the Cuban population, even though he grew up in a society that adhered fiercely to negrophobic paradigms.

The state of racial thought and feeling among the intelligentsia active in Cuba when Ortiz was a child might be gleaned from the interest that some of the country's most distinguished naturalists, physicians, anthropologists, and, of course, phrenologists had in the skull of famed Afro-Cuban independence fighter Antonio Maceo, the "Bronze Titan." After Maceo's death in 1896, his interred remains elicited the morbid attraction of scholars intrigued by his record of achievements *despite* his blackness. They viewed his corpse as a potential portal to unique racial knowledge. Intrigued by the widespread recognition of the "Bronze Titan" as a supposedly superior human being, scholars José R. Montalvo Covarrubias, Carlos de la Torre Huerta, and Luis Montané Dardé sought the proper permission from the family and exhumed Maceo's body on September 17, 1899. After their detailed study of every crevice of the warrior's skull, they could find comfort in their findings. For even though "many anthropological characteristics" would place Maceo in the "black type," he was apparently "closer to the white race." They could now scientifically affirm that indeed "Maceo may be considered a superior man" (Montalvo Covarrubias et al. 13). By establishing Maceo's closer proximity to "the white race," they confirmed the underlying premise of their study, namely, that "the crossing of whites and blacks produces an advantageous group when the influence of the former predominates but an inferior group when the two influences balance each other out, and even more so when the black influence exceeds the white" (2). With the Titan having his inconvenient blackness toned down by the powers of hybridity and "science," patriotic white Cubans could now continue to admire his greatness without the roadblock posed by his racial alterity.

Perhaps nothing other than the radical otherness of blackness can explain the extreme response of the Cuban government forces and the civilian militias that followed the civil rights demonstration organized by the Partido Independiente de Color on May 20, 1912. With a galvanizing force one would typically associate with a patriotic national resistance against foreign invaders, the government deployed a ruthless military offensive against the demonstrators that left over three thousand Afro-Cubans dead. The establishment press characterized the clash as a "race war," with the brunt of the casualties being black.[7] The recovery of Maceo's "whiteness" and the unwarranted military response to a rally of Afro-Cubans occurred in a country that, since 1898, alongside Puerto Rico, had belonged to the sphere of influence of the United States in a more literal way than any other Latin American nation. With the advent of that geopolitical reality, African-descended Cubans came to lose many of the gains they had accrued over generations of social-justice struggle.

Afro-Latinidad and Humane Solidarity

To be sure, while Cuba did not import its racism from the United States, the island country does grant us a glimpse of the social shifts that can occur when the Northern and Southern hemispheric traditions of racial othering coincide in one national jurisdiction. The Hispanic Caribbean, as the above discussions of Puerto Rico and Cuba would suggest, sets forth particularly disturbing examples of the confluence of Hispanic and Anglo legacies of negrophobia operating in unison through the history of direct US intervention in those areas, as well as through the immigrant and diasporic presence of their populations in the US mainland. The United States has played a role in the affairs of the Dominican Republic since the late 1860s, when Ulysses S. Grant's administration obsessed about annexing the country, an objective that did not receive the necessary votes in Congress. The decades that followed witnessed the control of Dominican customs revenue by the San Domingo Improvement Company, a private US corporation as of 1893. A State Department arbitration on behalf of the company would lead to turning the Dominican Republic into a US protectorate, beginning in 1905. The US military occupation of the country from 1916 to 1924 followed. Occurring under the watch of Woodrow Wilson, a bona fide negrophobe who resegregated all federal offices the very moment he stepped into the White House in 1913, the US occupation had an unsurprising racial dimension, as Dominicans belonged among those peoples whom Wilson viewed as "incapable of governing themselves" (García-Peña 74–75). More specifically, the occupying forces placed a high premium on attacking folk rituals and religious practices of African origin prevalent in the country's rural areas, as Lorgia García Peña, for example, has shown.

Raised in Santo Domingo during those years marked by pronounced US involvement in Dominican society, the literary scholar Pedro Henríquez Ureña came to the United States in 1901, right after high school, and received his higher education at the University of Minnesota. Henríquez Ureña says nothing about race in his much-admired study *La cultura y las letras coloniales en Santo Domingo* (1936), a book that sets out to document the flourishing of literature and the arts in the island during the early period of the conquest and colonization of the Americas. Hispaniola had been at the core of the Spanish settlers' project to recreate their world on the ruins of the societies they dismantled. They transplanted their arts and cultures to the island while simultaneously crushing the local expressions rooted in Indigenous and African-descended experience. Henríquez Ureña's contemporary, Américo Lugo, the author of the first twentieth-century survey of Dominican literature, similarly evoked the efflorescence of artistic and intellectual life in early Santo Domingo. The creative ebullience of the settlers at the time encouraged them to apply the epithet "Athens of the New World" to the colony, a feat that Lugo credited to the motherland, Spain, "because she weaned us on her breast, and in her arms she lulled us to sleep" (94–95).

Henríquez Ureña evoked the glories of Imperial Spain's cultural legacy in the Americas, largely omitting reference to the accompanying violence and genocide. Such a selective memory would become the cultural frame of reference for the conquered peoples and their descendants. We might note his highlighting, for instance, the rise in seventeenth-century Santo Domingo of Tomás Rodríguez de Sosa. Born on the island to an enslaved mother, Rodríguez de Sosa escaped his captivity to become "a venerated priest and a famous orator" (*La cultura* 358–359). One easily discerns that what renders Rodríguez de Sosa worthy of memorializing in the eyes of Henríquez Ureña is his mastery of the bodies of knowledge and ways of knowing that correspond to the cultural legacy of the conquerors. Henríquez Ureña's account of Santo Domingo's colonial culture covers strictly the arts and expressive forms of the settlers; it makes little, if any, reference to cultural survival tools derived from the traditions of the Indigenous inhabitants and black captives of the land. It would take a long time for memory, imagination, or desire for self-expression to become a national interest—at least eight decades after he published *La cultura y las letras coloniales en Santo Domingo*. The Eurocentric narrative of the island's history had become normative by the mid-nineteenth century when the colony of Santo Domingo became the Dominican Republic. The nation's story extolled the glories of Spain's first colony in the Americas, along with the caliber of the families that lived there, many of whom had to emigrate due to the gradual loss of significance of Santo Domingo, once greater wealth was to be found elsewhere as the economy of pillage expanded to the South American mainland. A study of the island today, following the same chronology outlined by Henríquez Ureña—especially if done by a Dominican in the US academy—would probably stress the place of Santo Domingo as the "cradle of blackness in the Americas" (Torres-Saillant, "Dominican Republic" 110). But before the mid-twentieth century, such a perspective would have tried the imagination of the learned elites throughout Latin America and the Caribbean, a region whose intelligentsia and political leaders were, in most cases, the descendants of the settlers who came to the hemisphere during the colonial transaction.

Indeed, examining and rectifying the story of race relations in the country, with an eye on justice, equality, and inclusion, now constitutes the bulk of the research conducted by Dominican studies scholars in the US academy. By the time Henríquez Ureña reached adolescence, the national intelligentsia still lacked a language with which to speak of equality across ancestries, phenotypes, and cultural heritages. Negrophobia, Eurocentrism, and the white supremacist imaginary had been baked into the very idea of Dominicanness, in spite of the dark hue and diverse origins of the majority of the population. A 1907 general guide to Dominican society prepared for visitors by journalist, educator, and diplomat Enrique Deschamps sets forth a representative sample of racial thoughts and feelings at the time. In the section of his *guía* that evokes the early years of the colony of Santo Domingo, Deschamps cites the comeliness of the Taínos encountered by Christopher Columbus in 1492 using this problematic praise: "with beautiful and attractive figures, fine and soft skin *despite* their dark color" (72, my emphasis). Of the African workers brought forcibly to fuel the colonial machine, Deschamps speaks thusly: "In spite of the abuses to which their captivity made them victims, and although the number of males among them exceeded that of the females, the African race, contrary to the indigenous population, multiplied rapidly, *deriving physical and moral advantages* from their crossing with the European and indigenous races with which they immediately came into contact" (72, my emphasis). Since Deschamps also indicts the abusive treatment to which the white masters subjected their enslaved blacks as "inhumane and shameful," the reader will find it hard to imagine what could possibly qualify such depraved merchants of human flesh to pass on "moral advantages" to their captives (73). Strange as it may sound, the answer seems to be that whiteness of the skin itself signified superior morality, irrespective of any questionable conduct by the individual whose body was encased in such skin.

In keeping with the flexibility of race, which, as it names nothing concrete, has the power to attach to anything, the government of Haitian-descended Dominican tyrant Rafael Leónidas Trujillo used race as a tool to control and unify his malevolent regime. The dictatorship defined the Dominican population as being white, Catholic, heterosexual, capitalist, and Hispanic. The intelligentsia working in the employ of the dictatorship profited richly from the standard historical narrative that had left over three hundred years of Afro-Dominican resistance against slavery and colonial oppression out of the national story. Blackness continued to be stigmatized with fervency, including by writers and pundits who themselves had African ancestry. Joaquín Balaguer, a writer and thinker of modest intellectual merits, enjoyed national prestige because of the fifty-two years he spent in positions of power, thirty as the loyal servant of Trujillo and twenty-two as president in his own right. In 1983, he published a negrophobic pamphlet titled *La isla al revés* that attributes the country's insufficient development to the progressive blackening of the population. Decline was inevitable given the Dominican Republic's sharing of Hispaniola with Haiti and the influx of immigrants from that neighboring country. The caudillo even proposed measures to halt "the [A]fricanization of the Dominican people" (97) so that the population might "gradually improve its anthropological traits" (98), thus repairing the moral decay precipitated by "the contact with blacks" (45). Oddly, he also deemed the influence of Africa on Dominican culture to be "imperceptible" (211). When the leader attended the first Ibero-American Summit of Presidents and Heads of State in Mexico, he took time to extol "the tremendous vitality of our [Castilian] race" as a key to the survival of Santo Domingo ("Discurso").

Whether in Dominican society or in the United States, Afro-Dominicans are likely to respond to their country's pervasive negrophobia in different ways, depending on their level of political awareness or personal agendas. They may inscribe themselves into the long legacy of resistance that is represented in the contemporary era by the likes of Afro-Dominican singer Xiomara Fortuna. They may simply value themselves in their ancestry, while managing to plug their ears to surrounding antiblack discourses. Or they may join the voices of persons who make a living preaching anti-Haitianism and negrophobia, such as the pundit Manuel Núñez, whose opinions have earned him government jobs and literary prizes. An Afro-Dominican with highly pronounced negroid features, Núñez earned notoriety with the publication of *El ocaso de la nación dominicana* (*The Waning of the Dominican Nation*, 1990). In many respects a mere rewrite of Balaguer's *Las isla al revés*, *El ocaso* reads as an invective against progressive scholars and thinkers, especially those affiliated with the Autonomous University of Santo Domingo (UASD). Beginning in the 1960s, UASD intellectuals made strides to discredit the negrophobic, anti-Haitian, and Eurocentric narratives dominating discourses on Dominican national identity.

A Eurocentric ultranationalist, Núñez took on the task of upholding the theory of national identity promoted by the Trujillo dictatorship and its intellectual heir, the Balaguer regime. The latter was in power in 1990 when a government-appointed panel of jurors gave that year's National Book Award in nonfiction prose to *El ocaso*. In 2001, Núñez published an expanded edition, which retained the ultranationalist, Eurocentric, anti-Haitian, negrophobic, and anti-Dominican diaspora arguments of the original. The book offers a benign representation of the genocide of thousands of Haitian immigrants and their Dominican-born children in October 1937 as a "policy of nationalization" (656) that responded to the "denationalizing presence" of Haitian immigrants in the border regions (678). The author goes so far as to deny validity to Caribbean culture as a whole. He regards it as an invention of Afrocentric advocates taking advantage of their academic jobs to advance a deviant view of history that unnecessarily centers race in the story of humanity (531). Oddly, this second edition was accepted as a legitimate submission to the 2002 competition for that year's Premio E. Léon Jiménez, the highest literary honor with the largest monetary prize. Handpicked by Minister of Culture Tony Raful, a panel of jurors voted to give the coveted prize to Núñez's text, despite its many normally disqualifying features, not the least of which were the poverty of its writing and its failure to meet a modicum of academic standards. Minister Raful, a published poet and a liberal politician with former revolutionary sympathies, vigorously defended the prize being given to Núñez, against the barrage of criticism that came from numerous writers, journalists, scholars, and artists from Dominican society and the diaspora. The position adamantly maintained by Raful reminds us that racism and the white supremacist bias can very well cut across party affiliations and, thus, political ideologies.

The case of the Dominican Republic stands as a suitable unit of analysis with which to close this present discussion of Afro-Latinidad. As Afro-Latina/os must come to terms with the two equally vigorous negrophobic legacies that they straddle, perhaps they may have access to a wider lens through which to perceive the injustice, that is, in the society of civic belonging and in the ancestral homeland. This population may be uniquely poised to respond to instances of human rights violations (more specifically, racial oppression in their ancestral homelands), while continuing to advocate for justice and inclusion in the United States. The possibility that Afro-Latina/os might be in possession of a panhemispheric perspective to detect and respond to inequity has to remain tentative, since much will depend on the degree to which each individual is politicized, as well as their type and degree of ideological positioning. Too often, ethnonational loyalties can make us unconditional allies of governments that we have allowed to become integral to the construction of our identity. This happened in the case of several US Jews who felt obligated to defend the 2014 Benjamin Netanyahu–led offensive in Gaza, thus branding some critics who simply wished for an end to bombardments of public sites like hospitals, nurseries, and schools as "anti-Israel" or "anti-Semitic."

Giving the government of a land of origin an integral spot in the constitution of our ethnic identity may cause us to default on our human or, more importantly, our humane solidarity. We might learn to view the injustice committed by the government or the ruling elite against a vulnerable population *over there* as easier to stomach than what we might see happening against comparable victims *over here*. Likewise, we might lose the ability to recognize the similarity between the abuse perpetrated by Dominican authorities against a group to which we feel no allegiance, *over there*, and the disempowerment we ourselves might be suffering at the hands of corporate or political powers *over here*. In many respects, the writings of Dominican authors in the United States, most of whom own up to their African ancestry, can be read as a composite indictment of the white supremacist imaginary that continues to inform the official institutions of cultural promotion in their ancestral homeland. Works such as the novels *Geographies of Home* (1999), by Loida Maritza Pérez; *In the Name of Salomé* (2000), by Julia Alvarez; *Soledad* (2001), by Angie Cruz; *Song of the Water Saints* (2002), by Nelly Rosario; *Erzulie's Skirt* (2006), by Ana-Maurine Lara; and *The Brief Wondrous Life of Oscar Wao* (2007), by Junot Díaz, as well as the performance poetry of Josefina Báez and the formal verse of Rhina P. Espaillat, all partake in different ways and varying degrees of intensity the task of subverting the official narratives of national identity in the ancestral homeland. They do so alongside their advocacy for social justice and inclusion in US sites of civic belonging.

The Dominican diaspora, with African-descended compatriots at the forefront, has found itself involved deeply in various activist fora that convened in response to the September 2013 ruling of the Dominican Republic's Constitutional Court TC/0163/13, which revoked the citizenship status of Dominican-born people of Haitian ancestry, effective immediately and applying retroactively back to 1929. The result was that some 250 thousand compatriots of all ages became foreigners in their own country and were thus eligible for deportation overnight. Dominican Americans, many of whom have long accepted the burden of diasporic citizenship, namely, that of seeing to the enhancement of social relations "in more than one society at the same time," immediately became involved in the condemnation of an act of legislation that too closely resembled the denationalization of German Jews during the Third Reich and the removal of people of Indian background from citizenship rosters during the Idi Amin dictatorship in Uganda (Torres-Saillant, "Racism" 281). Nor can Dominican Americans fail to condemn a law that requires Haitian Dominicans to demonstrate that their forebears entered the country legally several generations prior. Here, the conservative right in the United States, which has so busily engaged in crafting voter-suppression laws since the first decade of the twenty-first century, echoes the Dominican court's disavowals of the principle of jus soli, which had previously been consecrated in Dominican jurisprudence. For many Dominican Americans, the impulse to challenge the annulment of citizenship for vulnerable populations in the ancestral homeland may stem from a necessarily self-interested altruism.

Since Afro-Latinidad is shaped by the pressures of negrophobic racism, it often comes prepared to respond to, rather than initiate, action. As an offspring of racism, it may lack a self-sustaining purpose other than to engage positively or negatively with the historic vilification of blackness that in the United States has informed some of the nation's most powerful public figures and their platforms. In the Western Hemisphere, we are racist by default; we are heirs of the conquerors as well as the descendants of the conquered. There is no exaggeration in proposing that the white supremacist dogma, pervasive othering, and radical racialization of populations with origins other than European are central pillars of the civilization born in the Americas from conquest and colonization. Furthermore, diasporic communities are not exempt from the complexities and contradictions of their counterparts who reside in ancestral homelands. As individuals, they demonstrate solidarity, betrayal, greed, generosity, selflessness, goodness, and malice in quite comparable proportions. The law that denationalized a major segment of the Dominican population based on race has not elicited wholesale condemnation from US Dominicans, many of whom find themselves speaking harshly against one another across the ideological divide or lambasting non-Dominican critics of the *sentencia* for "attacking the Dominican Republic." Just as some German patriots viewed any criticism of the Third Reich's denationalization laws against German Jews as "anti-German," many Dominican patriots construed the sentencia's external criticism as "anti-Dominican." Then, just as now, those who view the state in the land of origin as the anchor of their ethnonational identity will have a hard time realizing that the national victims of state violence also constitute "Germany," or, in this case, the "Dominican Republic." When we allow the state to monopolize the definition of our ethnonational belonging at the expense of our flesh-and-blood compatriots, we step forward as voluntary recruits in an oppressive regime that will have lasting consequences.

Afro-Dominicans in the United States exist on a political spectrum. We have someone like Carlos Cooks, born in 1913, a black nationalist from Samaná Bay who figured among the trusted lieutenants of Harlem-based pan-Africanist Marcus Garvey. We also have someone like baseball player Sammy Sosa, who after achieving fame for his athletic prowess, made headlines in 2009 for his altered appearance: he relaxed his coarse hair, lightened his dark skin, and traded his brown eyes for green ones. Dominicans on and off the island are entitled to inhabit their blackness as (un)problematically as any other segment of the African diaspora. Because racism follows a logic of its own, and because race usually becomes knowable only when it manifests itself in acts of racism, it is hard to predict what any Afro-Latina/o person will do at moments when a stance of ethnoracial solidarity might be expected. Afro-Latina/os are the offspring of societies that emerged from the Spanish, Dutch, French, and English conquest and colonization of the Americas. As such, they inherit the cultural logic of the conquerors, since it was the latter who set the terms of socialization in the former's world. The independence movements that sprang up in the hemisphere were led by descendants of the colonial masters. Not surprisingly, the societies they created did not commit to a new ethos of social relations but simply embraced the colonial status quo. They acted on the knowledge of what had worked before and assumed it could continue to do so. The conquerors and their heirs organized a civilization on Indigenous lands, fueled by the labor and resources they robbed from these subject peoples, indentured servants, and imported human chattel.

To become a force for good, Afro-Latinidad will need to put to productive use its potential to help dismantle the racist paradigms that continue to impoverish human relations on both sides of the Rio Grande, whether those paradigms come from the Anglo or the Hispanic world. It must also remain attentive to racism's need for victims (of any background) to refrain from replicating racist structures in the name of antiracist causes or sheer self-righteousness. Racism has ostensibly been the primary civilizing force in the Americas. In many respects, it is all we have known, except for those who have chanced upon alternative relational logics and have sought to acknowledge the worth of their fellow human beings with eyes unobstructed by race, ethnicity, gender, class, religion, sexual orientation, and cultural heritage, among other areas of social identity. We owe to Martin Luther King, Jr., the prescient thought that he articulated while fending off some of the fiercest violence from white racists: we cannot afford the luxury of fighting oppression without at the same time monitoring our own potential to oppress others. Convinced that "all life is interrelated" and that people "are caught in an inescapable network of mutuality, tied in a single garment of destiny," King had the foresight to warn African Americans against the temptation to be "victimized with a philosophy of 'black supremacy'" (*Testament of Hope* 121–122, 200).

The "blessing" someone might find in Puerto Rican music or Dominican food can enrich us all if these serve as links to other ancestries, other demographic lineages, and other social identities that ancestry and phenotype cannot account for. Afro-Latinidad can prosper in moral terms only to the extent that it can muster the humane solidarity required for attending to the needs of those who resemble us in ways unrelated to ancestry or phenotype, but whose kinship we recognize in our shared plight. Perhaps the story of barber Feidin Santana, a twenty-three-year-old Dominican immigrant, embodies a hopeful lesson about humane solidarity, the type that does not depend on tribal allegiance or blood ties. This young Afro-Dominican man in North Charleston, South Carolina, had occasion to witness and film the killing of a fifty-year-old African American, Walter Scott, by white police officer Michael Slager in April 2015. Eligible for deportation due to his precarious immigration status, he feared police retaliation, which he knew could happen both in the Dominican Republic and the United States. The sense that the unjustified use of lethal force "was not right" proved strong enough for Santana to bring his smartphone video to the press, prompting an investigation that resulted in Slager having to face a murder charge (Belliard). A moral compulsion prompted Santana to push back against a wrongdoing in which both the victim and the perpetrator were strangers to him. Although he could claim ethnic kinship with neither Slager nor Scott, he knew one thing for sure: what he had witnessed was "not right" and merited inspired (if risky) action.

To remain viable as a serious and worthwhile identity location, Afro-Latinidad will need to show its value beyond the mere act of self-affirmation. The field of Latino studies and the Afro-Latino component within it must face the challenge of articulating a discourse that encourages us to fight for the general even as we focus—as we undoubtedly will—on the specific. Thinking of the new economy that emerged from the conquest and colonization of the Americas, which required ongoing mistreatment and dehumanization as key facilitators of accumulation and development, we will do well to identify and activate our solidarity with the demographic groups most disempowered by that system at any given time, whether it is "us" or somebody else.

Notes

1. As explained in the Note on Terminology, "Afro-Latina/o" will be used when referring to human subjects in general terms (for example, Afro-Latina/o faculty; the majority of Afro-Latina/os) and "Afro-Latino" for the adjectival form in the abstract (for instance, Afro-Latino politics). An implicit acknowledgment of gender diversity and fluidity should be noted in this usage.

2. See, for instance, Alegría; Restall.

3. The treasurer is the accountant of the voyage. The Crown expected this expedition to yield a satisfactory return on the investment.

4. See de Niza.

5. *Muñocismo* in Puerto Rican political discourse names the ideology and leadership of Governor Luis Muñoz Marín.

6. An American Civil Liberties Union report entitled *Island of Impunity: Puerto Rico's Outlaw Police Force* that draws its data from 2005 to the time of publication in 2012 has added "non-violent political protestors" to the social sectors suffering the impact of police brutality.

7. See Helg.

CHAPTER 9

RACISM IN THE AMERICAS AND THE LATINO SCHOLAR

This chapter outlines a history of racial oppression in the hemisphere, from conquest and colonization centuries ago to the impact of that legacy on current structures of social relations across ethnoracial difference. While acknowledging the difficulties and dangers involved for marginalized academics of color in the US, Torres-Saillant urges Latina/o intellectuals to take a stand on political injustices in their ancestral homelands. He declares, "Latinos are historically poised . . . to exercise their civil intervention simultaneously in the United States and in their lands of origin." He points out the disparities between scholars situated in the Global South and those in the North, giving examples of differential access to channels of scholarship, funding, safety, resistance, and community building. As such, "academics, intellectuals, activists, and cultural workers can make a difference in the possible amelioration of real-life conditions." The author invokes the greater ability of US-based scholars, in view of the tradition of respect for academic freedom, to enunciate a greater degree of contestation than is available at institutions of higher learning on the other side of the hemisphere. This relative advantage entails a proportionate measure of responsibility to those Latin American and Caribbean colleagues who may have less access to platforms of free intellectual exchange.

Torres-Saillant also posits a psychological explanation for why US-based scholars are quick to call out injustices where they live but slow to condemn them when dealing with the Old Country. He cautions, "The danger, of course, lies in deactivating the political eye when looking at the ancestral homeland during our restorative trips abroad; doing so entails a measure of self-deception that carries serious moral implications." Broaching such topics as the politics of miscegenation—and unpersuaded by the argument that mestizaje will neutralize racial strife, coun-

tering that it may instead occlude it—Torres-Saillant shares multiple examples of injustice, racism, and classism throughout Latin America and the Caribbean. The author points out, for instance, Mexico's penchant for representing the face of the nation as white (as evidenced by features preferred by television and other visual media), the Dominican Republic's drastic legal impediments to citizenship targeting Dominicans of Haitian ancestry, and the long history of exploitation of Indigenous peoples in Guatemala, Ecuador, Chile, and Bolivia, among others. He laments the ongoing toll of the colonial legacy on Indigenous peoples, including subsistence living, land dispossession, cultural erasure, and the reverberations of genocide in various forms. The writer concludes by once again reminding us of the pivotal role that Afro-Latina/os can play from their unique social location within the Latino panethnicity by "open[ing] doors of communication" and raising awareness as a crucial first step toward making a meaningful contribution to a more just world through diasporic social justice.

The Presence of the Past

Citizens become most deserving of their civic rank when they recognize themselves as agents of change. They possess the power to help society embrace the goal of "becoming truly human," as education theorist Paulo Freire would put it, by earnestly upholding the tenets of inclusion, equality, and justice across all differentiated segments of the population (57–59, 75, 95). With that premise in mind, I would propose that the burden of civic belonging that comes with the praxis of citizenship is likely to weigh more heavily on members of diasporic groups than on the more regular citizens, namely those with only one locus of ethnonational bonding or civic allegiance. One could argue that the latter can afford to concern themselves with the task of humanizing only one society. Among ethnic minorities in the United States, Latina/os face the civil overload of the former group quite distinctly. I can think of at least two reasons for this: first, Latina/os, for the most part, still retain meaningful ties to their ancestral homelands. This is true whether their insertion into the US population resulted from an act of US imperial conquest, such as those of 1848 and 1898, or from the massive migratory flows that poured in from Latin America and the Caribbean beginning in the first half of the twentieth century. Second, most Latin American societies have, in recent decades, made advances toward their respective émigré populations to secure the continued flow of remittances that have become practically indispensable to the region's economies. These advances include dual citizenship and voting rights abroad, initiatives whereby Latin American state authorities have sought to formalize legislatively their ties to their diasporas. Given this scenario, Latina/os can feel authorized to intervene on behalf of the downtrodden in the lands of their forebears without concern for the predictable charge that in seeking to influence Latin American societies from their location in the North, they might perpetuate ethnocentric assumptions of American cultural imperialism in the region.

It will become clear in the following pages that Latina/o spokespersons derive their moral ascendancy from a long record of resistance to hegemonic paradigms in American society, where they typically inhabit the margins rather than the center. After all, the social inequities that they would set out to challenge in Latin America have been perpetrated almost invariably by US-backed regimes there. In other words, the oppressors have strong allies in the North. There is hardly any sound reason to wish for the oppressed to fend for themselves on the other side of the hemisphere. Latina/os are historically poised, therefore, to exercise their civil intervention simultaneously in the United States and in their lands of origin. In fact, it may be that only insofar as they maintain upright positions toward racial oppression and other injustices in their ancestral homelands will Latina/o scholars activate the moral vision and political sensitivity necessary for addressing the tensions that often mar the rapport among distinct segments of the US Hispanic population.

For a long time, Mexican American, Puerto Rican, and other US Hispanic communities have accrued an estimable record of struggle for justice and equality, greatly contributing to the social movements that have brought US society slightly closer to living up to the meaning of its creed. In light of that legacy, I would like to explore whether Latina/os might also commit themselves to the equally necessary struggle against racial and ethnic prejudice in Latin America and the Caribbean. I refer here to a prejudice that has resulted in harsh policies and practices in an area where over 146 million primarily Indigenous and African-descended people suffer "poverty, stigmatization, and exclusion" caused by societal, structural, and systemic impediments (ECLAC 1). This subordination emanates from a long history, or what scholar Roberto Márquez has termed the "*Society of Race* and racial castes" in the Americas (13). Álvaro Bello and Marta Rangel's 2000 study *Etnicidad, "Raza" y Equidad en América Latina y el Caribe* (*Ethnicity, "Race" and Equity in Latin America and the Caribbean*) finds that inclusion of Afrodescendientes and Indigenous people in the region has remained "symbolic and discursive in nature, while in practice it has been denied" (qtd. in ECLAC 6). I deliberately underscore the role that US-based Hispanic scholars can play in mitigating the difficulties endured by certain ethnically differentiated populations south of the Rio Grande. As this opening commentary suggests, I believe that academics, intellectuals, activists, and cultural workers can make a difference in the possible amelioration of real-life conditions, especially when the existing injustices have come into being through the indirect or direct involvement of generations of scholars, writers, and social theorists who were elite warriors of white supremacy. From the moment the countries in the region secured their political independence from Spain and Portugal, they rushed to assess their populations and began to differentiate and stratify groups based on ancestry and phenotype, calculating their greater or lesser potential to contribute to development in the burgeoning republics. The US Hispanic intelligentsia, one might argue, is therefore obligated to help dismantle the paradigms that have historically condoned oppression against specific groups in the region. This proposition has particular significance at the present juncture. Perhaps more than ever before, with the rise of social media and other technological additions to our daily lives, an international climate seems to exist that encourages people to remain vigilant and even vocal about contemporary injustices committed abroad as well as at home. The sense also prevails that we in the present have a position to take regarding the atrocities perpetrated against our fellow human beings in the past. The resilient belief that construes any recollection of past conflicts as a source of disruption (echoed, for instance, by President Bill Clinton at the closing of his final State of the Union address to Congress in January 2000) appears at present to be outmatched by several persuasive arguments that urge us to confront the wrongs of previous generations so we can start the healing that must precede any practical efforts to achieve unity and harmony.

Two relatively recent gestures concerning the atrocities of former generations merit mention here for their unique value as examples of the need for contemporary societies to assume responsibility for the misdeeds of our elders. The first refers to the recommendation made in February 2000 by a state commission of the Oklahoma House of Representatives to pay reparations to the survivors and descendants of the victims of the white mob that on May 31, 1921, rampaged through Greenwood, a major black residential-and-business district of Tulsa. The chaos left a death toll of some three thousand and reduced to ashes thousands of homes and hundreds of businesses that had made the district one of the most prosperous in the city. The Tulsa Race Riot Commission (renamed Tulsa Race Massacre Commission in 2018), which the Oklahoma legislature had appointed to study the case, shared preliminary research findings that incriminated the government. The report stated that "city officials not only failed to protect the lives of black residents but also contributed to the riot by deputizing many members of the white mob that attacked Greenwood . . . many of whom were members of the Ku Klux Klan" (Yardley). The study implicated the local, state, and federal governments, whose laws tolerated racism and whose law enforcement personnel facilitated the violence (Ruble). In recommending reparations on behalf of the victims of the destroyed "Negro Wall Street of America," the Commission cited the precedent of a 1994 provision by the Florida legislature that had allocated $2 million to compensate survivors of a smaller riot in 1923, when racist whites destroyed the small town of Rosewood, killing at least six of its African American residents (Brand-Williams 7).

The other gesture concerns the "Déclaration de repentance des évêques de France" ("Declaration of Repentance of the Church of France"), issued by the French bishops in Drancy on September 30, 1997. Through this pronouncement, the Catholic hierarchy admitted its fault in remaining indifferent to the plight of the Jews during World War II. During the Vichy government, forty thousand Jews found themselves in French internment camps by February 1941. A few months before, on October 3, 1940, the French government, under Philippe Pétain, had issued its first anti-Jewish statutes, and the Church did not react. Under the gaze of the Catholic Church, a series of anti-Semitic pieces of legislation deprived French Jews of their citizenship, relegating them to the most inferior status in the nation, subjecting them to the horrors of the concentration camps. Starting from the realization that "no society, nor for that matter any individual, can live in peace with itself if it has a history of repression and deceit," the French prelacy announced that "the time has come" for the church "to submit her very own history to a critical reading, without hesitating to recognize the sins committed by her sons, and to demand pardon from God and man."[1] The clergymen reflected, "We are forced to acknowledge that the Bishops of France did not express publicly their outrage, acquiescing by their silence to the flagrant violations of the rights of man, allowing open season to a most deadly system." Their document laments the fact that while the Nazi crimes were occurring, "the hierarchy of the Church considered its first obligation to be that of insuring the practice of Catholicism, the promotion of its institutions, and the protection of her faithful." Such an institutional priority, which could be effectively pursued only by adhering to a code of behavior that the vicious regime found palatable, had the inescapable consequence of making the Church complicit in the genocide that the Third Reich was perpetrating.

Consistent with the ideological climate illustrated by these two instances, Pope John Paul II spoke out in a March 12, 2000, statement beseeching forgiveness for the sins of Catholics and the Church over the centuries, noting especially those committed against Jewish people. The pope further decried "the crimes of the past" during his trip to Israel and elsewhere in the Middle East later that same month. Speaking at Yad Vashem, the Holocaust memorial in Jerusalem, he commented, "I assure the Jewish people that the Catholic Church . . . is deeply saddened by the hatred, acts of persecution and displays of anti-Semitism directed against the Jews by Christians at any time and in any place. The Church rejects racism in any form as a denial of the image of the Creator inherent in every human" (qtd. in Griffin-Nolan 1). The foregoing positions, corresponding to the widespread and ongoing demand that we take a stand against past evils, were motivated by the realization that the present bears as much responsibility for the past as for the times to come. This "act of remembrance," remarked the bishops of France, "calls us ever the more to a vigilance with regard to humanity both now and in the future" (Griffin-Nolan 1).[2] If the memories of pain inflicted years ago on large numbers of people of an ethnicity or background other than ours fail to move us to righteous indignation, I seriously doubt whether we could muster the empathy necessary to feel emotionally and morally affected by the grief of the victims should the atrocity recur in our own time and place.

The Morality of Scholarship

As we tackle the thorny question of race and ethnicity in Latin America and the Caribbean, it behooves us to consider whether we might arrive at a stage in our academic conversations where we transcend the civil routine of respectable scholarly work in order to directly confront the horrors of our own past. We might entertain some harsh, theoretically uncouth questions regarding our relationship to the racial crimes that have been (and continue to be) committed by Latin American and Caribbean states against differentiated subsections of their respective populations. Too often in the academy we restrict our social interventions to producing "objective" (that is, arm's-length and advocacy-free) discourse that is supposedly the most suitable for the lecture hall or the scholarly monograph. In so doing, we may fail to interrogate the human value of the knowledge that we, in our research and writing, purport to create. Trained as we are in the humanities and the social sciences to increase the level of sophistication of our queries rather than delivering clear solutions to the problems that complicate the lives of the people we study, we often content ourselves with merely expanding the intellectual horizons of our own fields. The typical scholarly paper in the humanities and social sciences, even when dealing with life-and-death topics such as racial oppression or interethnic conflict in this or that country, often closes with a sedate paragraph in which the scholar points to pertinent questions requiring further exploration. The purpose of research, in the end, is self-perpetuation. One receives credit for having made contributions to the discipline by merely increasing the number of research questions in one's field, formulating catchy terms and signature phrases, and leaving as legacy a cycle that is vicious in more than one way.

Careers are thus built, grants awarded, and stellar positions earned, even as the trail of tears that may have served as our subject matter remains unabated and the oppressive structures that may have fueled our research continue to await redress, reform, and resolution.

I would argue that many of us scholars have too often done an insufficient job of recognizing and articulating our complicity in the depravity of the state in our respective homelands, whether present or ancestral. Many of us remain loath to take the appropriate steps to separate ourselves from the infamy of the society, the leaders, or the societal mechanisms in question. Latina/os trace their origins back to countries that have brought into being visions of progress and modernization vastly dependent on the devastation of countless habitats for animals, plants, and people. The Guarani in northern Argentina, the Yuqui in Bolivia, the Cofán in the Ecuadorian Amazon, and the Kuna Indians of eastern Panama, among other endangered peoples in the vanishing forests of Latin America, bear the brunt of a Faustian bargain between the developing nations of the hemisphere and the "developed" world. These nations have embraced a model of economic success that involves attracting investment from the United States, Europe, and Japan, as well as borrowing millions of dollars from foreign banks, which end up endangering the lifelines and folkways of Indigenous communities. Alan Weisman and Sandy Tolan traveled through fifteen countries of the hemisphere to document a "swift, often irreversible destruction." They attested to a Guarani village "burned to make way for yet another hotel. The next Indian village to the south is also gone, swallowed by the waters of a new reservoir" (221). From a government contract in the 1970s that turned the Ecuadorian Amazon over to Texaco to build the oil industry there, to the ancient hardwood rainforests of Tierra del Fuego that in the 1990s Canadian and Japanese companies would turn into paper products, these development strategies have seemed less horrific than they are because their devastating impact has fallen most directly on the lives of Indigenous communities. According to J. Halcro Ferguson, writing in the early 1960s, it is no secret that Indigenous lives tend to occupy the bottom rung—even as compared with blacks—of the socioeconomic ladder in the hemisphere (75).

The perception of vast ethnic and cultural distance that might separate the majority from the immediate victims of the ecological genocide (ecocide) that industrialization has wrought in Latin America may have made the calamity seem more tolerable than it ought to be. Perhaps to help us overcome the insufficient solidarity that ethnic difference stimulates in us, we might wish to pay heed to the suggestion of French writer Marguerite Duras. When referring to the Nazi horrors, we should "turn it into a crime committed by all humanity"; once we see ourselves implicated, we "share the crime" (83). We need this mental exercise so that our proximity to both the victims and the perpetrators can become apparent. Once we can feel the evil closer to our own skin, we can then come to terms with our level of involvement and genuinely take a stand on it. A soul-searching maneuver such as this will produce the effect that Pablo Neruda's "Ode to Paul Robeson" ("Oda a Paul Robeson") credits to the African American athlete, singer, actor, and civil rights activist. The Chilean poet evokes Robeson's undaunted devotion to the cause of human justice in the following lines: "Your voice / separated us from crime / once more / it rescued the light from the darkness" ("Tu voz / nos separó del crimen / una vez más / apartó / la luz de las tinieblas"; my trans.; 1232–1233). I would say that especially when we study the history and the abiding legacy of racial oppression in Latin America and the Caribbean, we tread a delicate moral ground if we do not make an effort to separate ourselves from the crimes that our research activities may bring us into contact with, directly or indirectly.

Urgent Words, Compulsory Silences

Latina/o and US-based Latin American scholars who have chosen the study of their people as subjects of academic inquiry share membership in a community of knowledge with undeniable political privileges, irrespective of the challenges they might face because of their relative marginality in American institutions of higher learning. In many respects, that uneasy location between privilege and marginality constitutes the greatest asset that émigré and diasporic communities can boast. Working mostly from our intellectual trenches at university-based ethnic- or area-studies units, we enjoy the creative tension of inhabiting a space marked by challenge as much as by potential. We enjoy the dual perspective of the outsider who has accessed significant degrees of insiderness. We have succeeded at gaining entry to an industry that permits us to make a living by participating in thought production. No one can deny the considerable empowerment involved in wielding the weapons of discourse for pay. Yet, as evidenced by our marginality vis-à-vis mainstream bodies of knowledge that the academy values most, we achieve only partial inclusion. That mediated, conditional access encourages in us a perspective that enables us to look critically at American society's questionable record of racial disharmony and all its economic and political implications. By the same token, we achieve, as members of émigré or diasporic communities, a critical distance from our homelands or the homelands of our elders, which makes it possible for us to become demanding, even judgmental, concerning questions of equality and social justice in the "old" countries. Elsewhere, for instance, I have sought to demonstrate the extent to which, in the case of US Dominicans, one can speak of an "alternative epistemic community" in view of the models that prevail for standard definitions of nation in the Dominican Republic. Examples might include describing the "diasporic perspective" typically deployed by the émigré community in its critical assessment of cultural myths and political behaviors "back home" (Torres-Saillant, *El retorno* 37, 393–404).

An illustration of the same phenomenon in Puerto Rico appears in Edgardo Rodríguez-Juliá's *Las tribulaciones de Jonás* (1981), where the author recollects an eventful visit paid in 1978 by him, his wife, a guide, and his Nuyorican friend Roberto Márquez to the house of the elder statesman and political legend Luis Muñoz Marín. From the author's mere description of Márquez's gait as they approached the patriarch's house (having "a self-assurance possible only for someone who learned about [Muñoz Marín] from afar"), it seems clear that the Nuyorican in the group was comparatively unfazed by the spell of obsequiousness that the presence of the ruling class can cast on the members of the citizenry in the homeland (22). Muñoz Marín was "a true prince of the Creole ruling caste," but Márquez, unlike the other visitors, opted not to use the respectful form "Don Luis" when addressing the elder (25, 31). As their jovial conversation proceeds, the most disquieting of the topics covered and the questions formulated invariably come from the lips of Márquez, "the black Puerto Rican brought up in a New York ghetto, one of the 'oppressed' [by Muñoz?] children of the emigrants" (30). Indeed, from Márquez—and from nobody else—came the million-dollar question posed that day to the champion of Operation Bootstrap, the famed development initiative that led to the massive exodus of Puerto Ricans from their homeland in the 1940s. Márquez asked the former governor of Puerto Rico, "What was the Partido Popular's policy on emigration?," to which the former Partido Popular leader answered, "We figured: After two generations the problem of the Puerto Ricans in New York would no longer exist, simply because by then they would no longer be Puerto Ricans" (39). The response probably contained a greater degree of honesty than Márquez had expected, but it likely confirmed a truth he had intuited and resented, hence his less-obeisant demeanor toward "Don Luis." I would contend that, whatever its degree of articulateness, this justifiable resentment toward the ruling elites of Latin America often appears in the utterances of Latina/os in the diaspora, sharpening our critical edge.

Though it entails a measure of trauma, the aforementioned situation, born of the uprooting that is often the source of diasporic identity, has the capacity to turn us into hyperconscious citizens—that is, people with an acute awareness of the implications of our connection to a particular state. One could think of such hyperconscious citizens as less susceptible than regular citizens to state-induced social, political, and cultural deception. Furthermore, US-based Hispanic scholars have a signal advantage in that they live and work (thus existing intellectually) outside the reach of the Latin American and Caribbean thought police. Speaking and writing in the United States, they are at relative liberty to expose the foibles and iniquities of presidents, cardinals, generals, legislators, and magnates in their home countries without risk of facing consequences as dire as those that might occur were they to voice their critiques locally. This chapter is hardly the place to recount the long history of intellectuals who have suffered harm for sharing unflattering (albeit truthful) indictments of those in power across the hemisphere. The possibility of suffering physical injury, being subjected to various forms of harassment, or even "disappearing" still exists. On April 28, 1998, Monsignor Juan José Gerardi Conedera met his death at the hands of hitmen two days after he, as head of the Guatemalan Archbishop's Human Rights Office, made public a report that summarized three decades of violence and human rights abuses, mostly by military personnel (Hayner 32).

In this atmosphere, one can hardly expect scholars in Latin America to be at the forefront of the struggle for equality and social justice. The 1990s witnessed a climate in which societies in the region committed themselves to effectuating a transition to democratic practices, while remaining acutely aware of the need to make flattering concessions to the old guard, with its authoritative, corrupt, and murderous schemes deeply entrenched as the norm. The intelligentsia had to learn to cope with an amoral climate in which the likes of Dominican caudillo Joaquín Balaguer and extreme right-wing Chilean dictator Augusto Pinochet called the shots regarding how the past would be interpreted, narrated, and remembered. In 1998, they stomached the deliberations among the Chilean multipartisan legislature that conferred upon Pinochet the near sacred rank of senator-for-life, in accordance with a clause dating from 1980, some years after his 1973 coup d'état, when his military regime reformed the constitution. In 1997, the year before Pinochet's anointment, Dominican legislators in Congress voted to bestow on Balaguer the title of "Gran Propulsor de la Democracia Dominicana" (Torres-Saillant, *El retorno* 72). In that unstable environment, dwelling on the need to narrate the past in a way that would do justice to the thousands of Chileans and Dominicans who lost their lives or had their safety compromised by state-sanctioned violence might be dismissed by the conservative status quo as antigovernment posturing or as fanning the flames of past conflicts to disrupt law, order, and peace. Worse still, the insistence on truthful and inclusive remembering risks eliciting the disfavor of deeply rooted sectors of power, engendering more violence. One could lose one's job and the use of established venues for intellectual exchange, at the very least. Though less likely, the possibility of suffering bodily harm on account of one's ideas is never zero. But the social ostracism, which inevitably translates into lack of access to necessary infrastructural resources, including funding, would suffice to scare Latin American intellectuals into compliance with the behavior dictated by the political forces in power in the region.

These complex situations afford Latina/o and Latin American scholars in the United States discernible advantages compared to their counterparts in the region. They enjoy a measure of freedom from the pressures endured by their colleagues in Latin America, from politicians, the military, the church, and other power sectors. A tenured faculty member employed by the City University of New York system, for instance, could in the year 2001 have published an essay that provoked the discomfort of Mayor Rudolph Giuliani, Governor George Pataki, and President George W. Bush without suffering a punitive loss of employment. Our colleagues in universities from Argentina to Uruguay could not have boasted of a comparable freedom. This discursive advantage must be kept firmly in mind when we speak of racial inequality in the hemisphere. That advantage would even seem to impose a dire responsibility. We, as US-based scholars, might see it as our moral obligation to use our relative safety and freedom to voice critiques and pose questions that our counterparts on the other side of the hemisphere simply cannot afford to broach. The silences they leave are those we have the power and obligation to fill.[3]

Latina/os and Racism: A Call for Coherence

We have another, perhaps more powerful reason for feeling a compulsion to pronounce our views on racial injustices in Latin America and the Caribbean: to avoid moral and political inconsistency. Due to the peculiar racial history of the United States and the circumstances under which non-white ethnic minorities have gained access to the corridors of academia, Latina/o scholars, like their African American, Native American, and Asian American counterparts, have become quite adept at detecting race-based privilege and types of exclusion. We have sharpened our instincts to recognize inequality when we see it and quickly stand up against injustice, which still infiltrates the Ivory Tower. We stand out as natural advocates of diversity, inclusion, and proper representation in public spaces, including the job market. Therefore, we might wish to take appropriate measures to ensure an ongoing commitment to moral coherence. We can all begin by asking ourselves how well we have measured up. At least since the rise of the Chicano Movement, Mexican American colleagues have advocated effectively for social equity and respect on this side of the Rio Grande. We can ask, have they mobilized in comparable ways on behalf of the Indigenous populations of the Republic of Mexico? I recall a memorable visit to Guadalajara during the meeting of the Latin American Studies Association in the spring of 1997. During each of the three days of the conference, I bought a copy of the newspaper *El Excélsior* and two other major dailies, expressly to examine the phenotype of the people featured in the photographs and advertisements. I flipped through what felt like hundreds of pages a day looking specifically for spotlights on diverse faces of Indigenous or African-descended persons but to no avail.

Latina/os have persuasively laid their claim to a social space in which the rest of the US population recognizes the community's "cultural citizenship." Renato Rosaldo and William Flores define the concept of cultural citizenship as "the right to be different (in terms of race, ethnicity, or native language) with respect to the norms of the dominant national community, without compromising one's right to belong, in the sense of participating in the nation-state's democratic processes" (57). But one wonders if we have allowed ourselves a sort of double standard when it comes to witnessing denials of full citizenship to ethnically differentiated groups in our ancestral lands. One could ask whether Chicano spokespersons have effectively challenged *güero*[4] society in Mexico in a way that accords with their long trajectory of social justice struggle in the United States since the 1940s. Ironically, one observes instead a tendency among Latina/os to speak up stridently about issues of equality and diversity in American society while proceeding leniently when their countries of origin overtly practice racially and ethnically based exclusions. When mainland Puerto Ricans and US Dominicans travel back to the lands of their elders, they seldom analyze the quality of life on those islands with the same zeal and political urgency that they normally display in their examination of US society. Perhaps the numbing of one's political edge when looking at the ancestral land has a psychological explanation, such as permissiveness rooted in loyalty, sentimentality, guilt, or fear.

One could say that uprooting oneself from the original homeland to settle in the United States, where one must perpetually negotiate ethnic antipathy by remaining politically vigilant, is exhausting. The original homeland thus becomes a source of spiritual strength that confirms our cultural identity. In effect, we conjure our collective Aztlán as a near-transcendental realm, where history gives way to myth. When we travel, we experience an existential homecoming that permits us to reconnect with the food, music, landscape, family, and attendant feelings of guilt, obligation, and allegiance at all costs. Even a US writer as radical as Cherríe Moraga, who owes her celebrity to her blanket defiance of such oppressive structures as heteronormativity and white supremacy, reveals an ideological soft spot when describing her frequent travels to Mexico. In her deconstruction of patriarchal Latino culture, including references to Malinche (conquistador Hernán Cortés's Indigenous translator and mistress), she does not spare her own "Chicana mother," whom she places in the Mexican "wifely" tradition, which extends to Malinche's mother as well. The older woman betrays her daughter Cherríe by "putting the male first" ("Long Line" 152). Yet Moraga does not dissect the deep structure of Mexican society, namely, the internal injustices that people in every country perpetrate against their compatriots, with politically informed eyes; she limits her critique to the geopolitical concern over "the colonial relationship between the United States and Mexico." In a memorable interview, she enthused as follows:

> The land, that is the best! That is the reason I like to go there, especially the southern part. I've visited the pyramids, the *ruinas*. I have also studied a lot of Mesoamerican, pre-Columbian history. It is always very relaxing for me, and it also affects my work as you have seen. . . . There is no home for me in Mexico, except the land. The desert. I spent time in Sonora and Chihuahua a couple of summers ago. It's the land. These are my *raíces*. My family is from Sonora. The land calms me down, opens me up. I feel it is a rich resource in my writing. I experience a quietness there that is difficult to conjure in this country. ("City of Desire" 108)

Regarding the likelihood of ever residing in Mexico, the writer has remarked, "I hope to do that for periods of time. Particularly when you have a kid, your priorities change. I feel like I want to give my kid what I did not get: a direct sense of Mexican culture and some spots of land without gringo interference" ("City of Desire" 108).

Moraga's testimony evinces a process whereby, through contact with the ancestral land, we may undergo a kind of cultural reboot. This social renewal energizes us, enhancing our ability to confront the challenges of living as part of a disempowered ethnic minority upon our return to the United States. The danger, of course, lies in deactivating the political eye when looking at the ancestral homeland during our restorative trips there. Doing so entails a measure of self-deception that carries serious moral implications. We shield ourselves psychologically to remain unmoved by the injustices we see happening in the land of our forebears. We go to Guadalajara or Mexico City and rely on the invaluable services of Indigenous people, from the porter in the baggage-claim area of the airport to the housekeeper in the hotel or residence, to the taxi driver who brings us back to catch the return flight. These same faces do not appear in the mainstream media, except in the most unflattering of circumstances, rarely visible when watching Mexico on small or large screens or reading about triumphant national events in the newspaper.

We might travel to the Dominican Republic, stay at a hotel or in a relative's house in the capital, and see blacks and mulatta/os everywhere—as well we should, for they constitute nearly 90 percent of the country's population. The African presence in the hemisphere was first evident in this city in 1502. In 1521, this land also witnessed the first black slave insurrection registered in the history of the Americas. Certain neighborhoods, such as San Carlos de los Minas—initially known as San Carlos de los Negros—began as townships populated specifically by residents of African descent. Yet blackness magically disappears when one watches the Dominican family beaming out of TV commercials or the representative visage of the nation as reflected in the society pages of the major dailies. If we find nothing disturbingly wrong with such absences, one could argue that we have learned to tolerate in the ancestral land the same social ills that we call out in American society. We have become morally bifurcated, and our apparent indifference to the pain endured by the sectors of the population that suffer exclusion turns us into accomplices in oppressions that we know so much about because we make our living studying them in the United States.

As we reflect on issues related to race and ethnicity in Latin America and the Caribbean, it pays to examine the privilege of our positionality as US-based Hispanic scholars. We must not forget that in exploring the issues in question, we will inevitably discern serious crimes, and we cannot maneuver around the need to take a stand on that which our research brings into visibility for ourselves and others. We can recognize the crimes easily because of their pervasiveness. They arise almost invariably from formulations of national identity that not only fail to account for the racial and ethnic diversity of most Latin American and Caribbean populations, but also tend to embrace definitions of nationhood reeking of antipathy toward ethnically differentiated sectors of those populations. Formal European colonialism in the Americas began to recede in the mid-1800s, with abolition coming soon thereafter. During the 1880s, Cuba and Brazil freed their slaves, putting an end to the official practice of bondage in the Americas. Yet, as Peter Winn has noted, slavery's "legacies—racism, poverty, inequality—remain, a burden that the region's 100 million people of African descent still bear today" (279). The aftermath of colonial oppression ever impacts millions of Indigenous peoples. Nor should we forget the reverberations of such experiences on people of Asian descent, many of whom had elders survive indentured servitude and much ill-treatment that rarely arises as a legitimate part of the national storyline. Too often these populations are ignored or forgotten in discussions that focus exclusively on black and Indigenous peoples, leading to continued erasure of their unique dilemmas and the sense of perpetual foreignness, exacerbated by ignorance, from multiple populations, not just the ruling classes.

Builders of nations in the region were the political and cultural heirs of the Iberian conquerors who had robbed the Indigenous peoples of their lands and massacred their ancestors during the colonial transaction centuries before. Ironically, the advent of independence brought "increasing encroachments on communal lands by a creole and mestizo elite freed from imperial constraints" (Winn 250). In June 1990, the Ecuadorian peasant uprising in the region around Cayambe, led by the Confederation of Indigenous Nationalities of Ecuador, responded to the disempowerment to which original inhabitants of that country, as well as Peru and Bolivia, had been subjected since the conquest. Excluded from power, deprived of their homes, and deemed irrelevant in the land of their ancestors, they reasonably lost patience, much to the chagrin of the government that chastised the "agitators" who led the movement for their lack of "a sense of nationality" and their desire "to divide the country" (Winn 262). In Guatemala, during the counterinsurgency years of 1978–1985, the armed forces destroyed over four hundred communities and took the lives of some 200 thousand people, mostly "unarmed Indians." Little doubt existed in the minds of the dispossessed that their ethnicity made them easy targets, as the army was certain that no retaliation would arise, since they were "just Indians" (Winn 266). Despite the renown of a Guatemalan Maya activist like Rigoberta Menchú, winner of the 1992 Nobel Peace Prize for her defense of the human rights of Indigenous people, a constitutional reform that would acknowledge Guatemala as a "multiethnic, multicultural, multilingual society" did not receive enough votes to pass during the May 1999 referendum (Winn 269).

Racial Fictions, Fictional Harmony, and Genocide

The conceptual manipulations implicit in the intelligentsia's construction of the idea of the Latin American nation require extended discussion. These manipulations arose steadily from the Eurocentric and white supremacist paradigms that the region's thinkers embraced, rather than from any discernibly malicious conspiratorial designs. The same applies to the intellectual tradition that disputes the significance of race in social interactions and historical phenomena in the Americas. Many would earnestly subscribe to what scholar Anani Dzidzienyo describes as the "much admired non-contentiousness" of patterns relating to race relations ("Conclusions" 345). Rosángela Maria

Vieira references Dzidzienyo's key commentary on Edson Arantes do Nascimento, the former Brazilian sports minister better known as the extraordinary football player Pelé: "The 'King of Football' was an invaluable ally of the Brazilian authorities, constantly used to demonstrate the validity of their 'racial democracy,'" with Pelé going as far as to claim that there was "no racism in Brazil" (Dzidzienyo qtd. in Vieira 39). The fact that a black Brazilian should fail to see racism in his country has to do not only with the fact that his superior talents as an athlete elevated him socially, but also with the success of the narrative of racial non-contentiousness in that country. Afro-Brazilian scholar Abdias do Nascimento has stated in no uncertain terms that the black movement in Brazil "expends enormous energies trying to 'prove' to its own people that their situation is due to race" (106). Similarly, the Dominican case, which I have explored at greater length elsewhere, points to the possibility that discrete historical developments can lead to the emergence among blacks of a "deracialized consciousness" with the power to preclude the rise of "a discourse of black affirmation" (Torres-Saillant, *El retorno* 136). This impediment keeps the community from wielding the appropriate intellectual tools to counterbalance de facto negrophobia. Deracialization may also come from a particular state-sponsored ideology, as Afro-Cuban writer Carlos Moore argues was the case in Cuba with the advent of a Marxist revolution which advocated for the "non-racial" identity of Cubans ("Afro-Cubans" 219) and warned against the dangers of black self-affirmation (225).

Even more pernicious than the myth of noncontentiousness is the tradition that would have us believe in a harmonious process of miscegenation triggered by the colonial transaction. The standard wisdom, variously pastoralizing the emergence of the mestiza/o or the mulatta/o, posits that racial admixture leads to a state of pervasive hybridity devoid of racial tension. That tradition incorporates elements born of the "white legend" that Spanish thinkers promoted to counterattack the "black legend" that spokespersons for competing European colonial powers had deployed during the great imperial clashes of times past. Unlike their Dutch, French, and English counterparts, the Spanish, so the argument goes, thought nothing of the racial difference of the peoples they conquered. They intermingled carnally with the vanquished and produced well-liked mixed-race offspring. The distinguished Spanish essayist and physician Gregorio Marañón adhered fervently to that interpretation in a prologue he wrote in the mid-twentieth century for a book by archeologist José Pérez de Barradas on the mestizos of Spanish America. In self-congratulatory mode, Marañón announces, "If there is one thing that Hispanic peoples can undeniably feel proud of it, is not having ever assigned undue importance to the question of race" (my trans.; iii). But we cannot credit the Spanish with sole ownership of the tradition that presents miscegenation as a normal, concordant feature of the Latin American experience. Creole voices, even while at times harboring hostile feelings toward Spain, often embraced pastoral visions of mestizaje from the early days of the independence movement to foster notions of national unity in the face of observable ethnic heterogeneity. Addressing the second National Congress of Venezuela, in Angostura, on February 15, 1819, the liberator Simón Bolívar tackled the political challenge posed by diversity, stating,

> We do not retain the vestiges of our original being. We are not Europeans; we are not Indians; we are but a mixed species of aborigines and Spaniards. Americans by birth and Europeans by law, we find ourselves engaged in a dual conflict: we are disputing with the natives for titles of ownership, and at the same time we are struggling to maintain ourselves in the country that gave us birth against the opposition of the invaders. (175–176)

His candid recognition of such complexity did not deter him from prescribing a clear solution: "Unity, unity, unity must be our motto in all things. The blood of our citizens is varied: let it be mixed for the sake of unity" (191).

Bolívar expressed his view of mestizaje as a desideratum, something that would be necessary for national unity. The Cuban poet and independence leader José Martí articulated a vision of mestizaje free of white supremacist assumptions, while naming racism as a major impediment to a healthy national formation, as Lourdes Martínez-Echazábal has shown in her helpful reading of Martí's essays "Nuestra América" (1891) and "Mi Raza" (1893) (30–32). Martí thus parted ways with mestizaje-focused thinkers preceding him and those coming after. Subsequent voices tended to speak of race-mixing as having solved the racial problem. The Spanish writer and erstwhile diplomat Salvador de Madariaga evoked a historical process whereby the diverse ethnic contingents of the region, including blacks, communally blended into a well-integrated hybrid state. "Whatever statistics might say," he confidently affirms, "the soul of the Americas is, in effect, an essentially mestizo soul" (my trans.; qtd. in Mörner 11).

Assuming the smooth fusion of different races predictably leads to the claim that recognizable racial distinctions have disappeared in Latin America. As William Bollinger and Daniel Manny Lund have pointed out, the idea upheld by intellectuals during the first half of the twentieth century, that no racial problems per se existed in the region, and the assumption that the great degree of miscegenation occurring there diminished the racial dimensions of human interaction, have actually presented a serious obstacle to the development of a theory of Latin American racism (228). According to the prevailing interpretation, the sources of intergroup tension and conflict in the region gesture to other causes. One is class difference, which would normally merit a lengthy discussion in its own right, but which I will simply acknowledge here by posing a rhetorical question. What do we make of the fact that in Honduras during the mid-1990s, 99 percent of Garifuna communities contended with no access to postal, radio, or even telegraph services? Where available, these basic services were either unreliable or scarce. This faulty infrastructure exacerbated the fact that most Garifuna settlements also faced "no water, electricity or latrine services" and struggled without a public transportation system (Guevara Arzu 243). One would have a hard time proving the absence of a link between Garifuna destitution, class oppression, and ethnic difference when compared to non-black Hondurans.[5]

But perhaps the most resilient rhetoric against the significance of race in Latin America has been the contention that miscegenation has made racial distinctions vanish, subsumed under the more powerful, unifying mantle of culture. Dominican intellectual Pedro Henríquez Ureña articulated this position most succinctly when he disseminated his peculiar definition of Spanish America as constituting the location of a unified race despite "the multicolor multiplicity of peoples speaking our language in the world." He posits that "what unites and unifies this race, not so much a real as an ideal race, is its community of culture, which is predicated, mainly, on its linguistic commonality" (my trans.; *La utopia* 12–13). Race and ethnicity, then, evaporate into the vaster mists of culture and language. As the eminent philologist himself indicated, the evaporation would not occur haphazardly. He did not have in mind a symmetrical fusion of ethnicities. The West—not Africa, Indigenous America, or even the East—would provide the structure into which the various ethnicities would fuse. Henríquez Ureña had no qualms about tracing the cultural roots of Hispanic America to the Roman Empire, as Argentine intellectual and politician Domingo Faustino Sarmiento had suggested (*La utopia* 13). Henríquez Ureña's model presupposed the belief held by philosopher José Ingenieros that the Europeans who came to the Americas during the colonial transaction represented a higher stage in the evolution of the human species than the Indigenous peoples and blacks. The Dominican thinker did not overtly echo the claims of sociologist Carlos O. Bunge, who trumpeted the lesser capacity of blacks to think and work at the level of Europeans, and who charged Ibero-American Creoles with "impairing their own stock" by intermingling with these flawed peoples (Bunge 156). Yet Henríquez Ureña did go to considerable lengths in chapter 7 of his monograph *El español en*

Santo Domingo to deny that his country had had an African presence prior to 1916, when the United States invaded the Dominican Republic and promoted the flow of workers from Haiti (130, 134). As a mulatto, he himself had encountered negrophobic hostility in Mexico and the United States, yet these experiences did not seem to discourage his view of blackness as foreign to his country (Díaz Quiñones, "Pedro Henríquez Ureña" 69). Interestingly, the negroid features of his mother, which he visibly inherited, and the embarrassment they caused to the family in late nineteenth-century Santo Domingo, as well as to him and his sister Camila in early twentieth-century Minnesota, appear as a leitmotif in the historical novel *In the Name of Salomé* (2000) by the renowned Dominican American writer Julia Alvarez.

The proponents of mestizaje as the historical outcome that defused racial tensions would have been hard-pressed to explain a series of racially charged clashes in the countries of Ibero-America. It was a realization of the racial nature of their subjection that led to the 1912 insurrection of black Cubans in Oriente Province headed by Evaristo Estenoz and Pedro Ivonet during the José Miguel Gómez administration. Some three hundred blacks met their deaths when the government troops responded, decisively crushing the insurgents (Levine 3). Nor has the discourse of noncontentious hybridity provided reasoning that would counteract the antipathy that the region's Indigenous peoples have endured. We know Sarmiento dismissed the possibility of the "Indian" being a valid contributor to Argentinian society, and we know that the Creoles did not limit themselves to rhetorical aggression. Bolívar's 1819 speech at the Congress of Angostura refers in passing to contemporary Venezuela's disputes "with the natives for the titles of ownership," a candid reminder that the nations of the Americas were built on Indigenous land. To colonize a country, the Creoles often had to begin by clearing the ground of its native inhabitants, taking for granted the dispensability of these communities, including their languages, spiritual beliefs, and folkways.

In 1868, the Bolivian government declared the Indigenous peoples to be an impediment to the development and stability of the nation and promoted the outright theft of their lands. Referring to the Quechua and Aymara groups, Bolivian policymakers spoke of "the hopelessness of trying to civilize" these subject peoples "through education and training in our institutions" (qtd. in Calderón 197). Beginning from such a premise, it seemed logical to regard the communities in question as unfit to own and manage any property associated with development. This pronouncement followed: "To remove these lands from the hands of the ignorant and backward Indians is to achieve the most salutary transformation in the social and economic order of Bolivia" (qtd. in Calderón 197). In keeping with that syllogistic line of reasoning, the government of General Mariano Melgarejo in 1868 declared "the lands hitherto possessed by the Indians" to be the sovereign property of the Bolivian state. The government would then sell the lands in question by public auction, with the proceeds going "to cover the internal debt and public service expenditure" (qtd. in Calderón 198). There should be no doubt that atrocities that further reduced the numbers of the Indigenous peoples of Latin America, though carried out by generals and soldiers bearing firearms, derived their inspiration and legitimacy from ideological formulations made by intellectuals. In other words, it was the intelligentsia who created the paradigms that facilitated these crimes against humanity. They provided definitions of national identity that rendered specific ethnically differentiated subsections of the population inimical to the very constitution of the nation. They gave respectability to ethnic oppression, exclusion, and extermination. The effects of that opprobrious legacy have hardly died out. They still run rampant in the twenty-first century.

Latino Racial Proficiency and the Ubiquity of White Supremacy

Latina/o scholars writing and speaking from US university settings about race and ethnicity in Latin America and the Caribbean have some serious issues to confront. South of the Rio Grande, the intelligentsia has collaborated in grievous crimes against humanity, and those of us working in the North face the moral imperative to take a stand regarding that legacy. If we are to deserve a platform when we speak out against racism in the United States, we must stand clear of double standards. Moral consistency must manifest itself in the willingness to oppose racism wherever it occurs and with comparable compassion for victims, whatever their background. There is absolutely nothing that makes the ideas of a negrophobe or anti-immigrant, xenophobic agitator in the Northeast significantly worse than those of a white supremacist journalist or politician in the Rio de la Plata region. If we somehow find something more palatable in the one than in the other, we must admit to a defect in our moral compass. The theory of mestizaje can indeed play tricks on the mind, but once we detect the racism inherent in formulations extolling the advantages of miscegenation, moral alarm bells should go off immediately. In *La raza cósmica* (1925), José Vasconcelos set forth a potentially admirable view of hybridity, culminating in a "synthetic race," which he called the "fifth universal race" (32). He made himself objectionable, however, as soon as he demonstrated his acceptance of the existing ideology of superior and inferior races. His prediction of a future "cosmic race" depended on the absorption of "the inferior races" by "the superior," with blacks, for example, becoming "redeemed, step by step, by voluntary extinction" (32). Ultimately, he assigns to whites, with their peerless beauty and intelligence, the power to correct the defects of the darker races. One wonders where exactly Chicana feminist poet and lesbian activist Gloria Anzaldúa stands in terms of racism when she uncritically upholds Vasconcelos as an advocate of "inclusivity," whose ideas present an antidote to the "racial purity that white America practices" (99).

The schemes of thought underlying mestizaje can thus have profoundly racist roots. Abdias do Nascimento has fleshed out this truth in his assessment of the "Luso-Tropicalism" of Brazilian writers like Gilberto Freyre and Jorge Amado. He has decried their mystification of racial admixture as a conceptual strategy that has helped consolidate the misleading concept of racial democracy in Brazil (112). Freyre's model of *metaracial brunettism* insists on the extent to which Indigenous and African women, by becoming the domestics, concubines, and occasionally wives of the white masters/employers, contributed meaningfully to the social democratization of Brazil. Amado produces a scenario wherein hypersexualized blackness finds its match and mirror in the reserved and rational white psyche (Nascimento 113, 114).

Ultimately, celebrating miscegenation as a harmonious blending of disparate ethnic elements that fuse into a new transracial Iberian American assumes that the Caucasian ideal will continue to predominate and regulate the place accorded to each of the constituent parts of the resulting aggregate entity. The mestizo model, in other words, allows for the persistence of normative whiteness. The white ideal and an unbendingly Eurocentric definition of culture prevail in the configuration of the nation in public discourse. According to Carlos Moore, the prevalence of this scheme encounters little opposition, given the "deeply ingrained belief" among people of all colors in the region that, in his words, "whites are naturally superior to all other races" (210). The rise of the mestizo as a conceptual paradigm creates an illusion that tricks non-white ethnic minorities into compliance with the white norm. Mestizo identity allows for acknowledgment of difference in theory while circumventing the need to practice de facto inclusion. Conceptual inclusion breeds tolerance for practical exclusion. With that scenario in place, Venezuelan society can admit to the racial heterogeneity of its population without necessarily discontinuing the practice of representing the visage of the nation through a stream of homogeneously white women chosen to compete in the Miss Universe Pageant every year. Colombia, for its part, can celebrate diversity while continuing to render the Indigenous and black segments of the population invisible even after the 1991 constitutional reform took the radical step of acknowledging different ethnoracial groups within the country's population

(Arocha 71). Likewise, the guardians of official Dominican culture can continue to privilege the 10-percent-white minority over the remaining black and mulatta/o portion of the population to display the nation's official face on the international stage.

Parting with Crime

Owing to our rootedness in American society, Latina/o scholars possess what I would call a hyperethnicified perception that disposes us to react strongly to the deceptions inherent in the Latin American scenarios just described. Nonwhite ethnic minorities in the United States have had to fight fiercely for the level of empowerment and access they may now enjoy, however precariously. Glib arguments that race is a mere social construction deliver no real consolation. The truth of race for them is concrete, and its implications impinge on their life chances and opportunities for prosperity. Our partaking in American society's overt racial contentiousness has honed our perception. Affirmative action and other compensatory measures inserted into the Civil Rights Act could not have more categorically admitted to the reality of that contentiousness. We can now look at Latin American social interactions and easily recognize the violence that the official, more harmonious discourse conceals. I do not refer here only to the moral violence leveled at large portions of the population that have to coexist in society with white supremacist legacies that systematically exclude them from visual representations of the nation. I refer also, and more importantly, to the economic, political, and genocidal violence that racist formulations tend to encourage. Eurocentric and negrophobic definitions of Dominican national identity made it expedient for the Trujillo dictatorship, in the fall of 1937, to murder several thousand unarmed Haitian immigrants and their Dominican-born offspring in an effort to extirpate an unwanted population and to strengthen the "Dominicanness" of the border regions long exposed to Haitian influence (Vega, *Trujillo et Haïti* 390–392).

A quarter of a century later, Dominican society again witnessed the massacre of several thousand peasants in the village of Palma Sola in San Juan Province on December 28, 1962. The event supposedly helped safeguard "Christian values" and the economic, political, and cultural mores of the modern Dominican nation (Ferreras 318–320, 328, 332). The people slaughtered in Palma Sola were predominantly Afro-Dominicans, and their deaths did not provoke widespread indignation against the government, just as, after the genocide of 1937, the living accomplices of Trujillo, such as Balaguer, did not find themselves repudiated or prosecuted. Nor did the 1996–2000 government of Leonel Fernández Reyna, of the Partido de la Liberación Dominicana (a group formerly known for its left-wing leanings), have to contend with collective reproach for the illegal practice of denying birth certificates to the Dominican-born children of Haitian immigrant mothers. Such a measure was meant to keep them from claiming Dominican citizenship. This status is something the country's constitution, in keeping with the principle of jus soli, would automatically grant them.

The Inter-American Commission on Human Rights of the Organization of American States, in an October 1999 report, expressed concern for the denial of "fundamental rights, such as the right to nationality of the country of birth, access to health care, and access to education," to "numerous children of Haitian origin" (82). The government took offense and retaliated by deporting thousands of Haitians. Cardinal Nicolás de Jesús López Rodríguez quickly seized the occasion to voice his unequivocal public support for the retaliatory action of the Dominican authorities, declaring, "We are a nation, and we have a Dominican identity, and we have a flag. . . . [W]e are Dominican and we wish to remain being that" (my trans.; Feliz 1, 6). Adding that all countries have "their own territory, their own citizenship, their own culture, their own language," he decried what he believed to be an opportunistic practice among Haitian women: nearing their delivery dates, they would cross over to the Dominican Republic to give birth and thus claim Dominican citizenship for their children (Feliz 6). Emboldened by the Cardinal, among other politically influential voices in the country, the government continued to escalate its anti-Haitian agenda. Over a decade later, in 2013, a newly created Constitutional Court issued its ruling TC/0168/13, which annulled the Dominican citizenship of any person of Haitian ancestry who could not prove that their forebears entered the country legally. Applied retroactively to 1929, the court ruling denationalized over 250 thousand Haitian Dominicans, who instantly became illegal aliens in their land of birth, subject to deportation on the whim of any army personnel. Cardinal López Rodríguez stepped up again to defend the Dominican government, urging President Danilo Medina to disregard any demand or request to revoke the court ruling that had denationalized a quarter of a million Dominicans of Haitian ancestry (Rosa 228). Especially when voices of protest came from international human rights groups abroad, the merciless cardinal would override them by uttering ultranationalist rallying cries such as, "Here, we Dominicans call the shots" (Aquino Méndez 510).

When we think of the stateless children of Haitians in Dominican society, lacking the documentation that would verify their birthplace, and when we reflect on the plight of numerous other ethnically differentiated peoples suffering injustice throughout the countries of Latin America and the Caribbean, it becomes difficult to look the other way. As US scholars with a connection to the societies that perpetrate such atrocities, we have compelling reasons to care. White supremacy has been the conceptual glue that holds together the cultural logic of dispossession, discrimination, compulsory invisibility, and genocide in the hemisphere. Whether by preserving the exclusionary discourse of mono-ethnicity in the face of observable diversity or by paying lip service to pluralism while promoting a homogeneous picture (literally and figuratively) of the nation, Eurocentric formulations of national culture and the seduction of the Caucasian ideal have lent credence to schemes of thought that endanger the mental and physical well-being of too many inhabitants who call Latin America and the Caribbean home. As a result of their adherence to ideologies that allow ethnic antipathy to creep into definitions of the nation, the region's intelligentsia has been complicit in serious hate crimes. We must keep that background firmly in mind when we tackle the realities of race and ethnicity in the Americas. These matters cannot remain strictly academic. We are inescapably involved in the subject of our inquiry. At the very least, we ought to explore the ways in which our efforts, namely our intellectual labor, could help to dismantle the pervasive paradigms that have caused such harms historically and into the present day.

Afro-Latina/os and the Future

Let us not be tempted to think that a confrontation with the legacy of Latin American racism stems purely from a moral imperative. We have equally powerful motivations rooted in convenience and self-interest, with serious implications for the US Hispanic population's own ability to achieve appropriate levels of economic and political empowerment. Racial tensions can obstruct the ability of non-white ethnic minorities with common needs to present a united front or to pursue shared goals in this country. The visionary scholar and alliance-builder Frank Bonilla reminded us in 1995 of the seriousness of interethnic distrust between African Americans and Latina/os by pointing to the failure, in the 1930s, of the political leadership in both communities to seize control of the assembly seat in Manhattan's Seventeenth Congressional District, even though black and Latina/o voters outnumbered whites ("Urban Challenges"). Similarly, scholar Suzanne Oboler has pointed to a comparable tension during the 1960s that may have prevented grassroots Chicano leader Reies López Tijerina, head of the Alianza Movement, from forging effective alliances with such African American activists as Martin Luther King, Jr. (63). New York City in the 1990s witnessed a breakdown of communication between the political voices of black and Latino communities, which no doubt contributed to the defeat of the city's first black mayor, David N. Dinkins, in his bid for reelection. This outcome enabled the ascent of Rudolph Giuliani, whose eight-year term proved traumatic for both communities.

In addition to impairing the ability of Latina/os to forge salutary alliances with other segments of the US population, the issue of racial animosity has had serious consequences for the various US Hispanic communities in search of intraethnic unity. I believe that our failure to look closely at the racial divides within the Latino population can have a grave impact on the political and economic initiatives that are based on the precarious notion that Latina/os constitute one community with a shared sense of identity. For instance, sociologist Ginetta E. B. Candelario has unearthed a lesser-known chapter in the history of Dominican migration to the United States. She centered dark-skinned Dominicans who came to Washington, DC, in the 1940s as domestic servants to diplomatic families representing the Trujillo dictatorship. Settling into a city under the shadow of legal segregation, these workers had no choice but to embrace African American identity practices, as they could not live on the same (white) side of the color line as their employers. The Jim Crow divide came between them spatially and, in time, even culturally, with notable impact on their lifestyles that set them apart from their elite compatriots. Candelario cites the case of Mariela Medina, a black Dominican who, after having attended Harvard University, became an articulate spokesperson for the concerns of her community. Medina understood that to insert herself in civil rights discourses as a non–Puerto Rican and non–Mexican American person would be difficult. A dark-skinned Dominican like herself had to take the African American route, as it were, to achieve necessary visibility in Washington (165–166).

That racial segregation in the 1940s could divide Dominicans of different skin hues once they entered the geographic confines of Jim Crow is made clear by Candelario's evocation of Medina's experience in the US capital. Outside these legal strictures, however, a parallel partition could occur psychologically in the Northeast, even within a family unit, if its members subscribed to varying paradigms of ethnoracial identity and belonging. We get a glimpse of this internal rift in the memoir *Down These Mean Streets* (1967) by New York–born Puerto Rican writer Piri Thomas. A harrowing account of the author's descent into (and eventual ascent from) social hell, the story provides a slice-of-life narrative centered upon disempowered Puerto Ricans in New York during the 1950s. This city initially became a key destination for displaced workers who left the island after Operation Bootstrap compelled many to try their luck on the US mainland. Growing up in poverty with only precarious parental guidance, young Piri becomes embroiled in violence, drugs, theft, and other perils of street gangs. But no source of disquiet looms larger in the text than the narrator's internal turmoil stemming from his negroid phenotype, which sets him noticeably apart from his light-skinned sibling. Piri had taken after their father, while José inherited the features of their mother. The narrator's sense that both his parents preferred his brother over him is so pervasive that it alienates him from the family. He reproaches his father for not identifying overtly as black and resents his brother for the color line that, in his view, divides them. He did not learn that in Puerto Rico, as in the Hispanophone Caribbean generally, couples with mixed phenotypes have abounded for centuries without their children feeling psychologically driven to address the lack of color consistency at home. Unaware of the normalcy of color spectrums in his parents' birthplace, Piri feels at a loss and must seek out a comfort zone wherein to situate himself existentially. After a series of traumatic episodes in which the young man's Afrocentric self-assertion leads him to part with the family, José movingly voices a farewell: "Piri, I can't help what I am, or what I look like, or how I feel, any more than you can. You wanna be Black. You wanna find out if you can fit better. That's you. You're still my brother, if you can overlook my color. That's me" (Thomas 151).

We no longer live in a world of suffocating racial boundaries as evoked by this memoir. Decades of struggle for racial justice within and outside the Civil Rights Movement have not been in vain. But dark-skinned Latina/os in the United States still deal with a greater share of social impediments than their light-skinned counterparts. While most Hispanics typically contend with the structural barriers erected by mainstream American society, Afro-Latina/os seem to face those barriers to a greater extent, as they must also wrestle with impediments stemming from negrophobia within their own panethnicity. A 2020 study of Afro-Latina/os in Massachusetts found them facing higher rates of unemployment than their non-black Latina/o counterparts, despite having higher levels of educational attainment than the latter (Mattos et al. 2). In that sense, then, while José is right in saying to his brother that he "can't help" the skin shade and overall phenotype that he was born with, the statistics suggest that when the time comes for him to seek home ownership and employment opportunities, his visible difference from Piri would likely come in handy and be to his notable advantage.

I have explained elsewhere that anyone watching Hispanic TV in the United States will easily recognize the white supremacist value system that informs the way the corporate media companies imagine the collective visage of the Latino population ("Problematic Paradigms" 444–447). *Washington Post* journalist Michael A. Fletcher has reported on "the rigid racial hierarchy" that controls Spanish-language television in this country, pointing to the "almost exclusively Caucasian face" that the industry puts forward for general consumption ("Blond, Blue-Eyed Face"). His article features the testimony of popular Spanish-language radio personality Malín Falú, a noted Afro–Puerto Rican talk show host who repeatedly failed to land a job on Hispanic television. The exclusion that black Latina/os have historically endured, save in the recreational fields of boxing, baseball, some pop music genres, and other manifestations of what I would loosely describe as the "gladiator's arena," resulted in the gradual development in dark-skinned Hispanics of a self-recognized otherness vis-à-vis their light-skinned counterparts. Thus, in the 1990s, we witnessed the emergence of the term *Afro-Latina/o* to designate a new category among the paradigms brandished by US Hispanics of African origin to label their distinct ethnoracial location. The efflorescence in the fall of 1999 of distinctly Afro-Latino events in Washington, DC, at the Smithsonian Institution's National Portrait Gallery and at the White House (among others), spoke to the growing visibility of black Latina/os as a fully differentiated constituency in American society.

There is a persuasive indication that Latina/os have the capacity to overturn the nefarious legacy of negrophobia that they inherited from their ancestral Latin American homelands, and which has been complemented and amplified by the white supremacist heritage of Anglo-American society. I am referring to the way US Dominicans interact with Haitians in New York and other American cities where the two communities share space. The history of animosity between the two nations that occupy the island of Hispaniola has been competently evoked in journalist Michele Wucker's *Why the Cocks Fight: Dominicans, Haitians, and the Struggle for Hispaniola* (1999). But the shared marginality that Haitians and Dominicans endure in the United States seems to awaken both groups to the realization of their commonality. Especially students at colleges and universities in the Northeast, as well as community activists in New York and elsewhere, have demonstrated compelling evidence of a radically new understanding of the Haitian–Dominican rapport. At City College of the City University of New York, for instance, the Haitian and Dominican student associations shared the same office space and supported each other's activities throughout the 1980s. In the fall of 1997, Haitian and Dominican students at Cornell University joined in an effort to celebrate their shared heritage, featuring among the events readings by Haitian American author Edwidge Danticat and her Dominican American counterpart Junot Díaz. I served as keynote speaker in fall 1998 for the fifth anniversary of the joint gala organized by the Haitian American Students Association and Casa Dominicana at the University of Massachusetts-Amherst. More strikingly still, in February 1999, the members of the Manhattan-based Dominican organization Centro Cultural Orlando Martínez brought together Haitian writers, speakers, and performers for a joint commemoration of the 155th anniversary of Dominican independence. Since Dominicans founded their sovereign state by separating from Haitian rule, one can imagine the many ideological hurdles the organizers had to overcome in the process of conceiving a way to memorialize Dominican independence that steered clear of antipathy toward their nation's political Other.

I am convinced that US Dominicans' more humanized rapport with Haitians, breaking with their ancestral homeland's inimical construction of their neighbors, has to do in large part with their enhanced appreciation of the African heritage that connects them to the people of Haiti. The racial history of the United States soon awakens Dominicans to their marginality with respect to mainstream society, making it untenable for them to engage in strategies of othering toward fellow African-descended peoples. They also recognize their relative marginality with respect to the larger segments of the US Hispanic population, namely Mexican Americans, Cubans, and Puerto Ricans who tend to be lighter skinned. In other words, their self-recognition as Afro-Latina/os contributes to their greater solidarity with Haitians. By the same token, a comparable dynamic could contribute to bridging the communication gap between US Hispanics and African Americans in the public sphere. The emergence of self-recognition among Afro-Latina/os as members of a differentiated ethnoracial constituency places them in an ideal position to mediate between members of various black communities and beyond. Their blackness can open doors of communication and vital collaboration with African Americans. The mediating role of Afro-Latina/os, coupled with the persuasive espousal of black symbols and urban youth culture within the Hispanic population, may very well hold the key to a salutary future in the relationship between Latina/os and African Americans.

By looking closely at the specific experience of Afro-Latina/os and drawing from the lessons contained therein, the Latina/o scholar will be better equipped to tackle one of the most serious impediments to the community's collective advancement, namely intra-Latino racism and the various forms of violence that accompany it. Without an understanding of this unsavory phenomenon in all its complexities, Latina/os have a very slim chance of making meaningful contributions to social justice, either in the United States or in their ancestral Latin American homelands. A failure to tackle the racial problems within the panethnicity and the legacies of our forebears will lessen our credibility when protesting instances of exclusion from access to full citizenship for ourselves at present or for our offspring in the generations to come.

Notes

1. Translations of "Déclaration de repentance" are by Laurence Thomas, former Professor of Religion at Syracuse University.

2. The apology and subsequent visit of Pope Francis in 2022 for the widespread abuse of First Nations, Métis, and Inuit children in Canadian residential schools from the nineteenth through the twentieth centuries is another, more recent example of the ongoing quest for acknowledgment of a racist past by Indigenous peoples in that country. See Parkhill.

3. At the time of writing the original text that became this chapter, the author had no way of predicting the rise of a government with dictatorial sway over intellectual production and expressed opinions, including the threat of job loss and public ostracism, as became the case in the United States after the presidential inauguration of January 2025.

4. *Güero/a* is similar to *rubio/a* (blond). The former is a popular term for a white or white-presenting person in the Mexican vernacular.

5. Likewise, it is difficult to deracialize the denial of citizenship rights to the Dominican-born children of Haitian immigrants by the Dominican government at the very end of the twentieth century. See, for instance, López and Azcona.

CHAPTER 10

AFRO-LATINOS AND THE RACIAL WALL

As the concluding chapter to Problematic Paradigms, *"Afro-Latinos and the Racial Wall" is a fitting capstone to Torres-Saillant's inquiry into pan-Latinx subjects from the point of view of a frontline participant in the growth of Latino studies in the US academy. The opening line dispassionately argues that "to merit attention in contemporary civil society, beyond the narrow confines of scholarly parlors, the academic engagement with questions of race and ethnicity must commit to advancing ideological dispositions and patterns of thought that aim to erode the bases of racism." This sentence exemplifies the writer's signature style, including the use of quaintly archaic word choices ("scholarly parlors") and a broad-ranging lexicon, underscored by the praxis and voice of a scholar-activist ("to erode the bases of racism"). A well-chosen Latin quotation later in the essay (*Homo sum, humani nihil a me alienum puto*) adds a rhetorical flourish to an argument about social identity and racial self-affirmation, putting on full display yet another hallmark of Torres-Saillant's prose that draws readers in: a propensity to season his writing with foreign expressions and "patterns of thought" often unfamiliar to readers. Overall, what emerges is a better understanding of—and closer proximity to—the geographical, cultural, and temporal Other.*

As announced in its opening salvo, this chapter seeks to dismantle the racial wall by interrogating the very ways we conceptualize and otherwise confront and process racial matters. Torres-Saillant interrogates the self-harming narrative in African American youth culture that associates dedication to school and learning with "acting white," a racial and cultural essentialism that he juxtaposes with the straightforward exhortation Martin Luther King, Jr., delivered to high school students: "Always feel that you count." He goes on to warn against the high cost of racial and ethnic essentialism more broadly, including "positive essentialisms" (stereotypes cast as favorable traits meant to affirm one's identity) about ethnic communities and the individuals who seemingly represent them. Building to a crescendo near the end of the essay, Torres-Saillant concludes succinctly, "There are no cultural genes."

Particularly poignant in this essay are the writer's personal reflections on racially and ethnically inflected experiences in the classroom and beyond. He analyzes personal interactions with students as they (often uncritically) describe and interpret their own experiences through racialist conceptions and phraseology. He observes that US college students tend to find themselves unmentored in the skills needed to engage with the "social, historical, and existential meaning of ancestry." They will easily gravitate toward simple allegiances—those narrowly conceived and construed—and hence hit the racial wall. What remains crucial to "knowing ourselves ethnoracially" is some cognizance of "the symbolic realm" of racialist discourse, including awareness and understanding of the social narratives (including from commercial media) that shape our thoughts and feelings. Coming full circle to the statement of purpose announced at the opening of the essay, the chapter concludes with a call for "self-deracialization" through the questioning of rituals, stereotypes, expectations, and flawed logic that typically inform identitarian discussions. Through it all, Torres-Saillant maintains the conviction that Afro-Latina/os, given their unique and sometimes confounding ethnoracial location, can be instrumental in scaling the racial wall that continues to hinder our attempts to achieve justice, equality, and peace in our time.

The present essay espouses the tenet that to merit attention in contemporary civil society, beyond the narrow confines of scholarly parlors, the academic engagement with questions of race and ethnicity must commit to advancing ideological dispositions and patterns of thought that aim to erode the bases of racism. In the United States, the courts, in response to the array of collective awakenings set in motion by the Civil Rights Movement, have proscribed legal racism. Today, a racially motivated lynching would occur only as an aberration, and the use of the topic as premise for humor on a college radio or television station would elicit the reproach of people of goodwill across racial lines on campus. In fact, whenever another of the country's customary mass shootings takes place (save for those instances when perpetrators make their racial aims overt), one finds law enforcement using any data they can gather to rule out its being a "racially motivated crime," as if wishing to reassure the public that the killing would have been worse had the racial factor played a role. Racism remains vibrant, however, in the symbolic and structural realms with practical consequences that influence the material conditions of differentiated segments of the population. Economist Sylvia Ann Hewlett's study of racialized-minority professionals establishes that they do not find themselves "promoted and advanced at a rate commensurate with their weight in the talent pool" (qtd. in Gardner 13). Despite sterling credentials, many members of minority groups find that in order to gain entrance to and thrive in the white- and male-dominated corporate world, they need to mitigate key markers of their difference, including hairstyles, accessories, communicative gestures, diction, and even given names. Companies may still attribute the overwhelmingly white complexion of their managerial staff to a dearth of "qualified minority candidates," regarding Asian American women executives as lacking a "commanding" tone of voice or thinking of African American managers as "too loud" or "threatening" (Gardner 16).

Race remains so much with us that, in the late 1990s, when African-descended and British-educated scholars Hazel Carby and Paul Gilroy called on colleagues to attenuate the focus on race in and of itself, and to foreground diasporic routes and interconnections, their appeal triggered impassioned refutations from such US-based African American scholars as Molefi Asante, Houston A. Baker, and Hortense Spillers (Shea 45–47). Structural racism has firm roots in centuries of legally sanctioned inequality. The long memory of condoned inequity may still inform the behaviors of some institutions, influencing their current practices even as they endeavor to better distribute opportunities or parcel out social prestige. At the receiving end, those exposed to generations of traumatic depersonalization may yet retain a scarred sense of self that conditions their acceptance of prevailing stereotypes generated and perpetuated by their detractors. The remnants of oppression persist in what scholars have termed "internalized racism," which can have consequences beyond the individual (Singer 393–394). We cannot fail to consider the role that the victims themselves, in their own efforts to affirm their personhood, may unwittingly play in upholding the racist paradigms that they purport to call out and dismantle.

The remainder of this discussion will meditate on the place of race-based thinking by racialized minorities in the context of the lingering practices that define and inform what we understand racism to be in the United States. I will isolate Afro-Latina/os as a segment of the population particularly suited to help transform American society into a more level playing field where the content of one's character, knowledge, and efforts can determine the position one occupies in society.

Situating Afro-Latina/os

Afro-Latina/os occupy a peculiar place in this country's ethnoracial makeup, insofar as the label that names them combines blackness (Afro-), as a racial designation that stretches across various ethnicities, with Hispanicity (Latina/o), as an ethnic label that encompasses multiple races. Conceivably, an Afro-Latina/o may come from two black parents of Latin American origin, a black and a non-black Latin American couple, a black non-Hispanic Caribbean parent and a Hispanic parent of any race, a US Hispanic of any race and a black African, or an African American and a US Hispanic of any race, among other variations of mixed parentage. The variegated nature of the ancestry of Afro-Latina/os further exposes the precarious constitution of official classifications that break down the US population into five presumably distinct communities of descent. In 1977 the US Census acknowledged one ethnic and four racial branches to catalogue the country's population. The category of Hispanic or Latina/o, consisting of people who, regardless of race, trace their origins to Latin American countries, constitute the one "ethnicity." Then follow the four groupings that designate the so-called races: *American Indian* or *Alaska Native* describes an individual ancestrally connected to the Indigenous peoples of the Americas; *Asian* or *Pacific Islander* refers to a person with origins traceable to the Far East and Oceania, Southeast Asia, or the Indian subcontinent, including such countries as Japan, China, Pakistan, and the Philippines, as well as to Hawaii, Guam, Samoa, or other Pacific Islands; *Black* or *African American* applies to a person who descends from any of the black racial groups of Africa; and *White* denotes a person of European, North African, or Middle Eastern origins.

The unstable nature of the foregoing classification system was borne out by the voices that contested it during the 1990s. Policymakers and activists, venting their dissatisfaction with its logic, contemplated the possibility of modifications prior to the 2000 Census. For instance, a national coalition of Asian Pacific Islander Americans lobbied for the inclusion of Cambodians and Laotians under the heading of Asian or Pacific Islander; the Arab American Institute argued for the removal of Middle Easterners from the White category and their placement in a protected category of their own; Hawaiian US Senator Daniel K. Akaka advocated the transfer of his people from the Asian or Pacific Islander designation to the American Indian or Alaska Native label to protect them from the misperception that they, the original inhabitants of the Hawaiian Islands, "somehow 'immigrated' to the United States like other Asian or Pacific Island groups"; and the National Council of La Raza wished for Hispanics to gain recognition as a full-fledged race rather than merely as an ethnic group (Wright 46). Still other voices agitated in favor of creating a new category for people of multiracial origin. The proponents of a multiracial box were unable to have the new category added to the existing ethnoracial classification system, but the fact that, for the first time ever, the 2000 US Census form allowed people to mark more than one racial group can be regarded as a small victory on their part. Political scientist Kim M. Williams's *Mark One or More: Civil Rights in Multiracial America* (2006) examines the long-term implications of the change, even though, as she noted in a 2005 interview with *Kennedy School Insight*, "only about 2.6 percent of Americans identified with more than one race in 2000."

However, neither the shifting statistical scenario nor the dubious nature of the existing ethnoracial taxonomy in question would strike me as justifiable grounds for recommending its outright dismissal. Such dismissal, in my view, would entail a reckless disregard for the civil rights agenda that the census categories came to address. Besides, epistemic dissatisfaction with the existing categories may be prompted by the equally disturbing expectation that some other classification system can successfully achieve an accurate rendition of dynamically configured segments of the human population. I have made my peace with the labels that classify the US population into distinct communities of descent by accepting them as expressive of a set of sociopolitical aspirations rather than as descriptive of an objective reality. The US Hispanic population, for instance, can reap whatever practical benefits the census categories may bring, in terms of allocation of federal funds to particular municipalities (including school districts), without allowing the statistical nomenclature of a federal agency to shape the way the "community" looks at itself, with any pretension of partaking of some sort of "essence." Promoting a Latino agenda does not preclude acknowledging the unstable and fractious nature of the very concept of Latina/o, an appellation—in all its evolving varieties—that has the improbable ambition of denoting the collective core of over sixty million US Hispanics, with disparate histories, heritages, and nation-specific experiences. By virtue of interlaced ethnoracial and multicultural experiences dating back to their colonial roots in the Americas, Latina/os have the historical wherewithal to discern the fragility of ethnoracial identity formulations and to help shake the conceptual edifices of the racial imagination. They can trouble the dominant racial logic, first, by stressing the US Hispanic population's own multiracial constitution. Foregrounding "the differentiated experiences of Latina/os of European ancestry, Indigenous Latina/os, Asian Latina/os, and Afro-Latina/os" (Torres-Saillant, "Problematic" 452), they can contribute to an expansion of the identity terrain currently available to the population, thus trespassing the territorial boundaries of what David Hollinger has termed "the ethnoracial pentagon" (7–9 et passim). The systematic fracturing of the Latino or Hispanic label may have several beneficial outcomes. A refashioning of the group's identity space could rid it of the "white supremacist assumptions" that often inform intra-Latino relations, potentially increasing the likelihood that the most marginalized subsections of the US Hispanic population will identify with national efforts to mobilize the whole so-called community around agendas of collective significance (Torres-Saillant, "Inventing" 147).

Afro-Latina/os, I would propose, have an even more central role to play in advancing this aspiration. Having borne the brunt of negrophobic practices and discourses in US society, as well as in their ancestral Caribbean and Latin American homelands, they may well boast of having an epistemically advantageous vantage point. Those Afro-Latina/os who have been enlightened rather than destroyed by their panhemispheric marginalization can muster the necessary wisdom to deploy their deeper understanding of the travesty of racist thought and challenge intra-Latino prejudices, foster collaboration with African Americans and other blacks from the global diaspora, valorize our large share of indigeneity, visibilize the Asian presence in our midst, and effectively participate in the struggle for social justice, equality, and inclusion on both sides of the Rio Grande. Seldom experiencing their "race" as natural, Afro-Latina/os often feel called upon to define themselves according to one or another of the components of their complex selves. Growing up in East Harlem, journalist Roberto Santiago often heard from the African American boys on the block that he did not "act black," while his lighter-skinned Puerto Rican friends jeered, "You're not black. You're a *boricua*, you ain't no *Moreno*" (46). The prevalent instinct of hypodescent racialization, which would favor blackness as the component that names a mixed-race person, does not seem to apply unproblematically to Afro-Latina/os. Evincing the hemispheric dimension of the phenomenon, scholars Suzanne Oboler and Anani Dzidzienyo stress the importance of focusing on the specificity of the life experience of "both Afro-Latin Americans and US-born and/or raised Afro-Latinos," since, while "the stigma of blackness" may operate similarly throughout the hemisphere, the various national-origin groups (Afro-Colombians, Afro-Puerto Ricans, Afro-Ecuadoreans, US-based Afro-Dominicans, and so on) experience it heterogeneously (16).

The Garifuna of Honduras, for instance, are among the least "Latinized" and most culturally distinct Afro-Latin American populations. In the United States, however, their insertion into the country's ethnoracial structure does not occur without ambivalence. In broad terms, they clearly assert their blackness, but they also tend to differentiate themselves from African Americans and for the most part settle for an "Afro-Hispanic" identity space (Anderson 112–113). Afro-Latina/os also enter the US Hispanic sphere with a measure of disadvantage. For instance, they show weaker socioeconomic indicators than other Latina/os. A 2003 study done by the Lewis Mumford Center at the State University of New York at Albany, as well as the 2002 National Survey of Latinos, conducted by the Pew Hispanic Center in Washington, DC, found many interviewees who reported feeling prejudice from other Latina/os (T. K. Hernández, "Afro-Latinos" 36).

We do not know the exact size of the Afro-Latino population. The 2000 US Census, which is the one that first enabled this panethnic group to claim more than one racial classification, counted over thirty-five million people of Hispanic descent in the country, making up 12.5 percent of the total population. With the option of marking more than one "race" category, some 2 percent of those who identified themselves as Hispanic or Latino also marked "Black," whereas nearly half marked "White," and 45.2 percent marked "some other race" (T. K. Hernández, "Afro-Latinos" 35). At the time, it seemed conceivable that the number of Afro-Latina/os would grow substantially as individuals became more comfortable with the census practice of allowing them to mark more than one ethnoracial category. It was noteworthy, however, that the majority of those marking both the "Black" *and* "Latino" boxes traced their origins to the Dominican Republic or Puerto Rico, with a contingent of approximately 250 thousand individuals of Mexican ancestry also classifying themselves as "Black" (35).

The identity of Afro-Latina/os may be met with suspicion in the eyes of African Americans, Hispanics, and whites. A few examples drawn from personal experience might help illustrate this point. Elsewhere in my writings I have narrated my encounter with the organizers of a black faculty and staff caucus at an institution where I formerly taught. The leaders of the initiative had weighed the question of whether to invite me to join, the degree of melanin on my skin seeming to qualify me while my Hispanophone roots appeared to place me in separate ethnoracial category. Unable to resolve their uncertainty and wishing to treat me fairly, they resorted to the reasonable solution of letting *me* decide. A colleague, serving as emissary, approached me and, after explaining the situation, posed this question: "Do you consider yourself *more* black than Hispanic or *more* Hispanic than black?" Dismayed by the task of having to quantify the immaterial, I hesitated, spending sentences galore in aimless circumlocution. My indecisiveness must have made me suspect in the eyes of my colleague, who clearly did not share my lack of clarity about matters of identity, with the result that I never heard from the black caucus again (Torres-Saillant, "Dominican Blackness" 283–284).

In addition to the living, the dead may also be subject to demands for ethnoracial precision. This stands out clearly in the case of a racially mixed labor activist who died in 1942, at the age of ninety, after a life devoted to promoting equality and justice. A biography written by Carolyn Ashbaugh, a researcher in women's labor history, calls her Lucy Parsons, privileges her black side, and dismisses the subject's self-attribution of Hispanic origin as an unfortunate repudiation of "her own black ancestry" (66, 268). Her Mexican American biographers, on the other hand, name the same labor advocate Lucía González Parsons and celebrate her as "an important early radical Chicana reformer" ("González Parsons, Lucía" 149). Scholars Alfredo Mirandé and Evangelina Enríquez succinctly capture the squabble over González Parsons's ethnicity in their book on Mexican American women. Like Ashbaugh, they champion only one of her ancestries when they declare her a full-fledged Chicana (91). A subtler manifestation of the same tension, largely devoid of acrimony, is the scholarly consensus formed around the figure of famed collector and historian Arturo Schomberg, who appears primarily black in African American sources but primarily Puerto Rican in Latino ones.

Another pertinent incident takes me back to the fall of 1998, when I served on the literature panel of the Mid-Atlantic Arts Foundation in Baltimore, Maryland. I recall bonding with the panel's two other males, one black and the other white. After completing the work, we found ourselves enjoying mirthful drinks at the bar of the hotel where we stayed. As the hours of our gleeful conversation passed, I noticed a distinct pattern in the triangular architecture of our exchange. The volume of animated words that flowed between my two companions greatly surpassed the number of utterances either of them exchanged with me. Though we had known one another for the same amount of time, a mere day and a half, and we all partook of a common interest in literature, as well as a shared disposition to serve in state arts councils, I sensed that I could not succeed at steering my third of the conversation. Try as I might, I failed to assert myself as a natural speaker at the table of conviviality. I, the Hispanic, my dark-skinned hue notwithstanding, could not compete with the attention and enthusiasm that kept my black and white associates going with reciprocal zest. I found myself resigned to playing a supporting role as a tributary to the main dialogue, intermittently expanding upon or wittily complementing the core chat between my black and white copanelists. While never desisting from my occasional feeder remarks to confirm my still-active presence, I mused about the long history of attraction and repulsion that mysteriously bonded my black and white interlocutors in a way that rendered my presence historically tertiary. In 1998, I had lived in the United States for a good twenty-five years; then, as now, my spoken English lacked the smoothness of a native speaker. Listeners wishing to locate the provenance of my accent often end up befuddled. Whether the dynamic at the table would have varied radically had my black and white acquaintances not detected in my voice the surviving trappings of the foreigner will have to remain a matter of conjecture.

I have come to expect that many Americans will experience my presence as less than natural, seldom looking at me without envisioning an elsewhere. I still find them at times inclined to edify me by fleshing out "American" social dynamics. These generous observations might start with, "The thing is, Silvio, we in the United States. . . ." At times, the age of the person speaking has been younger than the years of my American experience. Sometimes, the arsenal of assumptions has defied observable phenomena and intuition. I recall an experience with a white colleague who was an adjunct instructor in the English department of a college where I taught during the late 1980s. Never uttering a word in anything other than the King's English, she and I typically discussed various matters literary and political. When an essay of mine appeared in an academic journal and the publisher sent me twenty-five offprints, I thought of giving her one. As I tendered the copy and began to provide a minimal preface to frame the gesture, she amicably declined it without even glancing at the artifact in my hand, confessing politely, "Oh, no, I don't read Spanish." Dumbstruck, I withdrew at that point, judging it too insistent if I were to point out the Englishness of the words that made up the essay. I subsequently interpreted the episode as a situation in which my Hispanicity interfered with my colleague's ability to imagine me as a person in command of English, though we had never spoken anything else and had met as faculty members in an English department. Ironically, as a full-time instructor, I had a higher rank than she did, which meant that I taught the more advanced English and American literature survey courses. With that position, I enjoyed a greater measure of academic privilege, but clearly there remained impediments to inhabiting the role fully.

The preceding incident contrasts sharply with one that took place in the fall of 2002 at a Peruvian restaurant in Chicago, where a group of light-skinned Latina/o colleagues and I went to dine following a day-long editorial meeting as we prepared to launch the journal *Latino Studies*. Most of our cohort had been born in the United States and spoke English as their native tongue. On the other hand, I had come to the United States at the age of eighteen from a Spanish-speaking country, where I had completed my education through secondary school. By then, apart from a couple of texts in English, my book *El retorno de las yolas* (1999), written entirely in Spanish, had appeared in print. The gentleman server assigned to our table greeted the gathering in Spanish, explained the specials of the day, and proceeded counterclockwise to take our orders, beginning with the colleague to my right. When my turn arrived, the server—for some reason—felt compelled to dispense with Spanish and ask for my order in English. This switch did not escape the notice of my colleagues, and once the waiter was no longer within hearing range, we all proceeded to interpret it, as scholars are wont to do. In unison we concluded that my blackness had prevented the nice Peruvian gentleman from recognizing my Hispanicity. Another layer of irony emerges here. The waiter may have correctly identified us as academics on their way from a scholarly meeting. This was not an unreasonable supposition, given the proximity of the restaurant to the Chicago campus of the University of Illinois. If that was the case, one would have to forgive his blunder when he took me for a non-Latino. Prior experience had by then revealed to me that Afro-Latina/os seldom sat at the table of conversation in Latino scholarly fora. When participating in events in which Latina/o academics analyzed the past, present, and future of the US Hispanic population, I had often been among the very few (if not the only) Afro-Latina/o to address the august lecture hall or conference room. At any rate, these incidents should suffice to place in stark relief the difficult ethnoracial bind of African-descended Latina/os, an identitarian instability that ironically confers upon them a uniquely advantageous position from which to help advance modes of thought meant to effectuate the necessary deracialization of the national imaginary.

Enduring Disunities

The difficult rapport between Latina/os and African Americans merits serious attention, and Afro-Latina/os may be best qualified to take the lead in maintaining affable conversation. Due most likely to the combined effects of "unresolved racism within Latino communities" and "the frequently parochial way in which African Americans privilege the US-born black experience" (Sawyer 265), we in the twenty-first century still confront the legacy of "a history of conflict" between African Americans and Latina/os (Rowe and García Ramos 203). Scholars Daryl Rowe and Reyna García Ramos urge concerned members of each group to counterbalance the legacy of intergroup conflict by foregrounding the instances of collaboration and solidarity in the history of black and Latino contact. However, from the 1980s onwards, a growing tendency emerged in the mass media that seemed to pit one group against the other in a Darwinian contest. Particularly as corporations undertook to cash in on the continuing growth of the US Hispanic population, one would hear or read repeatedly that Latina/os had "replaced" blacks as the country's "largest minority," the oxymoron notwithstanding. The prominent Mexican American essayist Richard Rodriguez was on point when he noted that the country's "Hispanic political leadership has remained silent about the Census Bureau's grammar" (*Brown* 127). Rodriguez observes, not without grounds, that Hispanics have become "a population segment, an ad-agency target audience, a market share. Not coincidentally, it was an advertising agency that got the point of Hispanic totals as early as the 1980s. It was then that Coors Beer erected billboards throughout the Southwest that flattered 'The Decade of the Hispanic'" (127–128).

The most visible trends in conventional mass media, alongside new communications technologies, seem at present to conspire against harmonious relations between African Americans and Latina/os. On the one hand, the apparent business necessity of the corporate media to fuse all US Hispanic subgroups into a single panethnic market fuels the compulsion to promote homogenized representations of the whole (assorted) group. Such depictions tend to rely on the long-standing iconography of mestizaje as the signal representation of brownness. As a result, distinct Asiatic, Indigenous, and Negroid phenotypes fail to enter the picture. Thus the light mestizo visage has prevailed to suggest the Hispanicity of the Latina/o figures who grace the mainstream network screens. Examining beer commercials at the start of the twenty-first century on Univision, the Spanish-language television network, Frank G. Pérez concluded that the Hispanophone segment of corporate America was no less engaged in the exclusionary and strategic blending of the Latina/os represented on television (153). Furthermore, the multiple possibilities brought about by the latest developments in communications technologies have created new premises for ethnoracial separation. Media observers Don Umphrey and Alan B. Albarran have noted the practice of curtailing venues and program content discretely, according to the specifications of carefully differentiated market segments. Speculating on the sort of scenario that we might expect from the advent of new media, Umphrey and Albarran assert that in nurturing the taste of communities for their own material, at the exclusion of exposure to the differences of other groups, "a multichannel environment leads to polarization both between and among ethnic groups" (52). The immediate horizon, then, does not bode well for enhanced interactions between Latina/os and African Americans. Legal specialist Nicolás C. Vaca's emphasis on the contentiousness that has characterized the relationship between the two groups, and his dismissal of claims that assume a kind of rainbow coalition among disempowered minorities, merits special attention here. The racial attacks in the California state penitentiaries in February 2006 that caused the Pitchess Detention Center, on the northern fringes of Los Angeles County, to segregate Latino and black inmates would seem to affirm the need for ongoing vigilance and mindful awareness of the work that needs to be undertaken by both groups (Pomfret).

The Advent of Brown

The exponential numerical growth of US Hispanics has elicited the concern of doomsayers as much as it has emboldened the prophets of better days. On the neutral side, scholars seem to agree that "a 'browning' phenomenon is now more prominent than ever" in major American cities that boast a significant portion of non-white residents (Rios and Mohamed xi). Among the prognosticators of calamity, political scientist Samuel P. Huntington revived his dormancy in the public sphere by seeking to alarm white and black Americans with such forebodings as "One index foretells the future: In 1998 'José' replaced 'Michael' as the most popular name for newborn boys in both California and Texas" (44). Linguist Otto Santa Ana has meticulously examined the metaphors prevailing in American public discourse to stress the "dangerous" growth of the Hispanic population. Many of these tropes codified the language that went into the drafting of Proposition 187, the law passed by the California electorate on November 8, 1994, to deny healthcare, social services, and education to undocumented immigrants. The metaphors appealed to the citizenry's fear of "drowning by browning"; the nation was gasping "under a brown tide," with the "relentless flow" of immigrants who, "like waves on a beach," threatened to remake "the face of America" (Santa Ana 7).

Apparently fearful of the inundation, the City of Manassas, Virginia, a mere thirty-five miles from Washington, DC, established a new zoning ordinance that outlawed "households consisting of a family's cousins, uncles, aunts, nieces, and nephews," much to the indignation of the *Washington Post*, whose December 30, 2005, editorial issued a sobering reprimand of the regulation. "Like other suburban localities in this region," the editorial notes, "Manassas is undergoing a demographic shift as Hispanic immigrants, legal and undocumented, move into what were once relatively homogenous neighborhoods," where they often "share housing with their relatives to help out with the rent or mortgage" ("Manassas's War"). While some communities have welcomed this influx, Manassas city officials have opted "to harass" the newcomers, "sending inspectors into selected city households to interrogate hard-working people about the numbers and relationships of the inhabitants." The editorial mentions the case of Leyla and Juan Chavez, US citizens living in this country since the 1980s, who, found guilty of housing a "nephew as well as a renter couple who lived downstairs," endured "the city's persecution" and ultimately decided to depart. Evidently the management at the *Washington Post*, though presumably white, did not share the anxiety of the Manassas city officials about the "browning" of the population.

Similarly, there are those, mostly coming from Hispanic quarters, who herald the demographic change with an unabashedly celebratory attitude. Medical scholar David E. Hayes-Bautista confidently asserts that by virtue of their numerical growth, "Latinos today are defining what it is to be American" (176). Tracing the historical development of Hispanics in California and chronicling the uninterrupted presence of a Latino civil society in the state dating back to April 1769, the Mexican American academic regards Latina/os as "the new generation of Americans who will create American society and identity for the twenty-first century" (4). Hayes-Bautista seeks to allay the concerns of those who perceive the demographic shift as corrosive of the country's core values; instead of representing an "un-American" presence, Latina/os, like non-Latina/o Texans, merely represent a "distinctive way of being American" (11, 178).

Though complicated by conflicting desires and contradictory temptations, the foregoing pronouncements constitute a difficult but inevitable conversation about ethnoracial crossing and the future of race in the United States. It is an exchange in which Afro-Latina/os ought to have a natural, if not a leading, role. By virtue of their unstable ethnoracial location, they are ideally positioned to embody "public admissions of racial impurity," to escape the logic and the legacy of the "one-drop-rule," to subvert the racial imagination, and, as writer Richard Rodriguez concludes in *Brown: The Last Discovery of America* (2002), to undermine even the very "notion of race" (202). In his intensely personal meditation on ethnoracial identity, Rodriguez declares that "race is America's theme—not freedom, not democracy (as we say in company)," and envisions a time when the country will dare to speak the truth about its brownness (136). He also hopes for a reckoning with the history of miscegenation that the children of John Rolfe and Pocahontas, or Sally Hemings and Thomas Jefferson, would seem to epitomize. White supremacy in the United States gave rise to a situation in which only whites could enjoy the freedom to escape racial identity, embodying unmitigated personhood and humanity, while everyone else remained confined to the prison of their racialized blood (140–141). Provocatively, Rodriguez shares that he wants for African Americans the same freedom he would like for himself, namely the freedom "to admit brown" (142). During a 2002 interview on the program *Now with Bill Moyers*, the writer gave a poignant example of the country's resistance to acknowledging its brownness. He pointed to the irony that at the ceremony where the film industry congratulated itself for giving an Academy

Award to Halle Berry as a "black actress," the Oscar recipient was sitting right next to her white mother. When we learn further that Berry's parents divorced when she was only four, and that it was her mother who raised her, the irony that her absent African American father should count as the only racial progenitor becomes even more pronounced. The episode patently shows blacks and whites colluding in the preservation of a consensus that regards "a white woman capable of giving birth to a black child but denies that a black woman can give birth to a white child" (Fields 149).

Afro-Latina/os, again because of the discomfort of their ethnoracial location, bring to the conversation a history of necessary familiarity with the reality of brownness. We should acknowledge, however, an earlier use of the term *brown* that did not overtly denote racial crossing. The Research Institute of the Bureau of Negro Affairs in 1930 began publication in Philadelphia of a periodical that promoted the interests of the black community under the title *The Brown American*. The periodical ceased in 1940, and the following year the National Association of Negroes in American Industry revived it as its official organ until 1945, when it finally disappeared, having been superseded by *The Negro Statesman*. Still, the usage that Rodriguez invokes has meaningful precedents. In 1931, Edwin R. Embree opened his book *Brown America* with this tiding: "A new race is growing up in America. Its skin is brown. In its veins is the blood of the three principal branches of man—Black, white, and yellow-brown. The new race numbers twelve million in the United States, and other millions in the West Indies and Central America" (3). The emergence of the "new race" did not disturb Embree. On the contrary, he viewed it as the necessary solution to the race problem in the country: "As to the future of Brown Americans, I am a confirmed optimist. The race problem in the United States, which in the dark decades following the Civil War seemed completely baffling, no longer is among the difficult questions of the nation" (284–285).

Evidently, Embree's extreme optimism, expressed as if he were unaware of Jim Crow (which would remain legally in place for more than three decades after his writing), failed to do justice to the grave racial reality in the United States. Today, almost a century after his words appeared in print and the movement for civil rights having brought about significant transformations, we still cannot exclude race from what he characterizes as pivotal questions for the nation. Apart from ethnoracially differentiated statistics about incarcerations, unemployment, educational attrition, and substandard housing, the state of race today can be deduced from the statistical figures produced by specialists. An edited volume from 2001 titled *Beyond Racism* presents us with a good sampling of recognized specialists of that time who explored questions of racial inequality in Brazil, South Africa, and the United States. But rather than heralding the "end of racism," the volume closes with an appeal by political scientist Charles V. Hamilton to the societies in question to upgrade their investment in formal education to help the disempowered better protect themselves from the legacy of racism (597). The aspiration seems to be for the development of appropriate palliatives to treat the victims of a seemingly perpetual source of stress. But one need not grant racism such a timeless ontology and can instead assert that existing, as it does, in history and within the sphere of social relations, racism is subject to the perishability of all other products of human creation. Perhaps we have never been as well equipped to speed up its dismantling as we are at present.

Like others before me, I perceive a vulnerable spot in the constitution of racial separatism, namely, the clear propensity of the so-called races to undergo alteration by means of carnal intermingling, contributing to the process of browning that Rodriguez has explored. Naming it "amalgamation," David A. Hollinger has chronicled the trend's upward growth since the second half of the twentieth century. The 1990 Census reported rates of out-marriage for Latina/os at 33 percent, for Asian Americans at about 50 percent, for Native Americans at about 60 percent, and for African Americans—as defined by the hypodescent standard—at 10 percent ("Amalgamation" 1385). The persistence of negrophobia among the other ethnoracial minorities, as well as among whites, and a stronger sense of ethnic self-affirmation among blacks (which may express itself at times as a reticence to mingle carnally with whites) probably explain the lower rates of out-marriage for African Americans. Yet even the 1990 numbers represent a substantial increase as compared with the 1980 Census figures. Indeed, for all groups involved, we need to consider the significance of nonmarital cohabitation / common-law partnerships at a time when, as Hollinger observes, the percentage of formal marriages has continued to diminish ("Amalgamation" 1386). Furthermore, evolving genealogical research has shed new light on the history of interracial commingling since the violent period of slavery, with approximately 30 percent of African Americans who take DNA tests to determine their lineage finding Caucasian descent on their father's side (Willing 4A). The literary critic and historian Henry Louis Gates, Jr., host of the PBS documentary *African American Lives* (2006), which showcased nine black celebrities who underwent genetic testing, has found his own ancestry to be 50 percent white (Willing 4A). This type of discovery forces us to confront the irony of ethnoracial belonging, in light of Gates's leadership role in shaping black studies in the US academy. At the time, serving as chair of Harvard University's Department of African and African American Studies, he was particularly visible as spokesperson cum academic entrepreneur, promoting projects that sought to define the black experience.

Proposing amalgamation as an ethnoracial destination for the US population had by then a long history. To invoke racial interbreeding, says Hollinger, is to reclaim the vocabulary of Wendell Phillips, Frederick Douglass, and Ralph Waldo Emerson ("Amalgamation" 1386). Noting California's long history of Punjabi–Mexican intermarriage, Gary B. Nash recalls the period between 1913 and 1949, when "80 percent of Asian Indian [South Asian] men in California married Hispanic women" (948). Nash contends that racial intermingling has been a constant in American society, from the earliest colonial moment to the present (949). He draws attention to the attempts by Thomas Jefferson and John Hancock to promote intermarriage between American Indians and whites, and he cites the Afro-Indigenous ancestry of Crispus Attucks as emblematic of the long history of conjugal relations between Native Americans and African Americans (945–947). Nor could the idea of racial admixture have been entirely absent from the mind of Martin Luther King, Jr., who viewed integration as the necessary next step following desegregation. When people of different ethnoracial origins come together socially, politically, and in various professional capacities, interpersonal affinities—including sexual—are bound to make an appearance as well. In that respect, the 1967 United States Supreme Court ruling on the famous *Loving v. Virginia* case, which put an end to over three hundred years of antimiscegenation laws in the land, came to complete the fluid interracial mobility of bodies made legally possible by the 1954 *Brown v. Board of Education* ruling, the Supreme Court decision that struck down the 1896 *Plessy v. Ferguson* "separate but equal" precedent.

Toward a New Amalgamation

As a challenge to the structure of racism, amalgamation rarely stressed the agency of the less empowered when articulated by its early advocates. A new understanding of amalgamation would have to contemplate restoring to racialized peoples the full extent of the humanity that white supremacist reasoning had denied them. It would need to interrupt the white monopoly on the privilege to embody unmitigated personhood and resolve to delink from the tyrannical essentialisms of blood quanta. This new way of viewing intermixture would need to embrace a deracialized paradigm of amalgamation, withdrawing support for the notion that among the elements to be mixed, some are better than others. Put simply, this would be tantamount to delinking from racialized formulations in all constructions of identity. I am most interested in seeing this understanding embraced by ethnoracial minorities, with Afro-Latina/os playing a role among those at the helm, by virtue of their complex history.

Proponents of amalgamation of earlier generations rarely transcended racism in their formulations. The venerable Puerto Rican thinker Eugenio María de Hostos, in an article entitled "Cholo," published in Lima's *La Sociedad* on December 23, 1870, voiced one of the earliest known Latin American pronouncements on amalgamation. Meditating on the Peruvian *Cholo*, the name given to people of mixed European and Indigenous ancestry, Hostos regarded the "New World" as the oven or kiln (*horno*) where all the races would "melt." To him, the Latin American mestiza/o indicated that the process of melting was well on its way (372). Since he viewed the mestiza/o as "the hope of progress," he concluded that the future of the region hinged on "the fusion of the races" (373).

The African American essayist and fiction writer Charles W. Chesnutt, who by 1900 felt confident enough to speak of "the unity of the human race" as a proven fact, claimed that "the conception of a pure Aryan, Indo-European race has been abandoned in scientific circles, and the secret of the progress of Europe has been found in heterogeneity, rather than in racial purity" (18). He envisioned the American population as one "composed of octoroons, or persons only one-eighth Negro, who would probably call themselves white, if by this time there remained any particular advantage in being so considered" (21). As a result, "there would be no inferior race to domineer over" and no "superior race to oppress those who differed from them in racial externals" (21). Despite legislation aimed at preventing "race fusion," Chesnutt saw admixture as the inevitable historical process that would produce the future American. He conceived, just as Hostos did for Latin America and the Caribbean, the North American portion of "the New World" as a cauldron from which a new race and a less fractious pattern of social relations would emerge. Similarly, among Latina/o voices, several well-known authors have proclaimed their identity in terms that point directly to their distinctness as the product of amalgamation in the hemisphere. Thus, the speaker in "Child of the Americas," a poem by Puerto Rican writer Aurora Levins Morales, muses,

> I am not african. Africa is in me, but I cannot return.
> I am not taína. Taíno is in me, but there is no way back.
> I am not european. Europe lives in me, but I have no home there.
> I am new. History made me. (79)

The liminal locations that Chicana feminist writer Gloria Anzaldúa embraces to assert her transgressive identity also echo the semiotics of amalgamation. The title of her poem "To Live in the Borderlands Means You" creates the occasion for a definition of hybridity, intermixture, and borderlessness. The poem's speaker equates inhabiting the "borderlands" with the awareness of being a mélange of identities:

> neither *hispana india negra española*
> *ni gabacha, eres mestiza, mulata,* half-breed
> caught in the crossfire between camps
> while carrying all five races on your back (216)

The oven imagined by Hostos prefigured the melting-pot metaphor that would gain currency in American public discourse following the 1908 staging of Israel Zangwill's successful play *The Melting-Pot,* which presents the author's endorsement of amalgamation. Zangwill, however, did not believe in widespread, indiscriminate fusion, since blacks did not factor into his ethnoracial equation. His vision was unmistakably Eurocentric. Attributing to "the prognathous face" of blacks "an ugly and undesirable type of countenance" that "connotes a lower average of intellect and ethics," Zangwill believed black and white to be "as yet too far apart for profitable fusion" (206). Because, in his view—expressed using Mendelian language—"black traits" such as "negroid hair and complexion" were not "easy to eliminate from the hybrid posterity," he favored white America's scrupulous avoidance of "physical intermarriage with the Negro" (207). Marred by its naked negrophobia, Zangwill's idea of amalgamation endorsed the racial separation that it presumably aspired to contest, just as nearly four decades before, Hostos had favored the intermixture of all the races, while preserving in his scheme the hierarchy of racial values that associated the various branches of the human family with differentiated attributes. The Cholo represented a welcome specimen, for instance, because this hybrid type combined "the intelligence of the conquerors" with "the sensibility of the vanquished," and the "great moral caliber" of the "Indian race" with "the intellectual vigor he has received from the European race" (373–374). By the same token, though avoiding white supremacist formulations and declaring people of European descent "still susceptible of some improvement," Chesnutt conceived of a scenario in which "the more objectionable Negro traits" would disappear in the fusion, giving way to the development of "his better qualities" instead (32–33).

Latina/o voices have generally overlooked the racist presumptions that can go into uncritical conceptualizations of interracial fusion as a social ideal.

Both the aforementioned Rodriguez, arbiter of brownness, and Anzaldúa, proponent of crossracial borderlessness, pastoralized the view of amalgamation advanced by Mexican thinker José Vasconcelos in his 1925 essay *The Cosmic Race*. Neither took time to unpack Vasconcelos's aberrant presumptions about racial inferiority and superiority (Rodriguez, *Brown* 225; Anzaldúa 99). A characteristic passage, in which Vasconcelos articulates his vision of the "cosmic" race, illustrates this point:

> The lower types of the species will be absorbed by the superior type. In this manner, for example, the Black could be redeemed, and step by step, by voluntary extinction, the uglier stocks will give way to the more handsome. Inferior races, upon being educated, would become less prolific, and the better specimens would go on ascending a scale of ethnic improvement, whose maximum type is not precisely the white, but that new race to which the white himself will have to aspire with the object of conquering the synthesis. (32)

Vasconcelos's construction did not differ significantly from the predominant racial ideology current in his generation on both sides of the Rio Grande. Earlier in the twentieth century, John R. Commons, then a professor of political economy at the University of Wisconsin, spoke about the beneficial effect that amalgamation could have on blacks, attributing, for instance, the "natural" leadership of the mulatto to "the blood of white aristocracy" that runs in their veins. For while the supposedly superior races have the "mental capacities" necessary to conquer the obstacles of an adverse environment to advance themselves, the "inferior" races (such as "the children of the tropical zones") need to rely on amalgamation (209–210, 212, 213). Amalgamation cannot be deemed salutary if it is predicated on the presumption of one core superior race that provides the organizing principle of the fusion by mitigating the defects of the others and, in the process, exacting profit for itself. Such an arrangement will do nothing but create the conceptual conditions for whiteness to continue calling the shots, with white-presenting mestizos setting the pattern for the model of humanity that the rest should strive to attain. The triumph of the Latin American ideology of mestizaje points precisely to that outcome, hence the unspoken consensus whereby only a *güero* (a Mexican vernacular term for a blond or white-presenting person) even one of the humble talents of a Jorge Ramos, can climb to the position of anchor of the nightly news on the Spanish-language television network Univision.

A failure to liberate each of the amalgamated ingredients of the racist assumptions that inform them leads to a conceptual model that is still racist.

What is preserved is the *instinctual contempt* for non-white traits that prove difficult to, in Zangwill's words, "eliminate from the hybrid posterity" (207). Even in the mid-1990s we witnessed right-wing commentator Dinesh D'Souza's injunction to American liberals to "welcome the emerging *café au lait society*" and stop "treating mixed-race children as an embarrassment to the existing regime of head-counting," while also instructing the African American leadership to discontinue their adherence to the goals of civil rights and instead come to terms with the "dysfunctionalities" of their community so as more effectively to tackle the needs of "a people whose culture is frequently unsuited to the requirements of the modern world" (D'Souza 552–554). More disquietingly perhaps, *US News & World Report* journalist Michael Barone, a frequent panelist on the weekly public-affairs television program *The McLaughlin Group*, decided to have his say on the matter of the races and the future of the United States by revisiting the melting-pot metaphor in *The New Americans: How the Melting Pot Can Work Again* (2007).

I recall a panel held at Syracuse University on October 11, 2001, featuring sociologist Nathan Glazer and US Senator Daniel Patrick Moynihan, organized to reflect on the state of race and ethnicity in this country, nearly four decades since the publication of their coauthored study *Beyond the Melting Pot* (1963). Glazer and Moynihan summed up their reflections by sharing what they viewed as the clearest lesson to be drawn from the melting pot. They concluded that, though cherished as a metaphor purporting to describe the formation of the American people, sadly, the "melting pot simply did not happen." Also a participant on the panel, Barone insisted, while praising Moynihan and Glazer lavishly, that he did not disagree with their contention, apparently forgetting the claims of the book he had just published. Barone's *The New Americans* claims that the melting pot happened in the past, has every possibility of happening again, and has nothing obstructing its path other than "American guilt prompted by the civil rights movement and the Vietnam War" (279). Shunning complexity, he posits that through a feeling of guilt, American elites, starting in the 1960s, "began to doubt the fundamental goodness of the country they nevertheless felt entitled to lead. The elites became convinced that the white majority was obdurately racist and that racial quotas and preferences were needed to ensure that racism did not result in the exclusion of blacks" (278). Thoughtlessly, they proffered a similar gesture to Latina/os and Asians. "The goal of Americanization," reasons Barone, "seemed suspect, and elites sanctioned policies such as bilingual education on the theory that enabling immigrants' children to master the English language was to wrongfully detach them from their native culture" (278). Fortunately, in his view, the influence of the elites has gradually waned, and he assures us that the country will once again prove the descriptive accuracy of the motto *e pluribus unum*. With unwarranted epistemic self-sufficiency, Barone projects a scenario wherein blacks will assimilate just like the Irish did. Latina/os will follow the path to integration made by Italians generations before them. Asians will simply emulate the full Americanization embraced by European Jews. At least for Latina/os and Asians, the entire process could take fewer than eighty years (192, 274).

By the same token, Barone suggests that "the dysfunctional habits of mind blacks brought from the rural South," when their northward migration began over sixty years before, are dying out. Thus, he predicts, as they continue to exhibit "habits of mind similar to those that have helped other racial and ethnic minorities to move upward in American life," their prosperity and their assimilation will be assured (114). Barone's conclusions emanate predictably from his lax methodology and absence of data about the American past. He espouses what sounds like a migration history of his own making: immigrants come to the United States to flee from dysfunctional societies whose negative cultural freight they carry. The dysfunctionality of their ways impedes their progress here, but they eventually learn, since "in time the environment of the United States fosters different, more functional habits of mind—a process that can be called assimilation" (4–5). Since he assumes all ethnic minorities are immigrants, Native Americans do not emerge in his musings about the past or the future of the races in the United States. For the same reason, he locates the genesis of the African American experience in the period of the Great Migration (1910–1940 being the first phase, with a second lasting until the 1970s), so as better to accord with the "immigrant" narrative he applies to the other groups. He does not trouble himself with such complications as the centuries of slavery or the seventy-five years of postemancipation violence and dispossession under Jim Crow as enduring legacies for blacks, US imperial encroachment into the countries of Latin America for Latina/os, or labor importation followed by social exclusion for Asians.

Barone's story is simple: In the United States, proverbially abundant land of milk and honey, whoever does poorly does so on account of the defective baggage of their ancestry, which they are able to overcome eventually. Should that happen, they will manage to replicate the success story of every generation of immigrant that preceded them. Any explanation that tells a less triumphant story Barone rejects as a figment spawned by the febrile imagination of liberal elites, who lack the courage to speak with pride about the greatness of their country. The writer's analytically naive reasoning reclaims the thinking of an era, around the start of the twentieth century, when policymakers viewed the heritages of the non-English segments of the population as requiring repair, as can be gathered from *Race Improvement in the United States*, the title of one of the three issues published in 1909 by the American Academy of Political and Social Science. That in the twenty-first century Barone's unexamined melting-pot formulation, unaccompanied by any effort to delink from the white supremacist underpinnings of the paradigm, should still find a place in the market of ideas suggests that we remain far from the goal of dismantling the conceptual edifice that racism built.

Alliance between Detractors and Detracted

Espousing an antiracist configuration of amalgamation and fending off the logic of hypodescent racialization drilled by white supremacist structures into the consciousness of non-white minorities can possibly lead us out of the existential cul-de-sac of racial identity. This postulation concurs with the views of those who, skeptical of what has been termed the "dialectics of particularism," aspire to the emergence of a "pan-ethnic, pan-racial, anti-racist sensibility" to serve as the overarching logic that informs democratic ideals in American society (Nash 961–962). Ironically, the groups that have endured the throes of hypodescent racialization have a key role to play, hence my emphasis on the peculiar benefits that the odd location of Afro-Latina/os affords them. Not many will disagree that racism most brazenly flaunts its triumphs when it succeeds at enlisting its victims to further its logic and its rituals. At that point it can even afford to dispense with violence and tools of domination; that is, it becomes self-sustaining, boasting autonomy from the forces that brought it into being. Nor will many dispute the pointlessness of antiracist projects that cannot imagine an end to racism. One must believe that the indoctrination that reduces the dignity of human beings to blood quanta can and must be reversed, and that ideas matter in this regard, especially given the resilience of racist thought and action so many decades after the Civil Rights Act of 1964 outlawed racial discrimination. The racial imagination, then, merits an intense offensive, especially by racialized minority groups, because to fight racism, its targets must first be able to survive it. Those who adopt the prism of the perpetrators to look at themselves and others cannot claim to have achieved such survival.

This position, then, urges Afro-Latina/os and other racialized minority groups to recognize and act upon the special role assigned to them by their problematic location. Their difficult position enables them to embrace with conviction the scientific finding that denies validity to the very notion of race, not merely echoing the oft-repeated contention that "race is socially constructed," but also acting as if they in fact believed it. They occupy an unstable enough identitarian realm that they can probably muster the irony necessary to affirm their ethnoracial selves, in response to discernible instances of aggression, without succumbing to the insidious temptation to racialize themselves. Racialization generally diminishes the breadth of a person's humanity, and when excluded groups do it to themselves, they consequently endorse the logic that has harmed them. Racialization in the final analysis hampers one's solidarity with the other members of the species, delaying instead of advancing the cause of justice and equality. For instance, a person of Hispanic or African descent who prefaces a comment with the clause "As a black man, I . . ." or "Since I am a Latina . . ." cannot, for sanity's sake, lose sight of the circumstantial nature of the identity invoked. Mentally, the speaker of that preamble ought to display the alertness to produce its instant translation. The explanatory texture of the translation would necessarily result in something much larger: "As a person who, by virtue of my lesser position in our ethnoracially stratified social system has had to remain mindful of the economic and sociopolitical implications of my phenotype, I . . . ." If the translation does not happen and the speakers remain convinced that the *I* and the ethnoracial modifier are consubstantial, they have lost the battle against the forces responsible for their exclusion and inequity and have become casualties, psychologically speaking.

At no point did the urgency of promoting the disassembly of the conceptual edifice of racism become more compelling to me than during my encounter in the fall 2005 semester with a course titled Living in a Diverse Society. I had developed the module for students who chose to enroll in the Multicultural Living and Learning Community for first-year students. My course proposed the formal scrutiny of diversity as a field of inquiry, a phenomenon with multiple strands that, far from being reduced to issues of race and ethnicity, encompassed pressing intersectional questions of gender, class, culture, religion, sexualities, generations, disability, systems of thought, and other spheres of social interaction. During a gender-focused module that looked at some of the pressures that the patriarchal instincts of consumer society exert on women's bodies, I screened the PBS documentary *Dying to Be Thin*, a videorecording narrated by award-winning actress Susan Sarandon that delves into the search for thinness and the ideal body as imagined by mainstream US society. The film dwells on the sociology and psychopathology responsible for such potentially fatal eating disorders as anorexia and bulimia. The documentary exposes viewers to some disturbing images of emaciated women's bodies that call to mind some of the horrors of the Nazi concentration camps during the Second World War. Though skeletal and deformed, the women featured in the program, when they looked at themselves in the mirror, felt they still had more weight to lose before reaching the beauty ideal that had taken hold of their consciousness (*Dying* 2004).

Concerned that my students had not exhibited the measure of sympathy I had expected, and having detected the sound of giggling from a few in reaction to some of the more pitiable moments in the production, I undertook to turn the situation into a teachable moment by inviting discussion of the group's seemingly blasé response to the stories depicted in the documentary. The conversation that ensued revealed a prevailing understanding in the class that the victims of eating disorders had primarily themselves to blame for the choices they had made. Disquietingly, the class seemed to accept an African American male student's interpretation of their collectively jaded reaction to the appalling spectacle presented by the film, namely, that they—mostly African American, Asian American, and Latina/o students—did not regard bulimia and anorexia as problems likely to occur in "their" communities. It dawned on me after the student's comment that *Dying to Be Thin* featured primarily white women subjects. I valued the interpretation volunteered by the student, even as I desperately hoped that he had it wrong, because it invited us to reflect on human solidarity. The thought that my students had such a profoundly racialized view of themselves and others that they lacked the ability to recognize their bond to members of the species outside their immediate community of descent threatened to extinguish my hope to teach them anything about respect for difference and appreciation of diversity in all its forms.

I confronted the daunting pedagogical task of communicating some principles of human solidarity to a group of young Americans "of color" whose concern for humankind may reach no further than the range of their ethnoracial loyalty or affiliation. Those of us who embrace the vision encapsulated in the words of the Afro-Roman poet Terence, "Homo sum, humani nihil a me alienum puto" ("As I am a man, nothing human is alien to me"), have reason to tremble at the thought that the next generation may have curtailed the scope of their human solidarity to the diminutive dimension of their own race and ethnicity. If this disconcerting thought has the remotest possibility of approximating the truth, I would like to speculate that the root of the problem lies in the education the young have received from their elders, and that, by the same token, the hope of a solution lies in a corresponding unlearning that will reverse its effect. I allude here to the unintended consequence of stimulating their ethnoracial self-affirmation to shield them from the shame, damaged self-esteem, or outright self-loathing that could come from regular exposure to white supremacist structures and practices in American society. Having perhaps suffered the effects of dehumanizing racial barriers, their elders have probably sought to empower them psychologically by instilling in them a sense of self-worth and a heightened pride in their heritage. But perhaps this totally justifiable project failed to clarify to the young the limits and the traps inherent in such pride. It may have failed to restrict the value of ethnoracial self-affirmation to a strategy of self-defense against the venom unleashed by racist regimes. In other words, the potential targets of racism ought to regard racial pride as a disposable instrument that one casts aside at the end of every use, never allowing it to become either permanent or continuous. Racialized groups should never allow their racial pride to stabilize, lest they collude with the logic of the racist structures against which they seek to protect themselves.

I have tested the rigidity with which the young conceive of ethnoracial pride with two separate groups of college students: one predominantly white, made up of seniors, and the other mostly black, Latina/o, and Asian American, consisting of first-year students. In each case, at a moment when the class discussion gravitated toward questions of race and ethnicity, I interjected this disclaimer: "Me, I'm not proud of being black, of being Latino, or of being Dominican," causing wide-eyed, gaping disbelief in my audience. I then proceeded to break the heavy silence by urging them to consider the less flattering meanings of the word *pride*, namely haughtiness, conceit, stiff-neckedness, and arrogance. The word, I explained, turns positive when it denotes accomplishment, insofar as it involves a skill, an effort, or a talent deployed toward some creative end. In that respect, one can dismiss a feeling of pride over one's height, having brilliant parents, or winning the lottery as a fraudulent sentiment since it denotes conditions that involved no accomplishment by the individual feeling it. I further tested my students' anxiety over identity by contending that boasting of one's heredity causes a person to participate in a similar fraud, since it involves taking credit for an outcome that did not involve one's own ingenuity or labor. Even so, I still needed to apply myself to the task of allaying my students' concern about my psychological health, impoverished self-esteem, doubtful sense of identity, or even loyalty to my respective communities.

I had to escalate the argument by pointing to the seeming travesty of my allowing my chest to puff up over the mere awareness of my skin color, facial features, hair texture, ancestral background, or historical origins. I ventured to ask, rhetorically, was it not that sort of outlandish sense of self-worth that emboldened Nazi Germans to confer onto themselves the fraudulent authority to subject millions of their ethnically differentiated compatriots to exploitation, humiliation, and extermination? Did they not act on the conviction of their superiority over their victims, whom they had ranked as a lesser form of humanity? Uncritical pride in ancestry, I proposed, is dangerous. Why would I wish to risk moral collusion with Hitler's Third Reich (1933–1945) or with

South Africa's Apartheid regime (1948–1994), both of which, like their US precursor, Jim Crow (1870–1964) in the US South, executed rigid codes of mistreatment, exclusion, and disenfranchisement against millions of people whom the perpetrators deemed racially inferior? The state-endorsed institutional and physical violence committed by the warriors of white supremacy in the US South, Germany, and South Africa was fueled and ennobled by learned elites whose ethnoracial self-adulation and contempt for other ancestries lent credence to the armed mobs that went around lynching, bombing homes, or demolishing the livelihoods of racialized others. They were the angels of death and destruction in Tulsa, Oklahoma, in late May and early June 1921; throughout Germany during Kristallnacht in November 1938; and in the black township of Sharpeville, Gauteng Province, South Africa, in March 1960. Precisely the racial disparagement of non-Caucasian peoples earned the New York lawyer, zoology scholar, and reputed wildlife conservationist Madison Grant a place of honor in learned circles following publication of *The Passing of the Great Race* (1916), a text that overshadowed the author's previous zoological research. At a time in the early twentieth century when much of US social theory waddled through the unscientific ground of eugenics, he served as chairman of the New York Zoological Society, a trustee of the American Museum of Natural History, and councilor of the American Geographical Society. Grant's successful book glorified "Nordic" peoples as the only creators of civilization throughout human history and alerted readers to the degenerating effect of allowing the "great race" to mix with inferior peoples. A characteristic passage, with the contempt for amalgamation that pervades the entire volume, asserts:

> Negroes have demonstrated throughout recorded time that they are a stationary species, and that they do not possess the potentiality of progress or initiative from within. Progress from self-impulse must not be confounded with mimicry or with progress imposed from without by social pressure, or by the slaver's lash. Where two distinct species are located side by side history and biology teach that but one of the two things can happen: either one race drives the other out, as the Americans exterminated the Indians, or as the Negroes are now replacing the whites in various parts of the South; or else they amalgamate and form a population of race bastards in which the lower type ultimately preponderates. (69)

The impact of Grant's racist aberration was not small. As a leading figure of the US eugenics movement, he succeeded in shaping the racially inflected immigration act passed by Congress in 1921; he even counted Hitler among his admirers, in addition to consorting with the German proponents of racial hygiene during the Weimar period. Concluding my cautionary tale in the classroom, I pointed out that if we emulate the logic of those antecedents, we are basically conceding that they were right all along.

Identity Trivialized

In general, my students followed my argument, conceding the wisdom of distancing myself from the racist precedents I had outlined for them. Yet I noticed no appreciable change in the language they used, either in class discussion or in writing assignments, to speak about their ethnoracial selves. I had not expected a radical alteration of their manner of understanding race and ethnicity based merely on a set of teacherly exhortations, but I was surprised my lesson had no discernible impact on them. I had to conclude that these and the other groups of college students I have taught over the past years have difficulty seeing themselves through anything other than a racialist prism. The incident involving *Dying to Be Thin* would seem to suggest that the young people of color in front of me responded to the racialization inflicted on them by racializing themselves. The armor of reconstitutive self-esteem they received from their elders may have backfired. As a result, they may lack a healthy critical stance, the conceptual diligence necessary to discern the trap of all essentialisms, the deprecating as well as the flattering ones.

Rather than being equally skeptical of positive essentialisms that flatter (such as ethnoracial praise, for instance) they may gladly accept claims assuring them that Latina/os possess a more capacious soul than do Anglos, as exemplified by their deeper sensitivity to family ties, the greater quantum of affection generally harbored by Latina/o hearts, or even the spontaneous sense of musicality that supposedly infuses their blood. Unprepared to challenge metaphysical allegations concerning their ancestral attributes, they may resonate with representations of their identity that, apart from phenotype, invoke decalogues of distinct characteristics. Many of us have received humorous emails or seen reels on social media with subject headings that promise to spell out ethnoracial ontologies such as "Tell me you are Puerto Rican without telling me you are Puerto Rican," "You know that someone is Latina/o if . . . ," or "We're Dominican. Of course we. . . ." The contents tend to consist of a list of illustrative behaviors, characteristics, and attitudes that presumably amount to a composite picture of one's community of descent. These forms of media, which I read as only half tongue-in-cheek, usually originate from young people seeking validation, conversation, and a chance to show off both their sense of in-group belonging and their proficient knowledge about "their people."

The list of commandments that may seduce racialized peoples tends to follow a contrastive principle, operating in explicit or implicit opposition to a homogeneous and essentialized "White" or "Anglo" norm. The acceptance of such discursive maneuvers renders ethnoracial location measurable by degrees, conceivably allowing for an identity patrol of sorts to determine whether or not a person's set of attributes qualify them as a legitimate member of the group. A self-proclaimed gatekeeper of ethnoracial identity can muster the self-confidence to question someone else's Latino or black credentials. I recall a 1991 interview on the *Arsenio Hall Show* with African American singer Whitney Houston, in which she evoked her sad experience of being booed during a performance in 1989 on *Soul Train*, a musical television show whose predominantly black audience apparently deemed the texture of her voice, her delivery, and overall performance "too white" ("Whitney Houston"). Revealing the delirious extent to which intragroup identity policing can go, the booing seemed to come from the belief that race determines the texture, timbre, and "color" of a singer's voice, distinguishing it sharply from the vocal sounds of singers of a different stock. The presumption that one can measure ethnoracial identity based on a discrete inventory of qualities, demeanors, movements, or sounds can have severely deleterious consequences. Compendia of a discrete group's defining features will not likely emerge from the consensus reached by a council of elders or peers mindful of advancing the best interests of the community for present and future generations; rather, they are likely to come from the influential images wielded by the profit-hungry, amoral, and ideologically skewed commercial media.[1]

For a couple of generations now, the representation of blackness for the young has arguably been monopolized by rap and hip-hop performers whose songs, depending on the subgenre, are permeated with misogyny and homophobia, the pursuit of wealth at all costs, and the celebration of antisocial values, such as ostentatious displays of money, drugs, sex, and violence. In that context, young urban black males who apply themselves to the pursuit of academic excellence have mastered the standard variant of the English language (even as they remain proficient in the vernacular), keep their pants held by a belt at the waistline, opt not to wear the outfit of a basketball player or particular team on a daily basis, and refrain from patterning their body language after the motions and gesticulations of a performer on stage may elicit taunts from peers. A likely sneer could be, "Why are you trying to act white?" A concern over the mindset that equates educational attainment or propriety with whiteness came up during the lecture Henry Louis Gates, Jr., gave to the entering class at Syracuse University on October 5, 2004. After he spoke on the intellectual legacy of W. E. B. Du Bois, the discussion that followed tackled the present, and one of his responses stressed his faith in education as the most decisive factor to help reverse the African American community's unfavorable socioeconomic indicators, namely its over-representation among the country's unemployed, incarcerated, and socially disempowered populations. He then specifically identified a widespread aversion to school that many urban youths have somehow associated with affirming their black identity, a self-destructive idea that, in his view, demanded the immediate attention of concerned policymakers and parents. Besides, he found the equation of learning with whiteness "ridiculous," recalling that for his generation and that of his parents, showing intellectual aptitude was "the blackest thing you could [do]."[2]

Nearly four decades prior to Gates's lecture at Syracuse University, Martin Luther King, Jr., had combined the concepts of ethnoracial self-respect and commitment to learning in a message he addressed to an audience of black youths. His speech "What Is Your Life's Blueprint?," which he delivered before students at Barratt Junior High School in Philadelphia on October 26, 1967, bequeathed a model for their lives, one that consisted of self-affirmation and the pursuit of excellence:

> Number one in your life's blueprint should be a deep belief in your own dignity, your own worth, and your own somebodiness. Don't allow anybody to make you feel that you are a nobody. Always feel that you count. Always feel that you have worth, and always feel that your life has ultimate significance. Secondly, in your life's blueprint, you must have as the basic principle the determination to achieve excellence in your various fields of endeavor. (15)

While King's target audience was mostly African American, we should bear in mind that Latina/os are no less vulnerable to the deleterious consequences of allowing destructive social mythologies to determine the way the young understand and affirm their ethnoracial identity. Left to their own devices, unmentored in the difficulty of speaking meaningfully about the social, historical, and existential meaning of ancestry, they may fall prey to a facile sort of representation served to them by the commercial media, one that reduces their heritage to entertainment figures, glib stereotypes, and easily digestible formulas. They may thus fail to recognize the insults hurled at them via positive essentialisms that celebrate the community's warm, affectionate, and rhythmical nature, while the presumably less flattering qualities of sobriety, calculation, and thoughtfulness are assigned to the mainstream "Anglo" population. They may accept, in other words, a representation that relegates them to the realm of body and feeling, in contradistinction to whites, who inhabit the domain of spirit and reason.

As a result, a situation emerges that often allows the status quo to get away with including Latina/os only symbolically, granting them space in the realm of expressive culture, something that the 2000 National Convention of the Republican Party clearly demonstrated. Sprightly Ricky Martin appeared onstage, belting out "La Vida Loca" and dancing energetically as the party's nominee, George H. W. Bush, amid cheers and applause, braced himself for the challenge of the presidential election. In contrast, the party flaunted its inclusion of African Americans by doing more than just bringing them onstage to provide diversion and spectacle. Represented by Colin Powell and other prominent coethnics, they received speaking roles that enabled them to come to the podium to expound upon policy issues and conservative values as well as to share with the country and the world their vision of a future for blacks under the aegis of a Republican administration.

Unschooled in the complexities of ethnoracial identity, young Latina/os might fail to detect the offense involved in seemingly innocuous representations of themselves. I recall being particularly intrigued by a magazine ad that formed part of the promotional materials circulated in the weeks prior to the 4th Annual Latin Grammy Awards, held in Miami on September 3, 2003. The ad took up a full page of the magazine. It involved the image of a sensually sculpted, scantily clad young woman sitting with her hands resting on a drum placed between her widely open legs. With her bronzed skin oiled and her prominent breasts accentuated by slightly hunched shoulders, her head is bent backwards and leans gently to the right as her physique reflects some powerful surge coursing through her veins. Her closed eyes suggest a total surrender to some ineffable sensation. Beneath this alluring body, a slogan commands, "Feel the Latino." The ambiguous injunction invites at least two interpretations. By watching the Latin Grammy Awards, we can share in the "Latino" trance that the young woman is clearly enjoying, or, by consorting with the likes of her eroticized body, we can experience whatever she personifies. It is not clear whether the promoters had envisioned how the invitation to "feel the Latino" might register with Latina/os themselves, since one would suppose that they were well aware of the sensation and might not feel anything special. Most perturbingly, we have no grounds for supposing that young Latina/os will not embrace the understanding of "the Latino" as something that one "feels," as if possessed by a spirit, especially when summoned by the music's irresistible power. Their ethnoracial education, I insist, should prepare them well to defend themselves against anything they might find in overtly antagonistic representations, as well as in guilefully flattering idealizations of their bodies and minds.

The Composite Structure of *Latino* and *Afro*

In a 1995 essay that explores the "politics of racial identity" among US Puerto Ricans, social scientist Angelo Falcón evoked a 1972 paper presented at Yale University by junior scholars William E. Cross, Jr., and Manuel del Valle. As a black psychologist, Cross would gain renown for theorizing the conversion African Americans experience in the process of overcoming a white supremacy–induced stage of self-loathing to enter one of ethnoracial self-affirmation.[3] Del Valle, for his part, would contribute to empowerment of Puerto Ricans from the classroom to the courtroom. In their 1972 joint presentation at Yale, as recounted in Falcón's essay, del Valle and Cross espoused a model to strengthen the ethnic and racial identity of Puerto Ricans by adapting the racial-awakening praxis evident in the African American self-affirmation that had culminated in the successes of the Civil Rights Movement. Though still a graduate student at Princeton, Cross had by then begun to circulate the theory of racial-identity development for US blacks that would make him a salient figure in the field of psychology; his faith in the applicability of his model was understandable. But del Valle's acquiescence to the theory's fitness to explain the matter of racial identity among Puerto Ricans, including those of African descent, seems less understandable.

As a person who traces his origins to the Hispanic Caribbean, del Valle would know the difficulty of diagnosing Puerto Ricans in terms of their ethnic or racial development due to their varied ancestries and phenotypes. This is precisely the reality that the above-mentioned poem "Child of the Americas" by Aurora Levins Morales seeks to capture. Beyond poetic figurations, however, the view of Latina/os as an assemblage of ancestries and phenotypes, with distinct histories harkening back to sundry geographies and plights, informed federal authorities when the US government set out to classify the country's population based on origin. Dated May 12, 1977, Statistical Directive 15, issued by the Office of Management and Budget, officially qualified the term "Hispanic" to denote an "ethnic" grouping of peoples "regardless of race" as distinct from the terms meant to name the other four population segments (i.e., Asian, Black, Native American, and White) that denote "racial" groupings (Kang and Torres-Saillant, "Race" 175). Looking back, it is not clear whether the emerging scholars Cross and del Valle were, in 1972, in a position to fathom the extent of the complexity of racism outside the black-white binary prevalent in the United States up to the 1970s and beyond.

Falcón's essay quotes the conclusion reached by Cross and del Valle, namely that "an awareness of what [sic] the process of becoming conscious of one's Puerto Ricanness may allow the Puerto Rican to program Puerto Rican identity, resulting in that positive self-image which is the prerequisite for Puerto Rican pride and self-determination" (205). After quoting that conclusion, Falcón closes his essay with a sentence that embraces wholeheartedly the wisdom conveyed by the above words: "This represents, perhaps, a reckless optimism that may have been lost, but needs urgently to be rediscovered today in the Puerto Rican community" (205). Today the zeal of such a message would seem odd, bordering on the passion of religious conversion, rather than the practical political strategizing called for by agendas of community empowerment. Perhaps the formidable battles that the earlier generations of marginalized minority leaders had to wage in their time consumed their concentration and deprived them of the serenity to envision a time in the future when the terms of the struggle would no longer call for waving flags of reactive identity. They may not have imagined an occasion when their young, having been adversely racialized, would one day need to master the sensibility required for living in a diverse society in which they, too, would have to pass the moral test of refraining from diminishing the humanity of those differing from them in ancestry or phenotype. The proponents of the 1972 project set out to build up Puerto Rican self-image by replicating a model of strengthened racial identity created by an emerging black scholar to promote increased self-esteem among folks in his ethnoracially distinct group. One gets no sense of whether the copresenters at the Yale conference had any plans to operationalize Cross's model in del Valle's community, nor whether they sought to apply it to Puerto Ricans of all phenotypes, rather than just to Afro-Puerto Ricans. Cross and del Valle may have had to field questions concerning their methodology for diagnosing the degree to which community members were insufficiently "conscious of their Puerto Ricanness," needed to "program" their "identity," or lacked the "positive self-image" required for the nurturing of "pride and self-determination."

The audience must have wondered if the disparate manner by which Puerto Ricans were absorbed into the United States, compared to that of African Americans, would not be likely to yield a different social psychology for each group. Coming under US control only in 1898, as the North American empire expanded its dominions by going after Spain's remaining colonies in the Caribbean and the Pacific, Puerto Ricans did not experience seventy-five grueling years of Jim Crow, a system with the deliberate objective of annihilating in its victims any sense of pride or self-worth. By 1972, when Cross and del Valle presented their project for strengthening Puerto Rican identity, the community had lived in the United States in large numbers for some two generations. The difference in the historical conditions under which each experienced its subordination is so pronounced that it seems unlikely that both ended up with an identical sort of psychological dysfunction that is susceptible to rehabilitation by the same type of intervention. One should hope that spokespersons for racialized communities today would be less seduced by ethnoracial formulations that speak about identity with the degree of epistemic certainty shown by Cross and del Valle in their presentation, or that such formulations would not elicit the longing with which Falcón recalled it in his essay. The best we can do for the young is to encourage them to approach identity models with a healthy dose of skepticism, as something not so easily knowable, as susceptible to mutation in our varying circumstances and the intersections that cross us in the realm of social relations.

Race lacks materiality outside of a racist milieu, and even there its solidity is questionable in the presence of contravening factors. Afro-Cuban writer Carlos Moore credits African American writer Maya Angelou, whom he met in Harlem in the 1950s, with showing him the way toward embracing his black identity as the core of his being (*Pichón* 108–113). There is no small irony, however, in Angelou's own negotiation of identity when we learn that she had resorted to passing as an Afro-Cuban to obtain the record contracts that launched her singing career in the 1950s with the stage name "Miss Calypso." The biographical note on the back cover of an LP identifies her as "born in Cuba of a Watusi father, the tallest native tribe in the world" (111). She explained her trespass to Moore succinctly: "For a black artist to achieve anything here in music and theater, you must be from somewhere else" (111). The fact that Angelou could easily scale the racial wall by simply changing her country of origin must say something about the porosity—if not the fragility—of racial thought and feeling. Afro-Latina/os, as I have argued thus far, are predisposed to having a heightened awareness of white supremacy's situational instabilities. The young, especially, ought to have easy access to the complexities of ethnoracial identity, recognizing it as something fluid, unfinished, and in process rather than fixed in diamond hardness.

When asked how I classify myself ethnoracially, I dispense with any formulation that may aspire to name something permanent or essential. I usually resort to situational answers. I can be Dominican, Caribbean, or Afro-Latino, depending on the purpose that my answer is expected to serve, statistically or otherwise. I prefer to refrain from speaking of myself as a racial being. The fact that others may choose to racialize me constitutes no valid excuse for me to racialize myself or extend the same energy toward others, for either benign or for malignant purposes. Looking at the trajectories of Martin Luther King, Jr., and Desmond Tutu, I have marveled at their ability to fight white negrophobia while staying clear of anti-white racism. That one cannot fight racism while embracing a racist worldview seems clear. We cannot fight without first undergoing *self-deracialization*, lest we remain conceptual allies of the operative racist logic. We need to let go of the unwarranted assumption that as Afro-Latina/os, because we come from the flank of the racialized, we somehow "cannot be racist." Racism is a way of knowing our place in the world in relation to people of other ancestries or phenotypes. The ideology can be absorbed by the racialized, who may then proceed to racialize others in turn. Given the racialized context in which Afro-Latina/os may develop their sense of ethnoracial identity, caution and skepticism are the most prudent approaches to self-fashioning.

Caution, skepticism, and prudence are crucial factors in the way King kept his eye trained on the complexity of identity, even at the height of fierce anti-racist struggle. He promoted racial self-affirmation among African Americans as a protective shield. He did so while imagining a scenario in which the godliness of every individual was recognized, "'whiteness' and 'blackness' pass as determinants in a relationship[,] and 'son' and 'brother' are substituted" (*Testament* 122). As he made clear in his 1950 speech "The Rising Tide of Racial Consciousness," the reverend celebrated African American racial pride but never wavered in his resolve to proclaim "the solidarity of the human family." In his speeches, he repeatedly stressed commonalities, as when reminding us that "all life is interrelated. All men are caught in an inescapable network of mutuality, tied in a single garment of destiny" (121–122). He had the foresight to warn against becoming "victimized with a philosophy of 'black supremacy'" (*Testament* 200). King's atypical vision did not resonate strongly among many secular black or Latina/o leaders who, for the most part, remained absorbed by the tyranny of what was immediately before them. They sought to instill in the consciousnesses of their respective groups effective safeguards against the vilifications of the present. They thus bequeathed to the subsequent generations essentialized, hardened, and therefore simplified ideas of identity that the powerful commercial media have found all too easy to manipulate and trivialize.

Knowing Ourselves Ethnoracially

Heirs of reductive, retaliatory models of identity understand themselves on the basis of a homogeneous "us" whose ontology emerges in contradistinction to an equally homogeneous "them." Ignoring the barriers of gender, class, sexuality, and ideology (among others) that set certain segments apart, even within differentiated populations, they fail to recognize conflict, ambiguity, and contradiction as necessary features of any attempt at understanding the whole. It is difficult for those who regard their group monolithically to detect inequality and injustices, except when these wrongs originate outside the community. The "them" monopolizes the function of oppressor, while the essentialized "us" necessarily inhabits the rank of the oppressed. Thus, homophobia, misogyny, religious biases, and ideological conservatism have a field day when they occur within the identity group. Negrophobic exclusions and fundamentalist nationalism go unchecked when they occur internally. Worse still, hardened and simple ideas of identity overlook the inescapable fact that knowing one's ancestry takes work and that defending it requires analytical sophistication as well as humility.

During my initial contact with the leaders of the Quisqueya Club at Cornell University in the 1990s, I learned of an initiative to bring to campus a major figure from the Dominican Republic to highlight the importance of Dominican history and culture. I gasped when a young Dominican student leader mentioned politician Joaquín Balaguer as the guest under consideration. Having been born in the United States or in the ancestral homeland much later than the period when Balaguer ruled the country through theft, murder, incarcerations, and widespread corruption, the Cornell students did not share my contempt and moral aversion for the individual in question. They viewed him simply as a successful statesman. With three presidential terms under his belt, Balaguer had returned to power in 1986 to rule the country for yet another decade. At such a remove from events in the ancestral homeland, the students had few ways of knowing the fraudulent means by which he had won each of his elections. Fortunately, the plan to invite the crafty head of state to Cornell as a means of boosting Dominican pride fell through. I most certainly hope my words of discouragement contributed to that outcome.

The extremes to which historical ignorance or ideological indifference can mar celebrations of ethnoracial ancestry, especially in cases of monolithic understandings of one's people, became shockingly clear to me, once again, in the spring of 2000. During Syracuse University's Latino Awareness Week, sponsored by the sole Hispanic fraternity on campus at the time, among the salient activities on the program was a photo exhibit of great Latino and Latin American leaders from different historical periods. Held at one of the exhibition halls in the Schine Student Center, the event included portraits of former Mexican president Benito Juárez, Cuban intellectual José Martí, and US civil rights pioneer Cesar Chavez, each with a biographical note highlighting key achievements. My jaw dropped when I saw that the Dominican hero chosen to grace the Latino pride exhibit was none other than Rafael Leónidas Trujillo, whom the biographical sketch lauded for having served as president of his country for thirty years and having brought "stability and order" to Dominican society. I pulled the Dominican member of the organizing team aside to ask, with urgency in my quivering voice, if he knew that Trujillo's three decades as "president" were actually a blood-drenched dictatorship, with his regime carrying out a reign of terror that involved hundreds of political assassinations and thousands of prisoners, many of whom endured torture and other unspeakable acts. Indeed, the angel of fear haunted the Dominican population during every year of the tyrant's three-decade rule. I explained further that Trujillo managed the country as if it were his personal hacienda, appropriating for himself a vast portion of the state's wealth, and that, among other affronts to humanity, he perpetrated the genocidal massacre of thousands of Haitian immigrants and Dominicans of Haitian ancestry during the fall of 1937. I have no idea whether the Dominican student whom I tried to deter from this absurd choice had occasion to reflect on my objections. At the time, he defensively brought up differences of opinion, arguing that, for sure, "not all Dominicans" felt the same way about Trujillo as I did.

To me, these identitarian moments, from the Latin Grammy publicity campaign to the student-led anointment of Trujillo, encapsulate the urgency of conveying to young people from racialized ethnic groups that they cannot afford to approach who and what they are carelessly. Knowing their identity, which is fluid and complex, is a labor-intensive and intricate process that requires ongoing interrogation and analysis. If they fail to do the homework that the task requires, they put themselves at the mercy of the hardened ideas fed to them by the commercial media and by the most objectionable ideologues. They may also find themselves colluding with the logic and rituals of racism, invigorating its currency and relevance, and ultimately facilitating its continuance into the future. Afro-Latina/os are the one minority group that by virtue of its unstable location in the existing US paradigms of identity seems uniquely equipped to discredit the presumptions of ethnoracial ontology. Assailed by the various sides of their mixed ancestry, they cannot afford to remain complacent about their roots because they lack the luxury of boasting about "good genes" (that is, a preexisting genetic self-confidence) like racist whites think they can.

I would speculate that it came as no surprise to Afro-Latina/os that many Japanese musicians can play salsa and merengue with the kind of passion and finesse assumed to be the sole jurisdiction of Puerto Rican and Dominican performers. We might recall, for example, the popularity of the all-Japanese band Orquesta La Luz. That Dominicans do not hold a monopoly on the talent for merengue had already become evident by the 1980s, when a flowering of Puerto Rican performers of that musical form, especially women, rose to the top of the charts internationally. This cross-national or cross-ethnic "intrusion" may today unsettle militant cultural nationalists who would have much to say about what they term "cultural appropriation," an area of policing that has lately gained much traction, especially on social media. The refrain in "Honra y cultura," a 1991 song composed by the iconic Puerto Rican salsero Willie Colón, issues the injunction for everyone to sing their own songs, not somebody else's. This utterance seems to express a desire for performers to abide by the strictures of national borderlines when choosing their musical repertoires.

Had performers in the first half of the twentieth century needed to abide by the expectations of today's musical gatekeepers, the African American baritone, actor, and antiracist advocate Paul Robeson would have had to refrain from singing the Yiddish song "Zog nit keynmol" to pay tribute to the Jews who had courageously fought the Nazi war machine in the 1943 Warsaw Ghetto Uprising. He did so most meaningfully while in Russia as part of his 1949 tour of the Soviet Union. Similarly, if one is inclined to value the role that art can play when effectively applied to advancing social justice causes, one would applaud the songwriter and poet Abel Meeropol, a child of Russian Jewish immigrant parents, for daring to capture the horror of lynching with harrowing lyricism in his 1937 poem "Strange Fruit." He did so even though such a debased form of vigilante justice primarily targeted not his people but African Americans. Jim Crow leaders like South Carolina Senator Benjamin R. "Pitchfork Ben" Tillman would even extol the righteousness of that extralegal practice, as he did during his Senate address on March 23, 1900 ("Their Own Hotheadedness"). Fortunately, Meeropol's text, after 1939, would become a staple for African American singer Billie Holiday. Following her recording of "Strange Fruit" that same year, the piece would go on to become the biggest hit of her career (O'Dell). There is a good chance that the power of Meeropol's words, as inimitably performed by Lady Day, lent moral fortitude to the social struggles that catalyzed the passage of the Civil Rights Act of 1964.

The preceding pages have voiced a call for our greater recognition of, and engagement with, complexity when contending with issues of ethnoracial, national, and cultural identity. I would like to insist on the restraint needed when feeling compelled to hype up "the community" for the sake of self-esteem. Noble as such a compulsion may be, if done without caution, celebrating one's people could run the risk of treading conceptually dangerous ground. We might end up replicating the self-adulation that became the norm when the heirs of conquerors and settlers aggrandized themselves while effacing the humanity of Indigenous peoples during the colonial transaction. Essentializing the virtues of one's own people or touting any sort of unparalleled excellence could make us purveyors of baleful legacies worthy of distance and critical reckoning. To bring this meditation to a close, let us remind ourselves that *there are no cultural genes*. Afro-Latina/os are best poised to understand the overarching implications of this thought in the realm of social interactions. As such, they enjoy a unique vantage point from which to promote deracialization in the hope of corroding the logic and practices that have, for too long, built and sustained the racial wall in the US and overall hemispheric imaginary.

Notes

1. Since the original composition of this piece, new developments have gained currency in the discipline. Among the elements of "political correctness," the notions of "being woke" and "woke-ism" have become ideological and electoral tools that US politicians may use either to attack or to defend particular values, stigmatizing them as "anti-American."

2. A similar point came up in the PBS documentary *America Beyond the Color Line* (2003), a film on the present conditions of blacks hosted by Gates, especially during an interview with African American psychotherapist and political activist Lenora Fulani, former presidential candidate of the now defunct New Alliance Party. Demonstrating her awareness of the lore that associates "white" behavior with diligence, resourcefulness, and savvy on the job market, Fulani resigned herself to saying that one of her goals in her work with the community was to convey to young African Americans that they should "learn to be more white."

3. See, for instance, Cross's "The Negro-to-Black Conversion Experience."

EPILOGUE

ON BEING COLLECTED

Looking Backwards and the Perils of Baseball Nationalism

SILVIO TORRES-SAILLANT

The experience of finding myself collected has been odd. I have had to come to terms with the unusual position of seeing myself as an elder, reading myself as if in the third person, and conversing with earlier versions of my thought and diction. Perhaps this sensation is common to the oddity of retrospection, with the sobering effect of the backwards glance. The texts collected and edited by Nancy Kang and Michael Nieto Garcia span a quarter century of my published thoughts on the sociocultural history and identity quandaries of people of Latin American ancestry in the United States. Their careful framing of the recurring themes and ongoing concerns in my writings on subjects within the interdisciplinary field of Latinx studies may be useful to the generations of scholars coming after mine. The editors pinpoint the call to embrace complexity, to avoid the lure of self-essentializing (such as ascribing unexamined virtues to one's own group), and to exercise caution when construing some sixty-million-plus people with multiple origins, ancestries, belief systems, worldviews, and political histories as a "community." They capture my stubborn advocacy for critically recognizing internal divisions, stratifications, and zones of latent strife within the panethnicity, my claim that overlooking complexity renders communal ties less likely, while doing injustice to Latinx humanity. The editors have noted my fear that rushed assertions of unity and assumed solidarities may obscure the work needed for achieving greater solidarity across the various subgroups of Latinx peoples.

My conversations with Nancy and Michael during their editorial work have involved revisiting stages in my intellectual journey, recognizing in me a voice that has evolved while keeping much of the enthusiasm of the graduate student who once embraced the hope that words could matter. I was taken by the view that perhaps knowledge in the human sciences could help spread glad tidings, with the aim of reducing the predominance of hatred in societies that too quickly boast of their advancement based on technological development and military might. Four decades have now passed since I entered a higher-education classroom as a teacher. I now feel quite confident saying categorically to my students that I recognize nothing as advancement which does not contribute to enhancing the caliber of our social relations. If the hatred does not let up, the new technologies will only increase the efficacy of their users to inflict greater degrees of harm onto their targets. The editors humored my request to aim for an outcome that, while gathering a fair sampling of my essays from the last couple of decades as a sort of recognition of the work I have done, would render the chapters useful to newer generations of readers. We thus aimed to respect the integrity of the texts as originally published, while making some judicious changes to amplify their relevance for current readers. I hope that such selective tampering has updated the texts just enough for today's audience to find them valuable beyond the mere ceremony of saluting the work of an elder in the field.

On Dominican Baseball as Complicated Source of Pride

In their introduction, Nancy and Michael understood my insistence on embracing complexity, perhaps even contradiction, to bridle the temptation to self-essentialize when formulating any portrait of a collective as demographically diverse as the Latinx panethnicity. I would emphasize this point further by invoking an illustration that spotlights the place of baseball, specifically among Dominicans. On the surface, Dominican baseball yields occasions for joy and the pride often displayed when evoking the accomplishments of compatriots in that sport. It is not unusual for ordinary Dominicans to be heard boasting about the nation's special gift for the game, speaking at times as if claiming a genetic predisposition for excellence in it. But examined closely, noting the backdrop of geopolitical events, national traumas, and deleterious legacies of domination that form part of the history whereby baseball became a core Dominican pastime may complicate the ethics of our pride.

The value of finding ways to resist such instances of self-essentializing became plain to me when I witnessed the shock expressed by acquaintances of Dominican, Cuban, and Puerto Rican ancestry at the results of the first World Baseball Classic tournament held in Puerto Rico during the spring of 2006. Japan's victory over the teams representing the United States, the Hispanic Caribbean, and mainland Latin American countries where the sport is a national obsession left many befuddled. "How could they beat us?" lamented a Dominican neighbor who felt the game was "ours" by virtue of its centrality in the country. Admittedly, players of Dominican ancestry in the US Major Leagues have excelled across many generations. One thinks of pioneers Osvaldo "Ozzie" Virgil (1932–2024), Hall of Famer Juan Marichal (1937–), Ricardo "Rico" Carty (1939–2024), the Alou brothers (Mateo "Matty" [1938–2011], Felipe [1935–], and Jesús Rojas Alou [1942–2023]), César Cedeño (1951–), Pedro Martínez (1971–), Alex "A-Rod" Rodriguez (1975–), and their more recent counterparts. As it turns out, Japan's team would gracefully snatch first place again at the second triennial tournament of the World Baseball Classic in 2009, and once more in 2023, scoring the best record among the twenty-three participants in the five editions of the tournament to date. My perturbed Dominican neighbor found some consolation in the victory of his home country during the third edition (2013), with the United States earning the title during the fourth (2017). Americans, in fact, would seem more justified than folks hailing from the Dominican Republic, at an emotional level, to grieve over being outperformed at "their own game" by a team from an island country in Asia. Whatever roots it may have inherited from earlier forms of entertainment elsewhere, baseball as we know it began in the United States, becoming a popular sport there by the second half of the nineteenth century.

Baseball had, in fact, reached Japanese shores *before* Dominican ones. Horace Wilson, a US English teacher working at the Kaisei Academy, a preparatory school in Tokyo, introduced it there in 1872. Other US educators and missionaries further popularized the sport elsewhere in Japan, from the local to the national level. Its appeal grew rapidly, leading to the establishment of the country's first official baseball team, the Shimbashi Athletic Club, formed in 1878 and led by the American-trained engineer Hiroshi Hiraoka (Allen). In their affinity for baseball, the Japanese had greater seniority than Dominicans, whose contact with it began in the 1880s, when the sport was brought over by Cuban plantation owners. They had left their country to pursue their businesses in safer pastures during the independence struggle known as the Ten Years War (1868–1878). The sport had first arrived in Cuba in 1864, brought by returning students who had studied in the United States, and they created a baseball league on the island by the late 1870s (Jamail). The first baseball teams born on Dominican soil were Cuban, hence the names of the rivals in the 1886 match held between Santiago de Cuba and Angelina, both evoking places aligned with Cuban geography, the Oriente and Matanzas provinces, respectively. Actual Dominican teams would emerge only several years later.

Imperial Domination and National Pastime

Ironically, the historical circumstances that led to the incorporation of baseball as the Dominican national pastime offer little cause for exuberance and celebration. People there did come to view baseball as "their game," but only after the country became an informal US possession. The sport morphed into a national delight for Dominicans alongside their country's geopolitical subservience to the United States, as Washington encroached on the life and governance of countries across the Western Hemisphere. This spread occurred as US leaders applied themselves to making manifest the doctrine envisioned in President James Monroe's December 1823 message to Congress, affirming the role of the US as overseer of societies across the region. Thus, ostensibly to preclude the likelihood of European creditors landing troops in the country to collect debts owed by the Dominican State, President Theodore Roosevelt proceeded to take control of Dominican customs and border surveillance, turning the sovereign nation into a US protectorate. This arrangement started in 1905, by US presidential fiat, and became formalized as a binational treaty in 1907. The endpoint arrived in 1940 when the United States felt it could return the control of Dominican fiscal affairs to native hands, specifically those of Rafael Leónidas Trujillo, the Generalissimo, a megalomaniacal, thievish, murderous, and sexually rapacious tyrant, who by then had been ruling the Dominican Republic for ten years.

Before that time, between 1916 and 1924, the rulers of the country had been US military governors. The exception was Dominican interim president Juan Bautista Vicini Burgos, who served while the occupying forces began to ready themselves to allow Dominicans to hold national elections and set up their own government. With Dominican finances in US hands, the occupiers held sway over civil and political life. Before joining the US-created National Guard in 1918, Trujillo had been making a living through odd jobs, petty criminality, and freelancing as a cattle rustler. As a trainee of the invading army who had quickly risen to the rank of second lieutenant, namely with the support of key US officers, he enjoyed visibility by the time the country chose its own president in 1924. Horacio Vásquez, the newly elected leader, may have thought it strategic to include on his team someone who had a good rapport with US authorities. In 1925 President Vásquez appointed Trujillo to head the National Police with the rank of commander, only to be enticed by the crafty officer to promote him to brigadier general two years later. As head of the country's security forces, Trujillo worked assiduously on galvanizing the loyalty of soldiers around his person rather than around the president or the constitution. This he did while using his position for personal gain, such as privileging family members and himself with monopolies on government services linked to the armed forces that were under his jurisdiction.

By 1930, when President Vásquez had completed his first six years in office—the length of presidential terms at the time—and received a solid majority of the votes for reelection to the next six-year period, Trujillo had come to a point where he could advance his own agenda less cautiously. He conspired with a disaffected cabinet member, Minister of Justice and Public Education Rafael Estrella Ureña, to overthrow Vásquez by goading an armed rebellion that would seemingly come from civilian quarters. As the anti-Vásquez mob marched on the National Palace, the president pleaded with the commander of the armed forces to deter them, but snaky Trujillo kept the soldiers in the barracks, opting to invoke the "neutrality" of the military in the face of conflicts between civilian factions. Vásquez chose to save his own life by offering to resign, with his vice president following suit. Before leaving the National Palace, Vásquez was prevailed upon to name Estrella Ureña minister of Interior and Police Affairs, the cabinet position required by law to fill the interim presidency when the president and the vice president failed to complete their terms.

With Estrella Ureña as acting president, new elections took place. The Trujillo ticket ran unopposed as candidate for the Patriotic Coalition of Citizens. Candidates Federico Velázquez Hernández and Ángel Morales, who had announced their campaign for president and vice president, respectively, saw fit to withdraw, intimidated by the terrifying violence deployed by paramilitary bands loyal to Trujillo. After the schemer's electoral "victory," Velázquez Hernández and Morales, having dared to challenge Trujillo briefly during the election, went into exile, fearing for their lives. On Inauguration Day, August 16, 1930, Trujillo took hold of the Dominican State and would not let go of it until a volley of assassins' bullets stopped him on May 30, 1961. In the intervening three decades, a period known in Dominican history as the Era of Trujillo, the country changed dramatically. The tyrant exerted absolute control over the nation via his command of the army; the unrestricted use of the national treasury and the country's natural resources to enrich his family and cronies; the limitless deployment of murder, incarceration, and torture to silence the slightest form of dissent; and bankrolling a robust propaganda machine committed to glorifying him everywhere.

The official narrative disseminated by the mass media venues at the time—plus all state institutions and schools—cast Trujillo as an anointed soul (his debauchery and serial philandering notwithstanding), as a superior statesman, and as supreme benefactor of the nation. Citizens learned it was both good sense and elevated style to decorate their living rooms with a poster showing a photograph of the dictator, under which was the solemn declaration "In This House, Trujillo Is Boss." Likewise, they would make sure to convey their gratitude to the Almighty while acknowledging their concurrent debt to the Generalissimo. If any chance existed to be heard by others, they ostentatiously brayed, "Thanks to God and Trujillo!"

The Era of Trujillo was a thirty-year period of continually enforced adulation of the dictator and an ongoing assault on the moral integrity of citizens with any degree of self-respect. Learned elites helped fuel a cult of personality that turned the apotheosis of the tyrant into a civic duty. Opposition to Trujillo became a punishable offense. Therein emerged a nationwide circus of political hypocrisy. Whether out of fear or in search of acknowledgment and reward, adherents sought to outdo one another in their display of trujillophilia. They exhibited hyperbolic admiration to protect themselves from charges of anti-trujillismo cooked up by spiteful, envious, or simply scared neighbors wishing to ward off the chance of themselves becoming targets of the regime. That there were reasons galore for fearing one's neighbor—perhaps even one's own shadow—was clear to the generations who lived during the Era. Those who did not could piece together the abominations from the contents of the *Catálogo de víctimas* (*Catalogue of Victims*) published by the Dominican National Archives in 2020. A review of the *Catálogo* by the Latin American satellite news network teleSUR, focusing on the massive number of the dictatorship's victims, estimated that some fifty thousand people were killed by the leader whom the official narrative praised for having brought *prosperity and peace* to Dominican society ("Los crímenes").[1]

Baseball, Trujillo, and Racial Exclusion

The Era of Trujillo was also the period when Dominican society latched firmly onto baseball as the national pastime, a process that had begun during the US occupation. The population had been lured out of the dust of the cockfighting pit into that of the baseball diamond, the latter seeming more consistent with the idea of modernity that the United States promulgated in the regions that were under its influence. After the War of 1898, following the US takeover of the Philippines, the US sphere of influence expanded to encompass territories in the Pacific. Baseball followed suit. Anthropologist Andrew Mitchel conveys the happenings succinctly in his baseball-centered account of US–Dominican relations: "The nations that fell under US political and/or economic hegemony in the 20th century—the Spanish Caribbean, Central America, Mexico, Venezuela, Japan, and South Korea—remain the nations where baseball is most popular today." Dominicans owe their passion for baseball to the cultural heritage bequeathed by the imperial overseer that took it upon itself, ostensibly out of geopolitical necessity, to intervene in their country's political and economic affairs. Baseball as a quintessential Dominican pastime and the cataclysmic Era of Trujillo share a common rootedness in US geopolitical oversight, since the US control of Dominican customs and border surveillance started in 1905.

No less troubling, the denial of civil rights to Dominicans of Haitian ancestry, which in 2013 prompted a Constitutional Court ruling (TC/0168/13) that revoked the citizenship of over two hundred thousand individuals (applied retroactively back to 1929), forms part of the same legacy that gave rise to Dominican preeminence in the world of baseball. Historian Sabine F. Cadeau has foregrounded the transformation of the generally fluid borderlands between the two countries sharing the island of Hispaniola into a heavily policed dividing line, after US Navy Rear Admiral Thomas Snowden, military governor of the Dominican Republic, issued his Executive Order 372 in December 1919, which specified racial criteria for migrant workers to enter the country (60–61). As if safeguarding Dominicans from intermixture with non-whites, Executive Order 372 forbade "the immigration to the Dominican Republic of braceros of any race that is not Caucasian . . . except through the ports authorized [to receive them] and the prescribed points along the border" (qtd. in Cadeau 60). The establishment of what one might call a Jim Crow–style logic in the Dominican Republic's immigration law gave rise to the conditions that would strip thousands of Haitian Dominicans of their Dominican citizenship rights (Cadeau 61). Given their generally Eurocentric and white supremacist leanings—despite their own phenotypical particulars—elite Dominicans had no problem colluding with the negrophobic and anti-Haitian texture of the US military government's early immigration laws.

There is thus an ominous link between the extent to which Dominicans have excelled as baseball players and the subservience of their homeland to US foreign policy in the region. The Dominican government's 2024 seizure of Venezuelan President Nicolás Maduro's plane, to comply with the US policy of hostility toward a neighboring country that in 2019 had opted to leave the US sphere of influence, as Cuba had done in the 1960s, is a case in point. Another is the human rights abuses against Haitian immigrants and Dominicans of Haitian ancestry in the country's population from 2013 onwards. The former clearly stems from the obedience owed by a subject nation to its geopolitical overseer. The latter has clear roots in the white supremacist logic discernible in the immigration and border control laws instituted by the invading US military forces that dictated Dominican fiscal life for decades after 1907. Enabler of the Trujillo regime, US imperialism stands at the heart of the cultural logic that in Dominican society associates blackness with Haiti, despite the overwhelmingly African-descended, native-born population. The negrophobia generated by the US forces in the early twentieth century remained even after the invading troops left the country. *Trujillismo cultural*, a pragmatic matrix of undemocratic and exclusionary norms that even self-styled liberal leaders have relied on, has endured through many decades of Dominican governments led by the tyrant's heirs, disciples, and admirers.

With this checkered, even chaotic background in mind, those of Dominican ancestry must decide how to modulate their ethnonational pride to avoid the unwitting celebration of those parts of their heritage that might instead merit regret. Moral caution would advise that we consider the aforementioned scenarios when extolling the national identity of a Dominican, just as when boasting of the seamless panethnic unity of Latinx peoples. Of course, the power of critical insight ultimately lies within us. We help no one by too rapidly subscribing to feel-good formulations of who and what we are. It seems best for the panethnicity to remain hard to define, intent on making sense of the challenges presented by the twenty-first century's return of autocratic leaders throughout the Americas. We bear witness to the rise of politicians whose success is due, in part, to the audacity and alacrity with which they express their contempt for various segments of their own national populations. The present moment may be a time for the mutable, multiple, and even metamorphic nature of human identity to prevail as a kind of incubation period for a more salutary future.

Notes

1. Before the *Catálogo* appeared in book form, when the National Archives had just made its contents available to the public, journalist Ángela Peña wrote a revealing assessment of its contents. She underlined the numerous ordinances whereby the dictatorship sought to curtail the mobility, thought, power of assembly, and overall civil rights of the citizenry. A person could be punished for trying to "leave the country secretly," associating with "a group that has unconstitutional leanings," having "relatives who are hostile to the government," expressing "anti-government views," aiding "actions against public peace and State order," or joining "suspicious meetings," among many other equally cryptic interdictions. It would thus be left up to the authorities to decide on one's guilt or innocence, often on the spot.

ACKNOWLEDGMENTS

Completing this volume was no leisurely stroll through sunlit meadows. It was an unpredictable trek with a few dark valleys, including health challenges and a global pandemic. Despite these and other unexpected setbacks, we managed to reach our destination through the power of helpers and believers, chief among them Kerry E. Webb, senior acquisitions editor of the University of Texas Press, and our series editors Lorgia García Peña and Nicole Guidotti-Hernández. We must credit the UTP team, including thoughtful editorial assistant Christina Vargas, responsive and generous manuscript editor Laura Gauggel, and altogether superlative copyeditor Martin Ainsley. We also thank indexer Lisa Rivero for her quality work and overall reliability. This crew, with Kerry at the helm, shepherded the book into existence using gentle nudges, clear direction, and the alchemist's ability to transform imaginative solutions into practical results.

Though it is difficult to thank everyone who played a meaningful role, we will briefly mention those whose impact was most keenly felt on the long road from conceptualization to publication.

Nancy Kang expresses gratitude to her colleagues at the University of Manitoba's Women's and Gender Studies (WGS) Department for their enthusiasm, solidarity, and goodwill. The guidance of Dean Heidi Marx and Associate Dean Rob Hoppa was greatly appreciated, as was the unwavering support of WGS Chair Shawna Ferris. The research for this book was undertaken, in part, through the support of the Canada Research Chairs Program.

McGill University's Institute for Gender, Sexuality, and Feminist Studies under the leadership of Natalie Stoljar and with the exceptional kindness of Andrew Folco provided welcome time and space during my term as Muriel Gold Visiting Professor in 2024. In addition to my immediate family (Anna, Maria, Mark, Kevin, Natalie, Michael, and Dad), I remain indebted to many inspirational mentors, friends, and friendly colleagues, including Linda Hutcheon, George Elliott Clarke, Naomi Morgenstern, Lourdes Torres, Ginetta Candelario, Sarah Aponte, Rhina P. Espaillat, Alfred Nicol, Liz Millward, Lisa Bednar, Mylène Gamache, Adele Perry, Jocelyn Thorpe, Christine Stewart, Justin Jaron Lewis, Neil McArthur, and Kai M. A. Chan (whose commitment to hope will transform the world). I thank my closest friends Amy Huang, Elizabeth Underwood, Sarane Poon, Christine Yau, Cherise Pollard, Adam and Ashley Barkman, Ian Williams, Dena and Robert Mandel, and Paritosh Kasotia for their enduring strength and loving presence. Finally, I salute *mis hermanos* Michael Nieto Garcia and Silvio Torres-Saillant, both of whom defied major health hurdles to complete this project. I have grown upwards in the warmth of their good light. Michael embodies resilience, adaptability, humble brilliance, and a quiet kindness. Silvio's unconditional acceptance and wise counsel keep me aspiring to a greater humanity. Thank you for walking me home all those dark mornings from a country away.

Michael Nieto Garcia would like to thank his big, beautiful (and beautifully mixed) extended family—for the inspiration of their example, for the rich diversity of their points of view, and for unapologetically being themselves.

My greatest thanks go to Silvio and Nancy. Silvio, for his grace, openness, and kind presence, not to mention his decades of scholarship and intellectual contributions to the field. I have greatly enjoyed our stimulating conversations over the last few years. Nancy, not only for her insight and scholarship, but also for unstinting encouragement and support—along with a wicked sense of humor to keep us grounded and connected no matter what was going on in the real world at the time. Truly, the book would not have been completed without her tireless efforts, unflagging devotion, much-beloved cajoling, and expert project-management skills.

I am deeply grateful to have Elisabeth Arti Wulandari in my life, and to her big Indonesian family for welcoming me as one their own—though culturally and geographically we are from opposite sides of the globe.

As editors, we hope that this volume, in bringing together key writings by a respected scholar-activist whose praxis has helped develop the field of Latinx studies, will spur fruitful conversations on the subjects, contradictions, doubts, queries, and suppositions found across the diverse chapters that comprise the book. We trust that many of the concerns Torres-Saillant has raised over the past few decades remain (even starkly) relevant today. Understanding the author's distinct style and unique forms of utterance, as well as his location at the crossroads of varied geographies of knowledge, readers can anticipate thoughts and questions unprovoked by previous scholarship. In that respect, *Problematic Paradigms* may offer a bridge for newer scholars to formulate analyses using more complex and multipronged approaches than ever before. We sense that despite the troubles and uncertainties of the past and present, there remain deep seeds of hope embedded in this material that will nourish generations of thinkers to come.

CREDITS AND PUBLICATION HISTORY

Versions of material in the chapters of *Problematic Paradigms* previously appeared in the following venues. All original texts named below have undergone varying degrees of modification in content, style, and length as appropriate. We have added short summary statements of what the original publications aimed to accomplish when they first appeared.

Chapter 1: "Before the Diaspora: Early Dominican Literature in the United States." Published in *Recovering the US Hispanic Literary Heritage*, vol. 3, edited by Maria Herrera-Sobek and Virginia Sánchez Korrol, Arte Público Press, 2000, pp. 250–267. This piece made the call to elongate and add nuance to the memory of Dominican cultural participation in US Latinx life.

Chapter 2: "Visions of Dominicanness in the United States." Published in *Borderless Borders: US Latinos, Latin Americans, and the Paradox of Interdependence*, edited by Frank Bonilla et al. Temple UP, 1998, pp. 139–152. This piece traced the history of the Dominican presence in the United States, accounting for the complex relationship of immigrants with their coethnics back home against the backdrop of US imperial interests.

Chapter 3: "Pilgrims of Humane Remembrance at the Borderlands." Published in the *Border of Lights Reader*, edited by Megan Jeannette Myers and Edward Paulino, Amherst College P, 2021, pp. 91–100. This piece bore witness to the efforts of scholars, writers, and community leaders of both Dominican and Haitian ancestry to reckon with the terrible legacy of the 1937 Haitian Massacre ordered by Dominican dictator Rafael Leónidas Trujillo.

Chapter 4: "Latinismo(s) and Latinidad." Published in *The Oxford Encyclopedia of Latinos and Latinas in Contemporary Politics, Law, and Social Movements*, edited by Suzanne Oboler and Deena J. González, Oxford UP, 2015, vol. 1, pp. 566–572; "Latinos." Op. cit., vol. 1, pp. 507–510; "Nationalism," Op. cit., vol. 2, pp. 110–112. These entries contemplated group dynamics and ethnonationalism in the context of US Latinx identity.

Chapter 5: "The Latino Autobiography." Published in *Latino and Latina Writers*, edited by Alan West, Charles Scribner's Sons, 2004, pp. 61–79; "The Political Essay." *The Oxford Encyclopedia of Latinos and Latinas in Contemporary Politics, Law, and Social Movements*, edited by Suzanne Oboler and Deena J. González, Oxford UP, 2015, pp. 177–180; "Essayists." Op. cit., vol. 2, pp. 72–78; "Isabel Allende." Op. cit., vol. 1, pp. 161–163; "Introduction: Inscribing Latinos in the National Discourse." *Recovering the US Hispanic Literary Heritage*, vol. 4, edited by José F. Aranda and Silvio Torres-Saillant, Arte Público Press, 2002, pp. 1–10. These articles, consolidated in the chapter, showcased twenty-first century Latinx writers and literary genres, bringing to the fore the complexities of speaking about the panethnicity when most of the voices articulate their vision as individuals with differing degrees of power and access to the national spotlight.

Chapter 6: "Inventing the Race: Latinos and the Ethnoracial Pentagon." Published in *Latino Studies*, vol 1, no. 1, 2003, pp. 125–151. Appearing in the inaugural issue of the journal, this piece examined identitarian positionalities as they relate to the self, as well as to various groups. The writer encouraged prudence in readers, such as regarding both ethnicity and race as equally tentative in the US context, since neither defines an objective reality.

Chapter 7: "Problematic Paradigms: Racial Diversity and Corporate Identity in the Latino Community." Published in *Latinos: Remaking America*, edited by Marcelo M. Suárez-Orozco and Mariela M. Páez, U of California P, 2002, pp. 435–455. This piece exposed the palpable inequalities when representing Latinx bodies in the media and dominant discourses in the public sphere. It cast doubt on the benefits of assuming an unmessy Latinx "oneness."

Chapter 8: "Afro-Latinidad: Phoenix Rising from the Hemisphere's Racist Flames." Published in *The Cambridge History of Latina/o American Literature*, edited by John Morán González and Laura Lomas, Cambridge UP, 2018, pp. 276–305. This piece touched upon scenarios that may attest to the political and intellectual embrace of white supremacy by societies on both sides of the Rio Grande, much to the detriment of racialized populations.

Chapter 9: "Racism in the Americas and the Latino Scholar." Published in *Neither Enemies nor Friends: Latinos, Blacks, Afro-Latinos*, edited by Anani Dzidzienyo and Suzanne Oboler, Palgrave Macmillan, 2005, pp. 281–304. This piece meditated on the combined obligation and urgency of US Latinx scholars to remain vigilant on behalf of their counterparts in their ancestral homelands in relation to political and racial violence as well as threats to academic freedom.

Chapter 10: "Afro-Latina/os and the Racial Wall." Published in *A Companion to Latina/o Studies*, edited by Juan Flores and Renato Rosaldo, Blackwell, 2007, pp. 363–375; "One and Divisible: Meditations on Global Blackness." *Small Axe*, vol. 29, July 2009, pp. 4–25; "Divisible Blackness: Reflections on Heterogeneity and Racial Identity." *The Afro-Latin@ Reader: History and Culture in the United States*, edited by Miriam Jiménez Román and Juan Flores, Duke UP, 2010, pp. 453–466. These texts intermingled personal experiences with scholarly reflections to underscore the contradictory yet illuminating position occupied by Afro-Latinx peoples in various global locations.

WORKS CITED

Abalos, David T. *The Latino Family and the Politics of Transformation*. Praeger, 1993.

Acosta-Belén, Edna. "The Building of a Community: Puerto Rican Writers and Activists in New York City (1890s–1960s)." Gutiérrez and Padilla, pp. 179–195.

Agüeros, Jack. "Halfway to Dick and Jane: A Puerto Rican Pilgrimage." *The Immigrant Experience: The Anguish of Becoming American*, edited by Thomas C. Wheeler, Dial Press, 1971, pp. 85–105.

Ainslie, Ricardo C. "The Plasticity of Culture and Psychodynamic and Psychosocial Processes in Latino Immigrant Families." Suárez-Orozco and Páez, 289–301.

Alba, Richard, and Victor Nee. "Rethinking Assimilation Theory for a New Era of Immigration." *International Migration Review*, vol. 31, no. 4, Dec. 1997, pp. 826–874.

Alegría, Ricardo E. *Juan Garrido: El conquistador Negro en las Antillas, Florida, México y California, c. 1503–1540*. Centro de Estudios Avanzados de Puerto Rico y el Caribe, 1990.

Alexie, Sherman. "The Unauthorized Autobiography of Me." Krupat and Swann, pp. 3–14.

Alexis, Jacques Stéphen. *Compère Général Soleil* [*General Sun, My Brother*]. Gallimard, 1955.

Alford, Harold J. *The Proud Peoples: The Heritage and Culture of Spanish-Speaking Peoples in the United States*. McKay, 1972.

Alig, Wallace B. "Man with a Hammer." *Américas*, vol. 5, no. 5, May 1953, pp. 6+.

Allen, Jim. "Japanese Baseball: A 150-Year Journey of Transformation." *Japan Wire*, 7 Aug. 2022, https://english.kyodonews.net/articles/-/35127.

Alvarez, Julia. "An American Childhood in the Dominican Republic." *The American Scholar*, vol. 56, no. 1, winter 1987, pp. 71–85.

Alvarez, Julia. *The Other Side / El Otro Lado*. Dutton, 1995.

Alvarez, Julia. *Something to Declare*. Algonquin Books, 1998.

Alvarez, Julia. *¡Yo!* Algonquin Books, 1997.

America beyond the Color Line. Directed by Daniel Percival and Mary Crisp, written and presented by Henry Louis Gates, Jr., performances by Maya Angelou, Samuel L. Jackson, and Morgan Freeman, PBS, 2004. 4 episodes.

American Civil Liberties Union. *Island of Impunity: Puerto Rico's Outlaw Police Force*. American Civil Liberties Union, 2012.

Anderson, Mark. "Bad Boys and Peaceful Garifuna: Transnational Encounters between Racial Stereotypes of Honduras and the United States (and Their Implications for the Study of Race in the Americas)." Dzidzienyo and Oboler, pp. 101–115.

Anthony, Kathryn H. *Designing for Diversity: Gender, Race, and Ethnicity in the Architectural Profession*. U of Illinois P, 2001.

Anzaldúa, Gloria. *Borderlands / La Frontera: The New Mestiza*. 2nd ed. Aunt Lute Books, 1999.

Aparicio, Frances R. "(Re)constructing Latinidad: The Challenge of Latina/o Studies." *A Companion to Latina/o Studies*, edited by Juan Flores and Renato Rosaldo, Blackwell, 2007, pp. 39–48.

Aparicio, Frances R., and Susana Chávez-Silverman, editors. *Tropicalizations: Transcultural Representations of Latinidad.* UP of New England, 1997.

Aponte, Sarah. *Dominican Migration to the United States, 1970–1997: An Annotated Bibliography.* Dominican Research Monographs, CUNY Dominican Studies Institute, 1999.

Aquino Méndez, Tomás. "Trato injusto." Tribunal Constitucional, pp. 509–510.

Aranda, José, and Silvio Torres-Saillant, editors. *Recovering the US Hispanic Literary Heritage.* Vol. 4, Arte Público Press, 2002.

Arocha, Jaime. "Inclusion of Afro-Colombians: Unreachable National Goal?" *Latin American Perspectives,* vol. 25, no. 3, May 1998, pp. 70–89.

Arteaga, Alfred. *Chicano Poetics: Heterotexts and Hybridities.* Cambridge UP, 1997.

Ashbaugh, Carolyn. *Lucy Parsons: An American Revolutionary.* Charles H. Kerr / Illinois Labor History Society, 1976.

Atlas sociolingüístico de pueblos indígenas en América Latina. UNICEF / FUNPROEIB Andes, 2009.

Augenbraum, Harold, and Ilan Stavans, editors. *Growing Up Latino: Memoirs and Stories.* Houghton Mifflin, 1993.

Back, Les, and John Solomos, editors. *Theories of Race and Racism: A Reader.* Routledge, 2000.

Balaguer, Joaquín. "Discurso." *I Cumbre Iberoamericana de Jefes de Estado y de Gobierno.* Guadalajara, México, 18 June 1991, https://www.segib.org/cumbres-iberoamericanas/.

Balaguer, Joaquín. *La isla al revés: Haití y el destino dominicano.* 2nd ed., Librería Dominicana, 1984.

Barone, Michael. *The New Americans: How the Melting Pot Can Work Again.* Regnery, 2001.

Belliard, Marianella. "From Alejandro González Iñárritu to Feidin Santana: Colliding Lives, Disrupting Narratives." *Latino Rebels,* 24 Apr. 2015, https://www.latinorebels.com/2015/04/24/from-alejandro-gonzalez-inarritu-to-feidin-santana-colliding-lives-disrupting-narratives/.

Beveridge, Albert J. "The March of the Flag," anthologized as "Beveridge Trumpets Imperialism." *Colonials and Sojourners,* Vintage, 1971, pp. 333–335. Vol. 2 of *To Serve the Devil,* by Paul Jacobs et al., 2 vols.

Black, George. *The Good Neighbor: How the United States Wrote the History of Central America and the Caribbean.* Pantheon, 1988.

Bolívar, Simón. *Selected Writings of Bolívar, 1810–1822.* Compiled by Vicente Lecuna, edited by Harold A. Bierck, Jr., and translated by Lewis Bertrand, Colonial Press, 1951. Vol. 1 of *Selected Writings of Bolívar,* 2 vols.

Bollinger, William, and Daniel Manny Lund. "Minority Oppression: Toward Analyses That Clarify and Strategies That Liberate." *Race and Ethnicity in Latin America,* edited by Jorge I. Domínguez, Garland Publishing, 1994, pp. 218–244.

Bonilla, Frank. "Beyond Survival: Por qué seguiremos siendo puertorriqueños." *The Puerto Ricans: Their History, Culture, and Society,* edited by Adalberto López, Schenkman Publishing, 1980, pp. 453–464.

Bonilla, Frank. "Rethinking Latino/Latin American Interdependence: New Knowing, New Practice." *Borderless Borders: US Latinos, Latin Americans, and the Paradox of Interdependence,* edited by Frank Bonilla et al., Temple UP, 1998, pp. 217–230.

Bonilla, Frank. "Urban Challenges for Blacks and Latinos in the 1990s: Strategies of Contention and Collaboration." Collaboration and Contentions among African Americans and Latinos: A Working Conference, 7–9 Sep. 1995, Center for Urban Economic Development, University of Illinois at Chicago.

Bosch Carcuro, Matías, et al., editors. *Masacre de 1937, 80 años después: Reconstruyendo la memoria* (*80 Years after the Massacre: Reconstructing the Memory*). Fundación Juan Bosch/CLACSO, 2018.

Brand-Williams, Oralandar. "Oklahoma Raises Hopes for Slavery Reparations." *Detroit News*, 6 Feb. 2000, p. 7.

Bubnova, Tatiana. "Prefacio de la traductora." *Hacia una filosofía del acto ético: De los borradores y otros escritores*, by Mijaíl M. Bajtín and translated by Tatiana Bubnova, Anthropos Editorial, 1997, pp. xiii–xx.

Bunge, Carlos Octavio. *Nuestra América: Ensayo de psicología social.* Valerio Abeledo, 1905.

Burma, John H. *Spanish-Speaking Groups in the United States.* Duke UP, 1954.

Bursey, Brett. "The Day the Flag Went Up." *Point*, vol. 10, no. 97, fall 1999, https://www.scpronet.com/point/9909/p04.html.

Cabán, Pedro. "Moving from the Margins to Where? Three Decades of Latino/a Studies." *Latino Studies*, vol. 1, no. 1, 2003, pp. 5–35.

Cabeza de Vaca, Álvar Núñez. *The Account: Álvar Núñez Cabeza de Vaca's* Relación. Translated by Martin A. Favata and José B. Fernández, Arte Público Press, 1993.

Cadeau, Sabine F. *More Than a Massacre: Racial Violence and Citizenship in the Haitian-Dominican Borderlands.* Cambridge UP, 2022.

Calderón, Fernando G. "The Quechua and Aymara peoples in the Formation and Development of Bolivian Society." *Race and Class in Post-Colonial Society: A Study in Ethnic Group Relations in the English-Speaking Caribbean, Bolivia, Chile, and Mexico*, UNESCO, 1977, pp. 185–219.

Caminero-Santangelo, Marta. *On Latinidad: US Latino Literature and the Construction of Ethnicity.* UP of Florida, 2007.

Candelario, Ginetta E. B. *Black behind the Ears: Dominican Racial Identity from Museums to Beauty Shops.* Duke UP, 2007.

Cañizares Esguerra, Jorge. "New World, New Stars: Patriotic Astrology and the Invention of Indian and Creole Bodies in Colonial Spanish America, 1600–1650." *American Historical Review*, vol. 104, no. 1, 1999, pp. 33–68.

Cantú, Norma Elia. *Canícula: Snapshots of a Girlhood en la Frontera.* U of New Mexico P, 1995.

Cantú, Norma Elia. "Whose Story Is It Anyway? Autobiography on the Border." XXIV International Congress of the Latin American Studies Association, 6–8 Sep. 2001, Washington, DC.

Carrasco, Mario. "Progressive Latino Pollster: 98% of Latinos Do Not Identify with 'Latinx' Label." *ThinkNow*, 1 Nov. 2019, https://medium.com/@ThinkNowTweets/progressive-latino-pollster-trust-me-latinos-do-not-identify-with-latinx-63229adebcea.

Castro, Fidel. "Segunda Declaración de la Habana" ["Second Declaration of Havana"]. *Fidel Castro: Obras Escogidas, 1953–1963*, vol. 1, Editorial Fundamentos, 1976, pp. 101–134.

Castro, Max J., and Thomas D. Boswell. *The Dominican Diaspora Revisited: Dominicans and Dominican Americans in a New Century.* Dante B. Fascell North-South Center, 2002.

Catálogo de víctimas de la dictadura de Trujillo en los fondos del Archivo General de la Nación, vol. 385, Archivo General de la Nación, 2020.

Céspedes, Diógenes, and Silvio Torres-Saillant. "Fiction Is the Poor Man's Cinema: An Interview with Junot Díaz." *Callaloo*, vol. 23, no. 3, 2000, pp. 892–907.

Chavez, Linda. *Out of the Barrio: Toward a New Politics of Hispanic Assimilation.* Basic Books, 1991.

Chesnutt, Charles W. "The Future American." *Theories of Ethnicity: A Classical Reader*, edited by Werner Sollors, New York UP, 1996, pp. 17–33.

Coates, Carrol F., translator. *General Sun, My Brother*. By Jacques Stéphen Alexis, U of Virginia P, 1999. Originally published in French as *Compère Général Soleil*. Gallimard, 1955.

Commons, John R. *Races and Immigrants in America*. Macmillan, 1911.

Cook, Mercer. Review of *Les semences de la colère*, by Anthony Lespès. *Journal of Negro History*, vol. 34, no. 4, Oct. 1949, pp. 474–475.

Cossío y Cisneros, Evangelina. "To Free Cuba" (excerpt from *The Story of Evangelia Cisneros*, 1897). *Hispanic American Literature*, edited by Rodolfo Cortina, NTC Publishing, 1998, pp. 355–358.

Courtney, W. S. *The Gold Fields of St. Domingo*. Anson P. Norton, 1860.

Crenshaw, Kimberlé Williams. "Race, Reform, and Retrenchment: Transformation and Legitimation in Antidiscrimination Law." Back and Solomos, pp. 549–560.

Cross, William E., Jr. "The Negro-to-Black Conversion Experience." *Black World*, vol. 20, no. 9, July 1971, pp. 13–27.

Dana, Richard Henry, Jr. 1840. *Two Years Before the Mast, and Other Voyages*. Library of America, 2005.

Danticat, Edwidge. *The Farming of Bones*. Soho Press, 1998.

Danticat, Edwidge. Preface. Philoctète, pp. 7–9.

Darder, Antonia, and Rodolfo D. Torres. "Latinos and Society: Culture, Politics, and Class." Darder and Torres, pp. 3–26.

Darder, Antonia, and Rodolfo D. Torres, editors. *The Latino Studies Reader: Culture, Economy, and Society*. Blackwell, 1998.

Davis, Mike. *Magical Urbanism: Latinos Reinvent the US City*. Verso, 2000.

Day, Frances Ann. *Latina and Latino Voices for Children and Teenagers*. Heinemann, 1997.

"Déclaration de repentance des évêques de France" ("Declaration of Repentance of the Church of France"). *Conférence des évêques de France*, 30 Sep. 1997, https://eglise.catholique.fr/conference-des-eveques-de-france/textes-et-declarations/369207-declaration-de-repentance-des-eveques-de-france/.

De la Campa, Roman. *Latin Americanism*. U of Minnesota P, 1999.

De Lara, Juan Jacobo. *Pedro Henríquez Ureña: Su vida y su obra*. Universidad Nacional Pedro Henríquez, 1975.

Delgado, Richard. "Words That Wound: A Tort Action for Racial Insults, Epithets, and Name-Calling." *Critical Race Theory: The Cutting Edge*, edited by Richard Delgado and Jean Stefancic, Temple UP, 1995, pp. 159–168.

Delgado, Richard, and Jean Stefancic, editors. *The Latino/a Condition: A Critical Reader*. New York UP, 1998.

De Man, Paul. "Autobiography as De-facement." *MLN*, vol. 94, no. 5, Dec. 1979, pp. 919–930.

De Niza, Fray Marcos. "Discovery of the Seven Cities of Cibola (Excerpt)." *Herencia: The Anthology of Hispanic Literature of the United States*, edited by Nicolás Kanellos, Oxford UP, 2002, pp. 39–46.

Deschamps, Enrique. 1907. *La República Dominicana: directorio y guía general*. Sociedad Dominicana de Bibliófilos, Editora de Santo Domingo, 1974.

Díaz, Junot. *Drown*. Riverhead Books, 1996.

Díaz Quiñones, Arcadio. "Pedro Henríquez Ureña: Modernidad, diáspora y construcción de identidades." *Modernización e identidades sociales*, edited by Gilberto Giménez and

Ricardo Pozas Horcasitas, Universidad Nacional Autónoma de México, 1994, pp. 59–117.

Díaz Quiñones, Arcadio. *Sobre los principios: Los intelectuales caribeños y la tradición*. Universidad Nacional de Quilmes Editorial, 2006.

Díaz, Rubén, Sr. "Senator Rubén Díaz, Sr., Speaks on the Martin Luther King, Jr., Resolution." *YouTube*, uploaded by NYSenate, 23 Jan. 2014, www.youtube.com/watch?v=jcnGAJpbV28.

Domínguez, Jorge I. Commentary on "Gender and Citizenship in Latino Political Participation," by Lisa J. Montoya. Suárez-Orozco and Páez, pp. 430–433.

Dougherty, Tim. "Media versus Minorities." *Hispanic Business*, Oct. 1999, pp. 26–28.

Douglass, Frederick. *Narrative of the Life of Frederick Douglass, An American Slave*. *Narrative of the Life of Frederick Douglass, An American Slave and Incidents in the Life of a Slave Girl*, edited by Kwame Anthony Appiah, Modern Library, 2004, pp. 3–119.

D'Souza, Dinesh. *The End of Racism: Principles for a Multiracial Society*. Free Press, 1995.

Duany, Jorge. "Neither Golden Exile nor Dirty Worm: Ethnic Identity in Recent Cuban-American Novels." *Cuban Studies*, vol. 23, 1993, pp. 167–183, https://www.jstor.org/stable/24487023.

Duarte, Rosa. *Apuntes de Rosa Duarte: Archivo y versos de Juan Pablo Duarte*. Edited by E. Rodríguez Demorizi, et al., 2nd ed., Secretaría de Estado de Educación, Bellas Artes y Cultos, 1994.

Duras, Marguerite. "We Must Share the Crime." Translated by D. G. Luttinger. *On Prejudice: A Global Perspective*, edited by Daniela Gioseffi, Anchor Books, 1993, p. 83.

Dworkin y Méndez, Kenya. Introduction. *Black Cuban, Black American: A Memoir*, by Evelio Grillo, Arte Público Press, 2000, pp. vii–xiv.

Dying to Be Thin. Directed by Larkin McPhee, performances by Walter Kaye, Jennifer Schmid, and Kate Dillon, PBS, 2004.

Dzidzienyo, Anani. "Conclusions." *No Longer Invisible: Afro-Latin Americans Today*, edited by the Minority Rights Group, Minority Rights Publications, 1995, pp. 345–358.

Dzidzienyo, Anani, and Suzanne Oboler, editors. *Neither Enemies nor Friends: Latinos, Blacks, Afro-Latinos*. Palgrave Macmillan, 2005.

Eakin, Paul John. "Malcolm X and the Limits of Autobiography." Olney, *Autobiography*, pp. 181–183.

ECLAC. "Indigenous and Afro-American People Live in Poverty." *ECLAC Notes* (newsletter of the United Nations Economic Commission for Latin America and the Caribbean), no. 13, Nov. 2000, pp. l+.

Embree, Edwin R. *Brown America: The Story of a New Race*. Viking, 1931.

Emerson, Ralph Waldo. *Self-Reliance and Other Essays*. Dover, 1993.

Espino, Rodolfo, and David L. Leal. "Latino Politics—The State of the Discipline." Introduction. *Latino Politics: Identity, Mobilization, and Representation*, edited by Espino et al. U of Virginia P, 2007, pp. 1–13.

Fabens, Joseph Warren. *In the Tropics: By a Settler in Santo Domingo*. Introduction by Richard B. Kimball, G. W. Carleton, 1863.

Fabens, Joseph Warren. *Life in Santo Domingo: By a Settler*. Introduction by Richard B. Kimball, G. W. Carleton, 1873.

Falcón, Angelo. "Puerto Ricans and the Politics of Racial Identity." *Racial and Ethnic Identity: Psychological Development and Creative Expression*, edited by Herbert W. Harris et al., Routledge, 1995, pp. 193–207.

Falicov, Celia Jaes. "Ambiguous Loss: Risk and Resilience in Latino Immigrant Families." Suárez-Orozco and Páez, pp. 274–288.

Fanon, Frantz. *Black Skin, White Masks.* 1952. Translated by Charles Lam Markmann, Grove Press, 1998.

Feliz, Raysa. "Cardenal pide Gobierno no tema a EEUU." *Hoy,* 1 Nov. 1999, pp. 1+.

Ferguson, J. Halcro. *Latin America: The Balance of Race Redressed.* Oxford UP, 1961.

Fernández, Alfredo A. "Crónica de una guerra anunciada: A Critical Report about the USA Press in the Spanish American War (1898)." Aranda and Torres-Saillant, pp. 18–30.

Fernández, Roberta, editor. *In Other Words: Literature by Latinas of the United States.* Arte Público Press, 1994.

Ferré, Rosario. "The Battle of the Virgins." *Goddess of the Americas: Writings on the Virgin of Guadalupe,* edited by Ana Castillo, Riverhead Books, 1996, pp. 79–87.

Ferreras, Ramón Alberto. *Negros.* Vol. 4, Serie Media Isla, Editorial del Nordeste, 1983.

Fields, Barbara J. "Ideology and Race in American History." *Region, Race and Reconstruction: Essays in Honor of C. Vann Woodward,* edited by J. Morgan Kousser and James M. McPherson, Oxford UP, 1982, pp. 143–177.

Fletcher, Michael A. "The Blond, Blue-Eyed Face of Spanish TV." *The Washington Post,* 2 Aug. 2000, https://www.washingtonpost.com/archive/politics/2000/08/03/the-blond-blue-eyed-face-of-spanish-tv/bb1806c5-1f84-412c-a6b5-07b4f04ba46e/.

Fletcher, Michael A. "Latino Actors Cite Color Barrier in US." *Boston Sunday Globe,* 6 Aug. 2000.

Flores, Juan. "Living Borders / *Buscando América*: Languages of Latino Self-Formation." Coauthored with George Yúdice. *Divided Borders: Essays on Puerto Rican Identity,* Arte Público Press, 1993, pp. 199–224.

Flores, Juan. "Puerto Rican Literature in the United States: Stages and Perspectives." Gutiérrez and Padilla, pp. 53–88.

Flores, Juan. Review of *Harvest of Empire: A History of Latinos in America,* by Juan González. *ColorLines: Race Culture Action,* vol. 3, no. 3, 2000, p. 43.

Flores, William Vincent, and Rina Benmayor, editors. *Latino Cultural Citizenship: Claiming Identity, Space, and Rights.* Beacon Press, 1997.

Foner, Nancy. "West Indian Identity in the Diaspora: Comparative and Historical Perspectives." *Latin American Perspectives,* vol. 25, no. 3, May 1998, pp. 173–188.

Fox, Geoffrey E. *The Hispanic Nation: Culture, Politics, and the Constructing of Identity.* U of Arizona P, 1997.

Franklin, Benjamin. "Observations Concerning the Increase of Mankind." *The Papers of Benjamin Franklin,* edited by Leonard W. Labaree, vol. 4, Yale UP, 1961, pp. 225–234.

Freire, Paulo. *Pedagogy of the Oppressed.* Translated by Myra Bergman Ramos, Continuum, 1970.

Fumagalli, Maria Cristina. *On the Edge: Writing the Border between Haiti and the Dominican Republic.* Liverpool UP, 2018.

Fumagalli, Maria Cristina. "Story of a History." Foreword. Prestol Castillo, pp. v–xvii.

Galíndez, Jesús de. *The Era of Trujillo: Dominican Dictator.* Edited by Russell H. Fitzgibbon, U of Arizona P, 1973.

Ganivet, Ángel. *Idearium español.* 1897. 2nd ed., Librería General de Victoriano Suárez, 1905.

García, Alejandro. "Latinos, Be Wary of Election Talk." *Detroit Free Press,* 16 Sep. 2002, *ProQuest,* https://www.proquest.com/docview/436403894.

García Peña, Lorgia. *The Borders of Dominicanidad: Race, Nation, and the Archives of Contradiction*. Duke UP, 2016.

Gardner, Marilyn. "Is 'White' the Only Color of Success?" *The Christian Science Monitor*, 31 Oct. 2005, pp. 13+.

Gates, David. "English Lessons." *The New York Times*, 29 Sep. 1996, sec. 7, p. 9.

Gates, Henry Louis, Jr. *Colored People: A Memoir*. Viking, 1994.

Gates, Henry Louis, Jr. "W. E. B. Du Bois and the African Encyclopedia." Milton First-Year Lecture series, 5 Oct. 2004, Goldstein Auditorium, Syracuse University.

Gilroy, Paul. *The Black Atlantic: Modernity and Double Consciousness*. Harvard UP, 1993.

Goldberg, David Theo. *Racial Subjects: Writing on Race in America*. Routledge, 1997.

González, Gilbert G. *Culture of Empire: American Writers, Mexico, and Mexican Immigrants, 1880–1930*. U of Texas P, 2004.

González, Juan. *Harvest of Empire: A History of Latinos in America*. Penguin Books, 2000.

Gonzales, Rodolfo "Corky." "I Am Joaquín." *The Latino Reader: An American Literary Tradition from 1542 to the Present*, edited by Harold Augenbraum and Margarite Fernández Olmos, Harper Perennial, 1997, pp. 265–279.

"González Parsons, Lucía." *Dictionary of Mexican American History*, edited by Matt S. Meier and Feliciano Rivera, Greenwood, 1981, pp. 148–149.

Good, Graham. Preface. *Encyclopedia of the Essay*, edited by Tracy Chevalier, Fitzroy Dearborn Publishers, 1997, pp. xix–xx.

Gracia, Jorge J. E. *Hispanic/Latino Identity: A Philosophical Perspective*. Blackwell, 2000.

Grant, Madison. *The Passing of the Great Race; or, the Racial Basis of European History*. Charles Scribner's Sons, 1916.

Griffin-Nolan, Ed. "The Long Hard Road." *IRC News* (newsletter of the Inter-Religious Council of Central New York), May 2000, pp. 1+.

Grillo, Evelio. *Black Cuban, Black American: A Memoir*. Arte Público Press, 2000.

Guevara Arzu, Roy. "The Garifunas in Honduras." Moore et al., pp. 241–248.

Gusdorf, Georges. "Conditions and Limits of Autobiography." Translated by James Olney. Olney, *Autobiography*, pp. 28–48.

Gutiérrez, Ramón, and Genaro Padilla, editors. *Recovering the US Hispanic Literary Heritage*. Vol. 1, Arte Público Press, 1993.

Gutman, Huck. "Rousseau's *Confessions*: A Technology of the Self." *Technologies of the Self: A Seminar with Michel Foucault*, edited by Gutman et al., U of Massachusetts P, 1988, pp. 99–120.

Hamilton, Charles V. "Concluding Note." *Beyond Racism: Race and Inequality in Brazil, South Africa, and the United States*, edited by Hamilton et al., Lynne Rienner, 2001, pp. 591–598.

Hancock, Henry J. "The Situation in Santo Domingo." *The Annals of the American Academy of Political and Social Science*, vol. 26, July 1905, pp. 47–52.

Haney López, Ian F. "The Social Construction of Race." *Critical Race Theory: The Cutting Edge*, edited by Richard Delgado and Jean Stefancic, Temple UP, 1995, pp. 191–203.

Hansberry, Lorraine. *Les Blancs: The Collected Last Plays*. Edited by Robert Nemiroff, Vintage, 1994.

Hayes-Bautista, David E. *La Nueva California: Latinos in the Golden State*. U of California P, 2004.

Hayner, Priscilla. "Truth Commissions: Exhuming the Past." *NACLA Report on the Americas*, vol. 32, no. 2, Sep./Oct. 1998, pp. 30–32.

Heiskanen, Benita. "Where Are 'We' in Transnational Latino/a Studies?" *Diálogos Latinoamericanos*, no. 16, 2009, pp. 5–15.

Helg, Aline. *Our Rightful Share: The Afro-Cuban Struggle for Equality, 1886–1912*. U of North Carolina P, 1995.

Henríquez Ureña, Max. *Pedro Henríquez Ureña: antología*. Colección Pensamiento Dominicano, Libreria Dominicana, reprint ed., Feria Nacional del Libro, 1984.

Henríquez Ureña, Pedro. "De Pedro Henríquez Ureña a Ramona Ureña Díaz." *Familia Henríquez Ureña: Epistolario*, Secretaría de Estado de Educación, Bellas Artes y Cultos, 1994, pp. 289–290.

Henríquez Ureña, Pedro. *El español en Santo Domingo*. 4th ed., Editora Taller, 1982.

Henríquez Ureña, Pedro. *El nacimiento de Dionisos*. Edited by Juan Jacobo de Lara, Universidad Nacional Pedro Henríquez Ureña, 1976. Vol. 1 of *Obras completas*.

Henríquez Ureña, Pedro. *La cultura y las letras coloniales en Santo Domingo. Obra crítica*. Edited by Emma Susana Speratti-Piñero, Biblioteca Americana, Fondo de Cultura Económica, 1960, pp. 331–444.

Henríquez Ureña, Pedro. *La utopía de América*. Edited by Angel Rama and Rafael Gutiérrez Girardot, Biblioteca Ayacucho, 1978.

Henríquez Ureña, Pedro. *La versificación irregular en la poesía castellana*. Edited by Juan Jacobo de Lara, Universidad Nacional Pedro Henríquez Ureña, 1978. Vol. 4 of *Obras completas*.

Henríquez y Carvajal, Francisco. "De Francisco Henríquez y Carvajal a Pedro Henríquez Ureña." *Familia Henríquez Ureña: Epistolario*, Secretaría de Estado de Educación, Bellas Artes y Cultos, 1994, pp. 657–658.

Hernández, Ramona, and Silvio Torres-Saillant. "Marginality and Schooling." Foreword. *Minorities, Education, Empowerment*, special issue of *Punto 7 Review: A Journal of Marginal Discourse*, edited by Hernández and Torres-Saillant, vol. 2, no. 2, 1992, pp. 1–6.

Hernández, Ramona, et al. *Dominican New Yorkers: A Socioeconomic Profile, 1990*. Dominican Research Monographs, CUNY Dominican Studies Institute, 1995.

Hernández, Tanya Katerí. "Afro-Latinos." Oboler and González, https://www.oxfordreference.com/display/10.1093/acref/9780195156003.001.0001/acref-9780195156003-e-14.

Hilden, Patricia Penn. *When Nickels Were Indians: An Urban, Mixed-Blood Story*. Smithsonian Institution Press, 1995.

Hoffnung-Garskoff, Jesse. "The Migrations of Arturo Schomburg: On Being *Antillano*, Negro, and Puerto Rican in New York, 1891–1938." *Journal of American Ethnic History*, vol. 21, no. 1, fall 2001, pp. 3–49.

Hollinger, David A. "Amalgamation and Hypodescent: The Question of Ethnoracial Mixture in the History of the United States." *American Historical Review*, vol. 108, no. 5, Dec. 2003, pp. 1363–1390.

Hollinger, David A. *Postethnic America: Beyond Multiculturalism*. Basic Books, 1995.

Hostos, Eugenio María de. "El cholo." *Aproximaciones al estudio de la literatura hispánica*, edited by Carmelo Virgillo et al., 4th ed., McGraw-Hill Education, 1999, pp. 372–374.

Huntington, Samuel P. "The Hispanic Challenge." *Foreign Policy*, vol. 141, Mar.–Apr. 2004, pp. 30–45.

Inter-American Commission on Human Rights. *Report on the Situation of Human Rights in the Dominican Republic*. Organization of American States, 1999.

Jackson, Carlton. *Hattie: The Life of Hattie McDaniel*. Madison Books, 1990.

Jamail, Milton. "Cuban League." *Encyclopedia Britannica*, 19 Dec. 2014, https://www.britannica.com/topic/Cuban-League.

Jefferson, Thomas. *Works: Selections*. Literary Classics of the United States, 1984.

Jenks, Kevin. "The 'Dominican Vespers': The Cultural Roots of US Immigrants from the Dominican Republic." *The Social Contract*, vol. 7, no. 4, 1997, pp. 268–275.

Jiménez Román, Miriam, and Juan Flores, editors. *The Afro-Latin@ Reader: History and Culture in the United States*. Duke UP, 2010.

Johnston, Thomas E. "A Translation of Cotton Mather's Spanish Works: *La Fe del Cristiano* and *La Religion Pura*." *Early American Literature Newsletter*, vol. 2, no. 2, autumn 1967, pp. 7–21.

Kanellos, Nicolás, editor. *Herencia: The Anthology of Hispanic Literature of the United States*. Oxford UP, 2002.

Kanellos, Nicolás. *The Hispanic Almanac: From Columbus to Corporate America*. Visible Ink, 1994.

Kanellos, Nicolás, editor. *The Hispanic Literary Companion*. Visible Ink, 1997.

Kanellos, Nicolás. "Hispanics and Race." *Reference Library of Hispanic America*, edited by Kanellos, vol. 1, Gale Research Group, 1998, pp. 176–184.

Kang, Nancy, and Silvio Torres-Saillant. *The Once and Future Muse: The Poetry and Poetics of Rhina P. Espaillat*. U of Pittsburgh P, 2018.

Kang, Nancy, and Silvio Torres-Saillant. "Race." *Keywords for Latina/o Studies*, edited by Deborah R. Vargas et al., New York UP, 2017, pp. 175–180.

Kashatus, William C. "Hispanics in the Crosshairs." *Puerto Rico and the American Dream*, 10 Jan. 2010, http://www.prdream.com/wordpress/topics/2010/01/1682/.

Keim, De B. Randolph. *San Domingo: Pen Pictures and Leaves of Travel, Romance and History, from the Portfolio of a Correspondent in the American Tropics*. Claxton, Remsen, and Haffelfinger, 1870.

King, Lourdes Miranda. "The Spanish-Speaking American." *Ethnic American Minorities: A Guide to Media and Materials*, edited by Henry A. Johnson, R. R. Bowker Company, 1976, pp. 189–239.

King, Martin Luther, Jr. "Read Martin Luther King, Jr.'s 'I Have a Dream' Speech in Its Entirety." *Talk of the Nation*, hosted by Rebecca Roberts, *NPR*, 16 Jan. 2023, https://www.npr.org/2010/01/18/122701268/i-have-a-dream-speech-in-its-entirety.

King, Martin Luther, Jr. *A Testament of Hope: The Essential Writings of Martin Luther King, Jr.* Edited by James Melvin Washington, Harper & Row, 1986.

King, Martin Luther, Jr. "What Is Your Life's Blueprint?" *Scholastic Scope*, 10 Jan. 2003, pp. 15–16, www.voiceofoc.org/wp-content/uploads/2017/01/MLK-Lifes-Blueprint.pdf.

Klor de Alva, J. Jorge, et al. "Our Next Race Question: The Uneasiness between Blacks and Latinos." *Harper's Magazine*, vol. 292, no. 1751, Apr. 1996, pp. 55–63.

Klor de Alva, J. Jorge. "Telling Hispanics Apart: Latino Sociocultural Diversity." *The Hispanic Experience in the United States: Contemporary Issues and Perspectives*, edited by Edna Acosta-Belén and Barbara R. Sjostrom, Praeger, 1998, pp. 107–136.

Krupat, Arnold, and Brian Swann, editors. *Here First: Autobiographical Essays by Native American Writers*. Modern Library, 2000.

Laó-Montes, Agustín. "Mambo Montage: The Latinization of New York City." Introduction. Laó-Montes and Dávila, pp. 1–54.

Laó-Montes, Agustín. "Niuyol: Urban Regime, Latino Social Movements, Ideologies of Latinidad." Laó-Montes and Dávila, pp. 117–154.

Laó-Montes, Agustín, and Arlene Dávila, editors. *Mambo Montage: The Latinization of New York*. Columbia UP, 2001.

Lejeune, Philippe. "The Autobiographical Contract." *French Literary Theory Today: A Reader*, edited by Tzvetan Todorov, translated by R. Carter, Cambridge UP, 1982, pp. 192–222.

Lespès, Anthony. *Les semences de la colère*. Éditions Henri Deschamps, 1949.

Levine, Robert M. *Race and Ethnic Relations in Latin America and the Caribbean: An Historical Dictionary and Bibliography*. Scarecrow Press, 1980.

Levins Morales, Aurora. "Child of the Americas." *Boricuas: Influential Puerto Rican Writings—An Anthology*, edited by Roberto Santiago, One World, 1995, p. 79.

Lomas, Clara. "Revolutionary Women and the Alternative Press in the Borderlands." Introduction. *The Rebel*, by Leonor Villegas de Magnón, edited by Lomas, Arte Público Press, 1994, pp. xi–li.

López, David, and Yến Lê Espiritu. "Panethnicity in the United States: A Theoretical Framework." *Ethnic and Racial Studies*, vol. 13, no. 2, 1990, pp. 198–224.

López, Kleiner, and Manuel Azcona. "López Rodríguez: Los hijos de haitianos son haitianos." *Listín Diario*, 8 Nov. 1999, pp. Al, 4.

Lopez, Mark Hugo. "'Hispanic,' 'Latino,' Or 'Latinx'? Survey Says . . ." Interview by Shereen Marisol Meraji, *Code Sw!tch*, *NPR*, 11 Aug. 2020, https://www.npr.org/sections/codeswitch/2020/08/11/901398248/hispanic-latino-or-latinx-survey-says.

"Los crímenes del dictador Rafael Trujillo en República Dominicana." *Precision*, 30 May 2020, https://precision.com.do/los-crimenes-del-dictador-rafael-trujillo-en-republica-dominicana/.

Lugo, Américo. *Bibliografía*. Imprenta La Cuna de América, 1906.

Luis, William. *Dance between Two Cultures: Latino Caribbean Literature Written in the United States*. Vanderbilt UP, 1997.

Luis, William. "Latin American (Hispanic Caribbean) Literature Written in the United States." *The Cambridge History of Latin American Literature*, edited by Roberto González Echevarría and Enrique Pupo-Walker, vol. 2, Cambridge UP, 1996, pp. 526–556.

Magill, Frank, editor. *Masterpieces of Latino Literature*. HarperCollins, 1994.

"Manassas's War on Immigrants." *Washington Post*, 30 Dec. 2005, https://www.washingtonpost.com/archive/opinions/2005/12/30/manassass-war-on-immigrants/50fea861-4395-4a72-a0d5-acbe36060778/.

Marable, Manning. "We Need New and Critical Study of Race and Ethnicity." *The Chronicle of Higher Education*, vol. 46. no. 25, 25 Feb. 2000, https://www.chronicle.com/article/we-need-new-and-critical-study-of-race-and-ethnicity/.

Marañón, Gregorio. Prólogo. *Los mestizos de America*, by José Pérez de Barradas, Cultura Clásica y Moderna, 1948, pp. i–v.

Margolis, Maxine L. *An Invisible Minority: Brazilians in New York City*. Allyn and Bacon, 1998.

Marín, Gerardo, and Barbara VanOss Marín. *Research with Hispanic Populations*, Sage, 1991. Applied Social Research Methods 23.

Maritain, Jacques. *Réflexions sur l'Amérique*. Librairie Arthème Fayard, 1958.

Márquez, Roberto. "Raza, racismo, e historia: 'Are All My Bones from There?'" *Latino(a) Research Review*, vol. 4, no. 3, 2000, pp. 8–22.

Martí, José. "My Race." *José Martí: Selected Writings*, edited and translated by Esther Allen, Penguin Books, 2002, pp. 318–321.

Martínez-Echazábal, Lourdes. "*Mestizaje* and the Discourse of National/Cultural Identity in Latin America, 1845–1959." *Latin American Perspectives*, vol. 25, no. 3, 1998, pp. 21–42.

Martínez, Rufino. *Diccionario biográfico-histórico dominicano: 1821–1930*. Editora de la UASD, 1971. Historia y Sociedad 5.

Mather, Cotton. *Magnalia Christi Americana: Books I and II.* Edited by Kenneth B. Murdock and Elizabeth W. Miller, Harvard UP, 1977.

Mattos, Trevor, et al. "Latinos in Massachusetts: Afro-Latinos." *Gastón Institute Publications*, no. 262, Dec. 2020, https://scholarworks.umb.edu/gaston_pubs/262.

McAlary, Mike. "The Framing of a Cop: How a Clever Dominican Cartel Manipulated New York Politicians to Bust a Federal Agent." *New York Post*, 9 Oct. 1991, pp. 2+.

McAlary, Mike. "The Tragic Legacy of a 'Narco Village.'" *New York Daily News*, 20 Apr. 1994, pp. 5+.

McAlary, Mike. "Washington Heights' Deadly Dominican Connection." *New York Post*, 6 Sept. 1992, p. 3.

McCall, George J. "The Me and the Not-Me: Positive and Negative Poles of Identity." *Advances in Identity Theory and Research*, edited by Peter J. Burke et al., Kluwer Academic / Plenum Publishers, 2003, pp. 11–26.

McKnight, Kathryn Joy, and Leo J. Garofalo, editors. *Afro-Latino Voices: Narratives from the Early Modern Ibero-Atlantic World, 1550–1812.* Hackett, 2009.

Medina, Pablo. *Exiled Memories: A Cuban Childhood.* 1990. Persea Books, 2002.

Miller, Wayne Charles. *A Comprehensive Bibliography for the Study of American Minorities.* Vol. 2, New York UP, 1976.

Miranda, Francisco de. *The Diary of Francisco de Miranda: Tour of the United States, 1783–1784.* Edited by William Spence Robertson, Hispanic Society of America, 1928.

Mirandé, Alfredo, and Evangelina Enríquez. *La Chicana: The Mexican American Woman.* U of Chicago P, 1979.

Miščević, Nenad. "Nationalism." *The Stanford Encyclopedia of Philosophy*, edited by Edward N. Zalta and Uri Nodelman, fall 2023 ed., https://plato.stanford.edu/archives/fall2023/entries/nationalism/.

Mitchel, Andrew. "The Dominican Republic and the United States: A Baseball History." *Origins: Current Events in Historical Perspective*, June 2021, https://origins.osu.edu/article/dominican-republic-and-united-states-baseball-history?language_content_entity=en.

Mollenkopf, John, and Manuel Castells, editors. *Dual City: Restructuring in New York.* Russell Sage Foundation, 1991.

Montalvo Covarrubias, José R., et al. "El cráneo de Antonio Maceo." *Ahora*, Sección Dominical, Havana, 2 Dec. 1934. Reprinted in *Cuaderno de Historia*, vol. 82, 1997, pp. 1–13.

Montes Huidobro, Matías. Prólogo. *El laud del desterrado*, by Anonymous, edited by Matías Montes Huidobro, Arte Público Press, 1995, pp. vii–xix.

Moore, Carlos. "Afro-Cubans and the Communist Revolution." Moore et al., pp. 199–239.

Moore, Carlos. *Pichón: A Memoir—Race and Revolution in Castro's Cuba.* Lawrence Hill Books, 2008.

Moore, Carlos, et al., editors. *African Presence in the Americas.* Africa World Press, 1995.

Moraga, Cherríe. "City of Desire." Interview by Bridget Kevane and Juanita Heredia. *Latina Self-Portraits: Interviews with Contemporary Women Writers*, edited by Kevane and Heredia, U of New Mexico P, 2000, pp. 97–108.

Moraga, Cherríe. "A Long Line of Vendidas." *Border Texts: Cultural Readings for Contemporary Writers*, edited by Randall Bass, Houghton Mifflin, 1999, pp. 144–160.

Moraga, Cherríe. *Loving in the War Years: Lo que nunca pasó por sus labios.* South End Press, 1983.

Morbraz. Review of *Le peuple des terres mêlées* (1989), by René Philoctète. *Blues dans le Sud*, 13 Feb. 2010, https://philmorbraz.blogspot.com/2010/02/le-peuple-des-terres-melees-de-rene.html.

Moreno, Marisel C. *Family Matters: Puerto Rican Women Authors on the Island and the Mainland.* U of Virginia P, 2012.

Mörner, Magnus. *El mestizaje en la historia de Ibero-América.* Comisión de Historia, Instituto Panamericano de Historia y Geografía, 1961.

Morris, Aldon D. *The Origins of the Civil Rights Movement: Black Communities Organizing for Change.* Free Press, 1984.

Mostern, Kenneth. *Autobiography and Black Identity Politics: Racialization in Twentieth-Century America.* Cambridge UP, 1999.

Moya Pons, Frank. *The Dominican Republic: A National History.* Hispaniola Books, 1995.

Nascimento, Abdias do. "The African Experience in Brazil." Moore et al., pp. 97–117.

Nash, Gary B. "The Hidden History of Mestizo America." *Journal of American History*, vol. 82, no. 3, 1995, pp. 941–964.

National Institute for Latino Policy. "NY State Senator Rubén Díaz's Rant on MLK, White Puerto Ricans, and Governor Cuomo's Views on Extreme Conservatives." *NiLP Report on Latino Policy & Politics*, 24 Jan. 2014, www.latinopolicy.org.

Neruda, Pablo. "Oda a Paul Robeson." *Obras completas*, 3rd expanded ed., Editorial Losada, 1967, pp. 1310–1318, https://archive.org/details/trent_0116405264460_1/page/1310/mode/2up.

Noticias La Paz. "Jorge Ramos, Entrevista a Evo Morales." *Facebook*, 16 Dec. 2022, 7:44 p.m., https://m.facebook.com/NoticiasLPZ/videos/jorge-ramos-entrevista-a-evo-moralesse-dice-que-evo-morales-ha-recibido-todo-el-/1221709095427328/.

Núñez, Manuel. *El ocaso de la nación dominicana.* 2nd ed., Editorial Letra Gráfica, 2001.

Oboler, Suzanne. *Ethnic Labels, Latino Lives: Identity and the Politics of (Re)Presentation in the United States.* U of Minnesota P, 1995.

Oboler, Suzanne, and Anani Dzidzienyo. "Flows and Counterflows: Latinas/os, Blackness, and Racialization in Hemispheric Perspective." Dzidzienyo and Oboler, pp. 3–35.

Oboler, Suzanne, and Deena J. González, editors. *The Oxford Encyclopedia of Latinos and Latinas in the United States.* Oxford UP, 2005, https://doi.org/10.1093/acref/9780195156003.001.0001.

Ocampo, Anthony Christian. *The Latinos of Asia: How Filipino Americans Break the Rules of Race.* Stanford UP, 2016.

O'Dell, Cary. "'Strange Fruit': Billie Holiday (1939)." *Library of Congress*, National Recording Preservation Board, 2002, www.loc.gov/static/programs/national-recording-preservation-board/documents/StrangeFruit.pdf.

Olney, James. "Autobiography and the Cultural Moment: A Thematic, Historical, and Bibliographical Introduction." Olney, *Autobiography*, pp. 3–27.

Olney, James, editor. *Autobiography: Essays Theoretical and Critical*, Princeton UP, 1980.

Omi, Michael, and Howard Winant. *Racial Formation in the United States: From the 1960s to the 1980s.* Routledge, 1986.

Padilla, Felix M. *Latino Ethnic Consciousness: The Case of Mexican Americans and Puerto Ricans in Chicago.* Notre Dame UP, 1985.

Padilla, Genaro. "Imprisoned Narrative? Or Lies, Secrets and Silence in New Mexico Women's Autobiography." *Criticism in the Borderlands: Studies in Chicano Literature,*

Culture and Ideology, edited by Héctor Calderón and José David Saldívar, Duke UP, 1991, pp. 43–60.

Padilla, Genaro. "Recovering Mexican-American Autobiography." Gutiérrez and Padilla, pp. 153–178.

Parkhill, Maggie. "Read the Full Text of the Pope's Apology for Canada's Residential Schools." *CTV News*, 1 Apr. 2022, https://www.ctvnews.ca/canada/article/read-the-full-text-of-the-popes-apology-for-canadas-residential-schools/.

Peña, Ángela. "¡POR PRIMERA VEZ! *Catálogo de víctimas de la dictadura de Trujillo*." *Hoy*, 19 Aug. 2017, https://hoy.com.do/por-primera-vez-catalogo-de-victimas-de-la-dictadura-de-trujillo/.

Perdomo, Willie. *Where a Nickel Costs a Dime: Poems*. Norton, 1996.

Pereyra, Emilia. "El enfático interés del nieto de Trujillo por la Presidencia dominicana." *Diario Libre*, 7 Dec. 2017, https://www.diariolibre.com/actualidad/el-enfatico-interes-del-nieto-de-trujillo-por-la-presidencia-dominicana-XK8729563.

Pérez, Frank G. "Hispanics, Advertising, and Alcohol: Cultivation Theory and Panethnic Beer Commercials on the Univision Television Network." Rios and Mohamed, pp. 145–157.

Pérez, Sonja Z. "Auto/Ethnography and the Politics of Recovery: Narrative Anxiety in the Borderlands of Culture." Aranda and Torres-Saillant, pp. 277–290.

Pessar, Patricia. "The Dominicans: Women in the Household and the Garment Industry." *New Immigrants in New York*, edited by Nancy Foner, Columbia UP, 1987, pp. 103–129.

Philoctète, René. *The Massacre River*. Translated by Linda Coverdale, with a preface by Edwidge Danticat, New Directions Books, 2005. Originally published in French as *Les peuples des terres mêlées*. Éditions Henri Deschamps, 1989.

Pomfret, John. "Black-Latino Tensions on Rise in California." *NBC News*, 20 Feb. 2006, https://www.nbcnews.com/id/wbna11467974.

Portes, Alejandro, and Rubén G. Rumbaut. *Legacies: The Story of the Immigrant Second Generation*. U of California P, 2001.

Prestol Castillo, Freddy. *You Can Cross the Massacre on Foot*. Translated by Margaret Randall, with a foreword by Maria Cristina Fumagalli, Duke UP, 2019. Originally published in Spanish as *El Masacre se pasa a pie*. Editora Taller, 1998.

Ramírez, Yasmín. "Passing on Latinidad: An Analysis of Critical Responses to El Museo del Barrio's Pan-Latino Mission Statements." National Conference on the Interpretation and Representation of Latino Cultures: Research and Museums. Smithsonian Center for Latino Initiatives, 20–23 Nov. 2002, Washington, DC.

Ramos, Aarón Gamaliel, editor. *Las ideas anexionistas en Puerto Rico bajo la dominación norteamericana*. Ediciones Huracán, 1987.

Ramos, Jorge. *La otra cara de América: Historias de los immigrantes latinoamericanos que están cambiando a Estados Unidos*. Grijalbo, 2000.

Ramos, Paola. *Finding Latinx: In Search of the Voices Redefining Latino Identity*. Vintage, 2020.

Resina, Joan Ramon. "Whose Hispanism? Cultural Trauma, Disciplining Memory, and Symbolic Dominance." *Ideologies of Hispanism*, edited by Mabel Moraña, Vanderbilt UP, 2005, pp. 160–186.

Restall, Matthew. "Black Conquistadors: Armed Africans in Early Spanish America." *The Americas*, vol. 57, no. 2, Oct. 2000, pp. 171–205.

Rios, Diana I., and A. N. Mohamed, editors. *Brown and Black Communication: Latino and African American Conflict and Convergence in Mass Media.* Praeger, 2003.

Rodó, José Enrique. *Ariel.* 1900. Espasa-Calpe, 1971.

Rodríguez, Clara E. "Challenging Racial Hegemony: Puerto Ricans in the United States." *Race*, edited by Steven Gregory and Roger Sanjek, Rutgers UP, 1994, pp. 131–143.

Rodríguez, Clara E. *Changing Race: Latinos, the Census, and the History of Ethnicity in the United States.* New York UP, 2000.

Rodríguez Demorizi, Emilio, editor. *Papeles de Buenaventura Báez.* Editora Montalvo, 1969. Academia Dominicana de la Historia 21.

Rodríguez Demorizi, Emilio. *Próceres de la Restauración: Noticias biográficas.* Editora del Caribe, 1963. Academia Dominicana de la Historia 12.

Rodríguez, Joe. "United States Hispanic Autobiography and Biography: Legend for the Future." *Handbook of Hispanic Cultures in the United States: Literature and Art*, edited by Nicolás Kanellos and Claudio Esteva-Fabregat, Arte Público Press, 1993, pp. 268–290.

Rodríguez-Juliá, Edgardo. *Las tribulaciones de Jonás.* Ediciones Huracán, 1981.

Rodriguez, Richard. *Brown: The Last Discovery of America.* Viking, 2002.

Rodriguez, Richard. *Days of Obligation: An Argument with My Mexican Father.* Penguin Books, 1992.

Rodriguez, Richard. *Hunger of Memory: The Education of Richard Rodriguez.* Bantam Books, 1982.

Rodriguez, Richard. "Mixed Blood: Columbus's Legacy—A World Made *Mestizo.*" *Progressions: Readings for Writers*, edited by Betsy Hilbert, Norton, 1998, pp. 535–549.

Roggiano, Alfredo A. *Pedro Henríquez Ureña en los Estados Unidos.* Talleres de la Casa Editorial Cultura, 1961.

Roosevelt, Franklin Delano. "Message to Congress (January 11, 1944)." *The Public Papers and Addresses of Franklin Delano Roosevelt*, edited by Samuel I. Rosenman, vol. 12, Harper & Brothers, 1950, pp. 32–44.

Rosa, Guarionex. "Fallo del TC, caso complejo." Tribunal Constitucional, pp. 227–230.

Rosaldo, Renato, and William V. Flores. "Identity, Conflict, and Evolving Latino Communities: Cultural Citizenship in San Jose, California." Flores and Benmayor, pp. 57–59.

Rosenblatt, Roger. "Black Autobiography: Life as the Death Weapon." Olney, *Autobiography*, pp. 169–180.

Rowe, Daryl M., and Reyna García Ramos. "Latino and African American Relations in Academia: A Case Study of Solidarity between Faculty of Color." Rios and Mohamed, pp. 203–215.

Rúa, Mérida M. "Latinidades." Oboler and González, https://www.oxfordreference.com/view/10.1093/acref/9780195156003.001.0001/acref-9780195156003-e-491.

Ruble, Renée. "Victims of America's Worst Race Riot to Be Compensated: Up to 300 Killed in 1921 Rampage in Tulsa, Oklahoma." *Ottawa Citizen*, 5 Feb. 2000, p. 2.

Ruiz de Burton, María Amparo. *The Squatter and the Don.* Edited by Rosaura Sánchez and Beatrice Pita, Arte Público Press, 1992.

Ryan, Bryan, editor. *Hispanic Writers: A Selection of Sketches from Contemporary Authors.* Gale Research, 1991.

Salvo, Joseph J. *The Newest New Yorkers: An Analysis of Immigration into New York City during the 1980s.* New York Department of City Planning, 1992.

Sánchez Korrol, Virginia. "The Origins and Evolution of Latino History." *OAH Magazine of History*, vol. 10, no. 2, 1996, pp. 5–12.

Santa Ana, Otto. *Brown Tide Rising: Metaphors of Latinos in Contemporary American Public Discourse.* U of Texas P, 2002.

Santiago, Roberto. "Black *and* Latino." *America Now: Short Readings from Recent Periodicals*, edited by Robert Atwan, Bedford Books, 1994, pp. 46–49.

Santo Domingo: A Brief Sketch of the Island, Its Resources, and Commercial Possibilities with Special Reference to the Treaty Now Pending in the United States Senate. New York Commercial, 1906.

Saralegui, Cristina. *Cristina! Confidencias de una rubia.* Warner Books, 1998.

Sawyer, Mark. "Racial Politics in Multiethnic America: Black and Latina/o Identities and Coalitions." Dzidzienyo and Oboler, pp. 265–279.

Sayre, Robert F. "Autobiography and the Making of America." Olney, *Autobiography*, pp. 146–168.

Schoenrich, Otto. *Santo Domingo: A Country with a Future.* Macmillan, 1918.

Shea, Christopher. "A Blacker Shade of Yale: African-American Studies Takes a New Direction." *Lingua Franca*, vol. 11, no. 2, 2001, pp. 42–49.

Silfa, Nicolás. *Guerra, traición y exilio.* N. Silfa, 1980.

Singer, Merrill. "Internalized Racism." Oboler and González, https://www.oxfordreference.com/view/10.1093/acref/9780195156003.001.0001/acref-9780195156003-e-438.

Sitkoff, Harvard. *A New Deal for Blacks: The Emergence of Civil Rights as a National Issue; The Depression Decade.* Oxford UP, 1978.

Sleeper, Jim. "Should American Journalism Make Us American?" Discussion Paper D-38. Shorenstein Center on the Press, Politics and Public Policy and the John F. Kennedy School of Government, Harvard University, 1999, pp. 1–15.

Sollors, Werner. *Beyond Ethnicity: Consent and Descent in American Culture.* Oxford UP, 1986.

Sommers, Laurie Kay. "Inventing Latinismo: The Creation of 'Hispanic' Pan-Ethnicity in the United States." *Journal of American Folklore*, vol. 104, no. 411, 1991, pp. 32–53. https://doi.org/10.2307/541132.

Spivak, Gayatri Chakravorty. "Can the Subaltern Speak?" *Colonial Discourse and Post-Colonial Theory: A Reader*, edited by Patrick Williams and Laura Chrisman, Columbia UP, 1994, pp. 66–111.

Stanton, David. "Junot Diaz: On Home Ground." *Poets & Writers Magazine*, vol. 26, no. 4, 1998, pp. 27–37.

Stavans, Ilán, and Iván Jaksić. *What Is La Hispanidad? A Conversation.* U of Texas P, 2011.

Steinberg, Stephen. *The Ethnic Myth: Race, Ethnicity, and Class in America.* Atheneum, 1981.

Steinmetz, Katy. "Why 'Latinx' Is Succeeding While Other Gender-Neutral Terms Fail to Catch On." *Time*, 2 Apr. 2018, https://time.com/5191804/latinx-definition-meaning-latino-hispanic-gender-neutral/.

Stepick, Alex, and Carol Dutton Stepick. "Power and Identity: Miami Cubans." Suárez-Orozco and Páez, pp. 75–92.

Suárez-Orozco, Marcelo M., and Mariela M. Páez, editors. *Latinos: Remaking America.* U of California P, 2002.

Suárez-Orozco, Marcelo M., and Mariela M. Páez. "The Research Agenda." Introduction. Suárez-Orozco and Páez, pp. 1–37.

Sumner, Charles. *Charles Sumner: His Complete Works.* Lee and Shepard, 1899.

Suro, Roberto. *Strangers among US: Latino Lives in a Changing America.* Knopf, 1999.

Susann, Marian. "María Móntez: On and Off Camera." *Latino Stuff Review*, vol. 15, 1994, pp. 3–4.

Tansill, Charles Callan. *The United States and Santo Domingo: 1798–1873*. Johns Hopkins UP, 1938.

Tejada, Juan de Dios. "De Juan de Dios Tejada a Ramona Ureña." *Familia Henríquez Ureña: Epistolario*, Secretaría de Estado de Educación Bellas Artes y Cultos, 1994, pp. 281–283.

"'Their Own Hotheadedness': Senator Benjamin R. 'Pitchfork Ben' Tillman Justifies Violence against Southern Blacks." *History Matters: The US Survey Course on the Web*, https://historymatters.gmu.edu/d/55/.

Thomas, Piri. *Down These Mean Streets*. Vintage Books, 1997.

Thompson-Hernández, Walter. "What Does It Mean to Be Afro-Latino? The NBA's Charlie Villanueva Explains." *Remezcla*, 19 Oct. 2015, https://remezcla.com/sports/afro-latino-nba-charlie-villanueva-espn/.

Torres-Saillant, Silvio. "Before the Diaspora: Early Dominican Literature in the United States." *Recovering the US Hispanic Literary Heritage*, vol. 3, edited by María Herrera-Sobek and Virginia Sánchez Korrol, Arte Público Press, 2000, pp. 250–267.

Torres-Saillant, Silvio. "Dominican Blackness and the Modern World." *Perspectives on Las Américas: A Reader in Culture, History, and Representation*, edited by Matthew C. Gutmann et al., Blackwell, 2003, pp. 274–288.

Torres-Saillant, Silvio. "The Construction of the Other in Studies of Dominican Migration." XV International Congress of the Latin American Studies Association, 4-6 Dec. 1989, Miami, Florida.

Torres-Saillant, Silvio. "The Dominican Republic." *No Longer Invisible: Afro-Latin Americans Today*, edited by Miles Litvinoff, Minority Rights Group, 1995, pp. 109–138.

Torres-Saillant, Silvio. "El concepto de dominicanidad y la emigración." *Punto y Coma*, vol. 4, nos. 1–2, 1992–1993, pp. 161–169.

Torres-Saillant, Silvio. "Essayists." Oboler and González, https://www.oxfordreference.com/view/10.1093/acref/9780195156003.001.0001/acref-9780195156003-e-283.

Torres-Saillant, Silvio. *An Intellectual History of the Caribbean*. Palgrave Macmillan, 2006.

Torres-Saillant, Silvio. "Inventing the Race: Latinos and the Ethnoracial Pentagon." *Latino Studies*, vol. 1, no. 1, 2003, pp. 123–151.

Torres-Saillant, Silvio. "La literatura dominicana en los Estados Unidos y la periferia del margen." *Punto y Coma*, vol. 3, no. 1–2, 1991, pp. 139–149.

Torres-Saillant, Silvio. "Pilgrims of Humane Remembrance at the Borderlands." *Border of Lights Reader*, edited by Megan Jeannette Myers and Edward Paulino, Amherst College P, 2021, pp. 91–100.

Torres-Saillant, Silvio. "Problematic Paradigms: Racial Diversity and Corporate Identity in the Latino Community." Suárez-Orozco and Páez, pp. 435–455.

Torres-Saillant, Silvio. "Racism in the Americas and the Latino Scholar." Dzidzienyo and Oboler, pp. 281–304.

Torres-Saillant, Silvio. *El retorno de las yolas: Ensayos sobre diáspora, democracia y dominicanidad*. Ediciones Librería La Trinitaria / Editora Mantí, 1999.

Torres-Saillant, Silvio. *El tigueraje intelectual*. 2nd rev. ed., Editora Mediabyte, 2011.

Torres-Saillant, Silvio. "The Unlikely Latinos: Brazilians in the United States." *Latino Studies*, vol. 6, no. 4, 2008, pp. 466–477.

Torres-Saillant, Silvio. "Visions of Dominicanness in the United States." *Borderless Bor-*

ders: US Latinos, Latin Americans, and the Paradox of Interdependence, edited by Frank Bonilla et al., Temple UP, 1998, pp. 139–152.

Torres-Saillant, Silvio, and Ramona Hernández. "Community, Culture, and Collective Identity." *One Out of Three: Immigrant New York in the Twenty-First Century*, edited by Nancy Foner, Columbia UP, 2013, pp. 223–245.

Torres-Saillant, Silvio, and Ramona Hernández. *The Dominican Americans*. Greenwood, 1998.

Torres, Lourdes. "Latinx?" *Latino Studies*, vol. 16, no. 3, 24 Sep. 2018, pp. 283–285. *Proquest*, https://doi.org/10.1057/s41276-018-0142-y.

Torres, Lourdes. "The Construction of the Self in US Latino Autobiographies." *Women, Autobiography, Theory: A Reader*, edited by Sidonie Smith and Julia Watson, U of Wisconsin P, 1998, pp. 276–287.

Tribunal Constitucional de la República Dominicana. *La Sentencia 168-13: Antología de una defensa esencial*. Edited by Justo Pedro Castellanos Khoury, Editora Búho, 2014.

Trujillo Declassified. www.trujillodeclassified.com.

Trumpbour, John, and Elaine Bernard. "Unions and Latinos: Mutual Transformation." Suárez-Orozco and Páez, pp. 126–145.

"Two Former Shenandoah, Pennsylvania, Police Officers Convicted of Falsifying Information about Hate Crime." *Office of Public Affairs, United States Department of Justice*, 27 Jan. 2011, https://www.justice.gov/opa/pr/two-former-shenandoah-pennsylvania-police-officers-convicted-falsifying-information-about. Press release no. 11-116, accessed 25 Aug. 2015.

Umphrey, Don, and Alan B. Albarran. "Polarization of Minorities: Projecting Trends in the New Media Environment." Rios and Mohamed, pp. 43–54.

United States. *Dominican Republic: Report of the Commission of Inquiry to Santo Domingo*. Government Printing Office, 1871.

Vaca, Nicolás C. *The Presumed Alliance: The Unspoken Conflict between Latinos and Blacks and What It Means for America*. Rayo, 2004.

Valdés-Rodríguez, Alisa. *The Dirty Girls Social Club*. St. Martin's Press, 2003.

Vallejo de Paredes, Margarita. *Apuntes biográficos y bibliográficos de algunos escritos dominicanos del siglo XIX*. Vol. 1, Publicaciones ONAP, 1995.

Vasconcelos, José. *The Cosmic Race / La raza cósmica*. Edited and translated by Didier T. Jaén, Johns Hopkins UP, 1997.

Vega, Bernardo. "Bernardo Vega y Edwidge Danticat discuten la matanza de 1937." *Hoy*, 5 June 2004, https://hoy.com.do/bernardo-vega-y-edwidge-danticat-discuten-la-matanza-de-1937-2/.

Vega, Bernardo. *Trujillo et Haïti, 1930–1937*. Translated by Guillermo Piña Contreras and Françoise Mironneau, vol. 1, Fundación Cultural Dominicana, 1995.

Vélez-Ibáñez, Carlos G. *Border Visions: Mexican Cultures of the Southwest United States*. U of Arizona P, 1996.

Vetik, Raivo, et al. "Reactive Identity versus EU Integration." *Journal of Common Market Studies*, vol. 44, no. 5, 2006, pp. 1079–1102.

Victoriano-Martínez, Ramón Antonio. "'The Black Plague from the West': Haiti in Roberto Marcallé Abreu's Dystopia." *Racialized Visions: Haiti and the Hispanic Caribbean*, edited by Vanessa K. Valdés, SUNY P, 2020, pp. 191–207.

Vieira, Rosángela María. "Brazil." *No Longer Invisible: Afro-Latin Americans Today*, edited by Minority Rights Group, Minority Rights Publications, 1995, pp. 19–46.

Villegas de Magnón, Leonor. *The Rebel.* Edited by Clara Lomas, Arte Público Press, 1994.

Vizenor, Gerald. Interview by Helmbrecht Breinig and Klaus Losch. *American Contradictions: Interviews with Nine American Writers*, edited by Wolfgang Binder and Helmbrecht Breinig, Wesleyan UP, 1995, pp. 143–165.

Waters, Mary C. "Multiple Ethnic Identity Choices." *Beyond Pluralism: The Conception of Groups and Group Identities*, edited by Wendy F. Katkin et al., U of Illinois P, 1998, pp. 28–46.

Weber, David J. "The Spanish Legacy of North America and the Historical Imagination." *Western Historical Quarterly*, vol. 23, no. 1, Feb. 1992, pp. 5–24.

Weber, Max. "Ethnic Groups." *Theories of Society: Foundations of Modern Sociological Theory*, edited by Talcott Parsons et al., Free Press, 1965, pp. 305–309.

Weisman, Alan, and Sandy Tolan. "Central America: Vanishing Forests, Endangered Peoples." *On Prejudice: A Global Perspective*, edited by Daniela Gioseffi, Anchor Books, 1993, pp. 221–225.

Welles, Sumner. 1928. *Naboth's Vineyard: The Dominican Republic, 1844–1924.* Reprint ed., Paul P. Appel, 1966. 2 vols.

Wells, H. G. *The Future in America: A Search After Realities.* Harper & Brothers, 1906.

"Whitney Houston on *The Arsenio Hall Show*, 1991." *YouTube*, uploaded by Mariah, 18 Feb. 2010, https://www.youtube.com/watch?v=zTGk6QIxzvg.

Williams, Kim. Interview. *Kennedy School Insight*, 5 Dec. 2005, *www.ksg.harvard*.edu/ (magazine no longer available on website).

Willing, Richard. "DNA Rewrites History for African-Americans." *USA Today*, 2 Feb. 2006, p. 4A.

Winant, Howard. "Theoretical Status of the Concept of Race." Back and Solomos, pp. 181–190.

Winn, Peter. *Americas: The Changing Face of Latin America and the Caribbean.* U of California P, 1999.

Wirth, Louis. "The Problem of Minority Groups." Parsons et al., pp. 309–315.

Wright, Lawrence. "One Drop of Blood." *The New Yorker*, 25 July 1994, pp. 46–55.

Yardley, Jim. "Panel Recommends Reparations in Long-Ignored Tulsa Race Riot." *The New York Times*, 5 Feb. 2000, https://www.nytimes.com/2000/02/05/us/panel-recommends-reparations-in-long-ignored-tulsa-race-riot.html.

Yunqué, Edgardo Vega, et al. "Conversation: The Writers and the Audience." *Hispanic Immigrant Writers and the Question of Identity*, edited by Silvio Torres-Saillant, vol. 1, Ollantay Press, 1989, pp. 61–81. Literature/Conversation.

Zangwill, Israel. *The Melting-Pot: A Drama in Four Acts.* Rev. ed., Macmillan, 1921.

Zenón Cruz, Isabelo. *Narciso descubre su trasero: El negro en la cultura puertorriqueña.* 2nd ed., Editorial Fundi, 1975.

Zepeda, Ofelia. "Autobiography." Krupat and Swann, pp. 405–420.

INDEX

Contributors

ABOUT THE AUTHOR

Silvio Torres-Saillant, professor of English and Dean's Professor of the Humanities at Syracuse University, has authored *Caribbean Poetics: Toward an Aesthetic of West Indian Literature*, *El retorno de las yolas*, *El tigueraje intelectual*, and *An Intellectual History of the Caribbean*, among other books. Founder of the CUNY Dominican Studies Institute at the City College of New York and founding Director of the Latino-Latin American Studies Program at Syracuse University, he teaches courses in reading and interpretation, Latinx literature, and writings of the Caribbean diaspora.

ABOUT THE EDITORS

Nancy Kang is an associate professor of women's and gender studies at the University of Manitoba, where she holds the Canada Research Chair in Transnational Feminisms and Gender-Based Violence. She is coauthor of *The Once and Future Muse: The Poetry and Poetics of Rhina P. Espaillat* with Silvio Torres-Saillant, and coeditor of *The Culture and Philosophy of Ridley Scott* with Adam and Ashley Barkman. An advisory board member for such journals as *Meridians: Feminism, Race, Transnationalism* and *Latino Studies*, Kang also publishes creative writing. Her poetry appears in *Atlantis*, *Amerasia Journal*, *The Fiddlehead*, *Women's Studies Quarterly*, *ARIEL*, and *Canadian Literature*, among others.

Michael Nieto Garcia is a professor of literature at Clarkson University in upstate New York. He is the son of an immigrant farmworker, and grew up on a potato farm in rural Idaho. He is the author of *Autobiography in Black and Brown: Ethnic Identity in Richard Wright and Richard Rodriguez*. His essays appear in the critical collections *Identifying with Freedom* and *The Culture and Philosophy of Ridley Scott*. His essay, "Do Brown People Have Brown Thoughts?: Richard Rodriguez's Philosophy of Race, Culture, and Identity," traces the societal turn to tribalism, cultural essentialism, and divisive forms of identity politics. It is available via open access from the journal *Latino Studies*.